Solutions Manual to Accompany
Loss Models
From Data to Decisions
Second Edition

Solutions Manual to Accompany

Loss Models
From Data to Decisions
Second Edition

Stuart A. Klugman
Drake University

Harry H. Panjer
University of Waterloo

Gordon E. Willmot
University of Waterloo

WILEY-
INTERSCIENCE

A JOHN WILEY & SONS, INC., PUBLICATION

Library of Congress Cataloging in Publication Data:

ISBN 0-471-22762-5 (paper)

Printed in the United States of America

10 9 8 7 6 5 4 3 2 1

Contents

1	Introduction	1
2	Chapter 2 solutions	3
	2.1 Section 2.2	3
3	Chapter 3 solutions	9
	3.1 Section 3.1	9
	3.2 Section 3.2	14
	3.3 Section 3.3	15
4	Chapter 4 solutions	17
	4.1 Section 4.2	17
	4.2 Section 4.3	21
	4.3 Section 4.4	25
	4.4 Section 4.5	33
	4.5 Section 4.6	33
5	Chapter 5 solutions	47
	5.1 Section 5.2	47
	5.2 Section 5.3	49

5.3	Section 5.4	51
5.4	Section 5.5	52
5.5	Section 5.6	54
6	**Chapter 6 solutions**	**57**
6.1	Section 6.1	57
6.2	Section 6.2	57
6.3	Section 6.3	58
6.4	Section 6.4	65
6.5	Section 6.6	68
6.6	Section 6.7	73
6.7	Section 6.8	75
6.8	Section 6.9	76
6.9	Section 6.11	77
7	**Chapter 7 solutions**	**83**
7.1	Section 7.3	83
8	**Chapter 8 solutions**	**91**
8.1	Section 8.2	91
8.2	Section 8.3	98
8.3	Section 8.4	101
8.4	Section 8.5	106
9	**Chapter 9 solutions**	**113**
9.1	Section 9.2	113
9.2	Section 9.3	116
9.3	Section 9.4	116
10	**Chapter 10 solutions**	**119**
10.1	Section 10.2	119
10.2	Section 10.3	120
11	**Chapter 11 solutions**	**125**
11.1	Section 11.1	125
11.2	Section 11.2	130
11.3	Section 11.3	133
11.4	Section 11.4	135

12 Chapter 12 solutions   139
    12.1 Section 12.1   139
    12.2 Section 12.2   143
    12.3 Section 12.3   155
    12.4 Section 12.4   163
    12.5 Section 12.5   174
    12.6 Section 12.6   176
    12.7 Section 12.7   176

13 Chapter 13 solutions   179
    13.1 Section 13.3   179
    13.2 Section 13.4   180
    13.3 Section 13.5   189

14 Chapter 14 solutions   197
    14.1 Section 14.2   197
    14.2 Section 14.7   198

15 Chapter 15 solutions   203
    15.1 Section 15.2   203
    15.2 Section 15.3   204
    15.3 Section 15.4   207
    15.4 Section 15.5   207
    15.5 Section 15.6   208

16 Chapter 16 solutions   211
    16.1 Section 16.2   211
    16.2 Section 16.3   215
    16.3 Section 16.4   217
    16.4 Section 16.5   244

17 Chapter 17 solutions   251
    17.1 Section 17.1   251
    17.2 Section 17.2   252

1

Introduction

The solutions presented in this manual reflect the author's best attempt to provide insights and answers. While we have done our best to be complete and accurate, errors may occur and there may be more elegant solutions. Errata will be posted at the ftp site dedicated to the text and solutions manual:

ftp://ftp.wiley.com/public/sci_tech_med/loss_models/

Should you find errors or would like to provide improved solutions, please send your comments to Stuart Klugman at stuart.klugman@drake.edu.

Loss Models: From Data to Decisions, Solutions Manual, Second Edition.
By Stuart A. Klugman, Harry H. Panjer, and Gordon E. Willmot
ISBN 0-471-22762-5   Copyright © 2004 John Wiley & Sons, Inc.

2

Chapter 2 solutions

2.1 SECTION 2.2

2.1 $F_5(x) = 1 - S_5(x) = \begin{cases} 0.01x, & 0 \le x < 50 \\ 0.02x - 0.5, & 50 \le x < 75. \end{cases}$

$f_5(x) = F_5'(x) = \begin{cases} 0.01, & 0 < x < 50 \\ 0.02, & 50 \le x < 75. \end{cases}$

$h_5(x) = \frac{f_5(x)}{S_5(x)} = \begin{cases} \frac{1}{100-x}, & 0 < x < 50 \\ \frac{1}{75-x}, & 50 \le x < 75. \end{cases}$

2.2 The requested plots appear below. The triangular spike at zero in the density function for Model 4 indicates the 0.7 of discrete probability at zero.

Loss Models: From Data to Decisions, Solutions Manual, Second Edition.
By Stuart A. Klugman, Harry H. Panjer, and Gordon E. Willmot
ISBN 0-471-22762-5   Copyright © 2004 John Wiley & Sons, Inc.

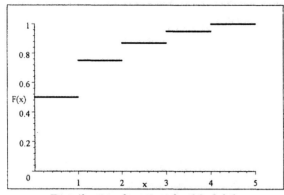

Distribution function for Model 3.

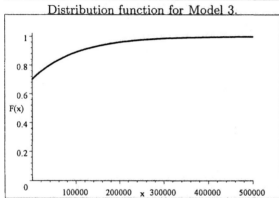

Distribution function for Model 4.

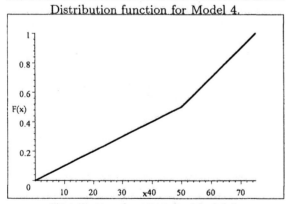

Distribution function for Model 5.

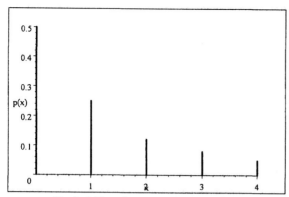

Probability function for Model 3.

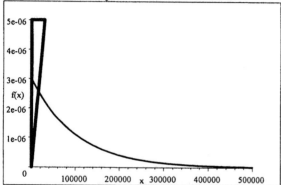

Density function for Model 4.

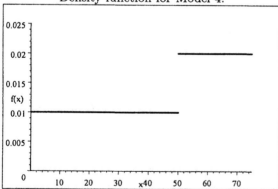

Density function for Model 5.

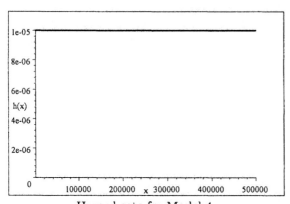

Hazard rate for Model 4.

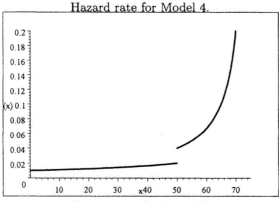

Hazard rate for Model 5.

2.3 $f'(x) = 4(1+x^2)^{-3} - 24x^2(1+x^2)^{-4}$. Setting the derivative equal to zero and multiplying by $(1+x^2)^4$ gives the equation $4(1+x^2) - 24x^2 = 0$. This is equivalent to $x^2 = 1/5$. The only positive solution is the mode of $1/\sqrt{5}$.

2.4 The survival function can be recovered as

$$
\begin{aligned}
0.5 &= S(0.4) = e^{-\int_0^{0.4} A + e^{2x} dx} \\
&= e^{-Ax - 0.5e^{2x}\big|_0^{0.4}} \\
&= e^{-0.4A - 0.5e^{0.8} + 0.5}.
\end{aligned}
$$

Taking logarithms gives

$$-0.693147 = -0.4A - 1.112770 + 0.5$$

and thus $A = 0.2009$.

2.5 The ratio is

$$
\begin{aligned}
r &= \frac{\left(\frac{10{,}000}{10{,}000+d}\right)^2}{\left(\frac{20{,}000}{20{,}000+d^2}\right)^2} \\
&= \left(\frac{20{,}000+d^2}{20{,}000+2d}\right)^2 \\
&= \frac{20{,}000^2 + 40{,}000d^2 + d^4}{20{,}000^2 + 80{,}000d + 4d^2}\,.
\end{aligned}
$$

From observation, or two applications of L'Hôpital's rule, we see that the limit is infinity.

3

Chapter 3 solutions

3.1 SECTION 3.1

3.1

$$\mu_3 = \int_{-\infty}^{\infty} (x-\mu)^3 f(x)dx = \int_{-\infty}^{\infty} (x^3 - 3x^2\mu + 3x\mu^2 - \mu^3)f(x)dx$$
$$= \mu_3' - 3\mu_2'\mu + 2\mu^3.$$

$$\mu_4 = \int_{-\infty}^{\infty} (x-\mu)^4 f(x)dx$$
$$= \int_{-\infty}^{\infty} (x^4 - 4x^3\mu + 6x^2\mu^2 - 4x\mu^3 + \mu^4)f(x)dx$$
$$= \mu_4' - 4\mu_3'\mu + 6\mu_2'\mu^2 - 3\mu^4.$$

3.2 For Model 1, $\sigma^2 = 3{,}333.33 - 50^2 = 833.33$, $\sigma = 28.8675$.
$\mu_3' = \int_0^{100} x^3(.01)dx = 250{,}000$, $\mu_3 = 0$, $\gamma_1 = 0$.
$\mu_4' = \int_0^{100} x^4(.01)dx = 20{,}000{,}000$, $\mu_4 = 1{,}250{,}000$, $\gamma_2 = 1.8$.

Loss Models: From Data to Decisions, Solutions Manual, Second Edition.
By Stuart A. Klugman, Harry H. Panjer, and Gordon E. Willmot
ISBN 0-471-22762-5   Copyright © 2004 John Wiley & Sons, Inc.

For Model 2, $\sigma^2 = 4{,}000{,}000 - 1000^2 = 3{,}000{,}000$, $\sigma = 1732.05$. μ_3' and μ_4' are both infinite so the skewness and kurtosis are not defined.

For Model 3, $\sigma^2 = 2.25 - .93^2 = 1.3851$, $\sigma = 1.1769$.
$\mu_3' = 0(.5) + 1(.25) + 8(.12) + 27(.08) + 64(.05) = 6.57$, $\mu_3 = 1.9012$, $\gamma_1 = 1.1663$.
$\mu_4' = 0(.5) + 1(.25) + 16(.12) + 81(.08) + 256(.05) = 21.45$, $\mu_4 = 6.4416$, $\gamma_2 = 3.3576$.

For Model 4, $\sigma^2 = 6{,}000{,}000{,}000 - 30{,}000^2 = 5{,}100{,}000{,}000$, $\sigma = 71{,}414$.
$\mu_3' = 0^3(.7) + \int_0^\infty x^3(.000003)e^{-.00001x}\,dx = 1.8 \times 10^{15}$, $\mu_3 = 1.314 \times 10^{15}$, $\gamma_1 = 3.6078$.
$\mu_4' = \int_0^\infty x^4(.000003)e^{-.00001x}\,dx = 7.2 \times 10^{20}$, $\mu_4 = 5.3397 \times 10^{20}$, $\gamma_2 = 20.5294$.

For Model 5, $\sigma^2 = 2395.83 - 43.75^2 = 481.77$, $\sigma = 21.95$.
$\mu_3' = \int_0^{50} x^3(.01)\,dx + \int_{50}^{75} x^3(.02)\,dx = 142{,}578.125$, $\mu_3 = -4394.53$, $\gamma_1 = -0.4156$.
$\mu_4' = \int_0^{50} x^4(.01)\,dx + \int_{50}^{75} x^4(.02)\,dx = 8{,}867{,}187.5$, $\mu_4 = 439{,}758.30$, $\gamma_2 = 1.8947$.

For Model 6, $\sigma^2 = 42.5 - 6.25^2 = 3.4375$, $\sigma = 1.8540$.
$\mu_3' = 310.75$, $\mu_3 = 2.15625$, $\gamma_1 = .3383$.
$\mu_4' = 2424.5$, $\mu_4 = 39.0508$, $\gamma_2 = 3.3048$.

3.3 The standard deviation is the mean times the coefficient of variation, or 4 and so the variance is 16. From (3.3) the second raw moment is $16 + 2^2 = 20$. The third central moment is (using Exercise 3.1) $136 - 3(20)(2) + 2(2)^3 = 32$. The skewness is the third central moment divided by the cube of the standard deviation, or $32/4^3 = 1/2$.

3.4 For a gamma distribution the mean is $\alpha\theta$. The second raw moment is $\alpha(\alpha + 1)\theta^2$ and so the variance is $\alpha\theta^2$. The coefficient of variation is $\sqrt{\alpha\theta^2}/\alpha\theta = \alpha^{-1/2} = 1$. Therefore $\alpha = 1$. The third raw moment is $\alpha(\alpha + 1)(\alpha + 2)\theta^3 = 6\theta^3$. From Exercise 3.1, the third central moment is $6\theta^3 - 3(2\theta^2)\theta + 2\theta^3 = 2\theta^3$ and the skewness is $2\theta^3/(\theta^2)^{3/2} = 2$.

3.5 For Model 1,

$$e(d) = \frac{\int_d^{100}(1 - .01x)\,dx}{1 - .01d} = \frac{100 - d}{2}.$$

For Model 2,

$$e(d) = \frac{\int_d^\infty \left(\frac{2000}{x+2000}\right)^3 dx}{\left(\frac{2000}{d+2000}\right)^3} = \frac{2000 + d}{2}.$$

For Model 3,

$$
e(d) = \begin{cases}
\frac{.25(1-d)+.12(2-d)+.08(3-d)+.05(4-d)}{.5} = 1.86 - d, & 0 \le d < 1 \\
\frac{.12(2-d)+.08(3-d)+.05(4-d)}{.25} = 2.72 - d, & 1 \le d < 2 \\
\frac{.08(3-d)+.05(4-d)}{.13} = 3.3846 - d, & 2 \le d < 3 \\
\frac{.05(4-d)}{.05} = 4 - d, & 3 \le d < 4.
\end{cases}
$$

For Model 4,

$$
e(d) = \frac{\int_d^\infty .3e^{-.00001x}dx}{.3e^{-.00001d}} = 100{,}000.
$$

The functions are straight lines for Models 1, 2, and 4. Model 1 has negative slope, Model 2 has positive slope, and Model 4 is horizontal.

3.6 For a uniform distribution on the interval from 0 to w the density function is $f(x) = 1/w$. The mean residual life is

$$
\begin{aligned}
e(d) &= \frac{\int_d^w (x - d)w^{-1}dx}{\int_d^w w^{-1}dx} \\
&= \frac{\frac{(x-d)^2}{2w}\Big|_d^w}{\frac{w-d}{w}} \\
&= \frac{(w - d)^2}{2(w - d)} \\
&= \frac{w - d}{2}.
\end{aligned}
$$

The equation becomes

$$
\frac{w - 30}{2} = \frac{100 - 30}{2} + 4
$$

with a solution of $w = 108$.

3.7 From the definition,

$$
e(\lambda) = \frac{\int_\lambda^\infty (x - \lambda)\lambda^{-1}e^{-x/\lambda}dx}{\int_\lambda^\infty \lambda^{-1}e^{-x/\lambda}dx} = \lambda.
$$

3.8

$$
\begin{aligned}
\mathrm{E}(X) &= \int_0^\infty xf(x)dx = \int_0^d xf(x)dx + \int_d^\infty df(x)dx + \int_d^\infty (x - d)f(x)dx \\
&= \int_0^d xf(x)dx + d[1 - F(d)] + e(d)S(d) = \mathrm{E}[X \wedge d] + e(d)S(d).
\end{aligned}
$$

3.9 For Model 1, from (3.8),

$$E[X \wedge u] = \int_0^u x(0.01)dx + u(1 - 0.01u) = u(1 - 0.005u)$$

and from (3.10),

$$E[X \wedge u] = 50 - \frac{100 - u}{2}(1 - 0.01u) = u(1 - 0.005u).$$

From (3.9),

$$E[X \wedge u] = -\int_{-\infty}^0 0dx + \int_0^u 1 - 0.01xdx = u - 0.01u^2/2 = u(1 - 0.005u).$$

For Model 2, from (3.8),

$$E[X \wedge u] = \int_0^u x\frac{3(2000)^3}{(x + 2000)^4}dx + u\frac{2000^3}{(2000 + u)^3} = 1000\left[1 - \frac{4,000,000}{(2000 + u)^2}\right]$$

and from (3.10),

$$E[X \wedge u] = 1000 - \frac{2000 + u}{2}\left(\frac{2000}{2000 + u}\right)^3 = 1000\left[1 - \frac{4,000,000}{(2000 + u)^2}\right].$$

From (3.9),

$$E[X \wedge u] = \int_0^u \left(\frac{2000}{2000 + x}\right)^3 dx = \frac{-2000^3}{2(2000 + x)^2}\bigg|_0^u = 1000\left[1 - \frac{4,000,000}{(2000 + u)^2}\right].$$

For Model 3, from (3.8),

$$E[X \wedge u] = \begin{cases} 0(.5) + u(.5) = .5u, & 0 \le u < 1 \\ 0(.5) + 1(.25) + u(.25) = .25 + .25u, & 1 \le u < 2 \\ 0(.5) + 1(.25) + 2(.12) + u(.13) \\ \quad = .49 + .13u, & 2 \le u < 3 \\ 0(.5) + 1(.25) + 2(.12) + 3(.08) + u(.05) \\ \quad = .73 + .05u, & 3 \le u < 4 \end{cases}$$

and from (3.10),

$$E[X \wedge u] = \begin{cases} .93 - (1.86 - u)(.5) = .5u, & 0 \le u < 1 \\ .93 - (2.72 - u)(.25) = .25 + .25u, & 1 \le u < 2 \\ .93 - (3.3846 - u)(.13) = .49 + .13u, & 2 \le u < 3 \\ .93 - (4 - u)(.05) = .73 + .05u, & 3 \le u < 4 \end{cases}$$

For Model 4, from (3.8),

$$E[X \wedge u] = \int_0^u x(.000003)e^{-.00001x}dx + u(.3)e^{-.00001u}$$
$$= 30,000[1 - e^{-.00001u}]$$

and from (3.10),

$$E[X \wedge u] = 30,000 - 100,000(.3e^{-.00001u}) = 30,000[1 - e^{-.00001u}].$$

3.10 For a discrete distribution (which all empirical distributions are), the mean residual life function is

$$e(d) = \frac{\sum_{x_j > d}(x_j - d)p(x_j)}{\sum_{x_j > d}p(x_j)}.$$

When d is equal to a possible value of X, the function cannot be continuous because there is jump in the denominator, but not in the numerator. For an exponential distribution, argue as in Exercise 3.7 to see that it is constant. For the Pareto distribution,

$$e(d) = \frac{E(X) - E(X \wedge d)}{S(d)}$$
$$= \frac{\frac{\theta}{\alpha - 1} - \frac{\theta}{\alpha - 1}\left[1 - \left(\frac{\theta}{\theta + d}\right)^{\alpha - 1}\right]}{\left(\frac{\theta}{\theta + d}\right)^{\alpha}}$$
$$= \frac{\theta}{\alpha - 1}\frac{\theta + d}{\theta} = \frac{\theta + d}{\alpha - 1}$$

which is increasing in d. Only the second statement is true.

3.11 Applying the formula from the solution to Exercise 3.10 gives

$$\frac{10,000 + 10,000}{0.5 - 1} = -40,000$$

which cannot be correct. Recall that the numerator of the mean residual life is $E(X) - E(X \wedge d)$. However, when $\alpha \le 1$ the expected value is infinite and so is the mean residual life.

3.12 The right truncated variable is defined as $Y = X$ given that $X \le u$. When $X > u$ this variable is not defined. The kth moment is

$$E(Y^k) = \frac{\int_0^u x^k f(x)dx}{F(u)} = \frac{\sum_{x_i \le u} x_i^k p(x_i)}{F(u)}.$$

3.13 This is a single parameter Pareto distribution with parameters $\alpha = 2.5$ and $\theta = 1$. The moments are $\mu_1 = 2.5/1.5 = 5/3$ and $\mu_2 = 2.5/.5 - (5/3)^2 = 20/9$. The coefficient of variation is $\sqrt{20/9}/(5/3) = 0.89443$.

3.14 $\mu = 0.05(100) + 0.2(200) + 0.5(300) + 0.2(400) + 0.05(500) = 300$.
$\sigma^2 = 0.05(-200)^2 + 0.2(-100)^2 + 0.5(0)^2 + 0.2(100)^2 + 0.05(200)^2 = 8,000$.
$\mu_3 = 0.05(-200)^3 + 0.2(-100)^3 + 0.5(0)^3 + 0.2(100)^3 + 0.05(200)^3 = 0$.
$\mu_4 = 0.05(-200)^4 + 0.2(-100)^4 + 0.5(0)^4 + 0.2(100)^4 + 0.05(200)^4 = 200,000,000$.
Skewness is $\gamma_1 = \mu_3/\sigma^3 = 0$. Kurtosis is $\gamma_2 = \mu_4/\sigma^4 = 200,000,000/8,000^2 = 3.125$.

3.15 The Pareto mean residual life function is, $e_X(d) = \frac{\int_d^\infty \theta^\alpha (x+\theta)^{-\alpha} dx}{\theta^\alpha (x+d)^{-\alpha}} = (d+\theta)/(\alpha - 1)$ and so $e_X(2\theta)/e_X(\theta) = (2\theta + \theta)/(\theta + \theta) = 1.5$.

3.2   SECTION 3.2

3.16 The *pdf* is $f(x) = 2x^{-3}$, $x \geq 1$. The mean is $\int_1^\infty 2x^{-2} dx = 2$. The median is the solution to $.5 = F(x) = 1 - x^{-2}$, which is 1.4142. The mode is the value where the *pdf* is highest. Because the *pdf* is strictly decreasing, the mode is at its smallest value, 1.

3.17 For Model 2, solve $p = 1 - \left(\frac{2000}{2000+\pi_p}\right)^3$ and so $\pi_p = 2000[(1-p)^{-1/3} - 1]$ and the requested percentiles are 519.84 and 1419.95.

For Model 4, the distribution function jumps from 0 to 0.7 at zero and so $\pi_{.5} = 0$. For percentile above 70, solve $p = 1 - 0.3e^{-0.00001\pi_p}$ and so $\pi_p = -100,000 \ln[(1 - p)/0.3]$ and so $\pi_{.8} = 40,546.51$.

For Model 5, the distribution function has two specifications. From $x = 0$ to $x = 50$ it rises from 0.0 to 0.5 and so for percentiles at 50 or below, the equation to solve is $p = 0.01\pi_p$ for $\pi_p = 100p$. For $50 < x \leq 75$ the distribution function rises from 0.5 to 1.0 and so for percentiles from 50 to 100 the equation to solve is $p = 0.02\pi_p - 0.5$ for $\pi_p = 50p + 25$. The requested percentiles are 50 and 65.

Model 6 is similar to Model 3 and so the requested percentiles are 6 and 7.

3.18 The two percentiles imply

$$0.1 = 1 - \left(\frac{\theta}{\theta + \theta - k}\right)^\alpha$$

$$0.9 = 1 - \left(\frac{\theta}{\theta + 5\theta - 3k}\right)^\alpha.$$

Rearranging the equations and taking their ratio yields

$$\frac{0.9}{0.1} = \left(\frac{6\theta - 3k}{2\theta - k}\right)^\alpha = 3^\alpha.$$

Taking logarithms of both sides gives $\ln 9 = \alpha \ln 3$ for $\alpha = \ln 9 / \ln 3 = 2$.

3.19 The two percentiles imply

$$0.25 = 1 - e^{-(1000/\theta)^\tau}$$

$$0.75 = 1 - e^{-(100,000/\theta)^\tau}.$$

Subtracting and then taking logarithms of both sides gives

$$\ln 0.75 = -(1000/\theta)^\tau$$

$$\ln 0.25 = -(100,000/\theta)^\tau.$$

Dividing the second equation by the first gives

$$\frac{\ln 0.25}{\ln 0.75} = 100^\tau.$$

Finally, taking logarithms of both sides gives $\tau \ln 100 = \ln[\ln 0.25 / \ln 0.75]$ for $\tau = 0.3415$.

3.3   SECTION 3.3

3.20 The sum has a gamma distribution with parameters $\alpha = 16$ and $\theta = 250$. Then, $\Pr(S_{16} > 6000) = 1 - \Gamma(16; 6000/250) = 1 - \Gamma(16; 24)$. From the Central Limit Theorem, the sum has an approximate normal distribution with mean $\alpha\theta = 4000$ and variance $\alpha\theta^2 = 1,000,000$ for a standard deviation of 1000. The probability of exceeding 6000 is $1 - \Phi[(6000 - 4000)/1000] = 1 - \Phi(2) = 0.0228$.

3.21 A single claim has mean $8,000/(5/3) = 4,800$ and variance

$$2(8,000)^2/[(5/3)(2/3)] - 4,800^2 = 92,160,000.$$

The sum of 100 claims has mean 480,000 and variance 9,216,000,000 which is a standard deviation of 96,000. The probability of exceeding 600,000 is approximately

$$1 - \Phi[(600{,}000 - 480{,}000)/96{,}000] = 1 - \Phi(1.25) = 0.106.$$

3.22 The mean of the gamma distribution is $5(1{,}000) = 5{,}000$ and the variance is $5(1{,}000)^2 = 5{,}000{,}000$. For 100 independent claims the mean is 500,000 and the variance is 500,000,000 for a standard deviation of 22,360.68. The probability of total claims exceeding 525,000 is

$$1 - \Phi[(525{,}000 - 500{,}000)/22{,}360.68] = 1 - \Phi(1.118) = 0.13178.$$

3.23 The sum of 2,500 contracts has an approximate normal distribution with mean $2{,}500(1{,}300) = 3{,}250{,}000$ and standard deviation $\sqrt{2{,}500}(400) = 20{,}000$. The answer is $\Pr(X > 3{,}282{,}500) \doteq \Pr[Z > (3{,}282{,}500 - 3{,}250{,}000)/20{,}000] = \Pr(Z > 1.625) = 0.052$.

3.24 The inverse Gaussian pdf is

$$f(x) = \frac{\mu}{\sqrt{2\pi\beta x^3}} \exp\left[-\frac{(x-\mu)^2}{2\beta x}\right] = \frac{\mu e^{\mu/\beta}}{\sqrt{2\pi\beta}} x^{-1.5} \exp\left(-\frac{x}{2\beta} - \frac{\mu^2}{2\beta x}\right), \quad x > 0.$$

Thus, $1 = \int_0^\infty f(x)dx$ may be restated as

$$\int_0^\infty x^{-1.5} \exp\left(-\frac{x}{2\beta} - \frac{\mu^2}{2\beta x}\right) dx = \frac{\sqrt{2\pi\beta}}{\mu e^{\mu/\beta}},$$

which is valid for any $\mu > 0, \beta > 0$. Then

$$\begin{aligned}
e^{tx} f(x) &= \frac{\mu e^{\mu/\beta}}{\sqrt{2\pi\beta}} x^{-1.5} \exp\left[-x\left(\frac{1}{2\beta} - t\right) - \frac{\mu^2}{2\beta x}\right] \\
&= \frac{\mu e^{\mu/\beta}}{\sqrt{2\pi\beta}} x^{-1.5} \exp\left(-\frac{x}{2\beta_t} - \frac{\mu_t^2}{2\beta_t x}\right)
\end{aligned}$$

where $\beta_t = \beta/(1 - 2\beta t)$ and $\mu_t = \mu/\sqrt{1 - 2\beta t}$. Therefore, if $t < 1/(2\beta)$, each of β_t and μ_t are positive, and the moment generating function is

$$\begin{aligned}
M(t) &= \int_0^\infty e^{tx} f(x)dx = \frac{\mu e^{\mu/\beta}}{\sqrt{2\pi\beta}} \int_0^\infty x^{-1.5} \exp\left(-\frac{x}{2\beta_t} - \frac{\mu_t^2}{2\beta_t x}\right) dx \\
&= \frac{\mu e^{\mu/\beta}}{\sqrt{2\pi\beta}} \frac{\sqrt{2\pi\beta_t}}{\mu_t e^{-\mu_t/\beta_t}} = \sqrt{\frac{\mu^2}{\beta} \cdot \frac{\beta_t}{\mu_t^2}} \exp\left(\frac{\mu}{\beta} - \frac{\mu_t}{\beta_t}\right) \\
&= \sqrt{\frac{\mu^2}{\beta} \cdot \frac{\beta}{\mu^2}} \exp\left(\frac{\mu}{\beta} - \frac{\mu}{\beta}\sqrt{1 - 2\beta t}\right).
\end{aligned}$$

Thus $M(t) = \int_0^\infty e^{tx} f(x)dx = \exp\left[\frac{\mu}{\beta}\left(1 - \sqrt{1 - 2\beta t}\right)\right], \quad t < 1/(2\beta)$.

4

Chapter 4 solutions

4.1   SECTION 4.2

Exercise 4.1 Arguing as in the examples,

$$
\begin{aligned}
F_Y(y) &= \Pr(X \le y/c) \\
&= \Phi\left[\frac{\ln(y/c) - \mu}{\sigma}\right] \\
&= \Phi\left[\frac{\ln y - (\ln c + \mu)}{\sigma}\right]
\end{aligned}
$$

which indicates that Y has the lognormal distribution with parameters $\mu + \ln c$ and σ. Because no parameter was multiplied by c, there is no scale parameter. To introduce a scale parameter, define the lognormal distribution function as $F(x) = \Phi\left(\frac{\ln x - \ln \nu}{\sigma}\right)$. Note that the new parameter ν is simply e^μ. Then,

Loss Models: From Data to Decisions, Solutions Manual, Second Edition.
By Stuart A. Klugman, Harry H. Panjer, and Gordon E. Willmot
ISBN 0-471-22762-5   Copyright © 2004 John Wiley & Sons, Inc.

arguing as above

$$
\begin{aligned}
F_Y(y) &= \Pr(X \le y/c) \\
&= \Phi\left[\frac{\ln(y/c) - \ln \nu}{\sigma}\right] \\
&= \Phi\left[\frac{\ln y - (\ln c + \ln \nu)}{\sigma}\right] \\
&= \Phi\left[\frac{\ln y - \ln c\nu}{\sigma}\right]
\end{aligned}
$$

demonstrating that ν is a scale parameter.

4.2 The following is not the only possible set of answers to this question. Model 1 is a uniform distribution on the interval 0 to 100 with parameters 0 and 100. It is also a beta distribution with parameters $a = 1$, $b = 1$, and $\theta = 100$. Model 2 is a Pareto distribution with parameters $\alpha = 3$ and $\theta = 2000$. Model 3 would not normally be considered a parametric distribution. However, we could define a parametric discrete distribution with arbitrary probabilities at $0, 1, 2, 3$, and 4 being the parameters. Conventional usage would not accept this as a parametric distribution. Similarly, Model 4 is not a standard parametric distribution, but we could define one as having arbitrary probability p at zero and an exponential distribution elsewhere. Model 5 could be from a parametric distribution with uniform probability from a to b and a different uniform probability from b to c. Model 6 is similar to Model 3.

4.3 For this year,

$$
\Pr(X > d) = 1 - F(d) = \left(\frac{\theta}{\theta + d}\right)^2.
$$

For next year, because θ is a scale parameter, claims will have a Pareto distribution with parameters $\alpha = 2$ and 1.06θ. That makes the probability $\left(\frac{1.06\theta}{1.06\theta+d}\right)^2$. Then

$$
\begin{aligned}
r &= \lim_{d\to\infty}\left[\frac{1.06(\theta + d)}{1.06\theta + d}\right]^2 \\
&= \lim_{d\to\infty}\frac{1.1236\theta^2 + 2.2472\theta d + 1.1236d^2}{1.1236\theta^2 + 2.12\theta d + d^2} \\
&= \lim_{d\to\infty}\frac{2.2472\theta + 2.2472d}{2.12\theta + 2d} \\
&= \lim_{d\to\infty}\frac{2.2472}{2} = 1.1236.
\end{aligned}
$$

4.4 The mth moment of a k-point mixture distribution is

$$
\begin{aligned}
\mathrm{E}(Y^m) &= \int y^m [a_1 f_{X_1}(y) + \cdots + a_k f_{X_k}(y)] dy \\
&= a_1 \mathrm{E}(Y_1^m) + \cdots + a_k \mathrm{E}(Y_k^m).
\end{aligned}
$$

For this problem, the first moment is

$$
a \frac{\theta_1}{\alpha - 1} + (1 - a) \frac{\theta_2}{\alpha + 1}, \text{ if } \alpha > 1.
$$

Similarly, the second moment is

$$
a \frac{2\theta_1^2}{(\alpha - 1)(\alpha - 2)} + (1 - a) \frac{2\theta_2^2}{(\alpha + 1)\alpha}, \text{ if } \alpha > 2.
$$

4.5 Using the results from Exercise 4.4, $\mathrm{E}(X) = \sum_{i=1}^{K} a_i \mu_i'$ and for the gamma distribution this becomes $\sum_{i=1}^{K} a_i \alpha_i \theta_i$. Similarly, for the second moment we have $\mathrm{E}(X^2) = \sum_{i=1}^{K} a_i \mu_2'$ which, for the gamma distribution, becomes $\sum_{i=1}^{K} a_i \alpha_i (\alpha_i + 1) \theta_i^2$.

4.6 Parametric distribution families: It would be difficult to consider the model in Model 1 as being from a parametric family (although the uniform distribution could be considered as a special case of the beta distribution). Model 2 is a Pareto distribution and as such is a member of the transformed beta family. As a stretch, Models 3 and 6 could be considered members of a family that places probability (the parameters) on a given number of non-negative integers. Model 4 could be a member of the "exponential plus family" where the plus means the possibility of discrete probability at zero. Creating a family for model 5 seems difficult.

Variable-component mixture distributions: Only model 5 seems to be a good candidate. It is a mixture of uniform distributions in which the component uniform distributions are on adjoining intervals.

4.7 For this mixture distribution,

$$
\begin{aligned}
F(5,000) &= 0.75\Phi\left(\frac{5,000 - 3,000}{1,000}\right) + 0.25\Phi\left(\frac{5,000 - 4,000}{1,000}\right) \\
&= 0.75\Phi(2) + 0.25\Phi(1) \\
&= 0.75(0.9772) + 0.25(0.8413) = 0.9432.
\end{aligned}
$$

The probability of exceeding 5000 is $1 - 0.9432 = 0.0568$.

4.8 The distribution function of Z is

$$
\begin{aligned}
F(z) &= 0.5\left[1 - \frac{1}{1 + (z/\sqrt{1,000})^2}\right] + 0.5\left[1 - \frac{1}{1 + z/1,000}\right] \\
&= 1 - 0.5\frac{1,000}{1,000 + z^2} - 0.5\frac{1,000}{1000 + z} \\
&= 1 - \frac{0.5(1,000^2 + 1,000z + 1,000^2 + 1,000z^2)}{(1,000 + z^2)(1,000 + z)}.
\end{aligned}
$$

The median is the solution to $0.5 = F(m)$ or

$$
\begin{aligned}
(1,000 + m^2)(1,000 + m) &= 2(1,000)^2 + 1,000m + 1,000m^2 \\
1,000^2 + 1,000m^2 + 1,000m + m^3 &= 2(1,000)^2 + 1,000m + 1,000m^2 \\
m^3 &= 1,000^2 \\
m &= 100.
\end{aligned}
$$

The distribution function of W is

$$
\begin{aligned}
F_W(w) &= \Pr(W \leq w) = \Pr(1.1Z \leq w) = \Pr(Z \leq w/1.1) = F_Z(w/1.1) \\
&= 0.5\left[1 - \frac{1}{1 + (w/1.1\sqrt{1,000})^2}\right] + 0.5\left[1 - \frac{1}{1 + z/1,100}\right].
\end{aligned}
$$

This is a 50/50 mixture of a Burr distribution with parameters $\alpha = 1$, $\gamma = 2$, and $\theta = 1.1\sqrt{1,000}$ and a Pareto distribution with parameters $\alpha = 1$ and $\theta = 1,100$.

4.9 Right censoring creates a mixed distribution with discrete probability at the censoring point. Therefore, Z is matched with (c). X is similar to Model 5 on Page 21 which has a continuous distribution function but the density function has a jump at 2. Therefore, X is matched with (b). The sum of two continuous random variables will be continuous as well, in this case over the interval from 0 to 5. Therefore, Y is matched with (a).

4.10 The density function is the sum of six functions. They are (where it is understood that the function is zero where not defined),

$$
\begin{aligned}
f_1(x) &= 0.03125, \ 1 \leq x \leq 5 \\
f_2(x) &= 0.03125, \ 3 \leq x \leq 7 \\
f_3(x) &= 0.09375, \ 4 \leq x \leq 8 \\
f_4(x) &= 0.06250, \ 5 \leq x \leq 9 \\
f_5(x) &= 0.03125, \ 8 \leq x \leq 12.
\end{aligned}
$$

Adding the functions yields

$$f(x) = \begin{cases} 0.03125, & 1 \le x < 3 \\ 0.06250, & 3 \le x < 4 \\ 0.15625, & 4 \le x < 5 \\ 0.18750, & 5 \le x < 7 \\ 0.15625, & 7 \le x < 8 \\ 0.09375, & 8 \le x < 9 \\ 0.03125, & 9 \le x < 12. \end{cases}$$

This is a mixture of seven uniform distributions, each being uniform over the indicated interval. The weight for mixing is the value of the density function multiplied by the width of the interval.

4.11

$$\begin{aligned} F_Y(y) &= \Phi\left[\frac{y/c - \mu}{\mu}\left(\frac{\theta c}{y}\right)^{1/2}\right] + \exp\left(\frac{2\theta}{\mu}\right)\Phi\left[-\frac{y/c + \mu}{\mu}\left(\frac{\theta c}{y}\right)^{1/2}\right] \\ &= \Phi\left[\frac{y - c\mu}{c\mu}\left(\frac{\theta c}{y}\right)^{1/2}\right] + \exp\left(\frac{2c\theta}{c\mu}\right)\Phi\left[-\frac{y + c\mu}{c\mu}\left(\frac{\theta c}{y}\right)^{1/2}\right] \end{aligned}$$

and so Y is inverse Gaussian with parameters $c\mu$ and $c\theta$. Because it is still inverse Gaussian, it is a scale family. Because both μ and θ change there is no scale parameter.

4.12 $F_Y(y) = F_X(y/c) = 1 - \exp[-(y/c\theta)^\tau]$ which is a Weibull distribution with parameters τ and $c\theta$.

4.2   SECTION 4.3

4.13 While the Weibull distribution has all positive moments, for the inverse Weibull moments exist only for $k < \tau$. Thus by this criterion, the inverse Weibull distribution has a heavier tail. With regard to the ratio of density functions, it is (with the inverse Weibull in the numerator and marking its parameters with asterisks)

$$\frac{\tau^* \theta^{*\tau^*} x^{-\tau^*-1} e^{-(\theta^*/x)^{\tau^*}}}{\tau \theta^{-\tau} x^{\tau-1} e^{-(x/\theta)^\tau}} \propto x^{-\tau-\tau^*} e^{-(\theta^*/x)^{\tau^*}+(x/\theta)^\tau}.$$

The logarithm is

$$(x/\theta)^\tau - (\theta^*/x)^{\tau^*} - (\tau + \tau^*)\ln x.$$

The middle term goes to zero, so the issue is the limit of $(x/\theta)^\tau - (\tau + \tau^*)\ln x$ which is clearly infinite. With regard to the hazard rate, for the Weibull

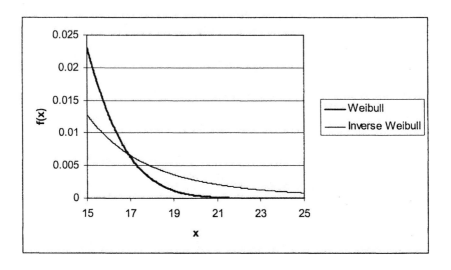

Fig. 4.1   Tails of a Weibull and inverse Weibull distribution.

distribution we have

$$h(x) = \frac{\tau x^{\tau-1}\theta^{-\tau}e^{-(x/\theta)^{\tau}}}{e^{-(x/\theta)^{\tau}}} = \tau x^{\tau-1}\theta^{-\tau}$$

which is clearly increasing when $\tau > 1$, constant when $\tau = 1$, and decreasing when $\tau < 1$. For the inverse Weibull,

$$h(x) = \frac{\tau x^{-\tau-1}\theta^{\tau}e^{-(\theta/x)^{\tau}}}{1 - e^{-(\theta/x)^{\tau}}} \propto \frac{1}{x^{\tau+1}[e^{(\theta/x)^{\tau}} - 1]}.$$

The derivative of the denominator is

$$(\tau+1)x^{\tau}[e^{(\theta/x)^{\tau}} - 1] + x^{\tau+1}e^{(\theta/x)^{\tau}}\theta^{\tau}(-\tau)x^{-\tau-1}$$

and the limiting value of this expression is $\theta^{\tau} > 0$. Therefore, in the limit, the denominator is increasing and thus the hazard rate is decreasing.

   Figure 4.1 displays a portion of the density function for Weibull ($\tau = 3$, $\theta = 10$) and inverse Weibull ($\tau = 4.4744$, $\theta = 7.4934$) distributions with the same mean and variance. The heavier tail of the inverse Weibull distribution is clear.

4.14 Means:

$$\begin{array}{lll} \text{Gamma} & : & 0.2(500) = 100 \\ \text{Lognormal} & : & \exp(3.70929 + 1.33856^2/2) = 99.9999 \\ \text{Pareto} & : & 150/(2.5 - 1) = 100. \end{array}$$

Second moments:

$$\begin{aligned}
\text{Gamma} \quad &: \quad 500^2(0.2)(1.2) = 60{,}000 \\
\text{Lognormal} \quad &: \quad \exp[2(3.70929) + 2(1.33856)^2] = 59{,}999.88 \\
\text{Pareto} \quad &: \quad 150^2(2)/[1.5(0.5)] = 60{,}000.
\end{aligned}$$

The density functions are:

$$\begin{aligned}
\text{Gamma} \quad &: \quad 0.754921x^{-0.8}e^{-0.002x} \\
\text{Lognormal} \quad &: \quad (2\pi)^{-1/2}(1.338566x)^{-1}\exp\left[-\frac{1}{2}\left(\frac{\ln x - 3.70929}{1.338566}\right)^2\right] \\
\text{Pareto} \quad &: \quad 688{,}919(x + 150)^{-3.5}.
\end{aligned}$$

The gamma and lognormal densities are equal when $x = 2{,}617$ while the lognormal and Pareto densities are equal when 9,678. Numerical evaluation indicates that the ordering is as expected.

4.15

$$\begin{aligned}
M_Y(t) &= \int_0^\infty e^{ty}\frac{S_X(y)}{E(X)}dy = \left.\frac{e^{ty}}{t}\frac{S_X(y)}{E(X)}\right|_0^\infty + \int_0^\infty \frac{e^{ty}}{t}\frac{f_X(y)}{E(X)}dy \\
&= -\frac{1}{tE(X)} + \frac{M_X(t)}{tE(X)} = \frac{M_X(t) - 1}{tE(X)}.
\end{aligned}$$

This result assumes $\lim_{y\to\infty} e^{ty}S_X(y) = 0$. An application of L'Hôpital's rule shows that this is the same limit as $(-t^{-1})\lim_{y\to\infty} e^{ty}f_X(y)$. This limit must be zero, otherwise the integral defining $M_X(t)$ will not converge.

4.16 (a)

$$\begin{aligned}
S(x) &= \int_x^\infty (1 + 2t^2)e^{-2t}dt \\
&= -(1 + t + t^2)e^{-2t}\big|_x^\infty \\
&= (1 + x + x^2)e^{-2x}, \quad x \ge 0.
\end{aligned}$$

(b) $\quad h(x) = -\frac{d}{dx}\ln S(x) = \frac{d}{dx}(2x) - \frac{d}{dx}\ln(1 + x + x^2)$

$$= 2 - \frac{1 + 2x}{1 + x + x^2}.$$

(c) For $y \ge 0$,

$$\begin{aligned}
\int_y^\infty S(t)dt &= \int_y^\infty (1 + t + t^2)e^{-2t}dt \\
&= -(1 + t + \tfrac{1}{2}t^2)e^{-2t}\big|_y^\infty = (1 + y + \tfrac{1}{2}y^2)e^{-2y}.
\end{aligned}$$

Thus,

$$S_e(x) = \frac{\int_x^\infty S(t)dt}{\int_0^\infty S(t)dt} = \left(1 + x + \tfrac{1}{2}x^2\right)e^{-2x}, \quad x \ge 0.$$

(d)

$$e(x) = \frac{\int_x^\infty S(t)dt}{S(x)} = \frac{1 + x + \frac{1}{2}x^2}{1 + x + x^2} \quad \text{from (a) and (c).}$$

(e) Using (b),

$$\lim_{x \to \infty} h(x) = \lim_{x \to \infty} \left(2 - \frac{1 + 2x}{1 + x + x^2} \right) = 2$$

$$\lim_{x \to \infty} e(x) = \frac{1}{\lim_{x \to \infty} h(x)} = \frac{1}{2}.$$

(f) Using (d), we have $e(x) = 1 - \frac{\frac{1}{2}x^2}{1 + x + x^2}$, and so

$$e'(x) = -\frac{x}{1 + x + x^2} + \frac{\frac{1}{2}x^2(1 + 2x)}{(1 + x + x^2)^2} = \frac{-x(1 + x + x^2) + \frac{1}{2}x^2 + x^3}{(1 + x + x^2)^2}$$

$$= -\frac{x + \frac{1}{2}x^2}{(1 + x + x^2)^2} \leq 0.$$

Also, from (b) and (e), $h(0) = 1, h(\frac{1}{2}) = \frac{6}{7}$, and $h(\infty) = 2$.

4.17 (a) Integration by parts yields

$$\int_x^\infty (y - x)f(y)dy = \int_x^\infty S(y)dy,$$

and hence $S_e(x) = \int_x^\infty f_e(y)dy = \frac{1}{E(X)} \int_x^\infty S(y)dy$, from which the result follows.

(b) It follows from (a) that

$$E(X)S_e(x) = \int_x^\infty yf(y)dy - x \int_x^\infty f(y)dy = \int_x^\infty yf(y)dy - xS(x),$$

which gives the result by addition of $xS(x)$ to both sides.

(c) Because $e(x) = E(X)S_e(x)/S(x)$, from (b)

$$\int_x^\infty yf(y)dy = S(x)\left[x + \frac{E(X)S_e(x)}{S(x)} \right] = S(x)[x + e(x)],$$

and the first result follows by division of both sides by $x + e(x)$. The inequality then follows from $E(X) = \int_0^\infty yf(y)dy \geq \int_x^\infty yf(y)dy$.

(d) Because $e(0) = E(X)$, the result follows from the inequality in (c) with $e(x)$ replaced by $E(X)$ in the denominator.

(e) As in (c), it follows from (b) that

$$\int_x^\infty yf(y)dy = S_e(x)\left\{ E(X) + \frac{xS(x)}{S_e(x)} \right\} = S_e(x)\left\{ E(X) + \frac{xE(X)}{e(x)} \right\},$$

i.e.

$$\int_x^\infty y f(y) dy = \mathrm{E}(X) S_e(x) \left\{ \frac{e(x) + x}{e(x)} \right\},$$

from which the first result follows by solving for $S_e(x)$. The inequality then follows from the first result since $\mathrm{E}(X) = \int_0^\infty y f(y) dy \geq \int_x^\infty y f(y) dy$.

4.3 SECTION 4.4

4.18 $F_Y(y) = 1 - (1 + y/\theta)^{-\alpha} = 1 - \left(\frac{\theta}{\theta+y} \right)^\alpha$. This is the cdf of the Pareto distribution. $f_Y(y) = dF_Y(y)/dy = \frac{\alpha\theta^\alpha}{(\theta+y)^{\alpha+1}}$.

4.19 After three years, values are inflated by 1.331. Let X be the 1995 variable and $Y = 1.331X$ be the 1998 variable. We want

$$\Pr(Y > 500) = \Pr(X > 500/1.331) = \Pr(X > 376).$$

From the given information we have $\Pr(X > 350) = 0.55$ and $\Pr(X > 400) = 0.50$. Therefore, the desired probability must be between these two values.

4.20 Inverse: $F_Y(y) = 1 - \left[1 - \left(\frac{\theta}{\theta+y^{-1}} \right)^\alpha \right] = \left(\frac{y}{y+\theta^{-1}} \right)^\alpha$. This is the inverse Pareto distribution with $\tau = \alpha$ and $\theta = 1/\theta$. Transformed: $F_Y(y) = 1 - \left(\frac{\theta}{\theta+y^\tau} \right)^\alpha$. This is the Burr distribution with $\alpha = \alpha$, $\gamma = \tau$, and $\theta = \theta^{1/\tau}$. Inverse transformed: $F_Y(y) = 1 - \left[1 - \left(\frac{\theta}{\theta+y^{-\tau}} \right)^\alpha \right] = \left[\frac{y^\tau}{y^\tau + (\theta^{-1/\tau})^\tau} \right]^\alpha$. This is the inverse Burr distribution with $\tau = \alpha$, $\gamma = \tau$, and $\theta = \theta^{-1/\tau}$.

4.21 $F_Y(y) = 1 - \frac{(y^{-1}/\theta)^\gamma}{1+(y^{-1}/\theta)^\gamma} = \frac{1}{1+(y^{-1}/\theta)^\gamma} = \frac{(y\theta)^\gamma}{1+(y\theta)^\gamma}$. This is the loglogistic distribution with γ unchanged and $\theta = 1/\theta$.

4.22 $F_Z(z) = \Phi \left[\frac{\ln(z/\theta)-\mu}{\sigma} \right] = \Phi \left[\frac{\ln z - \ln\theta - \mu}{\sigma} \right]$ which is the cdf of another lognormal distribution with $\mu = \ln\theta + \mu$, and $\sigma = \sigma$.

4.23 The distribution function of Y is

$$
\begin{aligned}
F_Y(y) &= \Pr(Y \le y) = \Pr[\ln(1 + X/\theta) \le y] \\
&= \Pr(1 + X/\theta \le e^y) \\
&= \Pr[X \le \theta(e^y - 1)] \\
&= 1 - \left[\frac{\theta}{\theta + \theta(e^y - 1)} \right]^\alpha \\
&= 1 - \left(\frac{1}{e^y} \right)^\alpha = 1 - e^{-\alpha y}.
\end{aligned}
$$

This is the distribution function of an exponential random variable with parameter $1/\alpha$.

4.24 $X|\Theta = \theta$ has pdf

$$
f_{X|\Theta}(x|\theta) = \frac{\tau\left[(x/\theta)^\tau\right]^\alpha \exp[-(x/\theta)^\tau]}{x\Gamma(\alpha)}
$$

and Θ has pdf

$$
f_\Theta(\theta) = \frac{\tau\left[(\delta/\theta)^\tau\right]^\beta \exp[-(\delta/\theta)^\tau]}{\theta\Gamma(\beta)}.
$$

The mixture distribution has pdf

$$
\begin{aligned}
f(x) &= \int_0^\infty \frac{\tau\left[(x/\theta)^\tau\right]^\alpha \exp[-(x/\theta)^\tau]}{x\Gamma(\alpha)} \frac{\tau\left[(\delta/\theta)^\tau\right]^\beta \exp[-(\delta/\theta)^\tau]}{\theta\Gamma(\beta)} d\theta \\
&= \frac{\tau^2 x^{\tau\alpha}\delta^{\tau\beta}}{x\Gamma(\alpha)\Gamma(\beta)} \int_0^\infty \theta^{-\tau\alpha - \tau\beta - 1} \exp[-\theta^{-\tau}(x^\tau + \delta^\tau)] d\theta \\
&= \frac{\tau^2 x^{\tau\alpha}\delta^{\tau\beta}}{x\Gamma(\alpha)\Gamma(\beta)} \frac{\Gamma(\alpha + \beta)}{\tau(x^\tau + \delta^\tau)^{\alpha+\beta}} = \frac{\Gamma(\alpha + \beta)\tau x^{\tau\alpha-1}\delta^{\tau\beta}}{\Gamma(\alpha)\Gamma(\beta)(x^\tau + \delta^\tau)^{\alpha+\beta}}
\end{aligned}
$$

which is a transformed beta pdf with $\gamma = \tau$, $\tau = \alpha$, $\alpha = \beta$, and $\theta = \delta$.

4.25 The requested gamma distribution has $\alpha\theta = 1$ and $\alpha\theta^2 = 2$ for $\alpha = 0.5$ and $\theta = 2$. Then

$$
\begin{aligned}
\Pr(N = 1) &= \int_0^\infty \frac{e^{-\lambda}\lambda^1}{1!} \frac{\lambda^{-0.5}e^{-0.5\lambda}}{2^{0.5}\Gamma(0.5)} \\
&= \frac{1}{\Gamma(0.5)\sqrt{2}} \int_0^\infty \lambda^{0.5}e^{-1.5\lambda}d\lambda \\
&= \frac{1}{1.5\Gamma(0.5)\sqrt{3}} \int_0^\infty y^{0.5}e^{-y}dy \\
&= \frac{\Gamma(1.5)}{1.5\Gamma(0.5)\sqrt{3}} \\
&= \frac{0.5}{1.5\sqrt{3}} = 0.19245.
\end{aligned}
$$

Line three follows from the substitution $y = 1.5\lambda$. Line five follows from the gamma function identity $\Gamma(1.5) = 0.5\Gamma(0.5)$. N has a negative binomial distribution and its parameters can be determined by matching moments. In particular, we have $\mathrm{E}(N) = \mathrm{E}[\mathrm{E}(N|\Lambda)] = \mathrm{E}(\Lambda) = 1$ and $\mathrm{Var}(N) = \mathrm{E}[\mathrm{Var}(N|\Lambda)] + \mathrm{Var}[\mathrm{E}(N|\Lambda)] = \mathrm{E}(\Lambda) + \mathrm{Var}(\Lambda) = 1 + 2 = 3$.

4.26 The hazard rate for an exponential distribution is $h(x) = f(x)/S(x) = \theta^{-1}$. Here θ is the parameter of the exponential distribution, not the value from the exercise. But this means that the θ in the exercise is the reciprocal of the exponential parameter and thus the density function is to be written $F(x) = 1 - e^{-\theta x}$. The unconditional distribution function is

$$
\begin{aligned}
F_X(x) &= \int_1^{11} (1 - e^{-\theta x})0.1d\theta \\
&= 0.1(\theta + x^{-1}e^{-\theta x})\big|_1^{11} \\
&= 1 + \frac{1}{10x}(e^{-11x} - e^{-x}).
\end{aligned}
$$

Then, $S_X(0.5) = 1 - F_X(0.5) = -\frac{1}{10(0.5)}(e^{-5.5} - e^{-0.5}) = 0.1205$.

4.27 We have

$$
\begin{aligned}
\Pr(N \geq 2) &= 1 - F_N(1) \\
&= 1 - \int_0^5 (e^{-\lambda} + \lambda e^{-\lambda})0.2d\lambda \\
&= 1 - [-(1 + \lambda)e^{-\lambda} - e^{-\lambda}]0.2\big|_0^5 \\
&= 1 + 1.2e^{-5} + 0.2e^{-5} - 0.2 - 0.2 \\
&= 0.6094.
\end{aligned}
$$

4.28 It follows from (4.5) that

$$f_X(x) = -S'(x) = -M'_\Lambda[-A(x)][-a(x)] = a(x)M'_\Lambda[-A(x)].$$

Then

$$h_X(x) = \frac{f_X(x)}{S_X(x)} = \frac{a(x)M'_\Lambda[-A(x)]}{M_\Lambda[-A(x)]}.$$

4.29 It follows from Example 4.32 with $\alpha = 1$ that $S_X(x) = (1+\theta x^\gamma)^{-1}$ which is a loglogistic distribution with the usual (i.e. in Appendix A) parameter θ replaced by $\theta^{-1/\gamma}$.

4.30 (a) Clearly, $a(x) > 0$, and we have

$$A(x) = \int_0^x a(t)dt = \frac{\theta}{2}\int_0^x (1+\theta t)^{-\frac{1}{2}}dt = \sqrt{1+\theta t}|_0^x = \sqrt{1+\theta x} - 1.$$

Because $A(\infty) = \infty$, it follows that $h_{X|\Lambda}(x|\lambda) = \lambda a(x)$ satisfies $h_{X|\Lambda}(x|\lambda) > 0$ and $\int_0^\infty h_{X|\Lambda}(x|\lambda)dx = \infty$.
(b) Using (a), we find that

$$S_{X|\Lambda}(x|\lambda) = e^{-\lambda(\sqrt{1+\theta x}-1)}.$$

It is useful to note that this conditional survival function may itself be shown to be an exponential mixture with inverse Gaussian frailty.
(c) It follows from Example 3.15 that $M_\Lambda(t) = (1-t)^{-2\alpha}$, and thus from (4.5) that X has a Pareto distribution with survival function $S_X(x) = M_\Lambda(1-\sqrt{1+\theta x}) = (1+\theta x)^{-\alpha}$.
(d) The survival function $S_X(x) = (1+\theta x)^{-\alpha}$ is also of the form given by (4.5) with mixed exponential survival function $S_{X|\Lambda}(x|\lambda) = e^{-\lambda x}$ and gamma frailty with moment generating function $M_\Lambda(t) = (1-\theta t)^{-\alpha}$, as in Example 3.15.

4.31 Write $F_X(x) = 1 - M_\Lambda[-A(x)]$, and thus

$$S_1(x) = \frac{1 - M_\Lambda[-A(x)]}{\mathrm{E}(\Lambda)A(x)} = M_1[-A(x)]$$

where

$$M_1(t) = \frac{M_\Lambda(t) - 1}{t\mathrm{E}(\Lambda)}$$

is the moment generating function of the equilibrium distribution of Λ, as is clear from Exercise 4.15. Therefore $S_1(x)$ is again of the form given by (4.5), but with the distribution of Λ now given by the equilibrium pdf $Pr(\Lambda > \lambda)/\mathrm{E}(\Lambda)$.

4.32 (a)

$$M_{\Lambda_s}(t) = \int_{\text{all } \lambda} e^{t\lambda} f_{\Lambda_s}(\lambda)d\lambda = \frac{1}{M_\Lambda(-s)} \int_{\text{all } \lambda} e^{(t-s)\lambda} f_{\Lambda_s}(\lambda)d\lambda$$

$$= \frac{M_\Lambda(t-s)}{M_\Lambda(-s)},$$

with the integral replaced by a sum if Λ is discrete.

(b) $M'_{\Lambda_s}(t) = \frac{M'_\Lambda(t-s)}{M_\Lambda(-s)}$, and thus $\text{E}(\Lambda_s) = M'_{\Lambda_s}(0) = \frac{M'_\Lambda(-s)}{M_\Lambda(-s)}$.

Also,

$M''_{\Lambda_s}(t) = \frac{M''_\Lambda(t-s)}{M_\Lambda(-s)}$, implying that $\text{E}(\Lambda_s^2) = M''_{\Lambda_s}(0) = \frac{M''_\Lambda(-s)}{M_\Lambda(-s)}$.

Now

$$c'_\Lambda(t) = \frac{M'_\Lambda(t)}{M_\Lambda(t)}, \text{ and replacement of } t \text{ by } -s \text{ yields}$$

$$c'_\Lambda(-s) = \text{E}(\Lambda_s). \text{ Similarly,}$$

$$c''_\Lambda(t) = \frac{M''_\Lambda(t)}{M_\Lambda(t)} - \left[\frac{M'_\Lambda(t)}{M_\Lambda(t)}\right]^2, \text{ and so}$$

$$c''_\Lambda(-s) = \frac{M''_\Lambda(-s)}{M_\Lambda(-s)} - \left[\frac{M'_\Lambda(-s)}{M_\Lambda(-s)}\right]^2 = \text{E}(\Lambda_s^2) - [\text{E}(\Lambda_s)]^2 = \text{Var}(\Lambda_s).$$

(c)

$$h_X(x) = -\frac{d}{dx}\ln S_X(x) = -\frac{d}{dx}\ln M_\Lambda[-A(x)] = -\frac{d}{dx}c_\Lambda[-A(x)]$$

$$= a(x)c'_\Lambda[-A(x)].$$

(d)

$$h'_X(x) = a'(x)c'_\Lambda[-A(x)] + a(x)\frac{d}{dx}c'_\Lambda[-A(x)]$$

$$= a'(x)c'_\Lambda[-A(x)] - [a(x)]^2 c''_\Lambda[-A(x)].$$

(e) Using (b) and (d), we have

$$h'_X(x) = a'(x)\text{E}[\Lambda_{A(x)}] - [a(x)]^2 \text{Var}[\Lambda_{A(x)}] \leq 0$$

if $a'(x) \leq 0$ because $\text{E}[\Lambda_{A(x)}] \geq 0$ and $\text{Var}[\Lambda_{A(x)}] \geq 0$. But $\frac{d}{dx}h_{X|\Lambda}(x|\lambda) = \lambda a'(x)$, and thus $a'(x) \leq 0$ when $\frac{d}{dx}h_{X|\Lambda}(x|\lambda) \leq 0$.

4.33 Using the first definition of a spliced model we have

$$f_X(x) = \begin{cases} \tau, & 0 < x < 1000 \\ \gamma e^{-x/\theta}, & x > 1000 \end{cases}$$

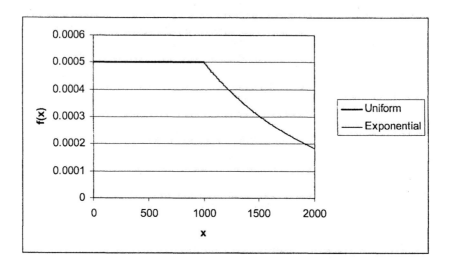

Fig. 4.2   Continuous spliced density function.

where the coefficient τ is a_1 multiplied by the the uniform density of .001 and the coefficient γ is a_2 multiplied by the scaled exponential coefficient. To ensure continuity we must have $\tau = \gamma e^{-1000/\theta}$. Finally, to ensure that the density integrates to 1, we have

$$
\begin{aligned}
1 &= \int_0^{1000} \gamma e^{-1000/\theta} dx + \int_{1000}^{\infty} \gamma e^{-x/\theta} dx \\
&= 1000\gamma e^{-1000/\theta} + \gamma\theta e^{-1000/\theta}
\end{aligned}
$$

which implies $\gamma = [(1000 + \theta)e^{-1000/\theta}]^{-1}$. The final density, a one parameter distribution, is

$$
f_X(x) = \begin{cases} \frac{1}{1000+\theta}, & 0 < x \le 1000 \\ \frac{e^{-x/\theta}}{(1000+\theta)e^{-1000/\theta}}, & x \ge 1000 \end{cases}.
$$

Figure 4.2 presents this density function for the value $\theta = 1000$.

4.34 $f_Y(y) = \exp(-|(\ln y)/\theta|)/2\theta y$, For $x \le 0$, $F_X(x) = \frac{1}{2\theta}\int_{-\infty}^x e^{t/\theta} dt = \frac{1}{2}e^{t/\theta}\big|_{-\infty}^x = \frac{1}{2}e^{x/\theta}$. For $x > 0$ it is $\frac{1}{2} + \frac{1}{2\theta}\int_0^x e^{-t/\theta} dt = 1 - \frac{1}{2}e^{-x/\theta}$. With exponentiation the two descriptions are $F_Y(y) = \frac{1}{2}e^{\ln y/\theta}$, $0 < y \le 1$, and $F_Y(y) = 1 - \frac{1}{2}e^{-\ln y/\theta}$, $y \ge 1$.

4.35 $F(x) = \int_1^x 3t^{-4} dt = 1 - x^{-3}$. $Y = 1.1X$. $F_Y(y) = 1 - (x/1.1)^{-3}$. $\Pr(Y > 2.2) = 1 - F_Y(2.2) = (2.2/1.1)^3 = 0.125$.

4.36 (a) $Pr\left(X^{-1} \le x\right) = Pr\left(X \ge 1/x\right) = Pr\left(X > 1/x\right)$, and the pdf is therefore

$$
\begin{aligned}
f_{1/X}(x) &= \frac{d}{dx}Pr\left(X > 1/x\right) \\[2mm]
&= \frac{1}{x^2}f\left(\frac{1}{x}\right) \\[2mm]
&= \sqrt{\frac{\theta x^3}{2\pi}}\exp\left[-\frac{\theta x}{2}\left(\frac{1-\mu x}{\mu x}\right)^2\right]\left(\frac{1}{x^2}\right) \\[2mm]
&= \sqrt{\frac{\theta}{2\pi x}}\exp\left[-\frac{\theta}{2x}\left(x-\frac{1}{\mu}\right)^2\right], \quad x > 0.
\end{aligned}
$$

(b) The inverse Gaussian pdf may be expressed as

$$
f(x) = \sqrt{\frac{\theta}{2\pi}}e^{\theta/\mu}x^{-1.5}\exp\left(-\frac{\theta x}{2\mu^2}-\frac{\theta}{2x}\right).
$$

Thus, $\int_0^\infty f(x)dx = 1$ may be expressed as

$$
\int_0^\infty x^{-1.5}\exp\left(-\frac{\theta x}{2\mu^2}-\frac{\theta}{2x}\right)dx = \sqrt{\frac{2\pi}{\theta}}e^{-\theta/\mu},
$$

valid for $\theta > 0$ and $\mu > 0$. Then

$$
\begin{aligned}
e^{t_1 x+t_2 x^{-1}}f(x) &= \sqrt{\frac{\theta}{2\pi}}e^{\theta/\mu}x^{-1.5}\exp\left[-\left(\frac{\theta}{2\mu^2}-t_1\right)x-\left(\frac{\theta}{2}-t_2\right)\frac{1}{x}\right] \\[2mm]
&= \sqrt{\frac{\theta}{2\pi}}e^{\theta/\mu}x^{-1.5}\exp\left(-\frac{\theta_* x}{2\mu_*^2}-\frac{\theta_*}{2x}\right)
\end{aligned}
$$

where $\theta_* = \theta - 2t_2$ and $\mu_* = \mu\sqrt{\frac{\theta-2t_2}{\theta-2\mu^2 t_1}}$. Therefore, if $\theta_* > 0$ and $\mu_* > 0$,

$$
\begin{aligned}
M\left(t_1,t_2\right) &= \int_0^\infty e^{t_1 x+t_2 x^{-1}}f(x)dx \\[2mm]
&= \sqrt{\frac{\theta}{2\pi}}e^{\theta/\mu}\int_0^\infty x^{-1.5}\exp\left(-\frac{\theta_* x}{2\mu_*^2}-\frac{\theta_*}{2x}\right)dx \\[2mm]
&= \sqrt{\frac{\theta}{2\pi}}e^{\theta/\mu}\sqrt{\frac{2\pi}{\theta_*}}e^{-\theta_*/\mu_*} \\[2mm]
&= \sqrt{\frac{\theta}{\theta-2t_2}}\exp\left[\frac{\theta}{\mu}-\frac{(\theta-2t_2)}{\mu}\sqrt{\frac{\theta-2\mu^2 t_1}{\theta-2t_2}}\right] \\[2mm]
&= \sqrt{\frac{\theta}{\theta-2t_2}}\exp\left[\frac{\theta-\sqrt{(\theta-2t_2)(\theta-2\mu^2 t_1)}}{\mu}\right].
\end{aligned}
$$

(c)

$$M_X(t) = M(t,0) = \exp\left(\frac{\theta - \sqrt{\theta\left(\theta - 2\mu^2 t\right)}}{\mu}\right) = \exp\left[\frac{\theta}{\mu}\left(1 - \sqrt{1 - \frac{2\mu^2}{\theta}t}\right)\right]$$

in agreement with the result in Exercise 3.24 because $\beta = \mu^2/\theta$, which implies that $\mu/\beta = \theta/\mu$.

(d)

$$
\begin{aligned}
M_{1/X}(t) &= M(0,t) \\
&= \sqrt{\frac{\theta}{\theta - 2t}}\,\exp\left(\frac{\theta - \sqrt{\theta(\theta - 2t)}}{\mu}\right) \\
&= \sqrt{\frac{\theta}{\theta - 2t}}\,\exp\left[\frac{\theta}{\mu}\left(1 - \sqrt{1 - \frac{2t}{\theta}}\right)\right] \\
&= \left(1 - \frac{2}{\theta}t\right)^{-1/2}\exp\left[\frac{\theta_1}{\mu_1}\left(1 - \sqrt{1 - \frac{2\mu_1^2}{\theta_1}t}\right)\right]
\end{aligned}
$$

where $\theta_1 = \theta/\mu^2$ and $\mu_1 = 1/\mu$. Thus $M_{1/X}(t) = M_{Z_1}(t)M_{Z_2}(t)$ with $M_{Z_1}(t) = \left(1 - \frac{2}{\theta}t\right)^{-1/2}$ the mgf of a gamma distribution with $\alpha = 1/2$ and θ replaced by $2/\theta$ (in the notation of Example 3.15). Also, $M_{Z_2}(t)$ is the mgf of an inverse Gaussian distribution with θ replaced by $\theta_1 = \theta/\mu^2$ and μ by $\mu_1 = 1/\mu$, as is clear from (c).

(e)

$$M_Z(t) = \mathrm{E}\left\{\exp\left[\frac{t}{X}\left(\frac{X - \mu}{\mu}\right)^2\right]\right\} = \mathrm{E}\left[\exp\left(\frac{t}{\mu^2}X - \frac{2t}{\mu} + \frac{t}{X}\right)\right],$$

and therefore

$$
\begin{aligned}
M_Z(t) &= e^{-\frac{2t}{\mu}}M\left(\frac{t}{\mu^2}, t\right) \\
&= e^{-\frac{2t}{\mu}}\sqrt{\frac{\theta}{\theta - 2t}}\,\exp\left[\frac{\theta - \sqrt{(\theta - 2t)^2}}{\mu}\right] \\
&= \sqrt{\frac{\theta}{\theta - 2t}}\,\exp\left[-\frac{2t}{\mu} + \frac{\theta - (\theta - 2t)}{\mu}\right] \\
&= \left(1 - \frac{2}{\theta}t\right)^{-1/2},
\end{aligned}
$$

the same gamma mgf discussed in (d).

4.4   SECTION 4.5

4.37 Let $\tau = \alpha/\theta$ and then in the Pareto distribution substitute $\tau\theta$ for α. The limiting distribution function is

$$\lim_{\theta\to\infty} 1 - \left(\frac{\theta}{x+\theta}\right)^{\tau\theta} = 1 - \lim_{\theta\to\infty} \left(\frac{\theta}{x+\theta}\right)^{\tau\theta}.$$

The limit of the logarithm is

$$
\begin{aligned}
\lim_{\theta\to\infty} \tau\theta[\ln\theta - \ln(x+\theta)] &= \tau \lim_{\theta\to\infty} \frac{\ln\theta - \ln(x+\theta)}{\theta^{-1}} \\
&= \tau \lim_{\theta\to\infty} \frac{\theta^{-1} - (x+\theta)^{-1}}{-\theta^{-2}} \\
&= -\tau \lim_{\theta\to\infty} \frac{x\theta}{x+\theta} = -\tau x.
\end{aligned}
$$

The second line and the final limit use L'Hôpital's rule. The limit of the distribution function is then $1 - \exp(-\tau x)$, an exponential distribution.

4.38 The generalized Pareto distribution is the transformed beta distribution with $\gamma = 1$. The limiting distribution is then transformed gamma with $\tau = 1$, which is a gamma distribution. The gamma parameters are $\alpha = \tau$ and $\theta = \xi$.

4.39 Hold α constant and let $\theta\tau^{1/\gamma} \to \xi$. Then let $\theta = \xi\tau^{-1/\gamma}$. Then

$$
\begin{aligned}
f(x) &= \frac{\Gamma(\alpha+\tau)\gamma x^{\gamma\tau-1}}{\Gamma(\alpha)\Gamma(\tau)\theta^{\gamma\tau}(1+x^\gamma\theta^{-\gamma})^{\alpha+\tau}} \\
&= \frac{e^{-\alpha-\tau}(\alpha+\tau)^{\alpha+\tau-1}(2\pi)^{1/2}\gamma x^{\gamma\tau-1}}{\Gamma(\alpha)e^{-\tau}\tau^{\tau-1}(2\pi)^{1/2}\xi^{\gamma\tau}\tau^{-\tau}(1+x^\gamma\xi^{-\gamma}\tau)^{\alpha+\tau}} \\
&= \frac{e^{-\alpha}\left(1+\frac{\alpha}{\tau}\right)^{\alpha+\tau-1}\gamma x^{-\gamma\alpha-1}}{\Gamma(\alpha)\tau^{-\alpha-\tau}\xi^{\gamma(\tau+\alpha)}\xi^{-\gamma\alpha}x^{-\gamma(\tau+\alpha)}(1+x^\gamma\xi^{-\gamma}\tau)^{\alpha+\tau}} \\
&= \frac{e^{-\alpha}\left(1+\frac{\alpha}{\tau}\right)^{\alpha+\tau-1}\gamma x^{-\gamma\alpha-1}}{\Gamma(\alpha)\xi^{-\gamma\alpha}\left[1+\frac{(\xi/x)^\gamma}{\tau}\right]^{\alpha+\tau}} \\
&\to \frac{\gamma\xi^{\gamma\alpha}}{\Gamma(\alpha)x^{\gamma\alpha+1}e^{(\xi/x)^\gamma}}.
\end{aligned}
$$

4.5   SECTION 4.6

4.40 For Exercise 12.96 the values at $k = 1, 2, 3$ are 0.1000, 0.0994, and 0.1333 which are nearly constant. The Poisson distribution is recommended.

For Exercise 12.98 the values at $k = 1, 2, 3, 4$ are 0.1405, 0.2149, 0.6923, and 1.3333 which is increasing. The geometric/negative binomial is recommended (although the pattern looks more quadratic than linear).

4.41 (a) $p_0 = e^{-4} = 0.01832$. $a = 0, b = 4$ and then $p_1 = 4p_0 = 0.07326$ and $p_2 = (4/2)p_1 = 0.14653$.

(b) $p_0 = 5^{-1} = 0.2$. $a = 4/5 = 0.8, b = 0$ and then $p_1 = (4/5)p_0 = 0.16$ and $p_2 = (4/5)p_1 = 0.128$.

(c) $p_0 = (1+2)^{-2} = 0.11111$. $a = 2/3, b = (2-1)(2/3) = 2/3$ and then $p_1 = (2/3 + 2/3)p_0 = 0.14815$ and $p_2 = (2/3 + 2/6)p_1 = 0.14815$.

(d) $p_0 = (1 - 0.5)^8 = 0.00391$. $a = -0.5/(1 - 0.5) = -1, b = (8+1)(1) = 9$ and then $p_1 = (-1 + 9)p_0 = 0.3125$ and $p_2 = (-1 + 9/2)p_1 = 0.10938$.

(e) $p_0 = 0$, $p_1 = 4/\ln(5) = 0.49707$. $a = 4/5 = 0.8, b = -0.8$ and then $p_2 = (0.8 - 0.8/2)p_1 = 0.14472$.

(f) $p_0 = 0$, $p_1 = \frac{-0.5(4)}{5^{0.5}-5} = 0.72361$. $a = 4/5 = 0.8, b = (-0.5 - 1)(0.8) = -1.2$ and then $p_2 = (0.8 - 1.2/2)p_1 = 0.14472$.

(g) The secondary probabilities were found in part (f). Then $g_0 = e^{-2} = 0.13534$, $g_1 = \frac{2}{1}(1)(0.72361)(0.13534) = 0.19587$, and

$$g_2 = \frac{2}{2}[1(0.723671)(0.19587) + 2(0.14472)(0.13534)] = 0.18091.$$

(h) $p_0^M = 0.5$ is given. $p_1^T = 1/5 = 0.2$ and then $p_1^M = (1 - 0.5)0.2 = 0.1$. From part (b), $a = 0.8, b = 0$ and then $p_2^M = (0.8)p_1^M = 0.08$.

(i) The secondary Poisson distribution has $f_0 = e^{-1} = 0.36788$, $f_1 = 0.36788$, and $f_2 = 0.18394$. Then, $g_0 = e^{-4(1-0.36788)} = 0.07978$. From the recursive formula, $g_1 = \frac{4}{1}(1)(0.36788)(0.07978) = 0.11740$ and $g_2 = \frac{4}{2}[1(0.36788)(0.11740) + 2(0.18394)(0.07978)] = 0.14508$.

(j) For the secondary ETNB distribution, $f_0 = 0, f_1 = \frac{2(0.5)}{1.5^3 - 1.5} = 0.53333$. With $a = b = 1/3$, $f_2 = (1/3 + 1/6)f_1 = 0.26667$. Then, $g_0 = e^{-4} = 0.01832$, $g_1 = \frac{4}{1}(1)(0.53333)(0.01832) = 0.03908$ and

$$g_2 = \frac{4}{2}[1(0.53333)(0.03908) + 2(0.26667)(0.01832)] = 0.06123.$$

(k) With $f_0 = 0.5$ (given) the other probabilities from part (j) must be multiplied by 0.5 to produce $f_1 = 0.26667$ and $f_2 = 0.13333$. Then, $g_0 = e^{-4(1-0.5)} = 0.01832$, $g_1 = \frac{8}{1}(1)(0.26667)(0.01832) = 0.03908$,

$$g_2 = \frac{8}{2}[1(0.26667)(0.03908) + 2(0.13333)(0.01832)] = 0.06123.$$

4.42

$$P_N(z) = \sum_{k=0}^{\infty} p_k z^k = \sum_{k=0}^{\infty} p_k e^{k \ln z} = M_N(\ln z)$$

$$P_N'(z) = z^{-1} M_N'(\ln z)$$

$$P_N'(1) = M_N'(0) = E(N)$$

$$P_N''(z) = -z^{-2} M_N'(\ln z) + z^{-2} M_N''(\ln z)$$

$$P_N''(1) = -E(N) + E(N^2) = E[N(N-1)]$$

4.43 For the Poisson, $\lambda > 0$ and so it must be $a = 0$ and $b > 0$. For the binomial, m must be a positive integer and $0 < q < 1$. This requires $a < 0$ and $b > 0$ provided $-b/a$ is an integer ≥ 2. For the negative binomial both r and β must be positive so $a > 0$ and b can be anything, provided $b/a > -1$.

The pair $a = -1$ and $b = 1.5$ cannot work because the binomial is the only possibility but $-b/a = 1.5$ which is not an integer. For proof, let p_0 be arbitrary. Then $p_1 = (-1 + 1.5/1)p = 0.5p$ and $p_2 = (-1 + 1.5/2)(0.5p) = -.125p < 0$.

4.44

$$p_k = p_{k-1}\left[\frac{\beta}{1+\beta} + \frac{r-1}{k}\frac{\beta}{1+\beta}\right] = p_{k-1}\frac{\beta}{1+\beta}\frac{k+r-1}{k}$$

$$= p_{k-2}\left(\frac{\beta}{1+\beta}\right)^2\frac{k+r-1}{k}\frac{k+r-2}{k-1}$$

$$= p_1\left(\frac{\beta}{1+\beta}\right)^{k-1}\frac{k+r-1}{k}\frac{k+r-2}{k-1}\cdots\frac{r+1}{2}.$$

The factors will be positive (and thus p_k will be positive) provided $p_1 > 0$, $\beta > 0$, $r > -1$, and $r \neq 0$.

To see that the probabilities sum to a finite amount,

$$\sum_{k=1}^{\infty} p_k = p_1 \sum_{k=1}^{\infty}\left(\frac{\beta}{1+\beta}\right)^{k-1}\frac{k+r-1}{k}\frac{k+r-2}{k-1}\cdots\frac{r+1}{2}$$

$$= p_1 \frac{1}{r}\sum_{k=1}^{\infty}\left(\frac{\beta}{1+\beta}\right)^{k-1}\binom{k+r-1}{k}$$

$$= p_1 \frac{(1+\beta)^{r+1}}{r\beta}\sum_{k=1}^{\infty}\left(\frac{1}{1+\beta}\right)^{r}\left(\frac{\beta}{1+\beta}\right)^{k}\binom{k+r-1}{k}.$$

The terms of the summand are the *pf* of the negative binomial distribution and so must sum to a number less than one (p_0 is missing) and so the original sum must converge.

4.45 From the previous solution (with $r = 0$),

$$
\begin{aligned}
1 &= \sum_{k=1}^{\infty} p_k = p_1 \sum_{k=1}^{\infty} \left(\frac{\beta}{1+\beta} \right)^{k-1} \frac{k-1}{k} \frac{k-2}{k-1} \cdots \frac{1}{2} \\
&= p_1 \sum_{k=1}^{\infty} \left(\frac{\beta}{1+\beta} \right)^{k-1} \frac{1}{k} \\
&= p_1 \frac{1+\beta}{\beta} \left[-\ln \left(1 - \frac{\beta}{1+\beta} \right) \right]
\end{aligned}
$$

using the Taylor series expansion for $\ln(1-x)$. Thus

$$
p_1 = \frac{\beta}{(1+\beta) \ln(1+\beta)}
$$

and

$$
p_k = \left(\frac{\beta}{1+\beta} \right)^k \frac{1}{k \ln(1+\beta)}.
$$

4.46

$$
\begin{aligned}
P(z) &= \frac{1}{\ln(1+\beta)} \sum_{k=1}^{\infty} \left(\frac{\beta}{1+\beta} \right)^k \frac{1}{k} z^k \\
&= \frac{1}{\ln(1+\beta)} \left[-\ln \left(1 - \frac{z\beta}{1+\beta} \right) \right] \\
&= \frac{\ln \left(\frac{1+\beta}{1+\beta-z\beta} \right)}{\ln(1+\beta)} \\
&= 1 - \frac{\ln[1 - \beta(z-1)]}{\ln(1+\beta)}
\end{aligned}
$$

4.47 The *pgf* goes to $1 - (1-z)^{-r}$ as $\beta \to \infty$. The derivative with respect to z is $-r(1-z)^{-r-1}$. The expected value is this derivative evaluated at $z = 1$, which is infinite due to the negative exponent.

4.48 $p_k / p_{k-1} = \left(\frac{k-1}{k} \right)^{\rho+1} \neq a + b/k$ for any choices of a, b, and ρ, and for all k.

4.49 Poisson: $P(z) = e^{\lambda(z-1)}$, $B(z) = e^z$, $\theta = \lambda$.
  Negative binomial: $P(z) = [1 - \beta(z-1)]^{-r}$, $B(z) = (1-z)^{-r}$, $\theta = \beta$.
  Binomial: $P(z) = [1 + q(z-1)]^m$, $B(z) = (1+z)^m$, $\theta = q$.

4.50

$$P_S(z) \;=\; \prod_{i=1}^{n} P_{S_i}(z) = \prod_{i=1}^{n} \exp\{\lambda_i[P_2(z) - 1]\}$$

$$=\; \exp\{(\sum_{i=1}^{n} \lambda_i)[P_2(z) - 1]\}.$$

This is a compound distribution. The primary distribution is Poisson with parameter $\sum_{i=1}^{n} m\lambda_i$. The secondary distribution has pgf $P_2(z)$.

4.51 The geometric-geometric distribution has pgf

$$P_{GG}(z) \;=\; (1 - \beta_1\{[1 - \beta_2(z - 1)]^{-1} - 1\})^{-1}$$

$$=\; \frac{1 - \beta_2(z - 1)}{1 - \beta_2(1 + \beta_1)(z - 1)}.$$

The Bernoulli-geometic distribution has pgf

$$P_{BG}(z) \;=\; 1 + q\{[1 - \beta(z - 1)]^{-1} - 1\}$$

$$=\; \frac{1 - \beta(1 - q)(z - 1)}{1 - \beta(z - 1)}.$$

The ZM geometric distribution has pgf

$$P_{ZMG}(z) \;=\; p_0 + (1 - p_0)\frac{[1 - \beta^*(z - 1)]^{-1} - (1 + \beta^*)^{-1}}{1 - (1 + \beta^*)^{-1}}$$

$$=\; \frac{1 - (p_0\beta^* + p_0 - 1)(z - 1)}{1 - \beta^*(z - 1)}.$$

In $P_{BG}(z)$, replace $1 - q$ with $(1 + \beta_1)^{-1}$ and replace β with $\beta_2(1 + \beta_1)$ to see that it matches $P_{GG}(z)$. It is clear that the new parameters will stay within the allowed ranges.

In $P_{GG}(z)$, replace q with $(1 - p_0)(1 + \beta^*)/\beta^*$ and replace β with β^*. Some algebra leads to $P_{ZMG}(z)$.

4.52 The binomial-geometric distribution has pgf

$$P_{BG}(z) \;=\; \left\{1 + q\left[\frac{1}{1 - \beta(z - 1)} - 1\right]\right\}^m$$

$$=\; \left[\frac{1 - \beta(1 - q)(z - 1)}{1 - \beta(z - 1)}\right]^m.$$

The negative binomial-geometric distribution has pgf

$$
\begin{aligned}
P_{NBG}(z) &= \left\{ 1 - \beta_1 \left[\frac{1}{1 - \beta_2(z-1)} - 1 \right] \right\}^{-r} \\
&= \left[\frac{1 - \beta_2(1+\beta_1)(z-1)}{1 - \beta_2(z-1)} \right]^{-r} \\
&= \left[\frac{1 - \beta_2(z-1)}{1 - \beta_2(1+\beta_1)(z-1)} \right]^{r} .
\end{aligned}
$$

In the binomial-geometric pgf, replace m with r, $\beta(1-q)$ with β_2, and β with $(1+\beta_1)\beta_2$ to obtain $P_{NBG}(z)$.

4.53 $P(z) = \sum_{k=0}^{\infty} z^k p_k,\ P^{(1)}(z) = \sum_{k=0}^{\infty} k z^{k-1} p_k,$

$$
\begin{aligned}
P^{(j)}(z) &= \sum_{k=0}^{\infty} k(k-1) \cdots (k-j+1) z^{k-j} p_k,\ P^{(j)}(1) \\
&= \sum_{k=0}^{\infty} k(k-1) \cdots (k-j+1) p_k \\
&= E[N(N-1) \cdots (N-j+1).
\end{aligned}
$$

$$
\begin{aligned}
P(z) &= \exp\{\lambda[P_2(z) - 1]\}, \\
P^{(1)}(z) &= \lambda P(z) P_2^{(1)}(z), \\
\mu &= P^{(1)}(1) = \lambda P(1) m_1' = \lambda m_1'.
\end{aligned}
$$

$$
\begin{aligned}
P^{(2)}(z) &= \lambda^2 P(z) \left[P_2^{(1)} \right]^2 + \lambda P(z) P_2^{(2)}(z), \\
\mu_2' - \mu &= P^{(2)}(1) = \lambda^2 (m_1')^2 + \lambda(m_2' - m_1').
\end{aligned}
$$

Then $\mu_2' = \lambda^2(m_1')^2 + \lambda m_2'$ and $\mu_2 = \mu_2' - \mu^2 = \lambda m_2'$.

$$
\begin{aligned}
P^{(3)}(z) &= \lambda^3 P(z) \left[P_2^{(1)} \right]^3 + 3\lambda^2 P(z) P_2^{(1)}(z) P_2^{(2)}(z) + \lambda P(z) P_2^{(3)}(z), \\
\mu_3' - 3\mu_2' + 2\mu &= \lambda^3(m_1')^3 + 3\lambda^2 m_1'(m_2' - m_1') + \lambda(m_3' - 3m_2' + 2m_1').
\end{aligned}
$$

Then,

$$
\begin{aligned}
\mu_3 &= \mu_3' - 3\mu_2'\mu + 2\mu^3 \\
&= (\mu_3' - 3\mu_2' + 2\mu) + 3\mu_2' - 2\mu - 3\mu_2'\mu + 2\mu^3 \\
&= \lambda^3(m_1')^3 + 3\lambda^2 m_1'(m_2' - m_1') + \lambda(m_3' - 3m_2' + 2m_1') \\
&\quad + 3[\lambda^2(m_1')^2 + \lambda m_2'] - 2\lambda m_1' - 3\lambda m_1'[\lambda^2(m_1')^2 + \lambda m_2'] + 2\lambda^3(m_1')^3 \\
&= \lambda^3[(m_1')^3 - 3(m_1')^3 + 2(m_1')^3] \\
&\quad + \lambda^2[3m_1'm_2' - 3(m_1')^2 + 3(m_1')^2 - 3m_1'm_2'] \\
&\quad + \lambda[m_3' - 3m_2' + 2m_1' + 3m_2' - 2m_1'] \\
&= \lambda m_3'.
\end{aligned}
$$

4.54 For the binomial distribution, $m_1' = mq$ and $m_2' = mq(1-q) + m^2 q^2$. For the third central moment, $P^{(3)}(z) = m(m-1)(m-2)[1 + q(z-1)]^{m-3} q^3$ and $P^{(3)}(1) = m(m-1)(m-2)q^3$. Then, $m_3' = m(m-1)(m-2)q^3 + 3mq - 3mq^2 + 3m^2 q^2 - 2mq$.
$\mu = \lambda m_1' = \lambda mq.$
$\sigma^2 = \lambda m_2' = \lambda(mq - mq^2 + m^2 q^2) = \lambda mq(1 - q + mq) = \mu[1 + q(m-1)].$

$$
\begin{aligned}
\mu_3 &= \lambda m_3' = \lambda mq(m^2 q^2 - 3mq^2 + 2q^2 + 3 - 3q + 3m - 2) \\
&= \lambda mq(3)(1 - q + mq) - \lambda mq(2) + \lambda mq(m^2 q^2 - 3mq^2 + 2q^2) \\
&= 3\sigma^2 - 2\mu + \lambda mq(m^2 q^2 - 3mq^2 + 2q^2) \\
&= 3\sigma^2 - 2\mu + \lambda mq(m-1)(m-2)q^2.
\end{aligned}
$$

Now, $\frac{m-2}{m-1}\frac{(\sigma^2 - \mu)^2}{\mu} = \frac{m-2}{m-1}\frac{\mu^2[q(m-1)]^2}{\mu} = (m-2)(m-1)\lambda mq^3$ and the relationship is shown.

4.55 For the compound distribution, the pgf is $P(z) = P_{NB}[P_P(z)]$ which is exactly the same as for the mixed distribution because mixing distribution goes on the outside.

4.56
$$
P_N(z) = \prod_{i=1}^n P_{N_i}(z) = \prod_{i=1}^n P_i[e^{\lambda(z-1)}]
$$

Then N is mixed Poisson. The mixing distribution has pgf $P(z) = \prod_{i=1}^n P_i(z)$.

4.57 Because Θ has a scale parameter, we can write $\Theta = cX$ where X has density (probability, if discrete) function $f_X(x)$. Then, for the mixed distribution

(with formulas for the continuous case)

$$p_k = \int \frac{e^{-\lambda\theta}(\lambda\theta)^k}{k!} f_\Theta(\theta)d\theta$$

$$= \frac{\lambda^k}{k!} \int e^{-\lambda\theta}\theta^k f_X(\theta/c)c^{-1}d\theta$$

$$= \frac{\lambda^k}{k!} \int e^{-\lambda c x}c^k x^k f_X(x)dx.$$

The parameter λ appears only as the product λc. Therefore, the mixed distribution does not depend on λ as a change in c will lead to the same distribution.

4.58 $$p_k = \int_0^\infty \frac{e^{-\theta}\theta^k}{k!} \frac{\alpha^2}{\alpha+1}(\theta+1)e^{-\alpha\theta}d\theta$$

$$= \frac{\alpha^2}{k!(\alpha+1)} \int_0^\infty \theta^k(\theta+1)e^{-(\alpha+1)\theta}d\theta$$

$$= \frac{\alpha^2}{k!(\alpha+1)} \int_0^\infty \beta^k(\alpha+1)^{-k-1}(\beta/(\alpha+1)+1)e^{-\beta}d\beta$$

$$= \frac{\alpha^2}{k!(\alpha+1)^{k+2}} [\Gamma(k+2)/(\alpha+1)+\Gamma(k+1)]$$

$$= \frac{\alpha^2[(k+1)/(\alpha+1)+1]}{(\alpha+1)^{k+2}}.$$

The pgf of the mixing distribution is

$$P(z) = \int_0^\infty z^\theta \frac{\alpha^2}{(\alpha+1)}(\theta+1)e^{-\alpha\theta}d\theta$$

$$= \frac{\alpha^2}{\alpha+1} \int_0^\infty (\theta+1)e^{-(\alpha-\ln z)\theta}d\theta$$

$$= \frac{\alpha^2}{\alpha+1} \left[-\frac{\theta+1}{\alpha-\ln z}e^{-(\alpha-\ln z)\theta} - \frac{\theta+1}{(\alpha-\ln z)^2}e^{-(\alpha-\ln z)\theta} \right]\Big|_0^\infty$$

$$= \frac{\alpha^2}{\alpha+1} \left[\frac{1}{\alpha-\ln z} + \frac{1}{(\alpha-\ln z)^2} \right]$$

and so the pgf of the mixed distribution (obtained by replacing $\ln z$ with $\lambda(z-1)$ is

$$P(z) = \frac{\alpha^2}{\alpha+1} \left\{ \frac{1}{\alpha-\lambda(z-1)} + \frac{1}{[\alpha-\lambda(z-1)]^2} \right\}$$

$$= \frac{\alpha}{\alpha+1}\frac{\alpha}{\alpha-\lambda(z-1)} + \frac{1}{\alpha+1}\left[\frac{\alpha}{\alpha-\lambda(z-1)} \right]^2$$

which is a two-point mixture of negative binomial variables with identical values of β. Each is also a Poisson-logarithmic distribution with identical logarithmic secondary distributions. The equivalent distribution has a logarithmic secondary distribution with $\beta = \lambda/\alpha$ and a primary distribution that is a mixture of Poissons. The first Poisson has $\lambda = \ln(1+\lambda/\alpha)$ and the second Poisson has $\lambda = 2\ln(1+\lambda/\alpha)$. To see that this is correct, note that the pgf is

$$
\begin{aligned}
P(z) &= \frac{\alpha}{\alpha+1} \exp\left\{ \ln(1+\lambda/\alpha)\frac{\ln[1-\lambda(z-1)/\alpha]}{\ln(1+\lambda/\alpha)} \right\} \\
&\quad + \frac{1}{\alpha+1} \exp\left\{ 2\ln(1+\lambda/\alpha)\frac{\ln[1-\lambda(z-1)/\alpha]}{\ln(1+\lambda/\alpha)} \right\} \\
&= \frac{\alpha}{\alpha+1} \ln[1-\lambda(z-1)/\alpha] + \frac{1}{\alpha+1}[1-\lambda(z-1)/\alpha]^2.
\end{aligned}
$$

4.59 (a)

$$
\sum_{n=0}^{\infty} a_n = \sum_{n=0}^{\infty}\sum_{k=n+1}^{\infty} p_k = \sum_{k=1}^{\infty}\sum_{n=0}^{k-1} p_k = \sum_{k=1}^{\infty} p_n \sum_{n=0}^{k-1}(1) = \sum_{k=1}^{\infty} k p_k = \mathrm{E}(N).
$$

(b) $\displaystyle\sum_{n=0}^{\infty} a_n z^n = \sum_{n=0}^{\infty} z^n \sum_{k=n+1}^{\infty} p_k = \sum_{k=1}^{\infty} p_k \sum_{n=0}^{k-1} z^n = \sum_{k=1}^{\infty} p_k \frac{1-z^k}{1-z}$. That is,

$$
A(z) = \frac{\displaystyle\sum_{k=1}^{\infty} p_k - \sum_{k=1}^{\infty} p_k z^k}{1-z} = \frac{1 - p_0 - [P(z) - p_0]}{1-z} = \frac{1 - P(z)}{1-z}.
$$

As $z \to 1$, $[1 - P(z)]/(1-z) \to \mathrm{E}(N)$, either using (a) or L'Hôpital's rule.
(c) A geometric series expansion implies using (b) that

$$
A(z) = \frac{1 - [1-\beta(z-1)]^{-r}}{1-z} = \beta\sum_{k=1}^{r}[1-\beta(z-1)]^{-k}.
$$

The coefficient of z^n on the right hand side is β times the sum from $k = 1$ to r of the negative binomial probabilities p_n, but with parameters r replaced by k and β. The coefficient on the left hand side is a_n.

(d) A binomial expansion yields

$$
\begin{aligned}
P(z) &= 1 - (1-z)^{-r} \\
&= -\sum_{n=1}^{\infty} \frac{(-r)(-r-1)...(-r-n+1)}{n!}(-z)^n \\
&= \sum_{n=1}^{\infty} \frac{(-r)(-r-1)...[-r-(n-1)](-1)^{n-1}}{n!} z^n \\
&= \sum_{n=1}^{\infty} \frac{(-r)(r+1)...(r+n-1)}{n!} z^n \\
&= \sum_{n=1}^{\infty} \frac{(-r)\Gamma(r+n)}{n!\,\Gamma(r+1)} z^n,
\end{aligned}
$$

and the expression for p_n follows by equating coefficients of z^n. Also, from (b),

$$
\begin{aligned}
A(z) &= \frac{1 - [1 - (1-z)^{-r}]}{1-z} \\
&= (1-z)^{-r-1} \\
&= \sum_{n=0}^{\infty} \frac{(-r-1)(-r-2)...(-r-n)}{n!}(-z)^n \\
&= \sum_{n=0}^{\infty} \frac{(r+1)(r+2)...(r+n)}{n!} z^n \\
&= \sum_{n=0}^{\infty} \binom{r+n}{n} z^n,
\end{aligned}
$$

and the result follows by equating coefficients of z^n.

(e)

$$
\begin{aligned}
a_n &= \sum_{k=n+1}^{\infty} p_k \\
&= \sum_{k=n+1}^{\infty} \int_0^{\infty} \frac{(\lambda\theta)^k e^{-\lambda\theta}}{k!} \, dU(\theta) \\
&= \int_0^{\infty} \left[e^{-\lambda\theta} \sum_{k=n+1}^{\infty} \frac{(\lambda\theta)^k}{k!} \right] dU(\theta) \\
&= \int_0^{\infty} \left[\int_0^{\theta} \frac{\lambda(\lambda x)^n e^{-\lambda x}}{n!} \, dx \right] dU(\theta),
\end{aligned}
$$

where the last line follows from the expression for the gamma cumulative distribution function in Appendix A with integer α. Interchanging the order of integration yields

$$a_n = \int_0^\infty \left[\int_x^\infty dU(\theta) \right] \frac{\lambda(\lambda x)^n e^{-\lambda x}}{n!} dx$$

$$= \lambda \int_0^\infty \frac{(\lambda x)^n e^{-\lambda x}}{n!} [1 - U(x)] dx,$$

and the result follows by changing the variable of integration from x to θ.

4.60 (a) Because $U'(\theta) = k(1 - \theta)^{k-1}$, $0 < \theta < 1$, we have

$$p_n = \frac{k\lambda^n}{n!} \int_0^1 \theta^n (1 - \theta)^{k-1} e^{-\lambda\theta} d\theta.$$

Change the variable of integration from θ to $x = 1 - \theta$ to get

$$p_n = \frac{k\lambda^n}{n!} \int_0^1 (1 - x)^n x^{k-1} e^{-\lambda(1-x)} dx$$

$$= \frac{k\lambda^n e^{-\lambda}}{n!} \int_0^1 x^{k-1} (1 - x)^n e^{\lambda x} dx.$$

Thus,

$$p_n = \frac{k\lambda^n e^{-\lambda}}{n!} \int_0^1 x^{k-1} (1 - x)^n \left[\sum_{m=0}^\infty \frac{(\lambda x)^m}{m!} \right] dx$$

$$= \frac{k\lambda^n e^{-\lambda}}{n!} \sum_{m=0}^\infty \frac{\lambda^m}{m!} \int_0^1 x^{m+k-1} (1 - x)^n dx.$$

But, from Appendix A, the beta distribution (with $\theta = \tau = 1$) satisfies $\int_0^1 f(x) dx = 1$, that is

$$\int_0^1 x^{a-1} (1 - x)^{b-1} dx = \frac{\Gamma(a)\Gamma(b)}{\Gamma(a + b)}.$$

Therefore, with $a = m + k$ and $b = n + 1$, we obtain

$$p_n = \frac{k\lambda^n e^{-\lambda}}{n!} \sum_{m=0}^\infty \frac{\lambda^m}{m!} \frac{\Gamma(m + k)\Gamma(n + 1)}{\Gamma(m + k + n + 1)}$$

$$= ke^{-\lambda} \sum_{m=0}^\infty \frac{\lambda^{m+n}(m + k - 1)!}{m!(m + k + n)!}.$$

(b) It follows from Exercise 4.59 that

$$Pr(N > n) = \lambda \int_0^1 \frac{(\lambda\theta)^n e^{-\lambda\theta}}{n!} (1 - \theta)^k d\theta.$$

This may be written as

$$\frac{k+1}{\lambda}Pr(N > n) = \frac{(k+1)\lambda^n}{n!} \int_0^1 \theta^n(1 - \theta)^k e^{-\lambda\theta} d\theta.$$

It is not hard to see from the solution to part (a) that the right hand side of this expression is simply p_n, but with k replaced by $k + 1$. Therefore, from (a),

$$\frac{k+1}{\lambda}Pr(N > n) = (k+1)e^{-\lambda} \sum_{m=0}^{\infty} \frac{\lambda^{m+n}(m+k)!}{m!(m+k+n+1)!},$$

that is

$$Pr(N > n) = e^{-\lambda} \sum_{m=0}^{\infty} \frac{\lambda^{m+n+1}(m+k)!}{m!(m+k+n+1)!}.$$

(c) When $k = 1$, the result in (a) becomes

$$p_n = e^{-\lambda} \sum_{m=0}^{\infty} \frac{\lambda^{m+n}}{(m+n+1)!} = \frac{e^{-\lambda}}{\lambda} \sum_{m=0}^{\infty} \frac{\lambda^{m+n+1}}{(m+n+1)!},$$

and by the series expansion of e^λ we thus have

$$\begin{aligned} p_n &= \frac{e^{-\lambda}}{\lambda}\left(e^\lambda - \sum_{m=0}^{n} \frac{\lambda^m}{m!}\right) \\ &= \frac{1 - \sum_{m=0}^{n} \frac{\lambda^m e^{-\lambda}}{m!}}{\lambda}. \end{aligned}$$

4.61

$$\begin{aligned} P(z) &= \sum_{n=0}^{\infty} p_n z^n \\ &= \int_0^{\infty} e^{\lambda\theta(z-1)} u(\theta) d\theta \\ &= e^{-[\lambda(1-z)]^\alpha} \\ &= e^{\lambda^\alpha[1-(1-z)^\alpha - 1]} \\ &= e^{\mu[Q(z)-1]}, \quad z \le 1, \end{aligned}$$

where the Poisson parameter is $\mu = \lambda^\alpha$ and $Q(z) = 1 - (1 - z)^\alpha$ is the pgf of a Sibuya distribution with parameter $r = -\alpha$.

4.62 (a) As shown in Exercise 4.36(c), the mixing distribution has mgf

$$M(t) = \sqrt{\frac{\theta}{\theta - 2t}} \exp\left[\frac{\theta}{\mu}\left(1 - \sqrt{1 - \frac{2}{\theta}t}\right)\right].$$

The mixed Poisson pgf is thus

$$
\begin{aligned}
P(z) &= M[\lambda(z-1)] \\
&= \sqrt{\frac{\theta}{\theta - 2\lambda(z-1)}} \exp\left\{\frac{\theta}{\mu}\left[1 - \sqrt{1 - \frac{2\lambda}{\theta}(z-1)}\right]\right\} \\
&= \{1 - \beta_1(z-1)\}^{-1/2} \exp\left\{\frac{\mu_2}{\beta_2}\left[1 - \sqrt{1 + 2\beta_2(1-z)}\right]\right\}
\end{aligned}
$$

where $\beta_1 = 2\lambda/\theta, \beta_2 = \lambda/\theta$, and $\mu_2 = \lambda/\mu$. That is

$$
P(z) = P_1(z)P_2(z)
$$

where $P_1(z)$ is a negative binomial pgf with parameters $r = 1/2$ and $\beta = \beta_1$, and $P_2(z)$ is a Poisson-inverse Gaussian pgf (from Example 4.71) with parameters $\mu = \mu_2$ and $\beta = \beta_2$.

(b) It follows from Example 4.53 that

$$
P_1(z) = \{1 - \beta_1(z-1)\}^{-1/2} = \exp\{\lambda_1[Q_1(z) - 1]\}
$$

where $\lambda_1 = [\ln(1 + \beta_1)]/2$, and

$$
Q_1(z) = 1 - \frac{\ln[1 - \beta_1(z-1)]}{\ln(1 + \beta_1)}
$$

is a logarithmic pgf with parameter β_1. Similarly, from Example 4.71,

$$
P_2(z) = \exp\left\{\frac{\mu_2}{\beta_2}\left[1 - \sqrt{1 + 2\beta_2(1-z)}\right]\right\} = \exp\{\lambda_2[Q_2(z) - 1]\}
$$

where $\lambda_2 = \mu_2\left(\sqrt{1 + 2\beta_2} - 1\right)/\beta_2$ and

$$
Q_2(z) = \frac{[1 - 2\beta_2(z-1)]^{1/2} - (1 + 2\beta_2)^{1/2}}{1 - (1 + 2\beta_2)^{1/2}}
$$

is an ETNB pgf with parameters $r = -1/2$ and $\beta = 2\beta_2$. Thus, by Theorem 4.58, $P(z) = \exp\{\lambda[Q(z) - 1]\}$ where

$$
\lambda = \lambda_1 + \lambda_2 = \frac{1}{2}\ln(1 + \beta_1) + \frac{\mu_2}{\beta_2}\left(\sqrt{1 + 2\beta_2} - 1\right)
$$

and

$$
Q(z) = \frac{\lambda_1}{\lambda_1 + \lambda_2}Q_1(z) + \frac{\lambda_2}{\lambda_1 + \lambda_2}Q_2(z)
$$

is the pgf of a mixture of logarithmic and ETNB pgfs.

5

Chapter 5 solutions

5.1 SECTION 5.2

Exercise 5.1 For the excess loss variable,

$$f_Y(y) = \frac{0.000003e^{-0.00001(y+5,000)}}{0.3e^{-.00001(5,000)}} = 0.00001e^{-0.00001y}, \; F_Y(y) = 1 - e^{-0.00001y}$$

For the left censored and shifted variable,

$$f_Y(y) = \begin{cases} 1 - 0.3e^{-0.05} = 0.71463, & y = 0 \\ 0.000003e^{-0.00001(y+5,000)}, & y > 0 \end{cases},$$

$$F_Y(y) = \begin{cases} 0.71463, & y = 0 \\ 1 - 0.3e^{-0.00001(y+5,000)}, & y > 0 \end{cases}$$

and it is interesting to note that the excess loss variable has an exponential distribution.

5.2 For the per payment variable,

$$f_Y(y) = \frac{0.000003e^{-0.00001y}}{0.3e^{-.00001(5,000)}} = 0.00001e^{-0.00001(y-5000)},$$

$$F_Y(y) = 1 - e^{-0.00001(y-5,000)}, \; y > 5000.$$

Loss Models: From Data to Decisions, Solutions Manual, Second Edition.
By Stuart A. Klugman, Harry H. Panjer, and Gordon E. Willmot
ISBN 0-471-22762-5   Copyright © 2004 John Wiley & Sons, Inc.

For the per loss variable,

$$f_Y(y) = \begin{cases} 1 - 0.3e^{-0.05} = 0.71463, & y = 0 \\ 0.000003e^{-0.00001y}, & y > 5,000 \end{cases},$$

$$F_Y(y) = \begin{cases} 0.71463, & 0 \leq y \leq 5,000 \\ 1 - 0.3e^{-0.00001y}, & y > 5,000. \end{cases}$$

5.3 From Example 3.2 $E(X) = 30,000$ and from Exercise 3.9,

$$E(X \wedge 5,000) = 30,000[1 - e^{-0.00001(5,000)}] = 1463.12.$$

Also $F(5,000) = 1 - 0.3e^{-0.00001(5,000)} = 0.71463$ and so for an ordinary deductible the expected cost per loss is 28,536.88 and per payment is 100,000. For the franchise deductible the expected costs are $28,536.88 + 5,000(0.28537) = 29,963.73$ per loss and $100,000 + 5,000 = 105,000$ per payment.

5.4 For risk 1,

$$E(X) - E(X \wedge d) = \frac{\theta}{\alpha - 1} - \frac{\theta}{\alpha - 1}\left[1 - \left(\frac{\theta}{\theta + k}\right)^{\alpha - 1}\right]$$

$$= \frac{\theta^{\alpha}}{(\alpha - 1)(\theta + k)^{\alpha - 1}}.$$

The ratio is then

$$\frac{\theta^{0.8\alpha}}{(0.8\alpha - 1)(\theta + k)^{0.8\alpha - 1}} \bigg/ \frac{\theta^{\alpha}}{(\alpha - 1)(\theta + k)^{\alpha - 1}} = \frac{(\theta + k)^{0.2\alpha}(\alpha - 1)}{\theta^{0.2\alpha}(0.8\alpha - 1)}.$$

As k goes to infinity, the limit is infinity.

5.5 The expected cost per payment with the 10,000 deductible is

$$\frac{E(X) - E(X \wedge 10,000)}{1 - F(10,000)} = \frac{20,000 - 6,000}{1 - 0.60} = 35,000.$$

At the old deductible, 40% of losses become payments. The new deductible must have 20% of losses become payments and so the new deductible is 22,500. The expected cost per payment is

$$\frac{E(X) - E(X \wedge 22,500)}{1 - F(22,500)} = \frac{20,000 - 9,500}{1 - 0.80} = 52,500.$$

The increase is $17,500/35,000 = 50\%$.

5.2   SECTION 5.3

5.6 From Exercise 5.3, the loss elimination ratio is
$(30,000 - 28,536.88)/30,000 = 0.0488$.

5.7 With inflation at 10% we need

$$E(X \wedge 5,000/1.1) = 30,000[1 - e^{-0.00001(5,000/1.1)}] = 1333.11.$$

After inflation, the expected cost per loss is $1.1(30,000 - 1333.11) = 31,533.58$ an increase of 10.50%. For the per payment calculation we need $F(5,000/1.1) = 1 - 0.3e^{-0.00001(5,000/1.1)} = 0.71333$ for an expected cost of 110,000, an increase of exactly 10%.

5.8 $E(X) = \exp(7 + 2^2/2) = \exp(9) = 8103.08$. The limited expected value is

$$
\begin{aligned}
E(X \wedge 2,000) &= e^9 \Phi\left(\frac{\ln 2,000 - 7 - 2^2}{2}\right) + 2,000\left[1 - \Phi\left(\frac{\ln 2,000 - 7}{2}\right)\right] \\
&= 8103.08\Phi(-1.7) + 2,000[1 - \Phi(0.3)] \\
&= 8103.08(0.0446) + 2,000(0.3821) = 1,125.60.
\end{aligned}
$$

The loss elimination ratio is $1,125.60/8103.08 = 0.139$. With 20% inflation, the probability of exceeding the deductible is

$$
\begin{aligned}
\Pr(1.2X > 2,000) &= \Pr(X > 2,000/1.2) \\
&= 1 - \Phi\left(\frac{\ln(2,000/1.2) - 7}{2}\right) \\
&= 1 - \Phi(0.2093) \\
&= 0.4171
\end{aligned}
$$

and therefore, 4.171 losses can be expected to produce payments.

5.9 The loss elimination ratio prior to inflation is

$$
\begin{aligned}
\frac{E(X \wedge 2k)}{E(X)} &= \frac{\frac{k}{2-1}\left[1 - \left(\frac{k}{2k+k}\right)^{2-1}\right]}{\frac{k}{2-1}} \\
&= \frac{2k}{2k + k} = \frac{2}{3}.
\end{aligned}
$$

Because θ is a scale parameter, inflation of 100% will double it to equal $2k$. Repeating the above gives the new loss elimination ratio of

$$1 - \left(\frac{2k}{2k + 2k}\right) = \frac{1}{2}.$$

5.10 The original loss elimination ratio is

$$\frac{E(X \wedge 500)}{E(X)} = \frac{1,000(1 - e^{-500/1,000})}{1,000} = 0.39347.$$

Doubling it produces the equation

$$0.78694 = \frac{1,000(1 - e^{-d/1,000})}{1,000} = 1 - e^{-d/1,000}.$$

The solution is $d = 1,546$.

5.11 For the current year the expected cost per payment is

$$\frac{E(X) - E(X \wedge 15,000)}{1 - F(15,000)} = \frac{20,000 - 7,700}{1 - 0.70} = 41,000.$$

After 50% inflation it is

$$\frac{1.5[E(X) - E(X \wedge 15,000/1.5)]}{1 - F(15,000/1.5)} = \frac{1.5[E(X) - E(X \wedge 10,000)]}{1 - F(10,000)}$$

$$= \frac{1.5(20,000 - 6,000)}{1 - 0.60} = 52,500.$$

5.12 The ratio desired is

$$\frac{E(X \wedge 10,000)}{E(X \wedge 1,000)} = \frac{e^{6.9078+1.5174^2/2}\Phi\left(\frac{\ln 10,000 - 6.9078 - 1.5174^2}{1.5174}\right) + 10,000\left[1 - \Phi\left(\frac{\ln 10,000 - 6.9078}{1.5174}\right)\right]}{e^{6.9078+1.5174^2/2}\Phi\left(\frac{\ln 1,000 - 6.9078 - 1.5174^2}{1.5174}\right) + 1,000\left[1 - \Phi\left(\frac{\ln 1,000 - 6.9078}{1.5174}\right)\right]}$$

$$= \frac{e^{8.059}\Phi(0) + 10,000[1 - \Phi(1.5174)]}{e^{8.059}\Phi(-1.5174) + 1,000[1 - \Phi(0)]}$$

$$= \frac{3162(0.5) + 10,000(0.0647)}{3162(0.0647) + 1,000(0.5)} = 3.162.$$

This year, the probability of exceeding 1000 is $\Pr(X > 1,000) = 1 - \Phi\left(\frac{\ln 1,000 - 6.9078}{1.5174}\right) = 0.5$. With 10% inflation the distribution is lognormal with parameters $\mu = 6.9078 + \ln 1.1 = 7.0031$ and $\mu = 1.5174$. The probability is $1 - \Phi\left(\frac{\ln 1,000 - 7.0031}{1.5174}\right) = 1 - \Phi(-0.0628) = 0.525$, an increase of

5%. Alternatively, the original lognormal distribution could be used and then $\Pr(X > 1{,}000/1.1)$ computed.

5.13 The desired quantity is the expected value of a right truncated variable. It is

$$\frac{\int_0^{1000} x f(x)}{F(1000)} = \frac{\mathrm{E}(X \wedge 1{,}000) - 1{,}000[1 - F(1{,}000)]}{F(1{,}000)} = \frac{\mathrm{E}(X \wedge 1{,}000) - 400}{0.6}.$$

From the loss elimination ratio,

$$0.3 = \frac{\mathrm{E}(X \wedge 1{,}000)}{\mathrm{E}(X)} = \frac{\mathrm{E}(X \wedge 1{,}000)}{2{,}000}$$

and so $\mathrm{E}(X \wedge 1{,}000) = 600$ making the answer $200/0.6 = 333$.

5.3   SECTION 5.4

5.14 From Exercise 3.9 we have

$$\mathrm{E}(X \wedge 150{,}000) = 30{,}000[1 - e^{-0.00001(150{,}000)}] = 23{,}306.10.$$

After 10% inflation the expected cost is

$$1.1\mathrm{E}(X \wedge 150{,}000/1.1) = 33{,}000[1 - e^{-0.00001(150{,}000/1.1)}] = 24{,}560.94$$

for an increase of 5.38%.

5.15 From Exercise 3.10 we have

$$e_X(d) = \frac{\theta + d}{\alpha - 1} = \frac{100 + d}{2 - 1} = 100 + d.$$

Therefore, the range is 100 to infinity. With 10% inflation, θ becomes 110 and the mean residual life is $e_Y(d) = 110 + d$. The ratio is $\frac{110+d}{100+d}$. As d increases, the ratio decreases from 1.1 to 1. The last one has not been encountered before. The mean residual life is

$$e_Z(d) = \frac{\int_d^{500} (x - d)f(x)dx + \int_{500}^\infty (500 - d)f(x)dx}{1 - F_X(d)}$$
$$= 100 + d - \frac{(100 + d)^2}{600}.$$

This is a quadratic function of d. It starts at 83.33, increases to a maximum of 150 at $d = 200$, and decreases to 0 when $d = 500$. The range is 0 to 150.

5.4   SECTION 5.5

5.16 $25 =\mathrm{E}(X) = \int_0^w (1-x/w)dx = w/2$ for $w = 50$. $S(10) = 1-10/50 = 0.8$.
Then

$$
\begin{aligned}
\mathrm{E}(Y) &= \int_{10}^{50} (x - 10)(1/50)dx/0.8 = 20 \\
\mathrm{E}(Y^2) &= \int_{10}^{50} (x - 10)^2(1/50)dx/0.8 = 533.33 \\
\mathrm{Var}(Y) &= 533.33 - 20^2 = 133.33.
\end{aligned}
$$

5.17 The bonus is $B = 500{,}000(0.7 - L/500{,}000)/3 = (350{,}000 - L)/3$, if
positive. The bonus is positive provided $L < 350{,}000$. The expected bonus is

$$
\begin{aligned}
\mathrm{E}(B) &= \frac{1}{3} \int_0^{350{,}000} (350{,}000 - l)f_L(l)dl \\
&= \frac{1}{3}\{350{,}000 F_L(350{,}000) - \mathrm{E}(L \wedge 350{,}000) \\
&\quad +350{,}000[1 - F_L(350{,}000)]\} \\
&= \frac{1}{3}\left\{ 350{,}000 - \frac{600{,}000}{2}\left[1 - \left(\frac{600{,}000}{950{,}000}\right)^2\right]\right\} \\
&= 56{,}556.
\end{aligned}
$$

5.18 The quantity we seek is

$$
\frac{1.1[\mathrm{E}(X \wedge 22/1.1) - \mathrm{E}(X \wedge 11/1.1)]}{\mathrm{E}(X \wedge 22) - \mathrm{E}(X \wedge 11)} = \frac{1.1(17.25 - 10)}{18.1 - 10.95} = 1.115.
$$

5.19 This exercise asks for quantities on a per loss basis. The expected value
is

$$
\mathrm{E}(X) - \mathrm{E}(X \wedge 100) = 1{,}000 - 1{,}000(1 - e^{-100/1{,}000}) = 904.84.
$$

To obtain the second moment, we need

$$
\begin{aligned}
\mathrm{E}[(X \wedge 100)^2] &= \int_0^{100} x^2 0.001 e^{-0.001x}dx + (100)^2 e^{-100/1{,}000} \\
&= -e^{-0.001x}(x^2 + 2{,}000x + 2{,}000{,}000)\big|_0^{100} + 9{,}048.37 \\
&= 9{,}357.68.
\end{aligned}
$$

The second moment is

$$E(X^2) - E[(X \wedge 100)^2] - 200E(X) + 200E(X \wedge 100)$$
$$= 2(1,000)^2 - 9,357.68 - 200(1,000) + 200(95.16)$$
$$= 1,809,674.32$$

for a variance of $1,809,674.32 - 904.84^2 = 990,938.89$.

5.20 Under the old plan the expected cost is $500/1 = 500$. Under the new plan the expected claim cost is K. The bonus is

$$B = \begin{cases} 0.5(500 - X), & X < 500 \\ 0.5(500 - 500), & X \geq 500 \end{cases}$$

which is 250 less a benefit with a limit of 500 and a coinsurance of 0.5. Therefore,

$$\begin{aligned} E(B) &= 250 - 0.5E(X \wedge 500) \\ &= 250 - 0.5\frac{K}{1}\left[1 - \left(\frac{K}{K + 500}\right)\right] \\ &= 250 - \frac{K}{2} + \frac{K^2}{2K + 1,000}. \end{aligned}$$

The equation to solve is

$$500 = K + 250 - \frac{K}{2} + \frac{K^2}{2K + 1,000}$$

and the solution is $K = 354$.

5.21 For year a, expected losses per claim are 2000 and thus 5000 claims are expected. Per loss, the reinsurer's expected cost is

$$\begin{aligned} E(X) - E(X \wedge 3,000) &= 2,000 - 2,000\left[1 - \left(\frac{2,000}{2,000 + 3,000}\right)\right] \\ &= 800 \end{aligned}$$

and therefore the total reinsurance premium is $1.1(5,000)(800) = 4,400,000$. For year b, there are still 5000 claims expected. Per loss, the reinsurer's expected cost is

$$\begin{aligned} &1.05[E(X) - E(X \wedge 3,000/1.05)] \\ &= 1.05\left\{2,000 - 2,000\left[1 - \left(\frac{2,000}{2,000 + 3,000/1.05}\right)\right]\right\} \\ &= 864.706 \end{aligned}$$

and the total reinsurance premium is $1.1(5,000)(864.706) = 4,755,882$. The ratio is 1.0809.

5.22 For this uniform distribution,

$$
\begin{aligned}
\mathrm{E}(X \wedge u) &= \int_0^u x(0.00002)dx + \int_u^{50,000} u(0.00002)dx \\
&= 0.00001u^2 + 0.00002u(50,000 - u) \\
&= u - 0.00001u^2.
\end{aligned}
$$

From Theorem 5.13, the expected payment per payment is

$$
\frac{\mathrm{E}(X \wedge 25,000) - \mathrm{E}(X \wedge 5,000)}{1 - F(5000)} = \frac{18,750 - 4,750}{1 - \frac{5,000}{50,000}} = 15,556.
$$

5.23 This is a combination of franchise deductible and policy limit, so none of the results apply. From the definition of this policy, the expected cost per loss is

$$
\int_{50,000}^{100,000} x f(x)dx + 100,000[1 - F(100,000)]
$$

$$
= \int_0^{100,000} x f(x)dx + 100,000[1 - F(100,000)] - \int_0^{50,000} x f(x)dx
$$

$$
= \mathrm{E}(X \wedge 100,000) - \mathrm{E}(X \wedge 50,000) + 50,000[1 - F(50,000)].
$$

Alternatively, it could be argued that this policy has two components. The first is an ordinary deductible of 50,000 and the second is a bonus payment of 50,000 whenever there is a payment. The first two terms above reflect the cost of the ordinary deductible and the third term is the extra cost of the bonus. Using the lognormal distribution, the answer is

$$
e^{10.5}\Phi\left(\frac{\ln 100,000 - 10 - 1}{1}\right) + 100,000\left[1 - \Phi\left(\frac{\ln 100,000 - 10}{1}\right)\right]
$$

$$
-e^{10.5}\Phi\left(\frac{\ln 50,000 - 10 - 1}{1}\right)
$$

$$
= e^{10.5}\Phi(0.513) + 100,000[1 - \Phi(1.513)] - e^{10.5}\Phi(-0.180)
$$

$$
= e^{10.5}(0.6959) + 100,000(0.0652) - e^{10.5}(0.4285) = 16,231
$$

5.5 SECTION 5.6

5.24 (a) For frequency, the probability of a claim is 0.03 and for severity, the probability of a 10,000 claim is 1/3 and of a 20,000 claim is 2/3.

(b) $\Pr(X = 0) = 1/3$ and $\Pr(X = 10{,}000) = 2/3$.

(c) For frequency, the probability of a claim is 0.02 and the severity distribution places probability one at 10,000.

5.25 $\nu = [1 - F(1000)]/[1 - F(500)] = 9/16$. The original frequency distribution is P–ETNB with $\lambda = 3$, $r = -0.5$, and $\beta = 2$. The new frequency is P–ZMNB with $\lambda = 3$, $r = -0.5$, $\beta = 2(9/16) = 9/8$ and $p_0^T = \frac{0 - 3^{.5} + (17/8)^{.5} - 0(17/8)^{.5}}{1 - 3^{.5}} = 0.37472$. This is equivalent to a P–ETNB with $\lambda = 3(1 - 0.37472) = 1.87584$, $\beta = 9/8$, and $r = -0.5$. which is P–IG with $\lambda = 1.87584$ and $\beta = 9/8$.

The new severity distribution has cdf $F(x) = \frac{F(x+500) - F(500)}{1 - F(500)} = 1 - \left(\frac{1{,}500}{1{,}500+x}\right)^2$ which is Pareto with $\alpha = 2$ and $\theta = 1{,}500$.

5.26 The value of p_0^M will be negative and so there is no appropriate frequency distribution to describe effect of lowering the deductible.

5.27 We have

$$
\begin{aligned}
P_{N^P}(z) &= P_N(1 - v + vz) \\
&= 1 - [1 - (1 - v + vz)]^{-r} \\
&= 1 - (v - vz)^{-r} \\
&= 1 - v^{-r}(1 - z)^{-r} \\
&= 1 - v^{-r}[1 - P_{N^L}(z)] \\
&= 1 - v^{-r} + v^{-r}P_{N^L}(z).
\end{aligned}
$$

Therefore,

$$
Pr(N^P = 0) = 1 - v^{-r},
$$

and

$$
Pr\left(N^P = n\right) = \left[1 - Pr\left(N^P = 0\right)\right] Pr\left(N^L = n\right); \quad n = 1, 2, 3, \ldots.
$$

6

Chapter 6 solutions

6.1 SECTION 6.1

6.1 $(c) + (d) + (e)$ is:

For $X \le 1{,}000$, $\quad\quad\quad\quad\quad 0 + 0 + X = X$

For $1{,}000 < X \le 63{,}500$, $\quad 0.8(X - 1{,}000) + 800 + 0.2X = X$

For $63{,}500 < X \le 126{,}000$, $\quad 0.8(X - 63{,}500) + 50{,}000 + 800 + 0.2X = X$

For $X > 126{,}000$, $\quad\quad\quad\quad 50{,}000 + 50{,}000 + X - 100{,}000 = X.$

6.2 SECTION 6.2

6.2
$$
\begin{aligned}
\mathrm{E}(N) &= P^{(1)}(1), \\
P^{(1)}(z) &= \alpha Q(z)^{\alpha-1} Q^{(1)}(z), \\
P^{(1)}(1) &= \alpha Q(1)^{\alpha-1} Q^{(1)}(1) \propto \alpha.
\end{aligned}
$$

6.3 The Poisson and all compound distributions with a Poisson primary distribution have a pgf of the form $P(z) = \exp\{\lambda[P_2(z) - 1]\} = [Q(z)]^\lambda$ where $Q(z) = \exp[P_2(z) - 1]$.

Loss Models: From Data to Decisions, Solutions Manual, Second Edition.
By Stuart A. Klugman, Harry H. Panjer, and Gordon E. Willmot
ISBN 0-471-22762-5   Copyright © 2004 John Wiley & Sons, Inc.

The negative binomial and geometric distributions and all compound distributions with a negative binomial or geometric primary distribution have $P(z) = \{1 - \beta[P_2(z) - 1]\}^{-r} = [Q(z)]^r$ where $Q(z) = \{1 - \beta[P_2(z) - 1]\}^{-1}$.

The same is true for the binomial distribution and binomial-X compound distributions with $\alpha = m$ and $Q(z) = 1 + q[P_2(z) - 1]$.

The zero-truncated and zero-modified distributions cannot be written in this form.

6.3   SECTION 6.3

6.4 To simplify writing the expressions, let

$$
\begin{aligned}
Njp &= \mu'_{Nj} = \mathrm{E}(N^j) \\
Nj &= \mu_{Nj} = \mathrm{E}[(N - N1p)^j] \\
Xjp &= \mu'_{Xj} = \mathrm{E}(X^j) \\
Xj &= \mu_{Xj} = \mathrm{E}[(XN - X1p)^j]
\end{aligned}
$$

and similarly for S. For the first moment, $P_S^{(1)}(z) = P_N^{(1)}[P_X(z)]P_X^{(1)}(z)$ and so

$$
\begin{aligned}
\mathrm{E}(S) &= P_S^{(1)}(1) = P_N^{(1)}[P_X(1)]P_X^{(1)}(1) \\
&= P_N^{(1)}(1)P_X^{(1)}(1) = (N1p)(X1p) = \mathrm{E}(N)\mathrm{E}(X).
\end{aligned}
$$

For the second moment use

$$
\begin{aligned}
P_S^{(2)}(1) &= S2p - S1p = P_N^{(2)}[P_X(z)][P_X^{(1)}(z)]^2 + P_N^{(1)}[P_X(z)]P_X^{(2)}(z) \\
&= (N2p - N1p)(Xp1)^2 + N1p(X2p - X1p).
\end{aligned}
$$

$$
\begin{aligned}
\mathrm{Var}(S) &= S2 = S2p - (S1p)^2 = S2p - S1p + S1p - (S1p)^2 \\
&= (N2p - N1p)(X1p)^2 + N1p(X2p - X1p) + (N1p)(X1p) \\
&\quad - (N1p)^2(X1p)^2 \\
&= N1p[X2p - (X1p)^2] + [N2p - (N1p)^2](X1p)^2 \\
&= (N1p)(X2) + (N2)(X1p)^2.
\end{aligned}
$$

For the third moment use

$$
\begin{aligned}
P_S^{(3)} &= S3p - 3S2p + 2S1p = P_N^{(3)}[P_X(z)][P_X^{(1)}(z)]^3 \\
&\quad + 3P_N^{(2)}[P_X(z)]P_X^{(1)}(z)P_X^{(2)}(z) + P_N^{(1)}[P_X(z)]P_X^{(3)}(z) \\
&= (N3p - 3N2p + 2N1p)(X1p)^3 \\
&\quad + 3(N2p - N1p)(X1p)(X2p - X1p) \\
&\quad + N1p(X3p - 3X2p + 2X1p).
\end{aligned}
$$

$$
\begin{aligned}
S3 &= S3p - 3(S2p)(S1p) + 2(S1p)^3 \\
&= S3p - 3S2p + 2S1p + 3[S2 + (S1p)^2](1 - 3S1p) + 2(S1p)^3 \\
&= (N3p - 3N2p + 2N1p)(X1p)^3 \\
&\quad + 3(N2p - N1p)(X1p)(X2p - X1p) \\
&\quad + N1p(X3p - 3X2p + 2X1p) + 3\{N1p[X2p - (X1p)^2] \\
&\quad\quad + [N2p - (N1p)^2](X1p)^2 \\
&\quad\quad + (N1p)^2(X1p)^2\}[1 - 3(N1p)(X1p)] \\
&\quad + 2(N1p)^3(X1p)^3 \\
&= N1p(X3) + 3(N2)(X1p)(X2) + N3(X1p)^3.
\end{aligned}
$$

6.5

$$
\begin{aligned}
E(X) &= 1{,}000 + 0.8(500) = 1{,}400. \\
\mathrm{Var}(X) &= \mathrm{Var}(X_1) + \mathrm{Var}(X_2) + 2\mathrm{Cov}(X_1, X_2) \\
&= 500^2 + 0.64(300)^2 + 2(0.8)(100{,}000) \\
&= 467{,}600. \\
E(S) &= E(N)E(X) = 4(1{,}400) = 5{,}600, \\
\mathrm{Var}(S) &= E(N)\,\mathrm{Var}(X) + \mathrm{Var}(N)E(X)^2 \\
&= 4(467{,}600) + 4(1{,}400)^2 = 9{,}710{,}400.
\end{aligned}
$$

6.6 $E(S) = 15(5)(5) = 375.$
$\mathrm{Var}(S) = 15(5)(100/12) + 15(5)(6)(5)^2 = 11{,}875.$ $StDev(S) = 108.97.$
The 95th percentile is $375 + 1.645(108.97) = 554.26.$

6.7
$$
\begin{aligned}
\mathrm{Var}(N) &= E[\mathrm{Var}(N|\lambda)] + \mathrm{Var}[E(N|\lambda)] = E(\lambda) + \mathrm{Var}(\lambda), \\
E(\lambda) &= 0.25(5) + 0.25(3) + 0.5(2) = 3, \\
\mathrm{Var}(\lambda) &= 0.25(25) + 0.25(9) + 0.5(4) - 9 = 1.5, \\
\mathrm{Var}(N) &= 4.5.
\end{aligned}
$$

6.8 The calculations appear in Table 6.1.

6.9 The calculations appear in Table 6.2.
$0.06 = f_S(5) = 0.1 - 0.05p,\ p = 0.8.$

Table 6.1   Results for Exercise 6.8

x	$f_1(x)$	$f_2(x)$	$f_{1+2}(x)$	$f_3(x)$	$f_S(x)$
0	0.9	0.5	0.45	0.25	0.1125
1	0.1	0.3	0.32	0.25	0.1925
2		0.2	0.21	0.25	0.2450
3			0.02	0.25	0.2500
4					0.1375
5					0.0575
6					0.0050

Table 6.2   Results for Exercise 6.9

x	$f_2(x)$	$f_3(x)$	$f_{2+3}(x)$	$f_1(x)$	$f_S(x)$
0	0.6	0.25	0.150	p	$0.15p$
1	0.2	0.25	0.200	$1-p$	$0.15 + 0.05p$
2	0.1	0.25	0.225		$0.2 + 0.025p$
3	0.1	0.25	0.250		$0.225 + 0.025p$
4			0.100		$0.25 - 0.15p$
5			0.050		$0.1 - 0.05p$
6			0.025		$0.05 - .025p$
7					$0.025 - 0.025p$

6.10 If all 10 do not have AIDS,

$$\begin{aligned} \mathrm{E}(S) &= 10(1,000) = 10,000 \\ \mathrm{Var}(S) &= 10(250,000) = 2,500,000 \end{aligned}$$

and so the premium is $10,000 + 0.1(2,500,000)^{1/2} = 10,158$.

If the number with AIDS has the binomial distribution with $m = 10$ and $q = 0.01$, then, letting N be the number with AIDS,

$$\begin{aligned} \mathrm{E}(S) &= \mathrm{E}[\mathrm{E}(S|N)] = \mathrm{E}[70,000N + 1,000(10 - N)] \\ &= 10,000 + 69,000[10(0.01)] \\ &= 16,900 \\ \mathrm{Var}(S) &= \mathrm{Var}[\mathrm{E}(S|N)] + \mathrm{E}[\mathrm{Var}(S|N)] \\ &= \mathrm{Var}[70,000N + 1,000(10 - N)] \\ &\quad + \mathrm{E}[1,600,000N + 250,000(10 - N)] \\ &= 69,000^2[10(0.01)(0.99)] + 2,500,000 + 1,350,000[10(0.01)] \\ &= 473,974,000 \end{aligned}$$

and so the premium is $16,900 + 0.1(473,974,000)^{1/2} = 19,077$. The ratio is $10,158/19,077 = 0.532$.

6.11 Let M be the random number of males and C be the number of cigarettes smoked. Then $E(C) = E[E(C|M)] = E[6M + 3(8 - M)] = 3E(M) + 24$. But M has the binomial distribution with mean $8(0.4) = 3.2$ and so $E(C) = 3(3.2) + 24 = 33.6$.

$$
\begin{aligned}
\text{Var}(C) &= E[\text{Var}(C|M)] + \text{Var}[E(C|M)] \\
&= E[64M + 31(8 - M)] + \text{Var}(3M + 24) \\
&= 33E(M) + 248 + 9\,\text{Var}(M) \\
&= 33(3.2) + 9(8)(0.4)(0.6) = 370.88.
\end{aligned}
$$

The answer is $33.6 + \sqrt{370.88} = 52.86$.

6.12 For insurer A, the group pays the net premium, so the expected total cost is just the expected total claims, that is, $E(S) = 5$.

For insurer B, the cost to the group is $7 - D$ where D is the dividend. We have

$$
D = \begin{cases} 7k - S, & S < 7k \\ 0, & S \ge 7k. \end{cases}
$$

Then $E(D) = \int_0^{7k}(7k - s)(0.1)ds = 2.45k^2$. We want $5 = E(7 - D) = 7 - 2.45k^2$, and so $k = 0.9035$.

6.13 Let θ be the underwriter's estimated mean. The underwriter computes the premium as

$$
\begin{aligned}
2E[(S - 1.25\theta)_+] &= 2\int_{1.25\theta}^{\infty}(s - 1.25\theta)\theta^{-1}e^{-s/\theta}ds \\
&= -2(s - 1.25\theta)e^{-s/\theta} - 2\theta e^{-s/\theta}\Big|_{1.25\theta}^{\infty} \\
&= 2\theta e^{-1.25}.
\end{aligned}
$$

Let μ be the true mean. Then $\theta = .9\mu$. The true expected loss is

$$
E[(S - 1.25(.9)\mu)_+] = 2\int_{1.125\mu}^{\infty}(s - 1.125\mu)\mu^{-1}e^{-s/\mu}ds = \mu e^{-1.125}
$$

The loading is

$$
\frac{2(0.9)\mu e^{-1.25}}{\mu e^{-1.125}} - 1 = 0.5885.
$$

6.14 A convenient relationship is, for discrete distributions on whole numbers, $E[(X - d - 1)_+] = E[(X - d)_+] - 1 + F(d)$. For this problem, $E[(X - 0)_+] = E(X) = 4$. $E[(X - 1)_+] = 4 - 1 + 0.05 = 3.05$, $E[(X - 2)_+] = 3.05 - 1 + 0.11 = 2.16$, $E[(X - 3)_+] = 2.16 - 1 + 0.36 = 1.52$. Then, by linear interpolation, $d = 2 + (2 - 2.16)/(1.52 - 2.16) = 2.25$.

6.15 $15 = \int_{100}^{\infty}[1 - F(s)]ds$, $10 = \int_{120}^{\infty}[1 - F(s)]ds$, $F(120) - F(80) = 0$. Subtracting the second equality from the first yields $5 = \int_{100}^{120}[1 - F(s)]ds$, but over this range $F(s) = F(80)$ and so

$$5 = \int_{100}^{120}[1 - F(s)]ds = \int_{100}^{120}[1 - F(80)]ds = 20[1 - F(80)]$$

and therefore $F(80) = 0.75$.

6.16

$$E(A) = \int_{50k}^{100}\left(\frac{x}{k} - 50\right)(0.01)dx = \left(\frac{x^2}{2k} - 50x\right)(0.01)\Big|_{50k}^{100}$$
$$= 50k^{-1} - 50 + 25k.$$
$$E(B) = \int_{0}^{100}kx(0.01)dx = \frac{kx^2}{2}(0.01)\Big|_{50k}^{100} = 50k.$$

The solution to $50k^{-1} - 50 + 25k = 50k$ is $k = 2/3$.

6.17 $E(X) = 440$, $F(30) = 0.3$, $f(x) = 0.01$ for $0 < x \leq 30$.

$$E(\text{benefits}) = \int_{0}^{30}20x(0.01)dx + \int_{30}^{\infty}[600 + 100(x - 30)]f(x)dx$$
$$= 90 + \int_{30}^{\infty}(-2,400)f(x)dx + 100\int_{30}^{\infty}xf(x)dx$$
$$= 90 - 2,400[1 - F(30)] + 100\int_{0}^{\infty}xf(x)dx$$
$$\quad -100\int_{0}^{30}xf(x)dx$$
$$= 90 - 2,400(0.7) + 100(440) - 100\int_{0}^{30}x(0.01)dx$$
$$= 90 - 1,680 + 44,000 - 450 = 41,960.$$

6.18

$$E(S) = E(N)E(X) = [0(0.5) + 1(0.4) + 3(0.1)][1(0.9) + 10(0.1)]$$
$$= 0.7(1.9) = 1.33.$$

We require $\Pr(S > 3.99)$. Using the calculation in Table 6.3, $\Pr(S > 3.99) \doteq 1 - 0.5 - 0.36 - 0.0729 = 0.0671$.

Table 6.3   Calculations for Exercise 6.18

x	$f_X^{*0}(x)$	$f_X^{*1}(x)$	$f_X^{*2}(x)$	$f_X^{*3}(x)$	$f_S(x)$
0	1	0	0	0	0.5000
1	0	0.9	0	0	0.3600
2	0	0	0.81	0	0
3	0	0	0	0.729	0.0729
p_n	0.5	0.4	0	0.1	

6.19 For 100 independent lives, $E(S) = 100mq$ and $\mathrm{Var}(S) = 100m^2q(1-q) = 250{,}000$. The premium is $100mq + 500$. For this particular group,

$$\begin{aligned} E(S) &= 97(mq) + (3m)q = 100mq \\ \mathrm{Var}(S) &= 97m^2q(1-q) + (3m)^2q(1-q) \\ &= 106m^2q(1-q) = 265{,}000 \end{aligned}$$

and the premium is $100mq + 514.18$. The difference is 14.78.

6.20
$$\begin{aligned} E(S) &= 1(8{,}000)(0.025) + 2(8{,}000)(0.025) = 600 \\ \mathrm{Var}(S) &= 1(8{,}000)(0.025)(0.975) \\ &\quad + 2^2(8{,}000)(0.025)(0.975) = 975. \end{aligned}$$

The cost of reinsurance is $0.03(2)(4{,}500) = 270$.

$$\begin{aligned} \Pr(S + 270 > 1{,}000) &= \Pr(S > 730) \\ &= \Pr\left(\frac{S - 600}{\sqrt{975}} > \frac{730 - 600}{\sqrt{975}} = 4.163 \right) \end{aligned}$$

so $K = 4.163$.

6.21
$$\begin{aligned} E(Z) &= \int_{10}^{100} 0.8(y - 10)(0.02)(1 - 0.01y)dy \\ &= 0.016 \int_{10}^{100} -0.01y^2 + 1.1y - 10\, dy = 19.44. \end{aligned}$$

6.22
$$\begin{aligned} \Pr(S > 100) &= \sum_{n=0}^{3} \Pr(N = n)\Pr(X^{*n} > 100) \\ &= 0.5(0) + 0.2\Pr(X > 100) \\ &\quad + 0.2\Pr(X^{*2} > 100) + 0.1\Pr(X^{*3} > 100). \end{aligned}$$

Because $X \sim N(100, 9)$, $X^{*2} \sim N(200, 18)$, and $X^{*3} \sim N(300, 27)$ and so

$$
\begin{aligned}
\Pr(S > 100) &= 0.2 \Pr\left(Z > \frac{100 - 100}{3}\right) + 0.2 \Pr\left(Z > \frac{100 - 200}{\sqrt{18}}\right) \\
&\quad + 0.2 \Pr\left(Z > \frac{100 - 300}{\sqrt{27}}\right) \\
&= 0.2(0.5) + 0.2(1) + 0.1(1) = 0.4.
\end{aligned}
$$

6.23 The calculations are in Table 6.4. The expected retained payment is $2,000(0.1) + 3,000(0.15) + 4,000(0.06) + 5,000(0.6275) = 4,027.5$ and the total cost is $4,027.5 + 1,472 = 5,499.5$.

Table 6.4 Calculations for Exercise 6.23

x	$f_X^{*0}(x)$	$f_X^{*1}(x)$	$f_X^{*2}(x)$	$f_S(x)$
0	1	0	0	0.0625
1	0	0	0	0.0000
2	0	0.4	0	0.1000
3	0	0.6	0	0.1500
4	0	0	0.16	0.0600
p_k	1/16	1/4	3/8	

6.24 In general, paying for days a through b, the expected number of days is

$$
\begin{aligned}
&\sum_{k=a}^{b} (k - a + 1) p_k + (b - a + 1)[1 - F(b)] \\
={}& \sum_{k=a}^{b} \sum_{j=a}^{k} p_k + (b - a + 1)[1 - F(b)] \\
={}& \sum_{j=a}^{b} \sum_{k=j}^{b} p_k + (b - a + 1)[1 - F(b)] \\
={}& \sum_{j=a}^{b} [F(b) - F(j - 1)] + (b - a + 1)[1 - F(b)] \\
={}& \sum_{j=a}^{b} [1 - F(j - 1)] = \sum_{j=a}^{b} (0.8)^{j-1} \\
={}& \frac{(0.8)^{a-1} - (0.8)^{b}}{.2}.
\end{aligned}
$$

For the four through ten policy the expected numbered of days is $(0.8^3 - 0.8^{10})/0.2 = 2.02313$. For the four through seventeen policy the expected number of days is $(0.8^3 - 0.8^{17})/0.2 = 2.44741$. This is a 21% increase.

6.25

$$E(S) = \int_1^\infty x3x^{-4}dx = 3/2$$

$$E(X^2) = \int_1^\infty x^2 3x^{-4}dx = 3$$

$$Var(S) = 3 - (3/2)^2 = 3/4.$$

$$0.9 = Pr[S \le (1+\theta)(3/2)] = \int_1^{(1+\theta)(3/2)} 3x^{-4}dx$$

$$= 1 - [(1+\theta)(3/2)]^{-3},$$

and so $\theta = 0.43629$.

$$0.9 = Pr[S \le 1.5 + \lambda\sqrt{3/4}] = \int_1^{1.5+\lambda\sqrt{3/4}} 3x^{-4}dx$$

$$= 1 - [1.5 + \lambda\sqrt{3/4}]^{-3},$$

and so $\lambda = 0.75568$.

6.4 SECTION 6.4

6.26 (a) The gamma distribution has mgf $(1 - \theta z)^{-\alpha}$. Adding n such variables produces a random variable with mgf $(1 - \theta z)^{-n\alpha}$. This is a gamma distribution with parameters $n\alpha$ and θ. The inverse Gaussian distribution has mgf $\exp\{\theta[1 - (1 - 2\mu^2 z/\theta)^{1/2}]/\mu\}$. When raised to the nth power it becomes $\exp\{n\theta[1 - (1 - 2\mu^2 z/\theta)^{1/2}]/\mu\}$. This is an inverse Gaussian distribution with parameters $\mu^3/(n\theta^2)$ and μ^2/θ replacing μ and θ. Because both parameters change in the inverse Gaussian case, only the gamma has the desired property. However, when the inverse Gaussian distribution is reparameterized with $\beta = \mu^2/\theta$ replacing θ, the property will hold.
(b) All infinitely divisible distributions must be closed under convolutions. The answer is the same as that for Exercise 6.3. In (4.19), f_k^{*n} can be written explicitly. Note that this is the secondary distribution and so will not work for distributions such as the Poisson-ETNB in which the secondary distribution is truncated and so is not closed under convolution.

6.27 Because this is a compound distribution defined on the non-negative integers, we can use Theorem 4.54. With an appropriate adaptation of notation,

$$P_N[P_X(z;\beta)] = P_N\{P_X(z); \beta[1 - f_X(0)]\}.$$

So just replace β by $\beta^* = \beta[1 - f_X(0)]$.

6.28 (a)

$$
\begin{aligned}
f_S(x) &= \sum_{n=1}^{\infty} \frac{\beta^n}{n(1+\beta)^n \ln(1+\beta)} \frac{x^{n-1} e^{-x/\theta}}{\theta^n (n-1)!} \\
&= \frac{1}{\ln(1+\beta)} \sum_{n=1}^{\infty} \left[\frac{\beta}{\theta(1+\beta)} \right]^n \frac{1}{n!} x^{n-1} e^{-x/\theta}
\end{aligned}
$$

(b)

$$
\begin{aligned}
f_S(x) &= \frac{e^{-x/\theta}}{x \ln(1+\beta)} \sum_{n=1}^{\infty} \left[\frac{x\beta}{\theta(1+\beta)} \right]^n \frac{1}{n!} \\
&= \frac{e^{-x/\theta}}{x \ln(1+\beta)} \left\{ \exp\left[\frac{x\beta}{\theta(1+\beta)} \right] - 1 \right\} \\
&= \frac{\exp\left[-\frac{x}{\theta(1+\beta)} \right] - \exp\left(-\frac{x}{\theta}\right)}{x \ln(1+\beta)}
\end{aligned}
$$

6.29 The answer is the sum of
$0.80R_{100}$ pays 80% of all in excess of 100,
$0.10R_{1100}$ pays an additional 10% in excess of 1,100, and
$0.10R_{2100}$ pays an additional 10% in excess of 2,100.

6.30 $\Pr(S = 0) = \sum_{n=0}^{\infty} p_n \Pr(B_n = 0)$ where $B_n \tilde{} bin(n, 0.25)$. Thus

$$
\Pr(S = 0) = \sum_{n=0}^{\infty} \frac{e^{-2} 2^n}{n!} (0.75)^n = e^{-2} e^{1.5} = e^{-1/2}.
$$

6.31

$$
\begin{aligned}
E(S) &= \int_0^{\infty} x f(x) dx = \int_0^{\infty} x \int_2^4 f(x|\theta) u(\theta) d\theta \, dx \\
&= \int_2^4 \frac{1}{2} \int_0^{\infty} x f(x|\theta) dx \, d\theta = \frac{1}{2} \int_2^4 E(S|\theta) d\theta = \frac{1}{2} \int_2^4 \frac{1}{\theta} d\theta \\
&= \frac{1}{2} (\ln 4 - \ln 2)
\end{aligned}
$$

6.32 $\mathrm{E}(N) = 0.1$.

$$
\begin{aligned}
\mathrm{E}(X) &= \int_0^{30} 100t f(t)dt + 3{,}000\,\mathrm{Pr}(T > 30) \\
&= \int_0^{10} 100t(0.04)dt + \int_{10}^{20} 100t(0.035)dt \\
&\quad + \int_{20}^{30} 100t(0.02)dt + 3{,}000(0.05) \\
&= 200 + 525 + 500 + 150 = 1{,}350.
\end{aligned}
$$

$\mathrm{E}(S) = 0.1(1{,}350) = 135$.

6.33 Total claims are compound Poisson with $\lambda = 5$ and severity distribution

$$
\begin{aligned}
f_X(x) &= 0.4f_1(x) + 0.6f_2(x) \\
&= \begin{cases} 0.4(0.001) + 0.6(0.005) = 0.0034, & 0 < x \le 200 \\ 0.4(0.001) + 0.6(0) = 0.0004, & 200 < x \le 1{,}000. \end{cases}
\end{aligned}
$$

Then,

$$
\begin{aligned}
\mathrm{E}[(X - 100)_+] &= \int_{100}^{\infty} (x - 100) f_X(x) dx \\
&= \int_{100}^{200} (x - 100)(0.0034) dx \\
&\quad + \int_{200}^{\infty} (x - 100)(0.0004) dx \\
&= 177.
\end{aligned}
$$

6.34 The calculations appear in Table 6.5.

Table 6.5   Calculations for Exercise 6.34

s	$\mathrm{Pr}(S = s)$	d	$d\,\mathrm{Pr}(S = s)$
0	0.031676	4	0.12671
1	0.126705	3	0.38012
2	0.232293	2	0.46459
3	0.258104	1	0.25810
4+	0.351222	0	0
	Total		1.25952

6.35 (a)

$$M_X(z) = \sum_{k=1}^{r} q_k \int_0^\infty e^{zx} \theta^{-k} x^{k-1} e^{-x/\theta} \frac{1}{(n-1)!} dx$$

$$= \sum_{k=1}^{r} q_k (1 - \theta z)^{-k} = Q[(1-\theta z)^{-1}]$$

(b)

$$M_S(z) = P_N[M_X(z)] = P_N\{Q[(1-\theta z)^{-1}]\}$$
$$= C[(1-\theta z)^{-1}]$$

where $C(z) = P_N[Q(z)]$.

(c) Use Theorem 4.49 with f_j replaced by c_j and g_j replaced by $f_X(j)$.

(d) S has a compound distribution with "frequency" pf c_k and "severity" mgf $(1 - \theta z)^{-1}$ which corresponds to an exponential distribution with parameter θ. The cdf is as in (6.9) with p_n replaced by c_n. Then $\{c_k\}$ is a compound distribution with N primary and $\{q_k\}$ secondary.

6.5   SECTION 6.6

6.36

$$m_0^k = \int_{kh}^{(k+1)h} \frac{x - kh - h}{-h} f(x)dx$$

$$= -\int_0^{(k+1)h} \frac{x}{h} dx + \int_0^{kh} \frac{x}{h} dx + (k+1)\{F[(k+1)h] - F(kh)\}$$

$$= -\frac{1}{h}\mathrm{E}[X \wedge (k+1)h] + (k+1)\{1 - F[(k+1)h]\}$$

$$\quad +\frac{1}{h}\mathrm{E}(X \wedge kh) - k[1 - F(kh)]$$

$$\quad +(k+1)\{F[(k+1)h] - F(kh)\}$$

$$= \frac{1}{h}\mathrm{E}(X \wedge kh) - \frac{1}{h}\mathrm{E}[X \wedge (k+1)h] + 1 - F(kh)$$

$$m_1^k = \int_{kh}^{(k+1)h} \frac{x - kh}{h} f(x)dx$$

$$= \frac{1}{h}\mathrm{E}[X \wedge (k+1)h] - \frac{1}{h}\mathrm{E}(X \wedge kh) - 1 + F[(k+1)h]$$

For $k = 1, 2, \ldots,$

$$f_k = m_1^{k-1} + m_0^k$$

$$= \frac{1}{h}\mathrm{E}(X \wedge kh) - \frac{1}{h}\mathrm{E}[X \wedge (k-1)h] - 1 + F(kh)$$

$$\quad +\frac{1}{h}\mathrm{E}(X \wedge kh) - \frac{1}{h}\mathrm{E}[X \wedge (k+1)h] + 1 - F(kh)$$

$$= \frac{1}{h}\{2\mathrm{E}(X \wedge kh) - \mathrm{E}[X \wedge (k-1)h] - \mathrm{E}[X \wedge (k+1)h]\}.$$

Also, $f_0 = m_0^0 = 1 - E(X \wedge h)/h$. All of the m_j^k have non-negative integrands and therefore all of the f_k are non-negative. To be a valid probability function they must add to one:

$$
\begin{aligned}
f_0 + \sum_{k=1}^{\infty} f_k &= 1 - \frac{1}{h}E(X \wedge h) + \frac{1}{h}\sum_{k=1}^{\infty}\{E(X \wedge kh) - E[X \wedge (k-1)h]\} \\
&\quad + \frac{1}{h}\sum_{k=1}^{\infty}\{E(X \wedge kh) - E[X \wedge (k+1)h]\} \\
&= 1 - \frac{1}{h}E(X \wedge h) + \frac{1}{h}E(X \wedge h) = 1
\end{aligned}
$$

because both sums are telescoping.

The mean of the discretized distribution is

$$
\begin{aligned}
\sum_{k=1}^{\infty} hk f_k &= \sum_{k=1}^{\infty} k\{E(X \wedge kh) - E[X \wedge (k-1)h]\} \\
&\quad + \sum_{k=1}^{\infty} k\{E(X \wedge kh) - E[X \wedge (k+1)h]\} \\
&= E(X \wedge h) + \sum_{k=1}^{\infty}(k+1)\{E[X \wedge (k+1)h] - E(X \wedge (kh))\} \\
&\quad + \sum_{k=1}^{\infty} k\{E(X \wedge kh) - E[X \wedge (k+1)h]\} \\
&= E(X \wedge h) + \sum_{k=1}^{\infty}\{E[X \wedge (k+1)h] - E(X \wedge (kh))\} \\
&= E(X)
\end{aligned}
$$

because $E(X \wedge \infty) = E(X)$.

6.37 Assume $x = 1$. Then $g_0 = \exp[-200(1 - 0.76)] = \exp(-48)$. The recursive formula gives

$$
g_k = \frac{200}{k}(0.14g_{k-1} + 0.10g_{k-2} + 0.06g_{k-3} + 0.12g_{k-4})
$$

with $g_k = 0$ for $k < 0$. Now use a spreadsheet to recursively compute probabilities until the probabilities sum to 0.05. This happens at $k = 62$. Then $62x = 4{,}000{,}000$ for $x = 64{,}516$. The expected compensation is

$$
200(0.14 + 0.10 + 0.06 + 0.12)(64{,}516) = 5{,}419{,}344.
$$

6.38 (a) $P_N(z) = wP_1(z) + (1-w)P_2(z)$

(b)
$$P_S(z) = P_N(P_X(z))$$
$$= wP_1(P_X(z)) + (1-w)P_2(P_X(z))$$
$$= wP_{S_1}(z) + (1-w)P_{S_2}(z)$$
$$f_S(x) = wf_{S_1} + (1-w)f_{S_2}(x), \quad x = 0, 1, 2, ...$$

Hence, first use (6.16) to compute $f_{S_1}(x)$. Then take a weighted average of the results.

(c) Yes. Any distributions $P_1(z)$ and $P_2(z)$ using (6.16) can be used.

6.39 From (6.16), the recursion for the compound Poisson distribution,

$$f_S(0) = e^{-5}$$

$$f_S(x) = \frac{5}{x} \sum_{y=1}^{5} y f_X(y) f_S(x-y).$$

Then

$$f_S(1) = 5 f_X(1) e^{-5}$$

and so $f_X(1) = \frac{1}{5}$ since $f_S(1) = e^{-5}$.

$$f_S(2) = \frac{5}{2}[f_X(1)f_S(1) + 2f_X(2)f_S(0)]$$
$$= \frac{5}{2}[\frac{1}{5}e^{-5} + 2f_X(2)e^{-5}]$$

since $f_S(2) = \frac{5}{2}e^{-5}$, we obtain $f_X(2) = \frac{2}{5}$.

6.40 $f_S(7) = \frac{6}{7}[1f_X(1)f_S(6) + 2f_X(2)f_S(5) + 4f_X(4)f_S(3)]$. Therefore, $0.041 = \frac{6}{7}[\frac{1}{3}f_S(6) + \frac{2}{3}0.0271 + \frac{4}{3}0.0132]$ for $f_S(6) = 0.0365$.

6.41 From (6.15) with $f_X(0) = 0$ and x replaced by z:

$$f_S(z) = \sum_{y=1}^{M}\left(a + b\frac{y}{z}\right) f_X(y) f_S(z-y)$$

$$= \sum_{y=1}^{M-1}\left(a + b\frac{y}{z}\right) f_X(y) f_S(z-y)$$

$$+ \left(a + b\frac{M}{z}\right) f_X(M) f_S(z-M).$$

Let $z = x + M$

$$f_S(x+M) = \sum_{y=1}^{M-1}\left(a + b\frac{y}{x+M}\right) f_X(y) f_S(x+M-y)$$

$$+ \left(a + b\frac{M}{x+M}\right) f_X(M) f_S(x).$$

Rearrangement gives the result.

6.42 We are looking for $6 - E(S) - E(D)$.
$E(X) = \frac{1}{4}1 + \frac{3}{4}2 = \frac{7}{4}$. $E(S) = 2\frac{7}{4} = \frac{7}{2}$.

$$D = \begin{cases} 4.5 - S, & S < 4.5 \\ 0, & S \geq 4.5. \end{cases}$$

$$
\begin{aligned}
f_S(0) &= e^{-2}, \\
f_S(1) &= \frac{2}{1}1\frac{1}{4}e^{-2} = \frac{1}{2}e^{-2}, \\
f_S(2) &= \frac{2}{2}\left(1\frac{1}{4}\frac{1}{2}e^{-2} + 2\frac{3}{4}e^{-2}\right) = \frac{13}{8}e^{-2}, \\
f_S(3) &= \frac{2}{3}\left(1\frac{1}{4}\frac{13}{8}e^{-2} + 2\frac{3}{4}\frac{1}{2}e^{-2}\right) = \frac{37}{48}e^{-2}, \\
f_S(4) &= \frac{2}{4}\left(1\frac{1}{4}\frac{37}{48}e^{-2} + 2\frac{3}{4}\frac{13}{8}e^{-2}\right) = \frac{505}{384}e^{-2}.
\end{aligned}
$$

Then $E(D) = (4.5 + 3.5\frac{1}{2} + 2.5\frac{13}{8} + 1.5\frac{37}{48} + 0.5\frac{505}{384})e^{-2} = 1.6411$. The answer is $6 - 3.5 - 1.6411 = 0.8589$.

6.43 For adults, the distribution is compound Poisson with $\lambda = 3$ and severity distribution with probabilities 0.4 and 0.6 on 1 and 2 (in units of 200). For children it is $\lambda = 2$ and severity probabilities of 0.9 and 0.1. The sum of the two distributions is also compound Poisson, with $\lambda = 5$. The probability at 1 is $[3(0.4) + 2(0.9)]/5 = 0.6$ and the remaining probability is at 2. The initial aggregate probabilities are:

$$
\begin{aligned}
f_S(0) &= e^{-5}, \\
f_S(1) &= \frac{5}{1}1\frac{3}{5}e^{-5} = 3e^{-5}, \\
f_S(2) &= \frac{5}{2}\left(1\frac{3}{5}3e^{-5} + 2\frac{2}{5}e^{-5}\right) = \frac{13}{2}e^{-5}, \\
f_S(3) &= \frac{5}{3}\left(1\frac{3}{5}\frac{13}{2}e^{-5} + 2\frac{2}{5}3e^{-5}\right) = \frac{21}{2}e^{-5}, \\
f_S(4) &= \frac{5}{4}\left(1\frac{3}{5}\frac{21}{2}e^{-5} + 2\frac{2}{5}\frac{13}{2}e^{-5}\right) = \frac{115}{8}e^{-5}.
\end{aligned}
$$

The probability of claims being 800 or less is the sum

$$\left(1 + 3 + \frac{13}{2} + \frac{21}{2} + \frac{115}{8}\right)e^{-5} = 35.375e^{-5} = 0.2384.$$

6.44 The aggregate distribution is two times a Poisson variable. The probabilities are $\Pr(S = 0) = e^{-1}$, $\Pr(S = 2) = \Pr(N = 1) = e^{-1}$, $\Pr(S = 4) = \Pr(N = 2) = \frac{1}{2}e^{-1}$. $E(D) = (6-0)e^{-1} + (6-2)e^{-1} + (6-4)\frac{1}{2}e^{-1} = 11e^{-1} = 4.0467$.

6.45 $\lambda = 1 + 1 = 2$, $f_X(1) = [1(1) + 1(0.5)]/2 = 0.75$, $f_X(2) = 0.25$. The calculations appear in Table 6.6. The answer is $F_X^{*4}(6) = (81+108+54)/256 = 243/256 = 0.94922$.

Table 6.6 Calculations for Exercise 6.45

x	$f_X^{*0}(x)$	$f_X^{*1}(x)$	$f_X^{*2}(x)$	$f_X^{*3}(x)$	$f_X^{*4}(x)$
0	1	0	0	0	0
1	0	3/4	0	0	0
2	0	1/4	9/16	0	0
3	0	0	6/16	27/64	0
4	0	0	1/16	27/64	81/256
5	0	0	0	9/64	108/256
6	0	0	0	1/64	54/256

6.46 $56 = 29E(X)$, so $E(X) = 56/29$. $126 = 29E(X^2)$, so $E(X^2) = 126/29$. Let $f_i = \Pr(X = i)$. Then there are three equations:
$f_1 + f_2 + f_3 = 1$
$f_1 + 2f_2 + 3f_3 = 56/29$
$f_1 + 4f_2 + 9f_3 = 126/29$.
The solution is $f_2 = 11/29$. (Also, $f_1 = 10/29$ and $f_3 = 8/29$)

6.47 Let $f_j = \Pr(X = j)$. $0.16 = \lambda f_1$, $k = 2\lambda f_2$, $0.72 = 3\lambda f_3$. Then $f_1 = 0.16/\lambda$ and $f_3 = 0.24/\lambda$ and so $f_2 = 1 - 0.16/\lambda - 0.24/\lambda$. $1.68 = \lambda[1(0.16/\lambda) + 2(1 - 0.4/\lambda) + 3(0.24/\lambda)] = 0.08 + 2\lambda$ and so $\lambda = 0.8$.

6.48 $1 - F(6) = 0.04 - 0.02$, $F(6) = 0.98$. $1 - F(4) = 0.20 - 0.10$, $F(4) = 0.90$. $\Pr(S = 5 \text{ or } 6) = F(6) - F(4) = 0.08$.

6.49 For 1,500 lives $\lambda = 0.01(1,500) = 15$. In units of 20, the severity distribution is $\Pr(X = 0) = 0.5$ and $\Pr(X = x) = 0.1$ for $x = 1,2,3,4,5$. Then $E(X^2) = 0.5(0) + 0.1(1 + 4 + 9 + 16 + 25) = 5.5$ and $\text{Var}(S) = 15(5.5) = 82.5$. In payment units it is $20^2(82.5) = 33,000$.

6.50 $\Pr(N=2) = \frac{1}{4}\Pr(N=2|\text{class I}) + \frac{3}{4}\Pr(N=2|\text{class II})$. $\Pr(N=2|\text{class}$
I$) = \int_0^1 \frac{\beta^2}{(1+\beta)^3} 1 d\beta = 0.068147$. (Hint: Use the substitution $y = \beta/(1+\beta)$).
$\Pr(N=2|\text{class II}) = (0.25)^2/(1.25)^3 = 0.032$. $\Pr(N=2) = 0.25(0.068147) +$
$0.75(0.32) = 0.04104$.

6.51 The result is 0.016.

6.52 The result is 0.055. Using a normal approximation with a mean of 250
and a variance 8,000 the probability is 0.047.

6.53 If $F_X(x) = 1 - e^{-\mu x}, x > 0$, then

$$f_0 = F_X\left(\frac{h}{2}\right) = 1 - e^{-\frac{\mu h}{2}},$$

and for $j = 1, 2, 3, ...,$

$$
\begin{aligned}
f_j &= F_X\left[\left(j+\frac{1}{2}\right)h\right] - F_X\left[\left(j-\frac{1}{2}\right)h\right] \\
&= 1 - e^{-\mu h\left(j+\frac{1}{2}\right)} - 1 + e^{-\mu h\left(j-\frac{1}{2}\right)} \\
&= e^{-\mu h\left(j-\frac{1}{2}\right)}\left(1 - e^{-\mu h}\right) \\
&= e^{-\frac{\mu h}{2}}\left(1 - e^{-\mu h}\right)e^{-\mu h(j-1)} \\
&= (1 - f_0)(1 - \phi)\phi^{j-1},
\end{aligned}
$$

where $\phi = e^{-\mu h}$.

6.6   SECTION 6.7

6.54 In this case $v = 1 - F_X(d) = e^{-\mu d}$, and from (6.24),

$$P_{NP}(z) = B\left[\theta(1 - v + vz - 1)\right] = B\left[\theta v(z-1)\right] = B\left[\theta e^{-\mu d}(z-1)\right].$$

Also, $Y^P = \alpha Z$, where

$$Pr(Z > z) = Pr(X > z+d)/Pr(X > d) = e^{-\mu(z+d)}/e^{-\mu d} = e^{-\mu z}.$$

That is, $F_{Y^P}(y) = 1 - Pr\left(Y^P > y\right) = 1 - Pr(Z > y/\alpha) = 1 - e^{-\frac{\mu}{\alpha}y}$.

6.55 (a) The cumulative distribution function of the individual losses is, from
Appendix A, given by $F_X(x) = 1 - \left(1 + \frac{x}{100}\right)e^{-\frac{x}{100}}$, $x \geq 0$. Also, $\text{E}(X \wedge x) =$
$200\Gamma\left(3; \frac{x}{100}\right) + x\left[1 - \Gamma\left(2; \frac{x}{100}\right)\right]$. Then

$$
\begin{aligned}
\text{E}(X \wedge 175) &= 200(0.25603) + 175(1 - 0.52212) = 134.835, \\
\text{E}(X \wedge 50) &= 200(0.01439) + 50(1 - 0.09020) = 48.368,
\end{aligned}
$$

and the individual mean payment amount on a per loss basis is

$$E(Y^L) = E(X \wedge 175) - E(X \wedge 50) = 134.835 - 48.368 = 86.467.$$

Similarly, for the second moment,

$$E\left[(X \wedge x)^2\right] = 60,000\Gamma\left(4; \frac{x}{100}\right) + x^2\left[1 - \Gamma\left(2; \frac{x}{100}\right)\right],$$

and in particular,

$$
\begin{aligned}
E\left[(X \wedge 175)^2\right] &= 60,000(0.10081) + 30,625(1 - 0.52212) = 20,683.645, \\
E\left[(X \wedge 50)^2\right] &= 60,000(0.00175) + 2,500(1 - 0.09020) = 2,379.587.
\end{aligned}
$$

Therefore,

$$
\begin{aligned}
E\left[(Y^L)^2\right] &= E\left[(X \wedge 175)^2\right] - E\left[(X \wedge 50)^2\right] \\
&\quad -100E(X \wedge 175) + 100E(X \wedge 50) \\
&= 20,683.645 - 2,379.587 - 100(134.835) + 100(48.368) \\
&= 9,657.358.
\end{aligned}
$$

Consequently,

$$\operatorname{Var}(Y^L) = 9,657.358 - (86.467)^2 = 2,180.816 = (46.70)^2.$$

For the negative binomially distributed number of losses,

$$E(N^L) = (2)(1.5) = 3, \text{ and } \operatorname{Var}(N^L) = (2)(1.5)(1 + 1.5) = 7.5.$$

The mean of the aggregate payments is therefore

$$E(S) = E(N^L)E(Y^L) = (3)(86.467) = 259.401,$$

and using Equation (6.6), the variance is

$$
\begin{aligned}
\operatorname{Var}(S) &= E(N^L)\operatorname{Var}(Y^L) + \operatorname{Var}(N^L)\left[E(Y^L)\right]^2 \\
&= (3)(2,180.816) + (7.5)(86.467)^2 \\
&= 62,616.514 = (250.233)^2.
\end{aligned}
$$

(b) The number of payments N^P has a negative binomial distribution with $r^* = r = 2$ and $\beta^* = \beta\left[1 - F_X(50)\right] = (1.5)(1 - 0.09020) = 1.36469$.

(c) The maximum payment amount is $175 - 50 = 125$. Thus $F_{Y^P}(y) = 1$ for $y \geq 125$. For $y < 125$,

$$
\begin{aligned}
F_{Y^P}(y) &= 1 - Pr\left(X > y + 50\right) / Pr(X > 50) \\
&= 1 - \frac{\left(1 + \frac{y+50}{100}\right) e^{-\frac{y+50}{100}}}{\left(1 + \frac{50}{100}\right) e^{-\frac{50}{100}}} \\
&= 1 - \left(1 + \frac{y}{150}\right) e^{-\frac{y}{100}}.
\end{aligned}
$$

(d)

$$f_0 = F_{YP}(20) = 0.072105$$
$$f_1 = F_{YP}(60) - F_{YP}(20) = 0.231664 - 0.072105 = 0.159559$$
$$f_2 = F_{YP}(100) - F_{YP}(60) = 0.386868 - 0.231664 = 0.155204$$
$$f_3 = F_{YP}(140) - F_{YP}(100) = 1 - 0.386868 = 0.613132$$

(e)

$$g_0 = [1 + \beta^*(1 - 0.072105)]^{-2} = [1 + (1.36469)(1 - 0.072105)]^{-2}$$
$$= 0.194702$$
$$a = 1.36469/2.36469 = 0.577112, \quad b = (2-1)\, a = 0.577112.$$

$$g_x = \frac{\sum\limits_{y=1}^{x} \left(a + b\frac{y}{x}\right) f_y g_{x-y}}{1 - a f_0} = 0.602169 \sum\limits_{y=1}^{x} \left(1 + \frac{y}{x}\right) f_y g_{x-y}$$

$$g_1 = (0.602169)(2)(0.159559)(0.194702) = 0.037415$$
$$g_2 = (0.602169)\,[(1.5)(0.159559)(0.037415) + (2)(0.155204)(0.194702)]$$
$$= 0.041786$$
$$g_3 = 0.602169\,[(4/3)(0.159559)(0.041786) + (5/3)(0.155204)(0.037415) +$$
$$(2)(0.613132)(0.194702)] = 0.154953.$$

6.7   SECTION 6.8

6.56 With a deductible of 25 the probability of making a payment is $v = 1 - F(25) = 0.98101$. The frequency distribution for the number of payments remains negative binomial with $r = 2$ and $\beta = 0.98101(2) = 1.96202$. The discretized severity distribution for payments begins with $f_0 = [F(27.5) - F(25)]/[1 - F(25)] = 0.00688$ and $f_1 = [F(32.5) - F(27.5)]/[1 - F(25)] = 0.01770$. The first 41 values of the discretized distribution and the discretized aggregate distribution are given in Table 6.7. The estimate value of $F(200)$ is obtained by summing all but the last given aggregate probabilities and then adding half of the final one. The result is 0.44802. For the limited expected value use (6.27) to obtain 146.3925. We also have $g_0 = (1 + \beta)^{-r} = 0.11398$.

6.57 (a) The recursive formula was used with a discretization interval of 25 and a mean-preserving discretization. The answers are 6,192.69, 4,632.13, and 12,800.04.
(b) The individual deductible of 100 requires a change in the frequency distribution. The probability of exceeding 100 under the gamma distribution is 0.7772974 and so the new Poisson parameter is 5 times this probability or 3.886487. The results are 5,773.24, 4,578.78, and 12,073.35.

Table 6.7   Discretized severities and aggregate probabilites for an ordinary deductible

x	f_x	p_x	x	f_x	p_x
0	0.006884	0.115025			
5	0.017690	0.002708	105	0.026359	0.009622
10	0.022983	0.003566	110	0.024169	0.009589
15	0.028080	0.004424	115	0.022070	0.009549
20	0.032730	0.005246	120	0.020076	0.009505
25	0.036757	0.006008	125	0.018198	0.009456
30	0.040056	0.006696	130	0.016440	0.009403
35	0.042579	0.007301	135	0.014805	0.009347
40	0.044326	0.007822	140	0.013294	0.009289
45	0.045329	0.008260	145	0.011904	0.009228
50	0.045650	0.008622	150	0.010632	0.009165
55	0.045363	0.008914	155	0.009473	0.009101
60	0.044551	0.009145	160	0.008420	0.009034
65	0.043302	0.009322	165	0.007469	0.008965
70	0.041698	0.009453	170	0.006610	0.008895
75	0.039821	0.009547	175	0.005839	0.008823
80	0.037744	0.009609	180	0.005149	0.008750
85	0.035533	0.009645	185	0.004531	0.008675
90	0.033244	0.009661	190	0.003981	0.008598
95	0.030926	0.009660	195	0.003493	0.008520
100	0.028620	0.009646	200	0.003059	0.008441

(c) The frequency distribution is altered as in part (b). The results are 148.27, 909.44, and 0.

6.58 (a) Two passes of the recursive formula were used, first with the Poisson(4) distribution and the two point severity distribution. The second pass uses the output from the first pass as the severity distribution along with a Poisson(10) frequency. With an aggregate limit of 400 the result is 247.25.
(b) The answer is $E(X \wedge 300) + 0.2[E(X) - E(X \wedge 300)] = 0.2E(X) + 0.8E(X \wedge 300) = 236.22$.

6.8   SECTION 6.9

6.59 The answers are the same as for Exercises 6.51 and 6.52.

6.9   SECTION 6.11

6.60

$$E(S) = \sum_{j=1}^{n} E(I_j B_j) = \sum_{j=1}^{n} E[E(I_j B_j | I_j)]$$

and then, $E(I_j B_j | I_j) = 0$ with probability $1 - q_j$ and $= \mu_j$ with probability q_j. Then

$$E[E(I_j B_j | I_j)] = 0(1 - q_j) + \mu_j q_j = \mu_j q_j$$

thus establishing (6.36). For the variance,

$$\text{Var}(S) = \sum_{j=1}^{n} \text{Var}(I_j B_j) = \sum_{j=1}^{n} \text{Var}[E(I_j B_j | I_j)] + E[\text{Var}(I_j B_j | I_j)].$$

For the first term,

$$
\begin{aligned}
\text{Var}[E(I_j B_j | I_j)] &= 0^2(1 - q_j) + \mu_j^2 q_j - (\mu_j q_j)^2 \\
&= \mu_j^2 q_j (1 - q_j).
\end{aligned}
$$

For the second term, $\text{Var}(I_j B_j | I_j) = 0$ with probability $1 - q_j$ and $= \sigma_j^2$ with probability q_j. Then,

$$E[\text{Var}(I_j B_j | I_j)] = 0(1 - q_j) + \sigma_j^2 q_j.$$

Inserting the two terms into the sum establishes (6.37).

6.61 Let S be the true random variable and let S_1, S_2, and S_3 be the three approximations. For the true variable,

$$E(S) = \sum_{j=1}^{n} q_j b_j, \quad \text{Var}(S) = \sum_{j=1}^{n} q_j(1 - q_j) b_j^2.$$

For all three approximations,

$$E(S) = \sum_{j=1}^{n} \lambda_j b_j, \quad \text{Var}(S) = \sum_{j=1}^{n} \lambda_j b_j^2.$$

For the first approximation, with $\lambda_j = q_j$ it is clear that $E(S_1) = E(S_2)$ and because $q_j > q_j(1 - q_j)$, $\text{Var}(S_1) > \text{Var}(S)$.

For the second approximation with $\lambda_j = -\ln(1 - q_j)$, note that

$$-\ln(1 - q_j) = q_j + \frac{q_j^2}{2} + \frac{q_j^3}{3} + \cdots > q_j$$

and then it is clear that $E(S_2) > E(S_1)$ and because the variance also involves λ_j the same is true for the variance.

For the third approximation, again using a Taylor series expansion,

$$\frac{q_j}{1-q_j} = q_j + q_j^2 + q_j^3 + \cdots > q_j + \frac{q_j^2}{2} + \frac{q_j^3}{3} + \cdots$$

and therefore the quantities for this approximation are the highest of all.

6.62 $\quad\quad\quad B \;=\; E(S) + 2\text{SD}(S)$
$$= \; 40(2) + 60(4) + 2\sqrt{40(4) + 60(10)}$$
$$= \; 375.136.$$

For A, $\quad\quad E(S) \;=\; E[E(S|N)] = E[2N + 4(100 - N)]$
$$= \; 400 - 2E(N) = 400 - 2(40) = 320.$$

$$\begin{aligned}\text{Var}(S) \;&=\; \text{Var}[E(S|N)] + E[\text{Var}(S|N)]\\ &=\; \text{Var}(400 - 2N) + E[4N + 10(100 - N)]\\ &=\; 4\,\text{Var}(N) - 6E(N) + 1000\\ &=\; 4(100)(0.4)(0.6) - 6(100)(0.4) + 1{,}000 = 856.\end{aligned}$$

Therefore, $A = 320 + 2\sqrt{856} = 378.515$ and $A/B = 1.009$.

6.63 Premium per person is $1.1(1{,}000)[0.2(0.02) + 0.8(0.01)] = 13.20$. With 30% smokers,

$$\begin{aligned}E(S) \;&=\; 1{,}000[0.3(0.02) + 0.7(0.01)] = 13,\\ \text{Var}(S) \;&=\; 1{,}000^2[0.3(0.02)(0.98) + 0.7(0.01)0(0.99)] = 12{,}810.\end{aligned}$$

With n policies, the probability of claims exceeding premium is

$$\begin{aligned}\Pr(S > 13.2n) \;&=\; \Pr\left(Z > \frac{13.2n - 13n}{\sqrt{12{,}810n}}\right)\\ &=\; \Pr(Z > 0.0017671\sqrt{n}) = 0.20.\end{aligned}$$

Therefore, $0.0017671\sqrt{n} = 0.84162$ for $n = 226{,}836$.

6.64 Let the policy being changed be the nth policy and let $F_n(x)$ represent the distribution function using n policies. Then, originally, $F_n(x) = 0.8F_{n-1}(x) + 0.2F_{n-1}(x - 1)$. Starting with $x = 0$:

$$\begin{array}{ll} 0.40 = 0.80F_{n-1}(0) + 0.2(0), & F_{n-1}(0) = 0.50\\ 0.58 = 0.80F_{n-1}(1) + 0.2(0.50), & F_{n-1}(1) = 0.60\\ 0.64 = 0.80F_{n-1}(2) + 0.2(0.60), & F_{n-1}(2) = 0.65\\ 0.69 = 0.80F_{n-1}(3) + 0.2(0.65), & F_{n-1}(3) = 0.70\\ 0.70 = 0.80F_{n-1}(4) + 0.2(0.70), & F_{n-1}(4) = 0.70\\ 0.78 = 0.80F_{n-1}(5) + 0.2(0.70), & F_{n-1}(5) = 0.80\end{array}$$

With the amount changed, $F_n(5) = 0.8F_{n-1}(5) + 0.2F_{n-1}(3) = 0.8(0.8) + 0.2(0.7) = 0.78$.

6.65 $E(S) = 400(0.03)(5) + 300(0.07)(3) + 200(0.10)(2) = 163$.
    For a single insured with claim probability q and exponential mean θ,

$$
\begin{aligned}
\text{Var}(S) &= E(N)\,\text{Var}(X) + \text{Var}(N)E(X)^2 \\
&= q\theta^2 + q(1-q)\theta^2 \\
&= q(2-q)\theta^2 .
\end{aligned}
$$

$$
\begin{aligned}
\text{Var}(S) &= 400(0.03)(1.97)(25) + 300(0.07)(1.93)(9) \\
&\quad + 200(0.10)(1.90)(4) \\
&= 1{,}107.77
\end{aligned}
$$

$$P = E(S) + 1.645\text{SD}(S) = 163 + 1.645\sqrt{1{,}107.77} = 217.75.$$

6.66 For one member, the mean is

$$0.7(160) + 0.2(600) + 0.5(240) = 352$$

and the variance is

$$0.7(4{,}900) + 0.21(160)^2 + 0.2(20{,}000) + 0.16(600)^2$$
$$+0.5(8{,}100) + 0.25(240)^2 = 88{,}856 .$$

For n members, the goal is

$$
\begin{aligned}
0.1 &< \Pr\left[S > 1.15(352)n\right] \\
&= \Pr\left(Z > \frac{1.15(352)n - 352n}{\sqrt{88{,}856n}}\right)
\end{aligned}
$$

and thus,

$$\frac{1.15(352)n - 352n}{\sqrt{88{,}856n}} > 1.28155$$

which yields $n > 52.35$ and so 53 members are needed.

6.67 The mean is

$$100{,}000 = 0.2k(3{,}500) + 0.6\alpha k(2{,}000) = (700 + 1{,}200\alpha)k$$

and the variance is

$$
\begin{aligned}
\text{Var}(S) &= 0.2(0.8)k^2(3{,}500) + 0.6(0.4)(\alpha k)^2(2{,}000) \\
&= (560 + 480\alpha^2)k^2 .
\end{aligned}
$$

Solving the first equation for k and substituting gives

$$\text{Var}(S) = \frac{560 + 480\alpha^2}{(700 + 1200\alpha)^2} 100,000^2.$$

Because the goal is to minimize the variance, constants can be removed, such as all the zeros. This leaves

$$\frac{56 + 48\alpha^2}{(7 + 12\alpha)^2}.$$

Taking the derivatives leads to a numerator of (the denominator is not important because the next step is set the derivative equal to zero)

$$(7 + 12\alpha)^2 96\alpha - (56 + 48\alpha^2)2(7 + 12\alpha)12.$$

Setting this equal to zero, dividing by 96 and rearranging, leads to the quadratic equation

$$84\alpha^2 - 119\alpha - 98 = 0$$

and the only positive root is the solution, $\alpha = 2$.

6.68 $\lambda = 500(0.01) + 500(0.02) = 15$. $f_X(x) = 500(0.01)/15 = 1/3$, $f_X(2x) = 2/3$. $E(X^2) = (1/3)x^2 + (2/3)(2x)^2 = 3x^2$. $\text{Var}(S) = 15(3x^2) = 45x^2 = 4,500$. $x = 10$.

6.69 All work is done in units of 100,000. The first group of 500 policies is not relevant. The others have amounts 1, 2, 1, and 1.

$$
\begin{aligned}
E(S) &= 500(0.02)(1) + 500(0.02)(2) + 300(0.1)(1) + 500(0.1)(1) \\
&= 110 \\
\text{Var}(S) &= 500(0.02)(0.98)(1) + 500(0.02)(0.98)(4) \\
&\quad + 300(0.1)(0.9)(1) + 500(0.1)(0.9)(1) \\
&= 121
\end{aligned}
$$

(a) $P = 110 + 1.645\sqrt{121} = 128.095$.
(b) $\mu + \sigma^2/2 = \ln 110 = 4.70048$. $2\mu + 2\sigma^2 = \ln(121 + 110^2) = 9.41091$. $\mu = 4.695505$ and $\sigma = .0997497$. $\ln P = 4.695505 + 1.645(0.0997497) = 4.859593$, $P = 128.97$.
(c) $\alpha\theta = 110$, $\alpha\theta^2 = 121$, $\theta = 121/110 = 1.1$, $\alpha = 100$. This is a chi-square distribution with 200 degrees of freedom. The 95th percentile is (using the Excel®[1] GAMMAINV function) 128.70.

---

[1] Excel® is either a registered trademark or trademark of Microsoft Corporation in the United States and/or other countries.

(d) $\lambda = 500(0.02) + 500(0.02) + 300(0.10) + 500(0.10) = 100$. $f_X(1) = (10 + 30 + 50)/100 = 0.9$ and $f_X(2) = .1$. Using the recursive formula for compound Poisson distribution, we find $F_S(128) = 0.94454$ and $F_S(129) = 0.95320$ and so to be safe at the 5% level a premium of 129 is required.

(e) One way to use the software is to note that $S = X_1 + 2X_2 + X_3$ where each X is binomial with $m = 500$, 500, and 800 and $q = 0.02$, 0.02, and 0.10. The results are $F_S(128) = 0.94647$ and $F_S(129) = 0.95635$ and so to be safe at the 5% level a premium of 129 is required.

7

Chapter 7 solutions

7.1 SECTION 7.3

7.1 (a) $\tilde{\psi}(2,0) = 0$, $\quad f_1 = \Pr(U_0^* = 2) = 1$. Initial calculations are in Table 7.1

Table 7.1 Initial calculations for Exercise 7.1(a)

k	S_k	$w_{1,k} = 6 + (6+2) \times 10\% - S_k$	$u_0 + w_{1,k}$	$g_{1,k}$
1	0	6.8	8.8	0.40
2	5	1.8	3.8	0.30
3	10	−3.2	−1.2	0.15
4	15	−8.2	−6.2	0.10
5	20	−13.2	−11.2	0.05

$$\tilde{\psi}(2,1) = \Pr(w_{q,k} + 2 < 0) = 0.15 + 0.1 + 0.05 = 0.3.$$

The updating equation is $u_j + w_{j,k} = (u_j + 6) \times 1.1 - s_k$. The next calculations are in Table 7.2. Then,

Loss Models: From Data to Decisions, Solutions Manual, Second Edition.
By Stuart A. Klugman, Harry H. Panjer, and Gordon E. Willmot
ISBN 0-471-22762-5   Copyright © 2004 John Wiley & Sons, Inc.

Table 7.2 Calculations for Exercise 7.1, part (a)

			Calculations for year 2				
			$u_j + w_{j,ki}\, g_{j,k}$				
					k		
j	$U_1^* = u_j$	f_j	1	2	3	4	5
1	3.8	0.3	10.78;0.4	5.78;0.3	0.78;0.15	−4.22;0.1	−9.22;0.05
2	8.8	0.4	16.28;0.4	11.28;0.3	6.28;0.15	1.28;0.1	−3.72;0.05

			Calculations for year 3				
			$u_j + w_{j,ki}\, g_{j,k}$				
					k		
j	$U_2^* = u_j$	f_j	1	2	3	4	5
1	0.78	0.045	7.458;0.4	2.458;0.3	−2.542;0.15	−7.542;0.1	−12.542;0.05
2	1.28	0.04	8.008;0.4	3.008;0.3	−1.992;0.15	−6.992;0.1	−11.992;0.05
3	5.78	0.09	12.958;0.4	7.958;0.3	2.958;0.15	−2.042;0.1	−7.042;0.05
4	6.28	0.06	13.508;0.4	8.508;0.3	3.508;0.15	−1.492;0.1	−6.492;0.05
5	10.78	0.12	18.458;0.4	13.458;0.3	8.458;0.15	3.458;0.1	−1.542;0.05
6	11.28	0.12	19.008;0.4	14.008;0.3	9.008;0.15	4.008;0.1	−0.992;0.05
7	16.28	0.16	24.508;0.4	19.508;0.3	14.508;0.15	9.508;0.1	4.508;0.05

$$\tilde{\psi}(2,2) = \tilde{\psi}(2,1) + 0.3(0.1) + 0.3(0.05) + 0.4(0.05) = 0.365.$$

The next calculations are also in Table 7.2. Then,

$$
\begin{aligned}
\tilde{\psi}(2,3) &= \tilde{\psi}(2,2) + 0.15(0.045 + 0.04) + 0.1(-0.045 + 0.04 + 0.09 + 0.06) \\
&\quad + 0.05(0.045 + 0.04 + 0.09 + 0.06 + 0.12 + 0.12) \\
&= 0.365 + 0.06 = 0.425.
\end{aligned}
$$

(b) Initial calculations are in Table 7.3.

Table 7.3 Initial calculations for Exercise 7.1(b)

j	$U_1^* = u_j$	f_j
1	3.8	0.3
2	8.8	0.4

The next set of calculations appears in the first half of Table 7.5. Then,

$$
\begin{aligned}
\tilde{\psi}(2,2) &= \tilde{\psi}(2,1) + 0.072(0.15 + 0.1 + 0.05) + 0.324(0.1 + 0.05) \\
&\quad + 0.304(0.05) \\
&= 0.3 + 0.0854 = 0.3854
\end{aligned}
$$

Values at the end of year two are in Table 7.4.
The next set of calculations appears in the second half of Table 7.5. Then,

Table 7.4   Calculations for Exercise 7.1 part (b), year 2

j	$U_2^* = u_j$	f_j
1	1.6	0.0216
2	2.1	0.0486
3	2.6	0.0304
4	6.6	0.0288
5	7.1	0.0972
6	7.6	0.0456
7	12.1	0.1296
8	12.6	0.0912
9	17.6	0.1216

$$\tilde{\psi}(2,3) = \tilde{\psi}(2,2) + 0.057468(0.15 + 0.1 + 0.05) + 0.140980(0.1 + 0.05)$$
$$+ 0.192696(0.05)$$
$$= 0.3854 + 0.0480222 = 0.4334222 > 0.425.$$

Table 7.5   Calculations for Exercise 7.1, part (b)

				Calculations for year 2			
				$u_j + w_{j,k};\, g_{j,k}$			
					k		
j	$U_1^* = u_j$	f_j	1	2	3	4	5
1	0	0.072	6.6	0.4;1.6	0.3;−3.4	0.15;−8.4	0.10;−13.4;0 .05
2	5	0.324	12.1;0.4	7.1;0.3	2.1;0.15	−2.9;0.10	−7.9;0.05
3	10	0.304	17.6;0.4	12.6;0.3	7.6;0.15	2.6;0.10	−2.4;0.05
				Calculations for year 3			
				$u_j + w_{j,k};\, g_{j,k}$			
					k		
j	$U_2^* = u_j$	f_j	1	2	3	4	5
1	0	0.057468	6.6;0.4	1.6;0.3	3.4;0.15	−8.4;0.1	−13.4;−.05
2	5	0.140980	12.1;0.4	7.1;0.3	2.1;0.15	−2.9;0.1	−7.9;0.05
3	10	0.192696	17.6;0.4	12.6;0.3	7.6;0.15	2.6;0.1	−2.4;0.05
4	15	0.160224	23.1;0.4	18.1;0.3	13.1;0.15	8.1;0.1	3.1;0.05
5	20	0.063232	28.6;0.4	23.6;0.3	18.6;0.15	13.6;0.1	8.6;0.05

From (a) we get the calculations in Table 7.6, which, upon rounding, leads to Table 7.7.

7.2 The initial calculations are in Table 7.8.

$$\tilde{\psi}(2,1) = \tilde{\psi}(2,0) + (0.15 + 0.1 + 0.05)[(1 - \tilde{\psi}(2,0)] = 0.3$$

Calculations for the next year appear in Tables 7.9–7.12.

Table 7.6   Calculations for Exercise 7.1 year 3

j	$U_3^* = u_j$	f_j	j	$U_3^* = u_j$	f_j
1	1.6	0.0172404	11	12.6	0.0578088
2	2.1	0.0211470	12	13.1	0.0240336
3	2.6	0.0192696	13	13.6	0.0063232
4	3.1	0.0080112	14	17.6	0.0770784
5	6.6	0.0229872	15	18.1	0.0480672
6	7.1	0.0422940	16	18.6	0.0094848
7	7.6	0.0289044	17	23.1	0.0640896
8	8.1	0.0160224	18	23.6	0.0189696
9	8.6	0.0031616	19	28.6	0.0252928
10	12.1	0.0563920			

Table 7.7   Calculations for Exercise 7.1 year 3

j	$U_3^* = u_j$	f_j
1	0	0.0362824
2	5	0.0903955
3	10	0.1237188
4	15	0.1311177
5	20	0.1063770
6	25	0.0604756
7	30	0.0182108

Table 7.8   Calculations for Exercise 7.2

k	s_k	$w = 6(1 + 10\%) - s_k$	$\Pr(W = w)$	$u_1 = u_0(1 + 10\%) + w$
1	0	6.6	0.4	8.8
2	5	1.6	0.3	3.8
3	10	−3.4	0.15	−1.2
4	15	−8.4	0.1	−6.2
5	20	−13.4	0.05	−11.2

The Fourier calculations appear in Tables 7.15 and 7.16.

$$\tilde{\psi}(2,2) = \tilde{\psi}(2,1) + (0.00239 + 0.01933 + 0.06077)[1 - \tilde{\psi}(2,1)] = 0.35774.$$

The next set of calculations appear in Tables 7.13 and 7.14.

The Fourier calculations appear in Tables 7.17 and 7.18. Then

$$\tilde{\psi}(2,3) = \tilde{\psi}(2,2) + (0.00428 + 0.01723 + 0.04253)[1 - \tilde{\psi}(2,2)] = 0.39887.$$

Table 7.9   Calculations for Exercise 7.2

j	$u^* = u \times 1.1$	$\Pr(U_1^{**} = u^*)$
1	4.18	3/7
2	9.68	4/7

Table 7.10   Calculations for Exercise 7.2

j	$u^* = u \times 1.1$	$\Pr(U_1^{**} = u^*)$
1	0	0.492/7
2	5	2.764/7
3	10	3.744/7

Table 7.11   Calculations for Exercise 7.2

w	$\Pr(W = w)$
6.6	0.40
1.6	0.30
-2.4	0.15
-8.4	0.10
-13.4	0.05

Table 7.12   Calculations for Exercise 7.2

w	$w + 15$	$\Pr(W = w + 15)$
-15	0	0.034
-10	5	0.084
-5	10	0.134
0	15	0.252
5	20	0.368
10	25	0.128

Table 7.13   Calculations for Exercise 7.2

j	u_2	$u^* = u_2 \times 1.1$	$\Pr(U_2^{**} = u^*)$
1	0	0	0.12594
2	5	5.5	0.21476
3	10	11.0	0.31508
4	15	16.5	0.26961
5	20	22.0	0.07462

Table 7.14 Calculations for Exercise 7.2

j	u^*	$\Pr\left(U_2^{**} = u^*\right)$
1	0	0.12594
2	5	0.195714
3	10	0.271110
4	15	0.251743
5	20	0.125665
6	25	0.029848

Table 7.15 Fourier calculations for Exercise 7.2

u	$f_1^{**}(u)$	$f_W(u)$	$\varphi_{1,2}$	$\varphi_{2,2}$
0	$\frac{0.492}{7}$	0.034	1	1
5	$\frac{2.764}{7}$	0.084	$0.3495 - 0.8141i$	$-0.5433 - 0.2811i$
10	$\frac{3.744}{7}$	0.134	$-0.4646 - 0.3945i$	$0.2680 + 0.0400i$
15	0	0.252	$-0.2089 + 0.2557i$	$-0.1247 - 0.0131i$
20	0	0.368	0.2103	0.072
25	0	0.128	$-0.2089 - 0.2557i$	$-0.1247 + 0.0131i$
30	0	0	$-0.4646 + 0.3949i$	$0.2680 - 0.0400i$
35	0	0	$0.3495 + 0.8141i$	$-0.5433 + 0.2811i$

Table 7.16 Fourier calculations for Exercise 7.2

u	$\varphi_{3,2} = \varphi_{1,2} \times \varphi_{2,2}$	$f_2(u)$	$U_2 = u$	$\Pr\left(U_2^* = u\right)$
0	1	0.00239	-15	—
5	$-0.4187 + 0.3440i$	0.01933	-10	—
10	$-0.1087 - 0.1244i$	0.06077	-5	—
15	$0.0294 - 0.0291i$	0.11555	0	0.12594
20	0.0151	0.19704	5	0.21476
25	$0.0294 + 0.0291i$	0.28909	10	0.31508
30	$-0.1087 + 0.1244i$	0.24737	15	0.26961
35	$-0.4187 - 0.3440i$	0.06846	20	0.07462

Table 7.17   Fourier calculations for Exercise 7.2

u	$f_2^{**}(u)$	$f_W(u)$	$\varphi_{1,3}$	$\varphi_{2,3}$
0	0.12594	0.034	1	1
5	0.195714	0.084	$0.58338 - 0.65242i$	$0.25381 - 0.84597i$
10	0.271110	0.134	$-0.06045 - 0.56640i$	$-0.54330 - 0.28108i$
15	0.251743	0.252	$-0.19587 - 0.13909i$	$-0.14317 + 0.34106i$
20	0.125655	0.368	$-0.01951 + 0.02618i$	$0.26800 + 0.04000i$
25	0.029848	0.128	$0.06434 - 0.00702i$	$0.02166 - 0.20543i$
30	0	0	$0.06100 - 0.02418i$	$-0.12470 - 0.01308i$
35	0	0	$0.05191 - 0.01768i$	$0.00369 + 0.07953i$
40	0	0	0.04541	0.072
45	0	0	$0.05191 + 0.01768i$	$0.00369 - 0.07953i$
50	0	0	$0.06100 + 0.02418i$	$-0.12470 + 0.01308i$
55	0	0	$0.06434 + 0.00702i$	$0.02166 + 0.20543i$
60	0	0	$-0.01951 - 0.02618i$	$0.26800 - 0.04000i$
65	0	0	$-0.19587 + 0.13909i$	$-0.14317 - 0.34106i$
70	0	0	$-0.06045 + 0.56640i$	$-0.54330 + 0.28108i$
75	0	0	$0.58338 + 0.65242i$	$0.25381 + 0.84597i$

Table 7.18   Fourier calculations for Exercise 7.2

u	$\varphi_{3,3} = \varphi_{1,3} \times \varphi_{2,3}$	$f_3(u)$	$U_3 = u$
0	1	0.00428	-15
5	$-0.40386 - 0.65911i$	0.01723	-10
10	$-0.12636 + 0.32472i$	0.04253	-5
15	$0.07548 - 0.04689i$	0.08930	0
20	$-0.00627 + 0.00624i$	0.15741	5
25	$-0.00005 - 0.01337i$	0.20177	10
30	$-0.00792 + 0.00222i$	0.20761	15
35	$0.00160 + 0.00406i$	0.16301	20
40	0.00327	0.08599	25
45	$0.00160 - 0.00406i$	0.02707	30
50	$-0.00792 - 0.00222i$	0.00382	35
55	$-0.00005 + 0.0133i$	0	40
60	$-0.00627 - 0.00624i$	0	45
65	$0.07548 + 0.04689i$	0	50
70	$-0.12636 - 0.32472i$	0	55
75	$-0.40386 + 0.65911i$	0	60

8

Chapter 8 solutions

8.1 SECTION 8.2

8.1 κ is the smallest positive root of $1 + (1+\theta)2\beta\kappa = (1-\beta\kappa)^{-2}$, $\theta = 0.32 \Rightarrow$ $\beta\kappa(6\beta\kappa - 1)(11\beta\kappa - 16) = 0 \Rightarrow \kappa = \frac{1}{6\beta}$.

8.2 $f(x) \propto x^{-1/2}e^{-\beta x}$ and so X has the gamma distribution with $\alpha = 1/2$ and $\theta = 1/\beta$. Then $\mu = \mathrm{E}(X) = \frac{1}{2\beta}$, $M_X(t) = \mathrm{E}(e^{tX}) = \left(\frac{1}{1-t/\beta}\right)^{1/2}$, $t < \beta$. κ is the smallest positive root of $1 + (1+\theta)\mu\kappa = \mathrm{E}(e^{\kappa X})$ and so $1 + (1+\theta)\frac{1}{2\beta}\kappa = (1-\kappa/\beta)^{-1/2}$.

Let $y = \frac{\kappa}{\beta}$. Then $1 + (1+\theta)\frac{y}{2} = (1-y)^{-1/2}$. Square both sides to obtain $\left[1 + (1+\theta)\frac{y}{2}\right]^2 = (1-y)^{-1}$. Then multiply by $1-y$, divide by y, and multiply by 4 to obtain

$$(1+\theta)^2 y^2 + (1+\theta)(3-\theta)y - 4\theta = 0$$

Loss Models: From Data to Decisions, Solutions Manual, Second Edition.
By Stuart A. Klugman, Harry H. Panjer, and Gordon E. Willmot
ISBN 0-471-22762-5   Copyright © 2004 John Wiley & Sons, Inc.

The solutions to this quadratic equation are

$$y = \frac{-(1+\theta)(3-\theta) \pm \sqrt{[(1+\theta)(3-\theta)]^2 + 16\theta(1+\theta)^2}}{2(1+\theta)^2}$$

$$= \frac{(\theta-3) \pm \sqrt{(\theta+1)(\theta+9)}}{2(1+\theta)}$$

Because $\theta \geq 0$, $|\theta-3| < |\sqrt{(\theta+1)(\theta+3)}|$ and so the positive root is the only one which has a chance to yield a positive value for y. Because $(\theta+1)(\theta+9) = \theta^2 100 + 9 \geq 9$ when $\theta \geq 0$ a positive value for y is assured. Then we get $y = \frac{(\theta-3)+\sqrt{(\theta+1)(\theta+0)}}{2(1+\theta)}$ and so $\kappa = y\beta = \frac{(\theta-3)+\sqrt{(\theta+1)(\theta+9)}}{2(\theta+1)}\beta$

8.3

$$f(x) = \frac{1}{2}\left(2e^{-2x}\right) + \frac{1}{2}\left(3e^{-3x}\right)$$

$$E(X) = \frac{1}{2}\int_0^\infty 2xe^{-2x}dx + \frac{1}{2}\int_0^\infty 3xe^{-3x}dx = \frac{1}{2}\left(\frac{1}{2} + \frac{1}{3}\right) = \frac{5}{12}$$

$$3 = c = (1+\theta)\lambda\mu = (1+\theta)(4)\frac{5}{12} \Rightarrow \theta = \frac{4}{5}$$

$$E\left(e^{tX}\right) = \frac{1}{2}\left[2\int_0^\infty e^{-(2-t)x}dx + 3\int_0^\infty e^{-(3-t)x}dx\right]$$

$$= \frac{1}{2}\left(\frac{2}{2-t} + \frac{3}{3-t}\right), \; t < 2.$$

κ is the smallest positive root of $1 + (1+\theta)\mu\kappa = E\left(e^{\kappa X}\right)$. Therefore

$$1 + \left(1+\frac{4}{5}\right)\frac{5}{12}\kappa = E\left(e^{tX}\right) = \frac{1}{2}\left(\frac{2}{2-\kappa} + \frac{3}{3-\kappa}\right)$$

which implies $1 + \frac{3}{4}\kappa = \frac{1}{2}\left(\frac{2}{2-\kappa} + \frac{3}{3-\kappa}\right)$. The roots are $0,1$ and $\frac{8}{3}$ and so $\kappa = 1$.

8.4

$$\mu = E(X) = 1(0.2) + 2(0.3) + 3(0.5) = 2.3$$
$$E\left(X^2\right) = 1(0.2) + 4(0.3) + 9(0.5) = 5.9$$
$$c = (1+\theta)\mu\lambda \Rightarrow \theta\frac{c}{\mu\lambda} - 1 = \frac{2.99}{2.3} - 1 = 0.3$$

κ must be less than $\kappa_0 = 2\theta\mu/E\left(X^2\right) = 2(0.3)(2.3)/5.9 = 0.233898$. Let

$$H(t) = 1 + (1+\theta)\mu t - E\left(e^{tX}\right) = 1 + 2.99t - 0.2e^t - 0.3e^{2t} - 0.5e^{3t}$$
$$H'(t) = 2.99 - 0.2e^t - 0.6e^{2t} - 1.5e^{3t}$$

Use

$$\kappa_{n+1} = \kappa_n - \frac{H(\kappa_n)}{H'(\kappa_n)} = \kappa_n - \frac{1 + 2.99\kappa_n - 0.2e^{\kappa_n} - 0.3e^{2\kappa_n} - 0.5e^{3\kappa_n}}{2.99 - 0.2e^{\kappa_n} - 0.6e^{2\kappa_n} - 1.5e^{3\kappa_n}}.$$

With $\kappa_0 = 0.233898$, the iterations follow in Table 8.1 with the answer being $\kappa = 0.194273$.

Table 8.1   Iterations for the adjustment coefficient in Exercise 8.4

n	κ_n	
0	0.233898	
1	0.201104	
2	0.194539	
3	0.194274	
4	0.194273	$\leftarrow \kappa$ the adjustment coefficient

8.5 $f(x) = \frac{1}{2}\left[2e^{-2x} + 3e^{-3x}\right]$. From Exercise 8.3, $\theta = \frac{4}{5}, \mu = \frac{5}{12}$.

$$\begin{aligned}
E\left(X^2\right) &= \frac{1}{2}\left[2\int_0^\infty x^2 e^{-2x}\,dx + 3\int_0^\infty x^2 e^{-3x}\,dx\right] \\
&= \frac{1}{2}\left[2\Gamma(3)\left(\frac{1}{2}\right)^3 + 3\Gamma(3)\left(\frac{1}{3}\right)^3\right] = \frac{13}{36}.
\end{aligned}$$

κ must be less than $\kappa_0 = 2\theta\mu/E\left(X^2\right) = 2\frac{4}{5}\frac{5}{12}\frac{36}{13} = \frac{24}{13}$

$$\begin{aligned}
H(t) &= 1 + (1+\theta)\mu t - E\left(e^{tX}\right) = 1 + \frac{3}{4}t - \frac{1}{2}\left(\frac{2}{2-t} + \frac{3}{3-t}\right) \\
H'(t) &= \frac{3}{4} - \frac{1}{2}\left[\frac{2}{(2-t)^2} + \frac{3}{(3-t)^2}\right]
\end{aligned}$$

Use

$$\kappa_{n+1} = \kappa_n - \frac{H(\kappa_n)}{H'(\kappa_n)} = \kappa_n - \frac{1 + \frac{3}{4}\kappa_n - \frac{1}{2}\left(\frac{2}{2-\kappa_n} + \frac{3}{3-\kappa_n}\right)}{\frac{3}{4} - \frac{1}{2}\left[\frac{2}{(2-\kappa_n)^2} + \frac{3}{(3-\kappa_n)^2}\right]}.$$

With $\kappa_0 = \frac{24}{13}$ then the iterations are given in Table 8.2 with the solution being $\kappa = 1$.

Table 8.2   Iterations for the adjustment coefficient in Exercise 8.5

n	κ_n	
0	1.846154	
1	1.719112	
2	1.528918	
3	1.305120	
4	1.117793	
5	1.021670	
6	1.000856	
7	1.000001	
8	1.000000	$\leftarrow \kappa$ the adjustment coefficient.

8.6 κ satisfies

$$
\begin{aligned}
1 + (1+\theta)\mu\kappa &= \mathrm{E}\left(e^{\kappa X}\right) = E\left(1 + \kappa X + \frac{1}{2}\kappa^2 X^2 + \frac{1}{6}\kappa^3 X^3 + \cdots\right) \\
&> \mathrm{E}\left(1 + \kappa X + \frac{1}{2}\kappa^2 X^2 + \frac{1}{6}\kappa^3 X^3\right) \\
&= 1 + \kappa\mu + \frac{1}{2}\kappa^2 \mathrm{E}\left(X^2\right) + \frac{1}{6}\kappa^3 \mathrm{E}\left(X^3\right)
\end{aligned}
$$

This implies $\mathrm{E}(X^3)\,\kappa^2 + 3\mathrm{E}(X^2)\,\kappa - 6\theta\mu < 0$ and therefore

$$
\kappa < \frac{-3\mathrm{E}\left(X^2\right) + \sqrt{9[\mathrm{E}\left(X^2\right)]^2 + 24\theta\mu\mathrm{E}\left(X^3\right)}}{2\mathrm{E}\left(X^3\right)}.
$$

Then,

$$
\frac{-3\mathrm{E}\left(X^2\right) + \sqrt{9[\mathrm{E}\left(X^2\right)]^2 + 24\theta\mu\mathrm{E}\left(X^3\right)}}{2\mathrm{E}\left(X^3\right)} < \frac{2\theta\mu}{\mathrm{E}\left(X^2\right)}.
$$

Since $X \geq 0$, the following are true

$$
\begin{aligned}
\sqrt{9[\mathrm{E}\left(X^2\right)]^2 + 24\theta\mu\mathrm{E}\left(X^3\right)} &< \frac{2\theta\mu}{\mathrm{E}\left(X^2\right)}2\mathrm{E}\left(X^3\right) + 3\mathrm{E}\left(X^2\right) \\
9[\mathrm{E}\left(X^2\right)]^2 + 24\theta\mu\mathrm{E}\left(X^3\right) &< \left[\frac{4\theta\mu}{\mathrm{E}\left(X^2\right)}\mathrm{E}\left(X^3\right) + 3\mathrm{E}\left(X^2\right)\right]^2 \\
9[\mathrm{E}\left(X^2\right)]^2 + 24\theta\mu\mathrm{E}\left(X^3\right) &< \left[\frac{4\theta\mu}{\mathrm{E}\left(X^2\right)}\mathrm{E}\left(X^3\right)\right]^2 \\
& \quad + 24\theta\mu\mathrm{E}\left(X^3\right) + 9[\mathrm{E}\left(X^2\right)]^2
\end{aligned}
$$

which implies $0 < \left[\frac{4\theta\mu}{\mathrm{E}(X^2)}\mathrm{E}\left(X^3\right)\right]^2$

8.7 (a) $1 + \theta = \int_0^\infty e^{\kappa x} f_e(x)dx$ where $f_e(x) = \frac{1-f(x)}{\mu}, x > 0$.

Let $g(x) = e^x$ then $g''(x) = e^x \geq 0$ and then by Jensen's inequality,

$$
\begin{aligned}
1 + \theta &= \int_0^\infty e^{\kappa x} f_e(x)dx = \mathrm{E}\left(e^{\kappa X}\right) \\
&\geq e^{\mathrm{E}(\kappa X)} = e^{\int_0^\infty \kappa x f_e(x)dx} \\
&= e^{\kappa \mathrm{E}(X^2)/(2\mu)}.
\end{aligned}
$$

Therefore, $\ln(1 + \theta) \geq \kappa \mathrm{E}(X^2)/(2\mu)$ and so $\kappa \leq [2\mu \ln(1 + \theta)]/\mathrm{E}(X^2)$.

(b) Consider $h(\theta) = \theta - \ln(1+\theta)$, $\theta \geq 0$. Then $h'(\theta) = 1 - \frac{1}{1+\theta} > 0$ for $\theta > 0$. Thus $h(\theta)$ is absolutely increasing in $(0, \infty)$.

Since $h(0) = 0$, $h(\theta) > h(0) = 0$, $\theta > 0$, that is, $\theta > \ln(1 + \theta)$ for $\theta > 0$.

Hence, $\leq \frac{2\mu \ln(1+\theta)}{\mathrm{E}(X^2)} < \frac{2\mu\theta}{\mathrm{E}(X^2)}$.

(c) If there is a maximum claim size of m, then $X \leq m$ and (8.7) becomes

$$
\begin{aligned}
1 + \theta &= \int_0^\infty e^{\kappa x} f_e(x)dx = \int_0^m e^{\kappa x} f_e(x)dx \\
&\leq \int_0^m e^{\kappa m} f_e(x)dx = e^{\kappa m}\int_0^m f_e(x)dx = e^{\kappa m}.
\end{aligned}
$$

So $1 + \theta \leq e^{\kappa m}$ and therefore, $\kappa \geq \frac{1}{m} \ln(1 + \theta)$.

8.8 (a) We have $S_e(x) \geq S(x)$, or since the mean residual lifetime $e(x)$ satisfies

$$
\frac{e(x)}{e(0)} = \frac{S_e(x)}{S(x)},
$$

equivalently, $e(x) \geq e(0)$. Now, $S_e(y) \geq S(y)$ may be stated as $\Pr(Y > y) \geq \Pr(X > y)$. Since the function $e^{\kappa x}$ is monotone increasing in x, this is equivalent to stating that $\Pr\left(e^{\kappa Y} > e^{\kappa y}\right) \geq \Pr\left(e^{\kappa X} > e^{\kappa y}\right)$, or $\Pr\left(e^{\kappa Y} > t\right) \geq \Pr\left(e^{\kappa X} > t\right)$ where $t = e^{\kappa y} \geq 1$.

(b) For any non-negative random variable W, $\mathrm{E}(W) = \int_0^\infty \Pr(W > t)dt$. Thus, with $W = e^{\kappa Y}$ we have from (a)

$$
\mathrm{E}\left(e^{\kappa Y}\right) = \int_0^\infty \Pr\left(e^{\kappa Y} > t\right) dt \geq \int_0^\infty \Pr\left(e^{\kappa X} > t\right) dt = \mathrm{E}\left(e^{\kappa X}\right).
$$

(c) From (b) and (8.7),

$$
1 + \theta = \mathrm{E}\left(e^{\kappa Y}\right) \geq \mathrm{E}\left(e^{\kappa X}\right) = 1 + (1 + \theta)\mu\kappa.
$$

Thus,

$$
\kappa \leq \frac{\theta}{\mu(1 + \theta)}.
$$

(d) Simply reverse the inequalities in (a), (b), and (c).

8.9 Let $\psi_n(u)$ be the probability that ruin occurs on or before the nth claim for $n = 0, 1, 2, \cdots$. We will prove by induction on n that $\psi_n(u) \leq \rho e^{-\kappa u}$. Obviously $\psi_0(u) = 0 \leq \rho e^{-\kappa u}$. Now assume that $\psi_n(u) \leq \rho e^{-\kappa u}$. Then

$$
\begin{aligned}
\psi_{n+1}(u) &= \int_0^\infty \left[1 - F(u + ct) + \int_0^{u+ct} \psi_n(u + ct - x) dF(x) \right] \lambda e^{-\lambda t} dt \\
&= \int_0^\infty \left[\overline{F}(u + ct) + \int_0^{u+ct} \psi_n(u + ct - x) dF(x) \right] \lambda e^{-\lambda t} dt \\
&\leq \int_0^\infty \left[\rho e^{-\kappa(u+ct)} \int_{u+ct}^\infty e^{\kappa x} dF(x) \right. \\
&\qquad\qquad \left. + \int_0^{u+ct} \rho e^{-\kappa(u+ct-X)} dF(x) \right] \lambda e^{-\lambda t} dt \\
&= \rho \int_0^\infty \left[\int_0^\infty e^{-\kappa(u+ct-X)} dF(x) \right] \lambda e^{-\lambda t} dt \\
&= \rho e^{-\kappa u} \int_0^\infty e^{-\kappa ct} \left[\int_0^\infty e^{\kappa X} dF(x) \right] \lambda e^{-\lambda t} dt \\
&= \rho \lambda e^{-\kappa u} \int_0^\infty e^{-\lambda t - \kappa ct} \mathrm{E}\left(e^{\kappa X} \right) dt \\
&= \rho \lambda e^{-\kappa u} \mathrm{E}\left(e^{\kappa X} \right) \int_0^\infty e^{-(\lambda + \kappa c)t} dt \\
&= \rho \lambda e^{-\kappa u} \mathrm{E}\left(e^{\kappa X} \right) / (\lambda + \kappa c) \\
&= \rho e^{-\kappa u}
\end{aligned}
$$

since $\lambda \mathrm{E}\left(e^{\kappa X}\right) = \lambda[1 + (1+\theta)\kappa\mu] = \lambda + \kappa(1+\theta)\lambda\mu = \lambda + \kappa c$. So $\psi_n(u) \leq \rho e^{-\kappa u}$, $n = 0, 1, 2, \cdots$, which implies $\psi(u) = \lim_{n \to \infty} \psi_n(u) \leq \rho e^{-\kappa u}$

8.10
$$
\begin{aligned}
\int_x^\infty e^{\kappa y} dF(y) &= -\int_x^\infty e^{\kappa y} dS(y) \\
&= -e^{\kappa y} S(y) \big|_x^\infty + \kappa \int_x^\infty e^{\kappa y} S(y) dy \quad X \geq 0 \\
&= -\lim_{y \to \infty} e^{\kappa y} S(y) + e^{\kappa x} S(x) + \kappa \int_x^\infty e^{\kappa y} S(y) dy
\end{aligned}
$$

Since

$$
\begin{aligned}
0 &\leq e^{\kappa y} S(y) = e^{\kappa y}[1 - F(y)] \\
&= e^{\kappa y} \int_y^\infty dF(x) \leq \int_y^\infty e^{\kappa x} dF(x) \\
&\leq \int_0^\infty e^{\kappa x} dF(x) = \mathrm{E}\left(e^{\kappa X} \right) < \infty
\end{aligned}
$$

and $\lim_{y \to \infty} e^{\kappa y} S(y) \leq \lim_{y \to \infty} \int_y^\infty e^{\kappa x} dF(x) = 0$, we have $\lim_{y \to \infty} e^{\kappa y} S(y) = 0$.

8.11 Let $\mu(x) = \frac{f(x)}{\overline{F}(x)}$ be the failure rate. Then $\mu(x + t) \leq \mu(x)$ for each x and $t \geq 0$ by assumption, so $\frac{f(x+t)}{\overline{F}(x+t)} \leq \frac{f(x)}{\overline{F}(x)}$ and therefore $f(x + t)S(x) - f(x)S(x + t) < 0$ for all x, and all $t \geq 0$. For each fixed $t \geq 0$, consider $g_t(x) = S(x + t)/S(x)$. Then

$$\frac{d}{dx} g_t(x) = \frac{-S(x)f(x + t) + S(x + t)f(x)}{[S(x)]^2} \geq 0$$

which implies that $g_t(x)$ is increasing in x for each fixed t. So $g_t(x) \geq g_t(0)$, and therefore

$$\frac{S(x + t)}{S(x)} \geq \frac{S(t)}{S(0)} = S(t), \text{ or } S(x + t) \geq S(x)S(t).$$

Hence $S(y) = S[x + (y - x)] \geq S(x)S(y - x)$, for all $x \geq 0$ and $y \geq x$. then, by Exercise 8.10,

$$
\begin{aligned}
\rho e^{-\kappa x} \int_x^\infty e^{\kappa y} dF(y) &= \rho e^{-\kappa x} \left[e^{\kappa x} S(x) + \kappa \int_x^\infty e^{\kappa y} S(y) dy \right] \\
&\geq \rho S(x) + \rho \kappa e^{-\kappa x} \int_x^\infty e^{\kappa y} S(x) S(y - x) dy \\
&= \rho S(x) + \rho S(x) \kappa \int_x^\infty e^{\kappa(y-x)} S(y - x) dy \\
&= \rho S(x) \left[1 + \kappa \int_0^\infty e^{\kappa z} S(z) dz \right], \text{ where } z = y - x, \\
&= \rho S(x) \left[1 + \int_0^\infty S(x) de^{\kappa x} \right] \\
&= \rho S(x) \left[1 + S(x)e^{\kappa x} \big|_0^\infty + \int_0^\infty e^{\kappa x} f(x) dx \right] \\
&= \rho S(x) \left[1 + \lim_{x \to \infty} S(x)e^{\kappa x} - 1 + \mathrm{E}\left(e^{\kappa X}\right) \right] \\
&= \rho S(x) \mathrm{E}\left(e^{\kappa X}\right)
\end{aligned}
$$

If $\rho^{-1} = \mathrm{E}\left(e^{\kappa X}\right)$, then $\rho e^{-\kappa x} \int_x^\infty e^{\kappa y} dF(y) \geq \rho \overline{F}(x) \mathrm{E}\left(e^{\kappa X}\right) = \overline{F}(x)$. (8.13) is satisfied. From Exercise 8.9,

$$\psi(x) \leq \rho e^{-\kappa x} = \left[\mathrm{E}\left(e^{\kappa X}\right) \right]^{-1} e^{-\kappa x}$$

8.12 $\mu(x) = -\frac{d}{dx} \ln S(x) \Rightarrow S(x) = e^{-\int_0^x \mu(t)dt}$. For $y > x$,

$$
\begin{aligned}
\frac{S(y)}{S(x)} &= \frac{e^{-\int_0^y \mu(t)dt}}{e^{-\int_0^x \mu(t)dt}} = e^{-\int_x^y \mu(t)dt} \\
&\geq e^{-\int_x^y m dt} = e^{-(y-x)m}
\end{aligned}
$$

which implies $S(y) \geq S(x)e^{-(y-x)m}$. From Exercise 8.10,

$$
\begin{aligned}
\rho e^{-\kappa x} \int_x^\infty e^{\kappa y} dF(y) &= \rho e^{-\kappa x}\left[e^{\kappa x}S(x) + \kappa \int_x^\infty e^{\kappa y}S(y)dy\right] \\
&\geq \rho S(x)\left[+\rho\kappa e^{-\kappa X}\int_x^\infty e^{\kappa y}S(x)e^{-(y-x)m}dy\right] \\
&= \rho S(x)\left[1 + \kappa \int_x^\infty e^{\kappa(y-x)}e^{-(y-x)m}dy\right] \\
&= \rho S(x)\left[1 + \kappa \int_0^\infty e^{-(m-\kappa)z}dz\right], \text{ where } z = y - x, \\
&= \rho S(x)\left[1 - \frac{\kappa}{m-\kappa}e^{-(m-\kappa)z}\Big|_0^\infty\right] \\
&= \rho S(x)\left[1 + \frac{\kappa}{m-\kappa}\right], \text{ if } m > \kappa, \\
&= \rho S(x)\frac{m}{m-\kappa}.
\end{aligned}
$$

If $\rho = \left(\frac{m}{m-\kappa}\right)^{-1} = 1 - \frac{\kappa}{m}$, then $\rho e^{-\kappa x}\int_x^\infty e^{\kappa y}dF(y) \geq \rho S(x)\frac{m}{m-\kappa} = S(x)$, (8.13) is satisfied. From Exercise 8.9, $\psi(x) \leq \rho e^{-\kappa x} = \left(1 - \frac{\kappa}{m}\right)e^{-\kappa x}$, $x \geq 0$.

8.2   SECTION 8.3

8.13 (a) In this case (8.15) becomes

$$
\frac{\partial}{\partial u}G(u,y) = \frac{\lambda}{c}G(u,y) - \frac{\lambda}{\mu c}\int_0^u G(u-x,y)e^{-x/\mu}dx - \frac{\lambda F(y)}{c}e^{-u/\mu}.
$$

A change of the variable of integration from x to $t = u - x$ in the integral term results in

$$
\frac{\partial}{\partial u}G(u,y) = \frac{\lambda}{c}G(u,y) - \frac{\lambda}{\mu c}e^{-u/\mu}\left[\int_0^u e^{t/\mu}G(t,y)dt + \mu F(y)\right].
$$

In order to eliminate the integral term, we may differentiate with respect to u to obtain

$$
\begin{aligned}
\frac{\partial^2}{\partial u^2}G(u,y) = {} & \frac{\lambda}{c}\frac{\partial}{\partial u}G(u,y) + \frac{\lambda}{\mu^2 c}e^{-u/\mu}\left[\int_0^u e^{t/\mu}G(t,y)dt + \mu F(y)\right] \\
& - \frac{\lambda}{\mu c}e^{-u/\mu}\left[e^{u/\mu}G(u,y)\right],
\end{aligned}
$$

resulting in

$$
\frac{\partial^2}{\partial u^2}G(u,y) = \frac{\lambda}{c}\frac{\partial}{\partial u}G(u,y) + \frac{1}{\mu}\left[\frac{\lambda}{c}G(u,y) - \frac{\partial}{\partial u}G(u,y)\right] - \frac{\lambda}{\mu c}G(u,y).
$$

That is

$$\frac{\partial^2}{\partial u^2} G(u,y) = \left(\frac{\lambda}{c} - \frac{1}{\mu}\right) \frac{\partial}{\partial u} G(u,y) = -\frac{\theta}{\mu(1+\theta)} \cdot \frac{\partial}{\partial u} G(u,y).$$

This equation may be rewritten after multiplication by the integrating factor $e^{\frac{\theta u}{\mu(1+\theta)}}$ as

$$\frac{\partial}{\partial u}\left[e^{\frac{\theta u}{\mu(1+\theta)}} \frac{\partial}{\partial u} G(u,y)\right] = 0,$$

and integration yields

$$e^{\frac{\theta u}{\mu(1+\theta)}} \frac{\partial}{\partial u} G(u,y) = K_1(y).$$

To evaluate $K_1(y)$, we may substitute $u=0$ into this equation and (8.15) to obtain

$$K_1(y) = \frac{\partial}{\partial u} G(u,y)\bigg|_{u=0} = \frac{\lambda}{c} G(0,y) - \frac{\lambda}{c} F(y).$$

In this situation (8.16) yields

$$G(0,y) = \frac{\lambda}{c} \int_0^y e^{-x/\mu} dx = -\frac{\lambda\mu}{c} e^{-x/\mu}\bigg|_0^y = \frac{\lambda\mu}{c}\left(1 - e^{-y/\mu}\right) = \frac{F(y)}{1+\theta}.$$

Therefore,

$$K_1(y) = \frac{\lambda}{c(1+\theta)} F(y) - \frac{\lambda}{c} F(y) = -\frac{\theta F(y)}{\mu(1+\theta)^2},$$

and so

$$\frac{\partial}{\partial u} G(u,y) = -\frac{\theta F(y)}{\mu(1+\theta)^2} e^{-\frac{\theta u}{\mu(1+\theta)}}.$$

Integration of this result yields

$$G(u,y) = \frac{F(y)}{1+\theta} e^{-\frac{\theta u}{\mu(1+\theta)}} + K_2(y).$$

But $G(0,y) = F(y)/(1+\theta)$, and so $K_2(y) = 0$. Thus

$$G(u,y) = \frac{F(y)}{1+\theta} e^{-\frac{\theta u}{\mu(1+\theta)}} = \psi(u)F(y)$$

because $\psi(u) = e^{-\frac{\theta u}{\mu(1+\theta)}}/(1+\theta)$ from Example 8.14.

(b) The cumulative distribution function of the deficit immediately after ruin occurs, given that ruin does occur, is given by

$$G_u(y) = \frac{G(u,y)}{\psi(u)} = F(y)$$

using (a).

8.14 (a) From (8.15)

$$\int_0^t \left[\frac{\partial}{\partial u} G(u,y)\right] du = \frac{\lambda}{c}\int_0^t G(u,y)du - \frac{\lambda}{c}\int_0^t \int_0^u G(u-x,y)dF(x)du$$
$$- \frac{\lambda}{c}\int_0^t [F(u+y) - F(u)]du.$$

Thus, by the fundamental theorem of calculus, and reversing the order of integration in the double integral,

$$G(t,y) - G(0,y) = \frac{\lambda}{c}\int_0^t G(u,y)du - \frac{\lambda}{c}\int_0^t\left[\int_x^t G(u-x,y)du\right]dF(x)$$
$$- \frac{\lambda}{c}\int_0^t [F(u+y) - F(u)]du.$$

Using (8.16) and changing the variable of integration from u to $v = u - x$ in the inner integral of the double integral results in

$$G(t,y) = \frac{\lambda}{c}\int_0^t G(u,y)du - \frac{\lambda}{c}\int_0^t\left[\int_0^{t-x} G(v,y)dv\right]dF(x)$$
$$+ \frac{\lambda}{c}\int_0^y [1 - F(x)]dx - \frac{\lambda}{c}\int_0^t [F(u+y) - F(u)]du.$$

For notational convenience, let $\Lambda(x,y) = \int_0^x G(v,y)dv$. Then

$$G(t,y) = \frac{\lambda}{c}\Lambda(t,y) - \frac{\lambda}{c}\int_0^t \Lambda(t-x,y)dF(x) + \frac{\lambda}{c}\int_0^y [1 - F(x)]dx$$
$$- \frac{\lambda}{c}\int_0^t [1 - F(u)]du + \frac{\lambda}{c}\int_0^t [1 - F(u+y)]du.$$

(b)Integration by parts on the second integral on the right-hand side of the result in (a) and changing the variable of integration from u to $x = u + y$ in the first integral on the right-hand side gives

$$G(t,y) = \frac{\lambda}{c}\Lambda(t,y) - \frac{\lambda}{c}\left[\Lambda(t-x,y)F(x)|_0^t + \int_0^t G(t-x,y)F(x)dx\right]$$
$$+ \frac{\lambda}{c}\int_0^y [1 - F(x)]dx - \frac{\lambda}{c}\int_0^t [1 - F(u)]du$$
$$+ \frac{\lambda}{c}\int_y^{y+t} [1 - F(x)]dx.$$

Thus,

$$G(t,y) = \frac{\lambda}{c}\Lambda(t,y) - \frac{\lambda}{c}\left[0 - 0 + \int_0^t G(t-x,y)F(x)dx\right]$$
$$+ \frac{\lambda}{c}\int_0^{y+t} [1 - F(x)]dx - \frac{\lambda}{c}\int_0^t [1 - F(u)]du.$$

(c) Changing the variable of integration from u to x in the last integral of the result in (b) yields, with $\Lambda(t,y) = \int_0^t G(t-x,y)dx$

$$G(t,y) = \frac{\lambda}{c} \int_0^t G(t-x,y)dx - \frac{\lambda}{c} \int_0^t G(t-x,y)F(x)dx + \frac{\lambda}{c} \int_t^{y+t} [1 - F(x)]dx.$$

Finally, combining the first two integrals,

$$G(t,y) = \frac{\lambda}{c} \int_0^t G(t-x,y)[1 - F(x)]dx + \frac{\lambda}{c} \int_t^{y+t} [1 - F(x)]dx.$$

The result follows by changing the variable t to u.

(d) Because $\psi(u) = \lim_{y\to\infty} G(u,y)$, let $y \to \infty$ in (c).

8.3 SECTION 8.4

8.15 By Example 8.14, $\psi(u) = \frac{1}{1+\theta} \exp\left[-\frac{\theta u}{\mu(1+\theta)}\right]$.

$$\psi(1,000) = \frac{1}{1.1} \exp\left[-\frac{0.1(1,000)}{100(1.1)}\right] = \frac{1}{1.1} \exp\left(-\frac{1}{1.1}\right) = 0.36626 \quad \text{(exact)}.$$

$$
\begin{aligned}
F_X(u) &= 1 - \exp(-u/100), \mathrm{E}(X) = 100 \\
f_e(u) &= \frac{1 - F_x(u)}{\mathrm{E}(X)} = \frac{1}{100} e^{-\frac{u}{100}}
\end{aligned}
$$

and so $F_e(u) = 1 - \exp(-u/100)$. Discretize $F_e(u)$ with a span of 50:

$$
\begin{aligned}
f_X(50m) &= \Pr\left[(2m-1)25 < u \le (2m+1)25\right] \\
&= \exp\left[-\frac{(2m-1)}{100}25\right] - \exp\left[-\frac{(2m+1)}{100}25\right] \\
&= \exp\left(-\frac{2m-1}{4}\right) - \exp\left(-\frac{2m+1}{4}\right), \quad m = 1, 2, \ldots .
\end{aligned}
$$

$K \sim$ geometric with $p_k = \Pr(K = k) = \frac{\theta}{1+\theta}\left(\frac{1}{1+\theta}\right)^k$ and $p_k = \frac{1}{1+\theta}p_{k-1}$, $k = 1, 2, \ldots$ Using

$$f_S(x) = \frac{1}{1 - af_X(0)} \sum_{i=1}^x \left(a + b\frac{i}{x}\right) f_X(i)f_S(x-i)$$

with $a = \frac{1}{1+\theta}$, $b = 0$, $f_X(0) = 1 - \exp(-1/4)$ and

$$f_S(0) = \sum_{k=0}^\infty \frac{\theta}{1+\theta}\left(\frac{1}{1+\theta}\right)^k [f_X(0)]^k = \frac{\theta}{1+\theta - f_X(0)} = \frac{.1}{.1 + e^{-1/4}}$$

Table 8.3 Calculations for Exercise 8.15

x	$f_S(x)$	x	$f_S(x)$
0	0.113791	550	0.025097
50	0.039679	600	0.023973
100	0.037902	650	0.022900
150	0.036205	700	0.021875
200	0.034584	750	0.020895
250	0.033036	800	0.019960
300	0.031556	850	0.019066
350	0.030144	900	0.018212
400	0.028794	950	0.017397
450	0.027505	1,000	0.016618
500	0.026273		

Calculations appear in Table 8.3.
Using the method of Section 6.8 we have

$$\phi(1,000) = \sum_{i=0}^{19} f_S(50 \times i) + 0.5 f_S(1,000) = 0.637152.$$

Then, $\psi(1,000) = 1 - \phi(1,000) = 0.362858$. Using a span of 1 changes the result to 0.366263 which agrees with the analytical result to 5 decimal places.

8.16 By Example 8.19, $\psi(u) = \frac{2}{5}e^{-\frac{u}{2\beta}} - \frac{1}{15}e^{-\frac{4u}{3\beta}}$ and so

$$\psi(200) = \frac{2}{5}e^{-\frac{200}{100}} - \frac{1}{15}e^{-\frac{800}{150}} = \frac{2}{5}e^{-2} - \frac{1}{15}e^{-\frac{16}{3}} = 0.053812 \quad (\text{exact}).$$

$$
\begin{aligned}
f_X(x) &= \beta^{-2}xe^{-x/\beta} = 50^{-2}xe^{-x/50} \\
E(X) &= 2\beta = 100 \\
F_X(x) &= 1 - \frac{x}{50}e^{-x/50} - e^{-x/50} \\
f_e(u) &= \frac{1 - F_X(u)}{E(X)} = \frac{1}{5,000}ue^{-u/50} + \frac{1}{100}e^{-u/50} \\
F_e(u) &= 1 - \frac{1}{100}ue^{-u/50} - e^{-u/50}.
\end{aligned}
$$

Although not relevant, this distribution is a mixture of gamma$(2, 50)$ and gamma$(1, 50)$ with probability one-half assigned to each. Discretize $F_e(u)$

with a span of 25.

$$f_X(25m) = \Pr\left[(2m-1)12.5 < Y \le (2m+1)12.5\right]$$
$$= \frac{1}{100}\left[(2m-1)12.5 - (2m+1)12.5\right]$$
$$+ \left[e^{-(2m-1)/4} - e^{-(2m+1)/4}\right], \quad m = 1, 2, \ldots.$$

Using

$$f_X(x) = \frac{1}{1-af_x(0)} \sum_{i=1}^{x}\left(a + b\frac{i}{x}\right) f_X(i)f_S(x-i)$$

where $a = \frac{1}{1+\theta} = \frac{1}{3}$, $b = 0$, $f_X(0) = 1 - \frac{125}{100}\exp(-12.5/50) - \exp(-12.5/50)$
and

$$f_S(0) = \frac{\theta}{1+\theta - f_X(0)} = \frac{2}{2 + \frac{12.5}{100}e^{-1/4} + e^{-1/4}}.$$

Therefore,

$$f_S(x) = \frac{1}{3 - f_X(0)} \sum_{i=0}^{x} f_X(i)f_S(x-i)$$

We then have the calculations given in Table 8.4.

Table 8.4   Calculations for Exercise 8.16

x	$f_S(x)$
0	0.695374
25	0.054797
50	0.048788
75	0.041135
100	0.033649
125	0.027036
150	0.021483
175	0.016952
200	0.013317

Using the method of Section 6.8 we have

$$\phi(200) = \sum_{m=0}^{7} f_S(25m) + 0.5f_S(200) = 0.9458725$$

and $\psi(200) = 1 - \phi(200) = 0.0541275$.

8.17 (a) First, change the index of summation from k to j, yielding

$$F'(x) = \sum_{j=1}^{r} q_j \frac{\beta^{-j}x^{j-1}e^{-x/\beta}}{(j-1)!}.$$

Then, from Example 6.13,

$$F(x) = \int_0^x F'(y)dy = \sum_{j=1}^r q_j \int_0^x \frac{\beta^{-j}y^{j-1}e^{-y/\beta}}{(j-1)!}dy = \sum_{j=1}^r q_j\Gamma(j;x/\beta)$$

$$= \sum_{j=1}^r q_j\left\{1 - \sum_{k=1}^j \frac{(x/\beta)^{k-1}e^{-x/\beta}}{(k-1)!}\right\} = 1 - \sum_{j=1}^r\sum_{k=1}^j q_j\frac{(x/\beta)^{k-1}e^{-x/\beta}}{(k-1)!}$$

$$= 1 - \sum_{k=1}^r\sum_{j=k}^r q_j\frac{(x/\beta)^{k-1}e^{-x/\beta}}{(k-1)!} = 1 - \sum_{k=1}^r\frac{(x/\beta)^{k-1}e^{-x/\beta}}{(k-1)!}\sum_{j=k}^r q_j.$$

Also,

$$\mu = \int_0^\infty xF'(x)dx = \sum_{j=1}^r q_j\int_0^\infty x\cdot\frac{\beta^{-j}x^{j-1}e^{-x/\beta}}{(j-1)!}dx = \sum_{j=1}^r q_j(\beta j) = \beta\sum_{j=1}^r jq_j.$$

Thus,

$$f_e(x) = \frac{1-F(x)}{\mu} = \frac{\sum_{k=1}^r\frac{(x/\beta)^{k-1}e^{-x/\beta}}{(k-1)!}\sum_{j=k}^r q_j}{\beta\sum_{j=1}^r jq_j} = \sum_{k=1}^r q_k^*\frac{\beta^{-k}x^{k-1}e^{-x/\beta}}{(k-1)!}$$

It remains to show that $\sum_{k=1}^r q_k^* = 1$. By interchanging the order of summation,

$$\sum_{k=1}^r\sum_{j=k}^r q_j = \sum_{j=1}^r\sum_{k=1}^j q_j = \sum_{j=1}^r jq_j.$$

Division of both sides by $\sum_{j=1}^r jq_j$ gives the result. Thus, $f_e(x)$ is of the same form as $F'(x)$, but with the mixing weights $\{q_j; j = 1, 2, \ldots, r\}$ replaced by $\{q_j^*; j = 1, 2, \ldots, r\}$.
(b) From Exercise 6.35(a),

$$\int_0^\infty e^{zx}f_e(x)dx = Q^*\{(1-\beta z)^{-1}\}.$$

Thus, from Exercise 6.35(b), the maximum aggregate loss L has moment generating function

$$E(e^{zL}) = \sum_{k=0}^\infty \frac{\theta}{1+\theta}\left(\frac{1}{1+\theta}\right)^k(Q^*\{(1-\beta z)^{-1}\})^k$$

$$= \frac{\theta}{\theta+1-Q^*\{(1-\beta z)^{-1}\}}.$$

That is, $E(e^{zL}) = C\{(1 - \beta z)^{-1}\}$ after division of the numerator and denominator by θ. Clearly, $C(z) = \sum_{n=0}^{\infty} c_n z^n$ is the pgf of a compound geometric distribution with $a = (1 + \theta)^{-1}$ and $b = 0$, and secondary "claim size" pgf $Q^*(z)$. Thus, by Theorem 4.48, the probabilities $\{c_n; n = 0, 1, 2, \ldots\}$ may be computed recursively by

$$c_k = \frac{1}{1 + \theta} \sum_{j=1}^{k} q_j^* c_{k-j}; \quad k = 1, 2, \ldots$$

beginning with $c_0 = \theta(1 + \theta)^{-1}$. Then from Exercise 6.35,

$$\psi(u) = \sum_{n=1}^{\infty} c_n \sum_{j=0}^{n-1} \frac{(u/\beta)^j e^{-u/\beta}}{j!}, \quad u \geq 0.$$

(c) From (b), interchanging the order of summation,

$$\psi(u) = e^{-u/\beta} \sum_{j=0}^{\infty} \sum_{n=j+1}^{\infty} \frac{(u(\beta)^j}{j!} c_n = e^{-u/\beta} \sum_{j=0}^{\infty} \bar{C}_j \frac{(u/\beta)^j}{j!}.$$

Clearly, $\bar{C}_0 = 1 - c_0 = (1 + \theta)^{-1}$. By summing the recursion in (b),

$$\sum_{k=n+1}^{\infty} c_k = \frac{1}{1 + \theta} \sum_{k=n+1}^{\infty} \sum_{j=1}^{k} q_j^* c_{k-j}.$$

Interchanging the order of summation yields

$$\bar{C}_n = \frac{1}{1 + \theta} \sum_{j=1}^{n} q_j^* \sum_{k=n+1}^{\infty} c_{k-j} + \frac{1}{1 + \theta} \sum_{j=n+1}^{\infty} q_j^* \sum_{k=j}^{\infty} c_{k-j}.$$

But $\bar{C}_{n-j} = \sum_{k=n+1}^{\infty} c_{k-j}$ and $1 = \sum_{k=j}^{\infty} c_{k-j}$, yielding

$$\bar{C}_n = \frac{1}{1 + \theta} \sum_{j=1}^{n} q_j^* \bar{C}_{n-j} + \frac{1}{1 + \theta} \sum_{j=n+1}^{\infty} q_j^*.$$

8.18 (a) Note that

$$\frac{f_e(x)}{1 + \theta} = \frac{1 - F(x)}{\mu(1 + \theta)} = \frac{\lambda}{c}[1 - F(x)],$$

and replacement of the right-hand side by the left-hand side in the equations in Exercise 8.14(c) and 8.14(d), respectively, yields the results.

(b)Recall that $f_e(x)$ is the probability density function of the amount of a drop in surplus, given that there is a drop. Also, $1/(1+\theta)$ is the probability of a drop in surplus. Consider $G(u, y)$, which is the probability that ruin occurs beginning with initial reserve u, and the surplus when ruin does occur is between $-y$ and 0. We condition on the first drop in surplus which occurs with probability $1/(1+\theta)$, and suppose that the amount of this drop is x with "probability" $f_e(x)dx$. There are two possibilities: the first is that the first drop does cause ruin and the deficit at ruin is between $-y$ and 0. Since the initial surplus is $u \geq 0$, the amount of this drop must be greater than u (for ruin to occur) but no greater than $y + u$ (in order that the surplus be no less than $-y$). The probability of this first possibility is $\int_u^{u+y} f_e(x)dx/(1+\theta)$. The second possibility is that the first drop does not cause ruin and therefore the amount of this drop is at most u. If the amount of the drop is x, then the surplus immediately after the drop is $u - x$. The process then "begins again" (by the stationary and independent increments property), and the probability of ruin with a deficit (negative surplus) of at most y is $G(u-x, y)$. "Summing" (i.e. integrating) over x from 0 to u results in the probability of this second possibility as $\int_0^u G(u - x, y)f_e(x)dx/(1 + \theta)$, and the result for $G(u, y)$ in (a) then follows. The result for $\psi(u)$ follows from that of $G(u, y)$ with $y \to \infty$.

8.4   SECTION 8.5

8.19 Consider

$$\int_0^\infty e^{zx} F'(x)dx = \mathrm{E}(e^{zX}).$$

By integration by parts,

$$
\begin{aligned}
\int_0^\infty e^{zx} F'(x)dx &= -e^{zx}\{1 - F(x)\}|_0^\infty + z\int_0^\infty e^{zx}\{1 - F(x)\}dx \\
&= 1 + \mu z \int_0^\infty e^{zx} f_e(x)dx
\end{aligned}
$$

since $f_e(x) = \{1 - F(x)\}/\mu$. Also

$$0 \leq \lim_{x\to\infty} e^{zx}\{1 - F(x)\} = \lim_{x\to\infty} e^{zx}\int_x^\infty F'(y)dy \leq \lim_{x\to\infty}\int_x^\infty e^{\kappa y} F'(y)dy = 0$$

if $\mathrm{E}(e^{zx}) < \infty$. That is, $\lim_{x\to\infty} e^{zx}[1 - F(x)] = 0$. In other words, the moment generating functions of X and Y are related by

$$\mathrm{E}(e^{zx}) = 1 + \mu z \mathrm{E}(e^{zY}).$$

Differentiating with respect to z yields

$$E(Xe^{zX}) = \mu E(e^{zY}) + \mu z E(Ye^{zY}).$$

Thus, with $z = \kappa$,

$$
\begin{aligned}
E(Xe^{\kappa X}) &= \mu E(e^{\kappa Y}) + \mu \kappa E(Ye^{\kappa Y}) \\
&= \mu(1 + \theta) + \mu \kappa E(Ye^{\kappa Y})
\end{aligned}
$$

using (8.7). Thus, from the above and (8.22),

$$C = \frac{\theta \mu}{\mu \kappa E(Ye^{\kappa Y})} = \frac{\theta}{\kappa E(Ye^{\kappa Y})}.$$

In this case, from (b)

$$E(e^{zY}) = \int_0^\infty e^{zx} f_e(x)dx = Q^*\{(1 - \beta z)^{-1}\} = \sum_{k=1}^r q_k^*(1 - \beta z)^{-k}.$$

Differentiating with respect to z gives

$$E(Ye^{zY}) = \beta \sum_{k=1}^r k q_k^*(1 - \beta z)^{-k-1} = \beta \sum_{j=1}^r j q_j^*(1 - \beta z)^{-j-1}.$$

Thus, with z replaced by κ,

$$C = \frac{\theta}{\kappa E(Ye^{\kappa Y})} = \frac{\theta}{\kappa \beta \sum_{j=1}^r j q_j^*(1 - \beta \kappa)^{-j-1}}$$

and Cramér's asymptotic ruin formula gives $\psi(u) \sim Ce^{-\kappa u}, u \to \infty$. Finally, from (8.7), $\kappa > 0$ satisfies

$$
\begin{aligned}
1 + \theta &= E \int_0^\infty e^{\kappa y} f_e(y)dy = E(e^{\kappa Y}) \\
&= Q^*\{(1 - \beta \kappa)^{-1}\} = \sum_{j=1}^r q_j^*(1 - \beta \kappa)^{-j}.
\end{aligned}
$$

8.20 (a) Because $\psi(u) = \lim_{y \to \infty} G(u, y)$, it is clear from (8.22) that we need only verify that

$$\kappa \int_0^\infty e^{\kappa t} \int_t^\infty f_e(x)dxdt = \theta.$$

But integration by parts yields

$$\kappa \int_0^\infty e^{\kappa t} \int_t^\infty f_e(x)dxdt \;=\; e^{\kappa t} \int_t^\infty f_e(x)dx \big|_{t=0}^\infty + \int_0^\infty e^{\kappa t} f_e(t)dt$$

$$=\; \Big[\lim_{t\to\infty} e^{\kappa t} \int_t^\infty f_e(x)dx \Big] - 1 + (1+\theta),$$

where (8.7) has been used. Thus, it remains to verify that

$$\lim_{t\to\infty} e^{\kappa t} \int_t^\infty f_e(x)dx = 0.$$

Now, $0 \le e^{\kappa t} \int_t^\infty f_e(x)dx \le \int_t^\infty e^{\kappa x} f_e(x)dx$, and $\lim_{t\to\infty} \int_t^\infty e^{\kappa x} f_e(x)dx = 0$ because $\int_0^\infty e^{\kappa x} f_e(x)dx = 1 + \theta < \infty$. The result therefore holds.

(b) Recall from Example 8.18 that $M_X'(\kappa) = \mu(1+\theta)^2$. Thus

$$C(y) \;=\; \frac{\kappa \int_0^\infty e^{\kappa t} \int_t^{t+y} [1-F(x)]dxdt}{m_X'(\kappa) - \mu(1+\theta)}$$

$$=\; \frac{\kappa \int_0^\infty e^{\kappa t} \int_t^{t+y} e^{-x/\mu} dxdt}{\mu(1+\theta)^2 - \mu(1+\theta)}$$

$$=\; \frac{\kappa \int_0^\infty e^{\kappa t} \Big[-\mu e^{-x/\mu} \big|_t^{t+y} \Big] dt}{\mu(1+\theta)[(1+\theta)-1]}$$

$$=\; \frac{\mu\kappa \int_0^\infty e^{\kappa t} [e^{-t/\mu} - e^{-(t+y)/\mu}]dt}{\mu\theta(1+\theta)}$$

$$=\; \frac{\kappa(1-e^{-y/\mu}) \int_0^\infty e^{-t(\mu^{-1}-\kappa)} dt}{\theta(1+\theta)}.$$

But $\kappa = \theta/[\mu(1+\theta)]$ from Example 8.4, and thus $\mu^{-1} - \kappa = 1/[\mu(1+\theta)]$. Therefore

$$C(y) \;=\; \frac{\kappa F(y) \int_0^\infty e^{-t/[\mu(1+\theta)]} dt}{\theta(1+\theta)}$$

$$=\; \frac{F(y)}{1+\theta} \int_0^\infty \frac{e^{-t/[\mu(1+\theta)]}}{\mu(1+\theta)} dt$$

$$=\; \frac{F(y)}{1+\theta} \Big\{ -e^{-t/[\mu(1+\theta)]} \big|_{t=0}^\infty \Big\}$$

$$=\; \frac{F(y)}{1+\theta}.$$

Therefore, the asymptotic formula becomes

$$G(u,y) \sim \frac{F(y)}{1+\theta} e^{-\kappa u}, \quad u \to \infty,$$

and from Example 8.18, $\psi(u) = e^{-\kappa u}/(1+\theta)$. Thus, the asymptotic formula may be expressed as

$$G(u,y) \sim \psi(u)F(y), \quad u \to \infty.$$

But in Exercise 8.13(a), it was demonstrated that $G(u,y) = \psi(u)F(y)$.

8.21 (a)

$$\psi(0) = \frac{1}{1+\theta} = C_1 + C_2 \Rightarrow \theta = \frac{1}{C_1 + C_2} - 1.$$

(b)

$$\lim_{u \to \infty} e^{r_1 u} \psi(u) = \lim_{u \to \infty} \left[C_1 + C_2 e^{-(r_2 - r_1)u} \right] = C_1 \text{ because } r_2 > r_1.$$

But Cramér's asymptotic ruin formula states that $\lim_{u \to \infty} e^{-\kappa u} \psi(u) = C$, implying that $\kappa = r_1$.

(c) Lundberg's inequality yields $\psi(u) \le e^{-r_1 u}$ because $r_1 = \kappa$ from (b). Thus, $e^{r_1 u} \psi(u) \le 1$ and from (b) $\lim_{u \to \infty} e^{r_1 u} \psi(u) = C_1$. Clearly, $C_1 \le 1$ because if $C_1 > 1$ then it would follow that $e^{r_1 u} \psi(u) > 1$ for sufficiently large u. Also, $e^{r_1 u} \psi(u) \ge 0$ implies that $C_1 \ge 0$, and it is given that $C_1 \ne 0$.

(d) It follows from (b) that $\psi(u) \sim C_1 e^{-r_1 u}$, $u \to \infty$.

(e) Now, from (d), it follows that

$$\psi_T(u) = \left(\frac{1}{1+\theta} - C_1 \right) e^{-u/\alpha} + C_1 e^{-r_1 u}, \ u \ge 0,$$

and from (a), $(1+\theta)^{-1} - C_1 = (C_1 + C_2) - C_1 = C_2$. Hence,

$$\psi_T(u) = C_2 e^{-u/\alpha} + C_1 e^{-r_1 u},$$

and the Tijms' approximation matches the compound geometric mean, i.e.

$$\int_0^\infty \psi_T(u) du = \int_0^\infty \psi(u) du,$$

which may be restated as

$$\alpha C_2 + \frac{C_1}{r_1} = \frac{C_1}{r_1} + \frac{C_2}{r_2}.$$

Therefore, $\alpha = 1/r_2$ and $\psi_T(u) = \psi(u)$.

8.22 (a) First note that $f(x) = \frac{1}{3}(3e^{-3x}) + \frac{2}{3}(9xe^{-3x})$, and so the moment generating function is

$$M_X(t) = \frac{1}{3} \left(\frac{3}{3-t} \right) + \frac{2}{3} \left(\frac{3}{3-t} \right)^2 = (3-t)^{-1} + 6(3-t)^{-2}.$$

Therefore $M_X'(t) = (3-t)^{-2} + 12(3-t)^{-3}$, from which it follows that $\mu = M_X'(0) = \frac{1}{9} + \frac{12}{27} = \frac{5}{9}$. The adjustment coefficient satisfies $1 + (1 + \frac{4}{5})(\frac{5}{9})\kappa = M_X(\kappa)$, or $1 + \kappa = \frac{1}{(3-\kappa)} + \frac{6}{(3-\kappa)^2}$. Thus $(1 + \kappa)(3 - \kappa)^2 = (3 - \kappa) + 6$, or $(\kappa + 1)(\kappa^2 - 6\kappa + 9) = -\kappa + 9$, which may be rearranged as $0 = \kappa^3 - 5\kappa^2 + 4\kappa =$

$\kappa(\kappa-1)(\kappa-4)$, and so $\kappa = 1$. Therefore, $M'_X(\kappa) = M'_X(1) = \frac{1}{4} + \frac{12}{8} = \frac{7}{4}$. Equation (8.22) yields

$$C = \frac{\left(\frac{5}{9}\right)\left(\frac{4}{5}\right)}{\frac{7}{4} - \left(\frac{5}{9}\right)\left(1 + \frac{4}{5}\right)} = \frac{\frac{4}{9}}{\frac{3}{4}} = \frac{16}{27},$$

and thus $\psi(u) \sim \frac{16}{27} e^{-u}$, $u \to \infty$.

(b)It is clear from the expression for $f(x)$ given in (a) above and the comment in the paragraph preceding Example 8.19 that $\psi_T(u) = \psi(u)$ so we will compute $\psi_T(u)$. Clearly,

$$\psi_T(u) = \left(\frac{1}{1 + \frac{4}{5}} - \frac{16}{27}\right) e^{-u/\alpha} + \frac{16}{27} e^{-u} = -\frac{1}{27} e^{-u/\alpha} + \frac{16}{27} e^{-u}.$$

To determine α, first note that $M''_X(t) = 2(3-t)^{-3} + 36(3-t)^{-4}$, and $E(X^2) = M''_X(0) = \frac{2}{27} + \frac{36}{81} = \frac{14}{27}$. The compound geometric mean is thus

$$E(L) = \frac{\frac{14}{27}}{2\left(\frac{5}{9}\right)\left(\frac{4}{5}\right)} = \frac{7}{12}.$$

Hence, (8.24) yields

$$\alpha = \frac{\frac{7}{12} - \frac{16}{27}}{-\frac{1}{27}} = \frac{1}{4},$$

and thus $\psi(u) = \psi_T(u) = \frac{16}{27} e^{-u} - \frac{1}{27} e^{-4u}$, $u \geq 0$.

8.23 (a) The moment generating function is

$$M_X(t) = \int_0^\infty e^{tx} f(x) dx = 2(4 - t)^{-1} + \frac{7}{2}(7 - t)^{-1}.$$

Consequently, $M'_X(t) = 2(4 - t)^{-2} + \frac{7}{2}(7 - t)^{-2}$, and so $\mu = M'_X(0) = \frac{2}{16} + \frac{7}{98} = \frac{11}{56}$. The adjustment coefficient satisfies $1 + (1 + \frac{3}{11})(\frac{11}{56})\kappa = M_X(\kappa)$, or equivalently $1 + \frac{1}{4}\kappa = \frac{2}{4-\kappa} + \frac{7}{2(7-\kappa)}$. This may be expressed as $4(\kappa-7)(\kappa-4) + \kappa(\kappa-7)(\kappa-4) = 8(7-\kappa) + 14(4-\kappa)$, or $4\kappa^2 - 44\kappa + 112 + \kappa^3 - 11\kappa^2 + 28\kappa = 112 - 22\kappa$. That is, $0 = \kappa^3 - 7\kappa^2 + 6\kappa = \kappa(\kappa-1)(\kappa-6)$, implying that $\kappa = 1$. Hence $M'_X(\kappa) = M'_X(1) = \frac{2}{9} + \frac{7}{72} = \frac{23}{72}$. Substitution in (8.22) yields

$$C = \frac{\left(\frac{11}{56}\right)\left(\frac{3}{11}\right)}{\frac{23}{72} - \left(\frac{11}{56}\right)\left(1 + \frac{3}{11}\right)} = \frac{\frac{3}{56}}{\frac{5}{72}} = \frac{27}{35},$$

and thus $\psi(u) \sim \frac{27}{35} e^{-u}$, $u \to \infty$.

(b) Because $f(x) = \frac{1}{2}(4e^{-4x}) + \frac{1}{2}(7e^{-7x})$, it follows from the comment in the paragraph preceding Example 8.20 that $\psi_T(u) = \psi(u)$ and thus we will compute $\psi_T(u)$. Therefore $\psi_T(u) = \left(\frac{1}{1 + \frac{3}{11}} - \frac{27}{35}\right) e^{-u/\alpha} + \frac{27}{35} e^{-u} = \frac{1}{70} e^{-u/\alpha} +$

$\frac{27}{35}e^{-u}$. In order to determine α, we have $M_X''(t) = 4(4-t)^{-3} + 7(7-t)^{-3}$, from which it follows that $E(X^2) = M_X''(0) = \frac{1}{16} + \frac{1}{49} = \frac{65}{784}$. The compound geometric mean is therefore

$$E(L) = \frac{\left(\frac{65}{784}\right)}{2\left(\frac{11}{56}\right)\left(\frac{3}{11}\right)} = \frac{65}{84}.$$

Then (8.24) yields

$$\alpha = \frac{\frac{65}{84} - \frac{27}{35}}{\frac{1}{70}} = \frac{1}{6}.$$

Finally, $\psi(u) = \psi_T(u) = \frac{1}{70}e^{-6u} + \frac{27}{35}e^{-u}$, $u \geq 0$.

8.24 (a) The moment generating function is

$$M_X(t) = \int_0^\infty e^{tx} f(x)dx = 3(4-t)^{-1} + \frac{1}{2}(2-t)^{-1},$$

and so, $M_X'(t) = 3(4-t)^{-2} + \frac{1}{2}(2-t)^{-2}$, from which it follows that $\mu = M_X'(0) = \frac{3}{16} + \frac{1}{8} = \frac{5}{16}$. The adjustment coefficient satisfies $1 + (1+\frac{3}{5})(\frac{5}{16})\kappa = M_X(\kappa)$, i.e. $1 + \frac{1}{2}\kappa = \frac{3}{4-\kappa} + \frac{1}{2(2-\kappa)}$. Alternately, $2(\kappa-2)(\kappa-4) + \kappa(\kappa - 2)(\kappa-4) = 6(2-\kappa) + (4-\kappa)$, or $2\kappa^2 - 12\kappa + 16 + \kappa^3 - 6\kappa^2 + 8\kappa = -7\kappa + 16$. That is, $0 = \kappa^3 - 4\kappa^2 + 3\kappa = \kappa(\kappa-1)(\kappa-3)$, and so $\kappa = 1$. Therefore, $M_X'(\kappa) = M_X'(1) = \frac{1}{3} + \frac{1}{2} = \frac{5}{6}$. Substitution in (8.22) yields

$$C = \frac{\left(\frac{5}{16}\right)\left(\frac{3}{5}\right)}{\frac{5}{6} - \left(\frac{5}{16}\right)\left(1+\frac{3}{5}\right)} = \frac{\frac{3}{16}}{\frac{1}{3}} = \frac{9}{16},$$

and so $\psi(u) \sim \frac{9}{16}e^{-u}$, $u \to \infty$.

(b)Note that $f(x) = \frac{3}{4}(4e^{-4x}) + \frac{1}{4}(2e^{-2x})$, which implies from the comment in the paragraph preceding Example 8.20 that $\psi_T(u) = \psi(u)$ and so we will determine $\psi_T(u)$. Clearly, $\psi_T(u) = \left(\frac{1}{1+\frac{3}{5}} - \frac{9}{16}\right)e^{-u/\alpha} + \frac{9}{16}e^{-u} = \frac{1}{16}e^{-u/\alpha} + \frac{9}{16}e^{-u}$. It remains to determine α. We have $M_X''(t) = 6(4-t)^{-3} + (2-t)^{-3}$, and so $E(X^2) = M_X''(0) = \frac{6}{64} + \frac{1}{8} = \frac{7}{32}$. The compound geometric mean is therefore

$$E(L) = \frac{\left(\frac{7}{32}\right)}{2\left(\frac{5}{16}\right)\left(\frac{3}{5}\right)} = \frac{7}{12}.$$

Then (8.24) yields

$$\alpha = \frac{\frac{7}{12} - \frac{9}{16}}{\frac{1}{16}} = \frac{1}{3},$$

and therefore $\psi(u) = \psi_T(u) = \frac{1}{16}e^{-3u} + \frac{9}{16}e^{-u}$, $u \geq 0$.

8.25 (a) Clearly, $f(x) = 6e^{-3x} \int_0^x e^y dy = 6e^{-3x}(e^x - 1) = 6e^{-2x} - 6e^{-3x}$, $x \geq 0$. The moment generating function is therefore

$$M_X(t) = \int_0^\infty e^{tx} f(x) dx = 6(2-t)^{-1} - 6(3-t)^{-1},$$

and thus, $M_X'(t) = 6(2-t)^{-2} - 6(3-t)^{-2}$. The mean is $\mu = M_X'(0) = \frac{6}{4} - \frac{6}{9} = \frac{5}{6}$. The adjustment coefficient satisfies $1 + (1 + \frac{7}{5})(\frac{5}{6})\kappa = M_X(\kappa)$, that is $1 + 2\kappa = \frac{6}{2-\kappa} - \frac{6}{3-\kappa}$. This may be expressed as $(\kappa - 2)(\kappa - 3) + 2\kappa(\kappa - 2)(\kappa - 3) = 6(3 - \kappa) - 6(2 - \kappa)$, which in turn may be expressed as $\kappa^2 - 5\kappa + 6 + 2\kappa^3 - 10\kappa^2 + 12\kappa = 6$. That is, $0 = 2\kappa^3 - 9\kappa^2 + 7\kappa = \kappa(2\kappa - 7)(\kappa - 1)$, implying that $\kappa = 1$. Then, $M_X'(\kappa) = M_X'(1) = 6 - 6/4 = 9/2$, and from (8.22)

$$C = \frac{\left(\frac{5}{6}\right)\left(\frac{7}{5}\right)}{\frac{9}{2} - \left(\frac{5}{6}\right)\left(1 + \frac{7}{5}\right)} = \frac{\frac{7}{6}}{\frac{5}{2}} = \frac{7}{15},$$

implying that $\psi(u) \sim \frac{7}{15} e^{-u}$, $u \to \infty$.

(b) It follows from (a) that $f(x) = \left(\frac{3}{3-2}\right)(2e^{-2x}) + \left(1 - \frac{3}{3-2}\right)(3e^{-3x})$, which is of the form discussed in the paragraph preceding Example 8.20 implying that $\psi_T(u) = \psi(u)$ and so we will compute $\psi_T(u)$, i.e. $\psi_T(u) = \left(\frac{1}{1+\frac{7}{5}} - \frac{7}{15}\right)e^{-u/\alpha} + \frac{7}{15}e^{-u} = -\frac{1}{20}e^{-u/\alpha} + \frac{7}{15}e^{-u}$. To compute α, first note that $M_X''(t) = 12(2-t)^{-3} - 12(3-t)^{-3}$, and thus $E(X^2) = M_X''(0) = \frac{3}{2} - \frac{4}{9} = \frac{19}{18}$. The compound geometric mean is therefore

$$E(L) = \frac{\frac{19}{18}}{2\left(\frac{5}{6}\right)\left(\frac{7}{5}\right)} = \frac{19}{42}.$$

Then (8.24) yields

$$\alpha = \frac{\frac{19}{42} - \frac{7}{15}}{\frac{1}{20}} = \frac{2}{7},$$

which results in $\psi_T(u) = \psi(u) = \frac{7}{15}e^{-u} - \frac{1}{20}e^{-7u/2}$, $u \geq 0$.

9

Chapter 9 solutions

9.1 SECTION 9.2

9.1 When three observations are taken without replacement there are only four possible results. They are 1,3,5; 1,3,9; 1,5,9; and 3,5,9. The four sample means are 9/3, 13/3, 15/3, and 17/3. The expected value (each has probability 1/4) is 54/12 or 4.5, which equals the population mean. The four sample medians are 3, 3, 5, and 5. The expected value is 4 and so the median is biased.

9.2

$$
\begin{aligned}
E(\bar{X}) &= E\left[\frac{1}{n}(X_1 + \cdots + X_n)\right] = \frac{1}{n}\left[E(X_1) + \cdots + E(X_n)\right] \\
&= \frac{1}{n}(\mu + \cdots + \mu) = \mu.
\end{aligned}
$$

9.3 For a sample of size 3 from a continuous distribution, the density function of the median is $6f(x)F(x)[1 - F(x)]$. For this exercise, $F(x) = (x - \theta + 2)/4$,

Loss Models: From Data to Decisions, Solutions Manual, Second Edition.
By Stuart A. Klugman, Harry H. Panjer, and Gordon E. Willmot
ISBN 0-471-22762-5   Copyright © 2004 John Wiley & Sons, Inc.

$\theta - 2 < x < \theta + 2$. The density function for the median is

$$f_{med}(x) = 6(0.25)\frac{x - \theta + 2}{4} \frac{2 - x + \theta}{4}$$

and the expected value is

$$6 \int_{\theta-2}^{\theta+2} \frac{x(x - \theta + 2)(2 - x + \theta)}{64} dx = \frac{6}{64} \int_0^4 (y + \theta - 2)y(4 - y)dy$$

$$= \frac{6}{64} \int_0^4 -y^3 + (6 - \theta)y^2 + 4(\theta - 2)ydy$$

$$= \frac{6}{64} \left[-\frac{y^4}{4} + \frac{(6 - \theta)y^3}{3} + \frac{4(\theta - 2)y^2}{2} \right]\bigg|_0^4$$

$$= \frac{6}{64} \left[-64 + \frac{(6 - \theta)64}{3} + 32(\theta - 2) \right]$$

$$= \theta$$

where the first line used the substitution $y = x - \theta + 2$.

9.4 Because the mean of a Pareto distribution does not always exist, it is not reasonable to discuss unbiasedness or consistency. Had the problem been restricted to Pareto distributions with $\alpha > 1$, then consistency can be established. It turns out that for the sample mean to be consistent, only the first moment needs to exist (the variance having a limit of zero is a sufficient, but not a necessary, condition for consistency).

9.5 The mean is unbiased, so its MSE is its variance. It is

$$MSE_{mean}(\theta) = \text{Var}(X)/3 = \frac{4^2}{12(3)} = \frac{4}{9}.$$

The median is also unbiased. The variance is

$$6 \int_{\theta-2}^{\theta+2} \frac{(x - \theta)^2(x - \theta + 2)(2 - x + \theta)}{64} dx = \frac{6}{64} \int_0^4 (y - 2)^2 y(4 - y)dy$$

$$= \frac{6}{64} \int_0^4 -y^4 + 8y^3 - 20y^2 + 16ydy$$

$$= \frac{6}{64} \left[-\frac{4^5}{5} + \frac{8(4)^4}{4} - \frac{20(4)^3}{3} + \frac{16(4)^2}{2} \right]$$

$$= 4/5$$

and so the sample mean has the smaller mean squared error.

9.6 We have

$$
\begin{aligned}
\mathrm{Var}(\hat{\theta}_C) &= \mathrm{Var}[w\hat{\theta}_A + (1-w)\hat{\theta}_B] \\
&= w^2(160,000) + (1-w)^2(40,000) \\
&= 200,000w^2 - 80,000w + 40,000.
\end{aligned}
$$

The derivative is $400,000w - 80,000$ and setting it equal to zero provides the solution, $w = 0.2$.

9.7 $\mathrm{MSE} = \mathrm{Var} + \mathrm{bias}^2$. $1 = \mathrm{Var} + (0.2)^2$, $\mathrm{Var} = 0.96$.

9.8 To be unbiased,

$$
m = \mathrm{E}(Z) = \alpha(0.8m) + \beta m = (0.8\alpha + \beta)m
$$

and so $1 = 0.8\alpha + \beta$ or $\beta = 1 - 0.8\alpha$. Then

$$
\mathrm{Var}(Z) = \alpha^2 m^2 + \beta^2 1.5m^2 = [\alpha^2 + (1 - 0.8\alpha)^2 1.5]m^2
$$

which is minimized when $\alpha^2 + 1.5 - 2.4\alpha + 0.96\alpha^2$ is minimized. This occurs when $3.92\alpha - 2.4 = 0$ or $\alpha = 0.6122$. Then $\beta = 1 - 0.8(0.6122) = 0.5102$.

9.9 One way to solve this problem is to list the 20 possible samples of size three and assign probability 1/20 to each. The population mean is $(1 + 1 + 2 + 3 + 5 + 10)/6 = 11/3$.
(a) The twenty sample means have an average of 11/3 and so the bias is zero. The variance of the sample means (dividing by 20 because this is the population of sample means) is 1.9778 and this is also the MSE.
(b) The twenty sample medians have an average of 2.7 and so the bias is $2.7 - 11/3 = -0.9667$. The variance is 1.81 and the MSE is 2.7444.
(c) The twenty sample midranges have an average of 4.15 and so the bias is $4.15 - 11/3 = 0.4833$. The variance is 2.65 and the MSE is 2.8861.
(d) $E(aX_{(1)} + bX_{(2)} + cX_{(3)}) = 1.25a + 2.7b + 7.05c$ where the expected values of the order statistics can be found by averaging the twenty values from the enumerated population. To be unbiased the expected value must be 11/3 and so the restriction is $1.25a + 2.7b + 7.05c = 11/3$. With this restriction, the MSE is minimized at $a = 1.445337$, $b = 0.043733$, and $c = 0.247080$ with a MSE of 1.620325. With no restrictions, the minimum is at $a = 1.289870$, $b = 0.039029$, and $c = 0.220507$ with a MSE of 1.446047 (and a bias of -0.3944).

9.10 $\mathrm{bias}(\hat{\theta}_1) = 165/75 - 2 = 0.2$, $\mathrm{Var}(\hat{\theta}_1) = 375/75 - (165/75)^2 = 0.16$, $\mathrm{MSE}(\hat{\theta}_1) = 0.16 + (0.2)^2 = 0.2$. $\mathrm{bias}(\hat{\theta}_2) = 147/75 - 2 = -0.04$, $\mathrm{Var}(\hat{\theta}_2) = 312/75 - (147/75)^2 = 0.3184$, $\mathrm{MSE}(\hat{\theta}_2) = 0.3184 + (-0.04)^2 = 0.32$. The relative efficiency is $0.2/0.32 = 0.625$.

9.2   SECTION 9.3

9.11 (a) From the information given in the problem, we can begin with

$$0.95 = \Pr(a \le \bar{X}/\theta \le b)$$

where $\bar{X}/\theta$ is known to have the gamma distribution with $\alpha = 50$ and $\theta = 0.02$. This does not uniquely specify the endpoints. However, if 2.5% probability is allocated to each side, then $a = 0.7422$ and $b = 1.2956$. Inserting these values in the inequality, taking reciprocals, and multiplying through by $\bar{X}$ gives

$$0.95 = \Pr(0.7718\bar{X} \le \theta \le 1.3473\bar{X}).$$

Inserting the sample mean gives an interval of 212.25 to 370.51.

(b) The sample mean has $\mathrm{E}(\bar{X}) = \theta$ and $\mathrm{Var}(\bar{X}) = \theta^2/50$. Then, using $275^2/50$ as the approximate variance

$$
\begin{aligned}
0.95 &\doteq \Pr\left(-1.96 \le \frac{\bar{X}-\theta}{275/\sqrt{50}} \le 1.96\right) \\
&= \Pr(-76.23 \le \bar{X}-\theta \le 76.23).
\end{aligned}
$$

Inserting the sample mean of 275 gives the interval 275 ± 76.23 or 198.77 to 351.23.

(c) Leaving the θ in the variance alone,

$$
\begin{aligned}
0.95 &\doteq \Pr\left(-1.96 \le \frac{\bar{X}-\theta}{\theta/\sqrt{50}} \le 1.96\right) \\
&= \Pr(-0.2772\theta \le \bar{X}-\theta \le 0.2772\theta) \\
&= \Pr(\bar{X}/1.2772 \le \theta \le \bar{X}/0.7228)
\end{aligned}
$$

for an interval of 215.31 to 380.46.

9.3   SECTION 9.4

9.12 For the exact test, null should be rejected if $\bar{X} \le c$. The value of c comes from

$$
\begin{aligned}
0.05 &= \Pr(\bar{X} \le c | \theta = 325) \\
&= \Pr(\bar{X}/325 \le c/325)
\end{aligned}
$$

where $\bar{X}/325$ has the gamma distribution with parameters 50 and 0.02. From that distribution, $c/325 = 0.7793$ for $c = 253.27$. Because the sample mean of 275 is not below this value, the null hypothesis is not rejected. The p-value is obtained from

$$\Pr(\bar{X} \le 275 | \theta = 325) = \Pr(\bar{X}/325 \le 275/325).$$

From the gamma distribution with parameters 50 and 0.02, this probability is 0.1353.

For the normal approximation,

$$
\begin{aligned}
0.05 &= \Pr(\bar{X} \le c | \theta = 325) \\
&= \Pr\left(Z \le \frac{c - 325}{325/\sqrt{50}} \right).
\end{aligned}
$$

Solving $(c - 325)/(325/\sqrt{50}) = -1.645$ produces $c = 249.39$. Again the null hypothesis is not rejected. For the p-value,

$$
\Pr\left(Z \le \frac{275 - 325}{325/\sqrt{50}} = -1.0879 \right) = 0.1383.
$$

10

Chapter 10 solutions

10.1 SECTION 10.2

10.1 When all information is available, the calculations are in Table 10.1. As in Example 10.11, values apply from the current y-value to the next one.

10.2 (a) $\hat{\mu} = \sum x_i/35 = 204{,}900$. $\hat{\mu}'_2 = \sum x_i^2/35 = 1.4134 \times 10^{11}$. $\hat{\sigma} = 325{,}807$. $\hat{\mu}'_3 = 1.70087 \times 10^{17}$, $\hat{\mu}_3 = 9.62339 \times 10^{16}$, $\hat{c} = 325{,}807/204{,}900 = 1.590078$, $\hat{\gamma}_1 = 2.78257$.

(b) $\hat{\pi}_{0.5} = y_{18} = 59{,}917$. $\hat{\pi}_{0.75} = y_{27} = 227{,}338$. $\hat{\pi}_{0.9} = 0.6y_{32} + 0.4y_{33} = 627{,}622$. $\hat{\pi}_{0.95} = 0.8y_{34} + 0.2y_{35} = 1{,}018{,}705$.

(c) B has a binomial distribution with $n = 35$ and $p = 0.75$. From that distribution, $\Pr(22 \leq B < 31) = 0.9227$ while $\Pr(23 \leq B < 31) = 0.8834$. The CI is from Y_{22} to Y_{31} which is $(103{,}217{,}000, 513{,}586{,}000)$.

(d) $E_n(500{,}000) = [\sum_{j=1}^{30} y_j + 5(500{,}000)]/35 = 153{,}139$.

$E_n^{(2)}(500{,}000) = [\sum_{j=1}^{30} y_j^2 + 5(500{,}000)^2]/35 = 53{,}732{,}687{,}032$.

10.3 $\hat{\mu}'_1 = [2(2{,}000) + 6(4{,}000) + 12(6{,}000) + 10(8{,}000)]/30 = 6{,}000$,
$\hat{\mu}_2 = [2(-4{,}000)^2 + 6(-2{,}000)^2 + 12(0)^2 + 10(2{,}000)^2]/30 = 3{,}200{,}000$,
$\hat{\mu}_3 = [2(-4{,}000)^3 + 6(-2{,}000)^3 + 12(0)^3 + 10(2{,}000)^3]/30 = -3{,}200{,}000{,}000$.

Loss Models: From Data to Decisions, Solutions Manual, Second Edition.
By Stuart A. Klugman, Harry H. Panjer, and Gordon E. Willmot
ISBN 0-471-22762-5   Copyright © 2004 John Wiley & Sons, Inc.

Table 10.1 Calculations for Exercise 10.1

j	y_j	s_j	r_j	$F_{30}(x)$	$\hat{H}(x)$	$\hat{F}(x)^*$
1	0.1	1	30	$1 - 29/30 = 0.0333$	$1/30 = 0.0333$	0.0328
2	0.5	1	29	$1 - 28/30 = 0.0667$	$0.0333 + 1/29 = 0.0678$	0.0656
3	0.8	1	28	$1 - 27/30 = 0.1000$	$0.0678 + 1/28 = 0.1035$	0.0983
4	1.8	2	27	$1 - 25/30 = 0.1667$	$0.1035 + 2/27 = 0.1776$	0.1627
5	2.1	1	25	$1 - 24/30 = 0.2000$	$0.1776 + 1/25 = 0.2176$	0.1956
6	2.5	1	24	$1 - 23/30 = 0.2333$	$0.2176 + 1/24 = 0.2593$	0.2284
7	2.8	1	23	$1 - 22/30 = 0.2667$	$0.2593 + 1/23 = 0.3027$	0.2612
8	3.9	2	22	$1 - 20/30 = 0.3333$	$0.3027 + 2/22 = 0.3937$	0.3254
9	4.0	1	20	$1 - 19/30 = 0.3667$	$0.3937 + 1/20 = 0.4437$	0.3583
10	4.1	1	19	$1 - 18/30 = 0.4000$	$0.4437 + 1/19 = 0.4963$	0.3912
11	4.6	2	18	$1 - 16/30 = 0.4667$	$0.4963 + 2/18 = 0.6074$	0.4552
12	4.8	2	16	$1 - 14/30 = 0.5333$	$0.6074 + 2/16 = 0.7324$	0.5192
13	5.0	14	14	$1 - 0/30 = 1.0000$	$0.7324 + 14/14 = 1.7324$	0.8231

$^*\hat{F}(x) = 1 - e^{-\hat{H}(x)}$

$\hat{\gamma}_1 = -3{,}200{,}000{,}000/(3{,}200{,}000)^{1.5} = -0.55902.$

10.2 SECTION 10.3

10.4 There are 392 observations and the calculations are in Table 10.2. For each interval, the ogive value is for the right-hand endpoint of the interval while the histogram value is for the entire interval. Graphs of the ogive and histogram appear in Figures 10.1 and 10.2.

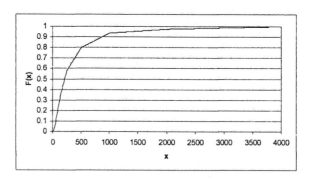

Fig. 10.1 Ogive for Exercise 10.4.

Table 10.2 Calculations for Exercise 10.4

Payment range	Number of payments	Ogive value	Histogram value
0–25	6	$\frac{6}{392} = 0.0153$	$\frac{6}{392(25)} = 0.000612$
25–50	24	$\frac{30}{392} = 0.0765$	$\frac{24}{392(25)} = 0.002449$
50–75	30	$\frac{60}{392} = 0.1531$	$\frac{30}{392(25)} = 0.003061$
75–100	31	$\frac{91}{392} = 0.2321$	$\frac{31}{392(25)} = 0.003163$
100–150	57	$\frac{148}{392} = 0.3776$	$\frac{57}{392(50)} = 0.002908$
150–250	80	$\frac{228}{392} = 0.5816$	$\frac{80}{392(100)} = 0.002041$
250–500	85	$\frac{313}{392} = 0.7985$	$\frac{85}{392(250)} = 0.000867$
500–1000	54	$\frac{367}{392} = 0.9362$	$\frac{54}{392(500)} = 0.000276$
1000–2000	15	$\frac{382}{392} = 0.9745$	$\frac{15}{392(1000)} = 0.000038$
2000–4000	10	$\frac{392}{392} = 1.0000$	$\frac{10}{392(2000)} = 0.000013$

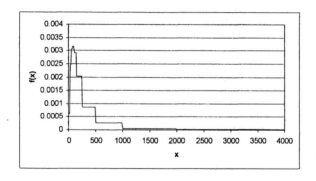

Fig. 10.2 Histogram for Exercise 10.4.

10.5 (a) We need the $0.75(21) = 15.75th$ smallest observation. It is $0.25(13) + 0.75(14) = 13.75$.

(b) The ogive connects the points $(0.5, 0)$, $(2.5, 0.35)$, $(8.5, 0.65)$, $(15.5, 0.85)$,, and $(29.5, 1)$.

(c) The histogram has height $0.35/2 = 0.175$ on the interval $(0.5, 2.5)$, height $0.3/6 = 0.05$ on the interval $(2.5, 8.5)$, height $0.2/7 = 0.028571$ on the interval $(8.5, 15.1)$, and height $0.15/14 = 0.010714$ on the interval $(15.5, 29.5)$.

10.6 The plot appears in Figure 10.3. The points are the complements of the survival probabilities at the indicated times.

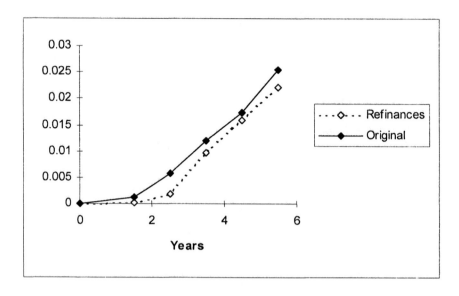

Fig. 10.3   Ogive for mortgage lifetime for Exercise 10.6.

Because one curve lies completely above the other it appears possible that original issues have a shorter lifetime.

10.7 The heights of the histogram bars are, respectively, $0.5/2 = 0.25$, $0.2/8 = 0.025$, $0.2/90 = 0.00222$, $0.1/900 = 0.000111$. The histogram appears in Figure 10.4.

10.8 The empirical model places probability $1/n$ at each data point. Then

$$
\begin{aligned}
\mathrm{E}(X \wedge 2) &= \sum_{x_j < 2} x_j(1/40) + \sum_{x_j \geq 2} 2(1/40) \\
&= (20 + 15)(1/40) + (14)(2)(1/40) \\
&= 1.575.
\end{aligned}
$$

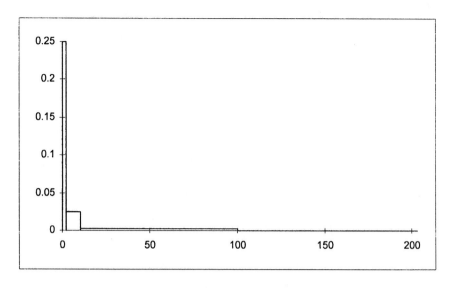

Fig. 10.4   Histogram for Exercise 10.7.

10.9 We have

$$
\begin{aligned}
\mathrm{E}(X \wedge 7000) &= \frac{1}{2000}\left(\sum_{x_j \leq 7000} x_j + \sum_{x_j > 7000} 7000\right) \\
&= \frac{1}{2000}\left(\sum_{x_j \leq 6000} x_j + \sum_{x_j > 6000} 6000\right. \\
&\quad \left. + \sum_{6000 < x_j \leq 7000} (x_j - 6000) + \sum_{x_j > 7000} 1000\right) \\
&= \mathrm{E}(X \wedge 6000) + [200{,}000 - 30(6000) + 270(1000)]/2000 \\
&= 1955.
\end{aligned}
$$

11

Chapter 11 solutions

11.1 SECTION 11.1

11.1 The calculations are in Tables 11.1 and 11.2.

Loss Models: From Data to Decisions, Solutions Manual, Second Edition.
By Stuart A. Klugman, Harry H. Panjer, and Gordon E. Willmot
ISBN 0-471-22762-5   Copyright © 2004 John Wiley & Sons, Inc.

Table 11.1   Calculations for Exercise 11.1

i	d_i	u_i	x_i	i	d_i	u_i	x_i
1	0	-	0.1	16	0	4.8	-
2	0	-	0.5	17	0	-	4.8
3	0	-	0.8	18	0	-	4.8
4	0	0.8	-	19–30	0	-	5.0
5	0	-	1.8	31	0.3	-	5.0
6	0	-	1.8	32	0.7	-	5.0
7	0	-	2.1	33	1.0	4.1	-
8	0	-	2.5	34	1.8	3.1	-
9	0	-	2.8	35	2.1	-	3.9
10	0	2.9	-	36	2.9	-	5.0
11	0	2.9	-	37	2.9	-	4.8
12	0	-	3.9	38	3.2	4.0	-
13	0	4.0	-	39	3.4	-	5.0
14	0	-	4.0	40	3.9	-	5.0
15	0	-	4.1				

Table 11.2   Further calculations for Exercise 11.1

j	y_j	s_j	r_j
1	0.1	1	$30 - 0 - 0 = 30$ or $0 + 30 - 0 - 0 = 30$
2	0.5	1	$31 - 1 - 0 = 30$ or $30 + 1 - 1 - 0 = 30$
3	0.8	1	$32 - 2 - 0 = 30$ or $30 + 1 - 1 - 0 = 30$
4	1.8	2	$33 - 3 - 1 = 29$ or $30 + 1 - 1 - 1 = 29$
5	2.1	1	$34 - 5 - 1 = 28$ or $29 + 1 - 2 - 0 = 28$
6	2.5	1	$35 - 6 - 1 = 28$ or $28 + 1 - 1 - 0 = 28$
7	2.8	1	$35 - 7 - 1 = 27$ or $28 + 0 - 1 - 0 = 27$
8	3.9	2	$39 - 8 - 4 = 27$ or $27 + 4 - 1 - 3 = 27$
9	4.0	1	$40 - 10 - 4 = 26$ or $27 + 1 - 2 - 0 = 26$
10	4.1	1	$40 - 11 - 6 = 23$ or $26 + 0 - 1 - 2 = 23$
11	4.8	3	$40 - 12 - 7 = 21$ or $23 + 0 - 1 - 1 = 21$
12	5.0	17	$40 - 15 - 8 = 17$ or $21 + 0 - 3 - 1 = 17$

11.2

$$S_{40}(t) = \begin{cases} 1, & 0 \le t < 0.1 \\ \frac{30-1}{30} = 0.9667, & 0.1 \le t < 0.5 \\ 0.9667\frac{30-1}{30} = 0.9344, & 0.5 \le t < 0.8 \\ 0.9344\frac{30-1}{30} = 0.9033, & 0.8 \le t < 1.8 \\ 0.9033\frac{29-2}{29} = 0.8410, & 1.8 \le t < 2.1 \\ 0.8410\frac{28-1}{28} = 0.8110, & 2.1 \le t < 2.5 \\ 0.8110\frac{28-1}{28} = 0.7820, & 2.5 \le t < 2.8 \\ 0.7820\frac{27-1}{27} = 0.7530, & 2.8 \le t < 3.9 \\ 0.7530\frac{27-2}{27} = 0.6973, & 3.9 \le t < 4.0 \\ 0.6973\frac{26-1}{26} = 0.6704, & 4.0 \le t < 4.1 \\ 0.6704\frac{23-1}{23} = 0.6413, & 4.1 \le t < 4.8 \\ 0.6413\frac{21-3}{21} = 0.5497, & 4.8 \le t < 5.0 \\ 0.5497\frac{17-17}{17} = 0, & t \ge 5.0. \end{cases}$$

11.3

$$
\hat{H}(t) = \begin{cases}
0, & 0 \le t < 0.1 \\
\frac{1}{30} = 0.0333, & 0.1 \le t < 0.5 \\
0.0333 + \frac{1}{30} = 0.0667, & 0.5 \le t < 0.8 \\
0.0667 + \frac{1}{30} = 0.1000, & 0.8 \le t < 1.8 \\
0.1000 + \frac{2}{29} = 0.1690, & 1.8 \le t < 2.1 \\
0.1690 + \frac{1}{28} = 0.2047, & 2.1 \le t < 2.5 \\
0.2047 + \frac{1}{28} = 0.2404, & 2.5 \le t < 2.8 \\
0.2404 + \frac{1}{27} = 0.2774, & 2.8 \le t < 3.9 \\
0.2774 + \frac{2}{27} = 0.3515, & 3.9 \le t < 4.0 \\
0.3515 + \frac{1}{26} = 0.3900, & 4.0 \le t < 4.1 \\
0.3900 + \frac{1}{23} = 0.4334, & 4.1 \le t < 4.8 \\
0.4334 + \frac{3}{21} = 0.5763, & 4.8 \le t < 5.0 \\
0.5763 + \frac{17}{17} = 1.5763, & t \ge 5.0.
\end{cases}
$$

$$
\hat{S}(t) = \begin{cases}
e^{-0} = 1, & 0 \le t < 0.1 \\
e^{-0.0333} = 0.9672, & 0.1 \le t < 0.5 \\
e^{-0.0667} = 0.9355, & 0.5 \le t < 0.8 \\
e^{-0.1000} = 0.9048, & 0.8 \le t < 1.8 \\
e^{-0.1690} = 0.8445, & 1.8 \le t < 2.1 \\
e^{-0.2047} = 0.8149, & 2.1 \le t < 2.5 \\
e^{-0.2404} = 0.7863, & 2.5 \le t < 2.8 \\
e^{-0.2774} = 0.7578, & 2.8 \le t < 3.9 \\
e^{-0.3515} = 0.7036, & 3.9 \le t < 4.0 \\
e^{-0.3900} = 0.6771, & 4.0 \le t < 4.1 \\
e^{-0.4334} = 0.6483, & 4.1 \le t < 4.8 \\
e^{-0.5763} = 0.5620, & 4.8 \le t < 5.0 \\
e^{-1.5763} = 0.2076, & t \ge 5.0.
\end{cases}
$$

11.4 Using the raw data, the results are in Table 11.3. When the deductible and limit are imposed, the results are as in Table 11.4. Because 1,000 is a censoring point and not an observed loss value, there is no change in the survival function at 1,000.

Table 11.3   Calculations for Exercise 11.4

value(x)	r	s	$S_{KM}(x)$	$H_{NA}(x)$	$S_{NA}(x)$
27	20	1	0.95	0.0500	0.9512
82	19	1	0.90	0.1026	0.9025
115	18	1	0.85	0.1582	0.8537
126	17	1	0.80	0.2170	0.8049
155	16	1	0.75	0.2795	0.7562
161	15	1	0.70	0.3462	0.7074
243	14	1	0.65	0.4176	0.6586
294	13	1	0.60	0.4945	0.6099
340	12	1	0.55	0.5779	0.5611
384	11	1	0.50	0.6688	0.5123
457	10	1	0.45	0.7688	0.4636
680	9	1	0.40	0.8799	0.4148
855	8	1	0.35	1.0049	0.3661
877	7	1	0.30	1.1477	0.3174
974	6	1	0.25	1.3144	0.2686
1,193	5	1	0.20	1.5144	0.2199
1,340	4	1	0.15	1.7644	0.1713
1,884	3	1	0.10	2.0977	0.1227
2,558	2	1	0.05	2.5977	0.0744
15,743	1	1	0.00	3.5977	0.0274

11.5 Suppose the lapse was at time 1. The estimate of $S(4)$ is $(3/4)(2/3)(1/2)$ $= 0.25$. If it is at time 2, the estimate is $(4/5)(2/3)(1/2)=0.27$. If it is at time 3, the estimate is $(4/5)(3/4)(1/2) = 0.3$. If it is at time 4, the estimate is $(4/5)(3/4)(2/3) = 0.4$. If it is at time 5, the estimate is $(4/5)(3/4)(2/3)(1/2)$ $= 0.20$. Therefore, the answer is time 5.

11.6 $\hat{H}(12) = \frac{2}{15} + \frac{1}{12} + \frac{1}{10} + \frac{2}{6} = 0.65$. The estimate of the survival function is $\hat{S}(12) = e^{-0.65} = 0.522$.

11.7 The information may be organized as in Table 11.5

11.8 $\hat{H}(t_{10}) - \hat{H}(t_9) = \frac{1}{n-9} = 0.077$, $n = 22$. $\hat{H}(t_3) = \frac{1}{22} + \frac{1}{21} + \frac{1}{20} = 0.14307$, $\hat{S}(t_3) = e^{-0.14307} = 0.8667$.

11.9 $0.60 = 0.72\frac{r_4-2}{r_4}$, $r_4 = 12$. $0.50 = 0.60\frac{r_5-1}{r_5}$, $r_5 = 6$. With two deaths at the fourth death time and the risk set decreasing by 6, there must have been four censored observations.

Table 11.4 Further calculations for Exercise 11.4

value(x)	r	s	$S_{KM}(x)$	$H_{NA}(x)$	$S_{NA}(x)$
115	18	1	0.9444	0.0556	0.9459
126	17	1	0.8889	0.1144	0.8919
155	16	1	0.8333	0.1769	0.8379
161	15	1	0.7778	0.2435	0.7839
243	14	1	0.7222	0.3150	0.7298
294	13	1	0.6667	0.3919	0.6758
340	12	1	0.6111	0.4752	0.6218
384	11	1	0.5556	0.5661	0.5677
457	10	1	0.5000	0.6661	0.5137
680	9	1	0.4444	0.7773	0.4596
855	8	1	0.3889	0.9023	0.4056
877	7	1	0.3333	1.0451	0.3517
974	6	1	0.2778	1.2118	0.2977

Table 11.5 Calculations for Exercise 11.7

age(t)	#ds	#xs	#us	r	$\hat{S}(t)$
0	300				
1		6		300	$\frac{294}{300} = 0.98$
2	20				
3		10		314	$0.98\frac{304}{314} = 0.94879$
4	30	10		304	$0.94879\frac{294}{304} = 0.91758$
5		a		324	$0.91758\frac{324-a}{324} = 0.892 \Longrightarrow a = 9$
7			45		
9		b		$279-a = 270$	$0.892\frac{270-b}{270}$
10			35		
12		6		$244-a-b = 235-b$	$0.892\frac{270-b}{270}\frac{229-b}{235-b} = 0.856 \Longrightarrow b = 4$
13			15		

11.2   SECTION 11.2

11.10 To proceed, we need the estimated survival function at whole number durations. From Exercise 10.1, we have $S_{30}(1) = 27/30$, $S_{30}(2) = 25/30$, $S_{30}(3) = 22/30$, $S_{30}(4) = 19/30$, and $S_{30}(5) = 14/30$. Then the mortality estimates are $\hat{q}_0 = 3/30$, $\hat{q}_1 = 2/27$, $\hat{q}_2 = 3/25$, $\hat{q}_3 = 3/22$, $\hat{q}_4 = 5/19$,

$_5\hat{p}_0 = 14/30$. The six variances are

$$
\begin{aligned}
\mathrm{Var}(\hat{q}_0) &= 3(27)/30^3 = 0.003 \\
\mathrm{Var}(\hat{q}_1) &= 2(25)/27^3 = 0.002540 \\
\mathrm{Var}(\hat{q}_2) &= 3(22)/25^3 = 0.004224 \\
\mathrm{Var}(\hat{q}_3) &= 3(19)/22^3 = 0.005353 \\
\mathrm{Var}(\hat{q}_4) &= 5(14)/19^3 = 0.010206 \\
\mathrm{Var}(_5\hat{p}_0) &= 14(16)/30^3 = 0.008296
\end{aligned}
$$

The first and last variances are unconditional.

11.11 From the data set, there were 1,915 out of 94,935 that had 2 or more accidents. The estimated probability is $1,915/94,935 = 0.02017$ and the estimated variance is

$$0.02017(0.97983)/94,935 = 2.08176 \times 10^{-7}.$$

11.12 From Exercise 11.10, $S_{30}(3) = 22/30$ and the direct estimate of its variance is $22(8)/30^3 = 0.0065185$. Using Greenwood's formula, the estimated variance is

$$
\left(\frac{22}{30}\right)^2 \left(\frac{1}{30(29)} + \frac{1}{29(28)} + \frac{1}{28(27)} + \frac{2}{27(25)} \right.
$$
$$
\left. + \frac{1}{25(24)} + \frac{1}{24(23)} + \frac{1}{23(22)} \right) = 22(8)/30^3.
$$

For $_2\hat{q}_3$, the point estimate is $8/22$ and the direct estimate of the variance is $8(14)/22^3 = 0.010518$. Greenwood's estimate is

$$
\left(\frac{14}{22}\right)^2 \left(\frac{2}{22(20)} + \frac{1}{20(19)} + \frac{1}{19(18)} + \frac{2}{18(16)} + \frac{2}{16(14)} \right) = 8(14)/22^3.
$$

11.13 From Exercise 11.2, $S_{40}(3) = 0.7530$ and Greenwood's formula provides a variance of

$$
0.7530^2 \left(\frac{1}{30(29)} + \frac{1}{30(29)} + \frac{1}{30(29)} + \frac{2}{29(27)} \right.
$$
$$
\left. + \frac{1}{28(27)} + \frac{1}{28(27)} + \frac{1}{27(26)} \right) = 0.00571.
$$

Also, $_2\hat{q}_3 = (0.7530 - 0.5497)/0.7530 = 0.26999$ and the variance is estimated as

$$0.73001^2 \left(\frac{2}{27(25)} + \frac{1}{26(25)} + \frac{1}{23(22)} + \frac{3}{21(18)} \right) = 0.00768.$$

11.14 Using the log-transformed method,

$$U = \exp \left(\frac{1.96\sqrt{0.00571}}{0.753 \ln 0.753} \right) = 0.49991.$$

The lower limit is $0.753^{1/0.49991} = 0.56695$ and the upper limit is $0.753^{0.49991} = 0.86778$.

11.15 From Exercise 11.3, $\hat{H}(3) = 0.2774$. The variance is estimated as

$$\widehat{\mathrm{Var}}[\hat{H}(3)] = \frac{1}{30^2} + \frac{1}{30^2} + \frac{1}{30^2} + \frac{2}{29^2} + \frac{1}{28^2} + \frac{1}{28^2} + \frac{1}{27^2} = 0.0096342.$$

The linear confidence interval is

$$0.2774 \pm 1.96\sqrt{0.0096342} \text{ or } 0.0850 \text{ to } 0.4698.$$

The log-transformed interval requires

$$U = \exp \left[\pm \frac{1.96\sqrt{0.0096342}}{0.2774} \right] = 2.00074 \text{ or } 0.49981.$$

The lower limit is $0.2774(0.49981) = 0.13865$
and the upper limit is $0.2774(2.00074) = 0.55501$.

11.16 Without any distributional assumptions, the variance is estimated as $(1/5)(4/5)/5 = 0.032$. From the distributional assumption, the true value of $_3q_7$ is $[(8/15) - (5/15)]/(8/15) = 3/8$ and the variance is $(3/8)(5/8)/5 = 0.046875$. The difference is -0.014875.

11.17 First, obtain the estimated survival probability as

$$\hat{S}(4) = \frac{12}{15} \frac{56}{80} \frac{20}{25} \frac{54}{60} = 0.4032.$$

Greenwood's formula gives

$$(0.4032)^2 \left(\frac{3}{15(12)} + \frac{24}{80(56)} + \frac{5}{25(20)} + \frac{6}{60(54)} \right) = 0.00551.$$

11.18 The Nelson-Åalen estimates are the centers of the confidence intervals, which are 0.15 and 0.27121. Therefore, $s_{i+1}/r_{i+1} = 0.12121$. From the first confidence interval, the estimated variance is $(0.07875/1.96)^2 = 0.0016143$ while for the second interval it is $(0.11514/1.96)^2 = 0.0034510$ and therefore $s_{i+1}/r_{i+1}^2 = 0.0018367$. Dividing the first result by the second gives $r_{i+1} = 66$. The first equation then yields $s_{i+1} = 8$.

11.19 Greenwood's estimate is

$$V = S^2 \left(\frac{2}{50(48)} + \frac{4}{45(41)} + \frac{8}{(41-c)(33-c)} \right).$$

Then,

$$0.011467 = \frac{V}{S^2} = 0.003001 + \frac{8}{(41-c)(33-c)}$$

$$(41-c)(33-c) = 8/(0.008466) = 945.$$

Solving the quadratic equation yields $c = 6$.

11.20 For the Nelson-Åalen estimate,

$$1.5641 = \hat{H}(35) = \frac{2}{15} + \frac{3}{13} + \frac{2}{10} + \frac{d}{8} + \frac{2}{8-d}$$

$$(1.5641 - 0.5641)8(8-d) = d(8-d) + 16$$

$$0 = d^2 - 16d + 48$$

$$d = 4.$$

The variance is

$$\frac{2}{15^2} + \frac{3}{13^2} + \frac{2}{10^2} + \frac{4}{8^2} + \frac{2}{4^2} = 0.23414.$$

11.21 The standard deviation is

$$\left(\frac{15}{100^2} + \frac{20}{65^2} + \frac{13}{40^2} \right)^{1/2} = 0.11983.$$

11.3   SECTION 11.3

11.22 In order for the mean to be equal to y, we must have $\theta/(\alpha - 1) = y$. Letting α be arbitrary (and greater than 1), use a Pareto distribution with

Table 11.6 Data for Exercise 11.23

y_j	$p(y_j)$
0.1	0.0333
0.5	0.0323
0.8	0.0311
1.8	0.0623
2.1	0.0300
2.5	0.0290
2.8	0.0290
3.9	0.0557
4.0	0.0269
4.1	0.0291
4.8	0.0916

$\theta = y(\alpha - 1)$. This makes the kernel function

$$k_y(x) = \frac{\alpha[(\alpha - 1)y]^\alpha}{[(\alpha - 1)y + x]^{\alpha+1}}.$$

11.23 The data points and probabilities can be taken from Exercise 11.2. They are given in Table 11.6

The probability at 5.0 is discrete and so should not be spread out by the kernel density estimator. Because of the value at 0.1, the largest available bandwidth is 0.1. Using this bandwidth and the triangular kernel produces the graph in Figure 11.1.

This is clearly not satisfactory. The gamma kernel is not available because there would be positive probability at values greater than 5. Your author tried to solve this by using the beta distribution. With θ known to be 5, the mean (to be set equal to y) is $5a/(a + b)$. In order to have some smoothing control and to determine parameter values, the sum $a + b$ was fixed. In the following graph, a value of 50 was used for the sum. The kernel is

$$k_y(x) = \frac{\Gamma(50)}{\Gamma(10y)\Gamma(50 - 10y)} \left(\frac{x}{5}\right)^{10y} \left(1 - \frac{x}{5}\right)^{50-10y-1} \frac{1}{x}, \quad 0 < x < 5$$

and the resulting smoothed estimate appears in Figure 11.2.

11.24 With a bandwidth of 60 the height of the kernel is $1/120$. At a value of 100, the following data points contribute probability $1/20 - 47$, 75, and 156. Therefore, the height is $3(1/20)(1/120) = 1/800$.

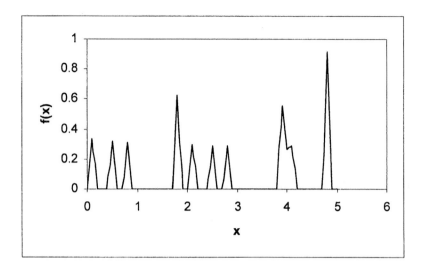

Fig. 11.1   Triangular kernel for Exercise 11.23.

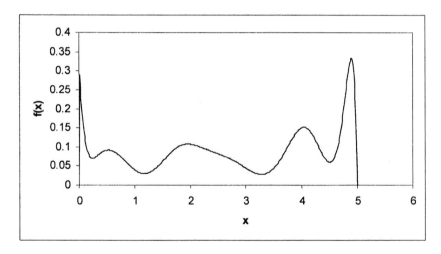

Fig. 11.2   Beta kernel for Exercise 11.23.

11.4   SECTION 11.4

11.25 The calculations for $q_j'^{(w)}$ are given in Table 11.7. The roles of u and x have been reversed. However, the 17 individuals who left at time 5 stay in the u column and are assigned $\beta = 0$. A sample calculation for the multiple

Table 11.7   Single decrement calculations for Exercise 11.25

j	d_j	u_j	x_j	P_j	r_j	$q_j'^{(d)}$
0	32	1	3	0	30.5	0.0984
1	2	0	2	28	29.0	0.0690
2	3	2	3	28	28.5	0.1053
3	3	3	3	26	26.0	0.1154
4	0	19	4	23	22.0	0.1818

Table 11.8   Kaplan-Meier calculations for Exercise 11.26

x	r	s	$\hat{S}(x)$
45.3	8	1	$7/8 = 0.875$
45.6	6	1	$0.875(5/6) = 0.729$
46.2	8	1	$0.729(7/8) = 0.638$
46.4	6	1	$0.638(5/6) = 0.532$
46.7	5	1	$0.532(4/5) = 0.425$

Table 11.9   Grouped calculations for Exercise 11.26

c_j	d_j	u_j	u_j^*	x_j	P_j	r_j	q_j
45	8	2	2	2	0	7	0.286
46	6	2	3	3	2	7	0.429

decrement probabilities is

$$q_2^T = 1 - (0.9286)(0.8947) = 0.1692$$

$$q_2^{(d)} = \frac{\ln 0.9286}{\ln 0.8308} 0.1692 = 0.0676$$

$$q_2^{(w)} = \frac{\ln 0.8947}{\ln 0.8308} 0.1692 = 0.1015.$$

11.26 The Kaplan-Meier calculations appear in Table 11.8. Then $\hat{q}_{45} = 1 - 0.729 = 0.271$ and $\hat{q}_{46} = 1 - 0.425/0.729 = 0.413$.

The calculations after grouping appear in Table 11.9. The u-values are those policies that terminated during the year of age while the u^*-values are those that terminated at the end of the year. The exposure formula used is $r_j = P_j + d_j - 0.5u_j$.

Table 11.10   Calculations for Exercise 11.27

c_j	d_j	u_j	x_j	P_j	r_j	$\hat{S}(c_j)$
250	7	0	1	0	7	1.000
500	8	0	2	6	14	$1.000(6/7) = 0.857$
1,000	7	1	4	12	19	$0.857(12/14) = 0.735$
2,750	0	1	1	14	14	$0.735(15/19) = 0.580$
3,000	0	0	0	12	12	$0.580(13/14) = 0.539$
3,500	0	1	6	12	12	$0.539(12/12) = 0.539$
5,250	0	1	0	5	5	$0.539(6/12) = 0.269$
5,500	0	1	1	4	4	$0.269(5/5) = 0.269$
6,000	0	0	1	2	2	$0.269(3/4) = 0.202$
10,250	0	1	0	1	1	$0.202(1/2) = 0.101$
10,500	0	0	0	0	0	$0.101(1/1) = 0.101$

11.27 The calculations are in Table 11.10. The intervals were selected so that all deductibles and limits are at the boundaries and so no assumption is needed because $\alpha = 1$ and $\beta = 0$ for all payments. When working with the observations, the deductible must be added to the payment in order to produce the loss amount. The requested probability is $\hat{S}(5{,}500)/\hat{S}(500) = 0.269/0.857 = 0.314$.

12

Chapter 12 solutions

12.1 SECTION 12.1

12.1 The mean of the data is $\hat{\mu}'_1 = [27 + 82 + 115 + 126 + 155 + 161 + 243 + 13(250)]/20 = 207.95$. The expected value of a single observation censored at 250 is $E(X \wedge 250) = \theta(1 - e^{-250/\theta})$. Setting the two equal and solving produces $\hat{\theta} = 657.26$.

12.2 The equations to solve are

$$\exp(\mu + \sigma^2/2) = 1{,}424.4$$
$$\exp(2\mu + 2\sigma^2) = 13{,}238{,}441.9.$$

Taking logarithms yields

$$\mu + \sigma^2/2 = 7.261506$$
$$2\mu + 2\sigma^2 = 16.398635.$$

The solution of these two equations is $\hat{\mu} = 6.323695$ and $\hat{\sigma}^2 = 1.875623$ and then $\hat{\sigma} = 1.369534$.

Loss Models: From Data to Decisions, Solutions Manual, Second Edition.
By Stuart A. Klugman, Harry H. Panjer, and Gordon E. Willmot
ISBN 0-471-22762-5   Copyright © 2004 John Wiley & Sons, Inc.

12.3 The two equations to solve are

$$0.2 = 1 - e^{-(5/\theta)^\tau}$$
$$0.8 = 1 - e^{-(12/\theta)^\tau}.$$

Moving the 1 to the left-hand side and taking logarithms produces

$$0.22314 = (5/\theta)^\tau$$
$$1.60944 = (12/\theta)^\tau.$$

Dividing the second equation by the first equation produces

$$7.21269 = 2.4^\tau.$$

Taking logarithms again produces

$$1.97584 = 0.87547\tau$$

and so $\hat\tau = 2.25689$. Using the first equation,

$$\hat\theta = 5/(0.22314^{1/2.25689}) = 9.71868.$$

Then $\hat S(8) = e^{-(8/9.71868)^{2.25689}} = 0.52490$.

12.4 The equations to solve are

$$0.5 = 1 - \exp[-(10{,}000/\theta)^\tau]$$
$$0.9 = 1 - \exp[-(100{,}000/\theta)^\tau].$$

Then

$$\ln 0.5 = -0.69315 = -(10{,}000/\theta)^\tau$$
$$\ln 0.1 = -2.30259 = -(100{,}000/\theta)^\tau.$$

Dividing the second equation by the first gives

$$3.32192 = 10^\tau$$
$$\ln 3.32192 = 1.20054 = \tau \ln 10 = 2.30259\tau$$
$$\hat\tau = 1.20054/2.30259 = 0.52139.$$

Then

$$0.69315 = (10{,}000/\theta)^{0.52139}$$
$$0.69315^{1/0.52139} = 0.49512 = 10{,}000/\theta$$
$$\hat\theta = 20{,}197.$$

12.5 The two moment equations are

$$\frac{4+5+21+99+421}{5} = 110 = \frac{\theta}{\alpha-1}$$

$$\frac{4^2+5^2+21^2+99^2+421^2}{5} = 37,504.8 = \frac{2\theta^2}{(\alpha-1)(\alpha-2)}.$$

Dividing the second equation by the square of the first equation gives

$$\frac{37,504.8}{110^2} = 3.0996 = \frac{2(\alpha-1)}{\alpha-2}.$$

The solution is $\hat{\alpha} = 3.8188$. From the first equation, $\hat{\theta} = 110(2.8188) = 310.068$. For the 95th percentile,

$$0.95 = 1 - \left(\frac{310.068}{310.068 + \pi_{0.95}}\right)^{3.8188}$$

for $\hat{\pi}_{0.95} = 369.37$.

12.6 After inflation the 100 claims from year 1 total $100(10,000)(1.1)^2 = 1,210,000$ and the 200 claims from year 2 total $200(12,500)(1.1) = 2,750,000$. The average of the 300 inflated claims is $3,960,000/300 = 13,200$. The moment equation is $13,200 = \theta/(3-1)$ which yields $\hat{\theta} = 26,400$.

12.7 The equations to solve are

$$0.2 = F(18.25) = \Phi\left(\frac{\ln 18.25 - \mu}{\sigma}\right)$$

$$0.8 = F(35.8) = \Phi\left(\frac{\ln 35.8 - \mu}{\sigma}\right).$$

The 20th and 80th percentiles of the normal distribution are -0.842 and 0.842 respectively. The equations become

$$-0.842 = \frac{2.904 - \mu}{\sigma}$$

$$0.842 = \frac{3.578 - \mu}{\sigma}.$$

Dividing the first equation by the second yields

$$-1 = \frac{2.904 - \mu}{3.578 - \mu}.$$

The solution is $\hat{\mu} = 3.241$ and substituting in either equation yields $\hat{\sigma} = 0.4$. The probability of exceeding 30 is

$$\Pr(X > 30) = 1 - F(30) = 1 - \Phi\left(\frac{\ln 30 - 3.241}{0.4}\right) = 1 - \Phi(0.4)$$

$$= 1 - \Phi(0.4) = 1 - 0.6554 = 0.3446.$$

12.8 For a mixture, the mean and second moment are a combination of the individual moments. The first two moments are

$$\begin{aligned}
\mathrm{E}(X) &= p(1) + (1-p)(10) = 10 - 9p \\
\mathrm{E}(X^2) &= p(2) + (1-p)(200) = 200 - 198p \\
\mathrm{Var}(X) &= 200 - 198p - (10-9p)^2 = 100 - 18p - 81p^2 = 4.
\end{aligned}$$

The only positive root of the quadratic equation is $\hat{p} = 0.983$.

12.9 We need the $0.6(21) = 12.6th$ smallest observation. It is $0.4(38) + 0.6(39) = 38.6$.

12.10 (a) We need the $0.75(21) = 15.75th$ smallest observation. It is $0.25(13) + 0.75(14) = 13.75$.
(b) The ogive connects the points $(0.5, 0)$, $(2.5, 0.35)$, $(8.5, 0.65)$, $(15.5, 0.85)$, and $(29.5, 1)$.
(c) The histogram has height $0.35/2 = 0.175$ on the interval $(0.5, 2.5)$, height $0.3/6 = 0.05$ on the interval $(2.5, 8.5)$, height $0.2/7 = 0.028571$ on the interval $(8.5, 15.1)$, and height $0.15/14 = 0.010714$ on the interval $(15.5, 29.5)$.

12.11 $\hat{\mu} = 975$, $\hat{\mu}'_2 = 977{,}916\frac{2}{3}$, $\hat{\sigma}^2 = 977{,}916\frac{2}{3} - 975^2 = 27{,}291\frac{2}{3}$. The moment equations are $975 = \alpha\theta$ and $27{,}291\frac{2}{3} = \alpha\theta^2$. The solutions are $\hat{\alpha} = 34.8321$ and $\hat{\theta} = 27.9915$.

12.12 $F(x) = (x/\theta)^\gamma/[1 + (x/\theta)^\gamma]$. The equations are $0.2 = (100/\theta)^\gamma/[1 + (100/\theta)^\gamma]$ and $0.8 = (400/\theta)^\gamma/[1 + (400/\theta)^\gamma]$. From the first equation $0.2 = 0.8(100/\theta)^\gamma$ or $\theta^\gamma = 4(100)^\gamma$. Insert this in the second equation to get $0.8 = 4^{\gamma-1}/(1 + 4^{\gamma-1})$ and so $\hat{\gamma} = 2$ and then $\hat{\theta} = 200$.

12.13 (a) $f(x) = px^{p-1}$, $L = p^n(\Pi x_j)^{p-1}$, $l = n\ln p + (p-1)\Sigma\ln x_j$; $l' = np^{-1} + \Sigma\ln x_j = 0$, $\hat{p} = -n/\Sigma\ln x_j$.
(b) $\mathrm{E}(X) = \int_0^1 px^p dx = p/(1+p) = \bar{x}$. $\hat{p} = \bar{x}/(1-\bar{x})$.

12.14 $\hat{\mu} = 3{,}800 = \alpha\theta$. $\mu'_2 = 16{,}332{,}000$, $\hat{\sigma}^2 = 1{,}892{,}000 = \alpha\theta^2$. $\hat{\alpha} = 7.6321$, $\hat{\theta} = 497.89$.

12.15 $\hat{\mu} = 2{,}000 = \exp(\mu + \sigma^2/2)$, $\hat{\mu}'_2 = 6{,}000{,}000 = \exp(2\mu + 2\sigma^2)$. $7.690090 = \mu + \sigma^2/2$ and $15.60727 = 2\mu + 2\sigma^2$. The solutions are $\hat{\mu} = 7.39817$ and

$\hat{\sigma} = 0.636761.$

$$
\begin{aligned}
\Pr(X > 4{,}500) \quad &= \quad 1 - \Phi[(\ln 4{,}500 - 7.39817)/0.636761] \\
&= \quad 1 - \Phi(1.5919) = 0.056.
\end{aligned}
$$

12.16 $\hat{\mu} = 4.2 = (\beta/2)\sqrt{2\pi}.$ $\hat{\beta} = 3.35112.$

12.17 X is Pareto and so $\mathrm{E}(X) = 1{,}000/(\alpha - 1) = \bar{x} = 318.4.$ $\hat{\alpha} = 4.141.$

12.18 $r\beta = 0.1001$, $r\beta(1 + \beta) = 0.1103 - 0.1001^2 = 0.10027999.$ $1 + \beta = 1.0017981$, $\hat{\beta} = 0.0017981$, $\hat{r} = 55.670.$

12.19 $r\beta = 0.166$, $r\beta(1 + \beta) = 0.252 - 0.166^2 = 0.224444.$ $1 + \beta = 1.352072$, $\hat{\beta} = 0.352072$, $\hat{r} = 0.47149.$

12.2   SECTION 12.2

12.20 For the inverse exponential distribution,

$$
\begin{aligned}
l(\theta) \quad &= \quad \sum_{j=1}^{n} (\ln \theta - \theta x_j^{-1} - 2\ln x_j) = n\ln\theta - ny\theta - 2\sum_{j=1}^{n} \ln x_j \\
l'(\theta) \quad &= \quad n\theta^{-1} - ny, \; \hat{\theta} = y^{-1}, \text{ where } y = \frac{1}{n}\sum_{j=1}^{n} \frac{1}{x_j}.
\end{aligned}
$$

For Data Set B, we have $\hat{\theta} = 197.72$ and the loglikelihood value is -159.78. Because the mean does not exist for the inverse exponential distribution, there is no traditional method of moments estimate available. However, it is possible to obtain a method of moments estimate using the negative first moment rather than the positive first moment. That is, equate the average reciprocal to the expected reciprocal:

$$
\frac{1}{n}\sum_{j=1}^{n} \frac{1}{x_j} = \mathrm{E}(X^{-1}) = \theta^{-1}.
$$

This special method of moments estimate is identical to the maximum likelihood estimate.

For the inverse gamma distribution with $\alpha = 2$,

$$f(x|\theta) = \frac{\theta^2 e^{-\theta/x}}{x^3\Gamma(2)}, \quad \ln f(x|\theta) = 2\ln\theta - \theta x^{-1} - 3\ln x$$

$$l(\theta) = \sum_{j=1}^{n}(2\ln\theta - \theta x_j^{-1} - 3\ln x_j) = 2n\ln\theta - ny\theta - 3\sum_{j=1}^{n}\ln x_j$$

$$l'(\theta) = 2n\theta^{-1} - ny, \quad \hat{\theta} = 2/y.$$

For Data Set B, $\hat{\theta} = 395.44$ and the value of the loglikelihood function is -169.07. The method of moments estimate solves the equation

$$1,424.4 = \frac{\theta}{\alpha - 1} = \frac{\theta}{2 - 1}, \quad \hat{\theta} = 1,424.4$$

which differs from the maximum likelihood estimate.

For the inverse gamma distribution with both parameters unknown,

$$f(x|\theta) = \frac{\theta^\alpha e^{-\theta/x}}{x^{\alpha+1}\Gamma(\alpha)}, \quad \ln f(x|\theta) = \alpha\ln\theta - \theta x^{-1} - (\alpha+1)\ln x - \ln\Gamma(\alpha).$$

The likelihood function must be maximized numerically. The answer is $\hat{\alpha} = 0.70888$ and $\hat{\theta} = 140.16$ and the loglikelihood value is -158.88. The methods of moments estimate is the solution to the two equations

$$1,424.4 = \frac{\theta}{\alpha - 1}$$

$$13,238,441.9 = \frac{\theta^2}{(\alpha - 1)(\alpha - 2)}.$$

Squaring the first equation and dividing it into the second equation gives

$$6.52489 = \frac{\alpha - 1}{\alpha - 2}$$

which leads to $\hat{\alpha} = 2.181$ and then $\hat{\theta} = 1,682.2$. This does not match the maximum likelihood estimate (which had to be the case because the mle produces a model that does not have a mean).

12.21 For the inverse exponential distribution, the cdf is $F(x) = e^{-\theta/x}$. Numerical maximization yields $\hat{\theta} = 6,662.39$ and the value of the loglikelihood function is -365.40. For the gamma distribution, the cdf requires numerical evaluation. In Excel® the function GAMMADIST(x, α, θ,true) can be used. The estimates are $\hat{\alpha} = 0.37139$ and $\hat{\theta} = 83,020$. The value of the loglikelihood function is -360.50. For the inverse gamma distribution, the cdf is available in Excel® as $1-$ GAMMADIST($1/x, \alpha, 1/\theta$,true). The estimates

Table 12.1   Estimatees for Exercise 12.22

Model	Original	Censored
exponential	$\hat{\theta} = 1,424.4$	$\hat{\theta} = 594.14$
gamma	$\hat{\alpha} = 0.55616, \hat{\theta} = 2,561.1$	$\hat{\alpha} = 1.5183, \hat{\theta} = 295.69$
inv. exponential	$\hat{\theta} = 197.72$	$\hat{\theta} = 189.78$
inv. gamma	$\hat{\alpha} = 0.70888, \hat{\theta} = 140.16$	$\hat{\alpha} = 0.41612, \hat{\theta} = 86.290$

are $\hat{\alpha} = 0.83556$ and $\hat{\theta} = 5,113$. The value of the loglikelihood function is -363.92.

12.22 In each case the likelihood function is $f(27)f(82) \cdots f(243)[1-F(250)]^{13}$. Table 12.1 provides the estimates for both the original and censored data sets. The censoring tended to disguise the true nature of these numbers and in general had a large impact on the estimates.

12.23 The calculations are done as in the example, but with θ unknown. The likelihood must be numerically maximized. For the shifted data the estimates are $\hat{\alpha} = 1.4521$ and $\hat{\theta} = 907.98$. The two expected costs are $907.98/0.4521 = 2,008$ and $1,107.98/0.4521 = 2,451$ for the 200 and 400 deductibles respectively. For the unshifted data the estimates are $\hat{\alpha} = 1.4521$ and $\hat{\theta} = 707.98$. The three expected costs are $707.98/0.4521 = 1,566$, $2,008$, and $2,451$ for the 0, 200, and 400 deductibles respectively. While it is always the case that for the Pareto distribution the two approaches produce identical answers, that will not be true in general.

12.24 The same table can be used. The only difference is that observations that were surrenders are now treated as x-values and deaths are treated as y-values. Observations that ended at 5.0 continue to be treated as y-values. Once again there is no estimate for a Pareto model. The gamma parameter estimates are $\hat{\alpha} = 1.229$ and $\hat{\theta} = 6.452$.

12.25 The contribution to the likelihood for the first five values (number of drivers having zero through four accidents) is unchanged. However, for the last seven drivers, the contribution is

$$[\Pr(X \geq 5)]^7 = [1 - p(0) - p(1) - p(2) - p(3) - p(4)]^7$$

and the maximum must be obtained numerically. The estimated values are $\hat{\lambda} = 0.16313$ and $\hat{q} = 0.02039$. These answers are similar to those for Example 12.12 because the probability of six or more accidents is so small.

Table 12.2 Probabilities for Exercise 12.26

Event	Probability
Observed at age 35.4 and died	$\frac{F(1)-F(0.4)}{1-F(0.4)} = \frac{w-0.4w}{1-0.4w} = \frac{0.6w}{1-0.4w}$
Observed at age 35.4 and survived	$1 - \frac{0.6w}{1-0.4w} = \frac{1-w}{1-0.4w}$
Observed at age 35 and died	$F(1) = w$
Observed at age 35 and survived	$1 - w$

12.26 There are four cases, with the likelihood function being the product of the probabilities for those cases raised to a power equal to the number of times each occurred. Table 12.2 provides the probabilities.

The likelihood function is

$$L = \left(\frac{0.6w}{1-0.4w}\right)^6 \left(\frac{1-w}{1-0.4w}\right)^4 w^8(1-w)^{12} \propto \frac{w^{14}(1-w)^{16}}{(1-0.4w)^{10}}$$

and its logarithm is

$$l = 14\ln w + 16\ln(1-w) - 10\ln(1-0.4w).$$

The derivative is

$$l' = \frac{14}{w} - \frac{16}{1-w} + \frac{4}{1-0.4w}.$$

Set the derivative equal to zero and clear the denominators to produce the equation

$$0 = 14(1-w)(1-0.4w) - 16w(1-0.4w) + 4w(1-w)$$
$$0 = 14 - 31.6w + 8w^2$$

and the solution is $w = q_{35} = 0.508$ (the other root is greater than one and so cannot be the solution).

12.27 The survival function is

$$S(t) = \begin{cases} e^{-\lambda_1 t}, & 0 \le t < 2 \\ e^{-2\lambda_1 - (t-2)\lambda_2}, & t \ge 2 \end{cases}$$

and the density function is

$$f(t) = -S'(t) = \begin{cases} \lambda_1 e^{-\lambda_1 t}, & 0 \le t < 2 \\ \lambda_2 e^{-2\lambda_1 - (t-2)\lambda_2}, & t \ge 2. \end{cases}$$

The likelihood function is

$$\begin{aligned} L &= f(1.7)S(1.5)S(2.6)f(3.3)S(3.5) \\ &= \lambda_1 e^{-1.7\lambda_1} e^{-1.5\lambda_1} e^{-2\lambda_1 - 0.6\lambda_2} \lambda_2 e^{-2\lambda_1 - 1.3\lambda_2} e^{-2\lambda_1 - 1.5\lambda_2} \\ &= \lambda_1 \lambda_2 e^{-9.2\lambda_1 - 3.4\lambda_2}. \end{aligned}$$

The logarithm and partial derivatives are

$$l = \ln \lambda_1 + \ln \lambda_2 - 9.2\lambda_1 - 3.4\lambda_2$$
$$\frac{\partial l}{\partial \lambda_1} = \frac{1}{\lambda_1} - 9.2 = 0$$
$$\frac{\partial l}{\partial \lambda_2} = \frac{1}{\lambda_2} - 3.4 = 0$$

and the solutions are $\hat{\lambda}_1 = 0.10870$ and $\hat{\lambda}_2 = 0.29412$.

12.28 Let $f(t) = w$ be the density function. For the eight lives that lived the full year, the contribution to the likelihood is $\Pr(T > 1) = 1 - w$. For the one censored life, the contribution is $\Pr(T > 0.5) = 1 - 0.5w$. For the one death, the contribution is $\Pr(T \leq 1) = w$. Then

$$L = (1 - w)^8 (1 - 0.5w)w$$
$$\ln L = 8\ln(1 - w) + \ln(1 - 0.5w) + \ln w$$
$$\frac{d\ln L}{dw} = -\frac{8}{1 - w} - \frac{0.5}{1 - 0.5w} + \frac{1}{w}.$$

Setting the derivative equal to zero and clearing the denominators gives

$$0 = -8w(1 - 0.5w) - 0.5w(1 - w) + (1 - w)(1 - 0.5w).$$

The only root of this quadratic that is less than one is $w = 0.10557 = \hat{q}_x$.

12.29 For the two lives that died, the contribution to the likelihood function is $f(10)$ while for the eight lives that were censored, the contribution is $S(10)$. We have

$$f(t) = -S'(t) = \frac{0.5}{k}\left(1 - \frac{t}{k}\right)^{-0.5}$$
$$L = f(10)^2 S(10)^8 = \left(\frac{0.5}{k}\right)^2 \left(1 - \frac{10}{k}\right)^{-1} \left(1 - \frac{10}{k}\right)^4 \propto \frac{(k - 10)^3}{k^5}$$
$$\ln L = 3\ln(k - 10) - 5\ln k$$
$$\frac{d\ln L}{dk} = \frac{3}{k - 10} - \frac{5}{k} = 0$$
$$0 = 3k - 5(k - 10) = 50 - 2k.$$

Therefore, $\hat{k} = 25$.

12.30 We have

$$
\begin{aligned}
L &= f(1,100)f(3,200)f(3,300)f(3,500)f(3,900)[S(4,000)]^{495} \\
&= \theta^{-1}e^{-1100/\theta}\theta^{-1}e^{-3,200/\theta}\theta^{-1}e^{-3300/\theta}\theta^{-1}e^{-3500/\theta} \\
&\quad \times \theta^{-1}e^{-3900/\theta}[e^{-4,000/\theta}]^{495} \\
&= \theta^{-5}e^{-1,995,000/\theta} \\
\ln L &= -5\ln\theta - \frac{1,995,000}{\theta} \\
\frac{d\ln L}{d\theta} &= -\frac{5}{\theta} + \frac{1,995,000}{\theta^2} = 0
\end{aligned}
$$

and the solution is $\hat{\theta} = 1,995,000/5 = 399,000$.

12.31 For maximum likelihood, the contributions to the likelihood function are (where q denotes the constant value of the time to death density function)

Event	Contribution
Survive to 36	$\Pr(T > 1) = 1 - q$
Censored at 35.6	$\Pr(T > 0.6) = 1 - 0.6q$
Die prior to 35.6	$\Pr(T \le 0.6) = 0.6q$
Die after 35.6	$\Pr(0.6 < T \le 1) = 0.4q.$

Then,

$$
\begin{aligned}
L &= (1-q)^{72}(1-0.6q)^{15}(0.6q)^{10}(0.4q)^3 \propto (1-q)^{72}(1-0.6q)^{15}q^{13} \\
\ln L &= 72\ln(1-q) + 15\ln(1-0.6q) + 13\ln q \\
\frac{d\ln L}{dq} &= -\frac{72}{1-q} - \frac{9}{1-0.6q} + \frac{13}{q} = 0.
\end{aligned}
$$

The solution to the quadratic equation is $\hat{q} = 0.13911 = \hat{q}_{35}$.

For the product-limit estimate, the risk set at time 0 has 100 members. The first 10 observations are all deaths, and so the successive factors are $(99/100)$, $(98/99)$, ..., $(90/91)$ and therefore $\hat{S}(0.6) = 90/100 = 0.9$. The 15 censored observations reduce the risk set to 75. The next three deaths each reduce the risk set by one and so $\hat{S}(1) = 0.9(74/75)(73/74)(72/73) = 0.864$. Then $\hat{q}_{35} = 1 - 0.864 = 0.136$.

12.32 The density function is $f(t) = -S'(t) = 1/w$. For Actuary X, the likelihood function is

$$
f(1)f(3)f(4)f(4)S(5) = \left(\frac{1}{w}\right)^4\left(1 - \frac{5}{w}\right) = \frac{1}{w^4} - \frac{5}{w^5}.
$$

Setting the derivative equal to zero gives

$$
0 = -\frac{4}{w^5} + \frac{25}{w^6}, \quad 4w = 25, \quad \hat{w} = 6.25.
$$

For Actuary Y the likelihood function is

$$f(1)f(3)f(4)f(4)f(6) = w^{-5}.$$

This function appears to be strictly decreasing and therefore is maximized at $w = 0$, an unsatisfactory answer. Most of the time the support of the random variable can be ignored, but not this time. In this case $f(t) = 1/w$ only for $0 \leq t \leq w$ and is 0 otherwise. Therefore, the likelihood function is only w^{-5} when all the observed values are less than or equal to w, otherwise the function is zero. In other words,

$$L(w) = \begin{cases} 0, & w < 6 \\ w^{-5}, & w \geq 6. \end{cases}$$

This makes sense because the likelihood that w is less than 6 should be zero. After all, such values of w are not possible, given the sampled values. This likelihood function is not continuous and therefore derivatives cannot be used to locate the maximum. Inspection quickly shows that the maximum occurs at $\hat{w} = 6$.

12.33 The likelihood function is

$$L(w) = \frac{f(4)f(5)f(7)S(3+r)}{S(3)^4} = \frac{w^{-1}w^{-1}w^{-1}(w-3-r)w^{-1}}{(w-3)^4 w^{-4}} = \frac{w-3-r}{(w-3)^4}$$

$$l(w) = \ln(w-3-r) - 4\ln(w-3).$$

The derivative of the logarithm is

$$l'(w) = \frac{1}{w-3-r} - \frac{4}{w-3}.$$

Inserting the estimate of w and setting the derivative equal to zero yields

$$0 = \frac{1}{10.67 - r} - \frac{4}{10.67}$$
$$0 = 10.67 - 4(10.67 - r) = -32.01 + 4r$$
$$r = 8.$$

12.34 The survival function is

$$S(t) = \begin{cases} e^{-t\lambda_1}, & 0 < t < 5 \\ e^{-5\lambda_1 - (t-5)\lambda_2}, & 5 \leq t < 10 \\ e^{-5\lambda_1 - 5\lambda_2 - (t-10)\lambda_3}, & t \geq 10 \end{cases}$$

and the density function is

$$f(t) = -S'(t) = \begin{cases} \lambda_1 e^{-t\lambda_1}, & 0 < t < 5 \\ \lambda_2 e^{-5\lambda_1 - (t-5)\lambda_2}, & 5 \leq t < 10 \\ \lambda_3 e^{-5\lambda_1 - 5\lambda_2 - (t-10)\lambda_3}, & t \geq 10. \end{cases}$$

The likelihood function and its logarithm are

$$
\begin{aligned}
L(\lambda_1, \lambda_2, \lambda_3) &= \lambda_1 e^{-3\lambda_1} \lambda_2^2 e^{-10\lambda_1-5\lambda_2} \lambda_3^4 e^{-20\lambda_1-20\lambda_2-11\lambda_3} \\
&\quad \times (e^{-5\lambda_1-5\lambda_2-5\lambda_3})^3 \\
&= \lambda_1 e^{-48\lambda_1} \lambda_2^2 e^{-40\lambda_2} \lambda_3^4 e^{-26\lambda_3} \\
\ln L(\lambda_1, \lambda_2, \lambda_3) &= \ln\lambda_1 - 48\lambda_1 + 2\ln\lambda_2 - 40\lambda_2 + 4\ln\lambda_3 - 26\lambda_3.
\end{aligned}
$$

The partial derivative with respect to λ_1 is $\lambda_1^{-1} - 48 = 0$ for $\hat{\lambda}_1 = 1/48$. Similarly, $\hat{\lambda}_2 = 2/40$ and $\hat{\lambda}_3 = 4/26$.

12.35 The density function is the derivative, $f(x) = \alpha 500^\alpha x^{-\alpha-1}$. The likelihood function is

$$
L(\alpha) = \alpha^5 500^{5\alpha} (\Pi x_j)^{-\alpha-1}
$$

and its logarithm is

$$
\begin{aligned}
l(\alpha) &= 5\ln\alpha + (5\alpha)\ln 500 - (\alpha+1)\Sigma\ln x_j \\
&= 5\ln\alpha + 31.073\alpha - 33.111(\alpha+1).
\end{aligned}
$$

Setting the derivative equal to zero gives

$$
0 = 5\alpha^{-1} - 2.038.
$$

The estimate is $\hat{\alpha} = 5/2.038 = 2.45$.

12.36 The coefficient $(2\pi x)^{-1/2}$ is not relevant because it does not involve μ. The logarithm of the likelihood function is

$$
l(\mu) = -\frac{1}{22}(11-\mu)^2 - \frac{1}{30.4}(15.2-\mu)^2 - \frac{1}{36}(18-\mu)^2 - \frac{1}{42}(21-\mu)^2 - \frac{1}{51.6}(25.8-\mu)^2.
$$

The derivative is

$$
l'(\mu) = \frac{11-\mu}{11} + \frac{15.2-\mu}{15.2} + \frac{18-\mu}{18} + \frac{21-\mu}{21} + \frac{25.8-\mu}{25.8} = 5 - 0.29863\mu.
$$

Setting the derivative equal to zero yields $\hat{\mu} = 16.74$.

12.37 The distribution and density function are

$$
F(x) = 1 - e^{-(x/\theta)^2}, \quad f(x) = \frac{2x}{\theta^2} e^{-(x/\theta)^2}.
$$

The likelihood function is

$$
\begin{aligned}
L(\theta) &= f(20)f(30)f(45)[1 - F(50)]^2 \\
&\propto \theta^{-2} e^{-(20/\theta)^2} \theta^{-2} e^{-(30/\theta)^2} \theta^{-2} e^{-(45/\theta)^2} \left[e^{-(50/\theta)^2} \right]^2 \\
&= \theta^{-6} e^{-8,325/\theta^2}.
\end{aligned}
$$

The logarithm and derivative are

$$l(\theta) = -6\ln\theta - 8{,}325\theta^{-2}$$
$$l'(\theta) = -6\theta^{-1} + 16{,}650\theta^{-3}.$$

Setting the derivative equal to zero yields $\hat\theta = (16{,}650/6)^{1/2} = 52.68$.

12.38 For the exponential distribution, the maximum likelihood estimate is the sample mean and so $\bar{x}_P = 1000$ and $\bar{x}_S = 1500$. The likelihood with the restriction is (using i to index observations from Phil's bulbs and j to index observations from Sylvia's bulbs)

$$\begin{aligned}
L(\theta^*) &= \prod_{i=1}^{20}(\theta^*)^{-1}\exp(-x_i/\theta^*)\prod_{j=1}^{10}(2\theta^*)^{-1}\exp(-x_j/2\theta^*)\\
&\propto (\theta^*)^{-30}\exp\left(-\sum_{i=1}^{20}\frac{x_i}{\theta^*} - \sum_{j=1}^{10}\frac{x_j}{2\theta^*}\right)\\
&= (\theta^*)^{-30}\exp(-20\bar{x}_P/\theta^* - 10\bar{x}_S/2\theta^*)\\
&= (\theta^*)^{-30}\exp(-20{,}000/\theta^* - 7{,}500/\theta^*).
\end{aligned}$$

Taking logarithms and differentiating yields

$$l(\theta^*) = -30\ln\theta^* - 27{,}500/\theta^*$$
$$l'(\theta^*) = -30(\theta^*)^{-1} + 27{,}500(\theta^*)^{-2}.$$

Setting the derivative equal to zero gives $\hat\theta^* = 27{,}500/30 = 916.67$.

12.39 For the first part,

$$\begin{aligned}
L(\theta) &= F(1{,}000)^{62}[1 - F(1{,}000)]^{38}\\
&= (1 - e^{-1{,}000/\theta})^{62}(e^{-1{,}000/\theta})^{38}.
\end{aligned}$$

Let $x = e^{-1{,}000/\theta}$. Then

$$\begin{aligned}
L(x) &= (1 - x)^{62}x^{38}\\
l(x) &= 62\ln(1 - x) + 38\ln x\\
l'(x) &= -\frac{62}{1 - x} + \frac{38}{x}.
\end{aligned}$$

Setting the derivative equal to zero yields

$$\begin{aligned}
0 &= -62x + 38(1 - x)\\
0 &= 38 - 100x\\
x &= 0.38
\end{aligned}$$

and then $\hat{\theta} = -1{,}000/\ln 0.38 = 1{,}033.50$.

With additional information

$$
\begin{aligned}
L(\theta) &= \left[\prod_{j=1}^{62} f(x_j)\right][1 - F(1{,}000)]^{38} = \left(\prod_{j=1}^{62} \theta^{-1} e^{-x_j/\theta}\right) e^{-38{,}000/\theta} \\
&= \theta^{-62} e^{-28{,}140/\theta} e^{-38{,}000/\theta} = \theta^{-62} e^{-66{,}140/\theta} \\
l(\theta) &= -62\ln\theta - 66{,}140/\theta \\
l'(\theta) &= -62/\theta + 66{,}140/\theta^2 = 0 \\
0 &= -62\theta + 66{,}140 \\
\hat{\theta} &= 66{,}140/62 = 1{,}066.77.
\end{aligned}
$$

12.40 The density function is

$$
f(x) = 0.5 x^{-0.5}\theta^{-0.5} e^{-(x/\theta)^{0.5}}.
$$

The likelihood function and subsequent calculations are

$$
\begin{aligned}
L(\theta) &= \prod_{j=1}^{10} 0.5 x_j^{-0.5}\theta^{-0.5} e^{-x_j^{0.5}\theta^{-0.5}} \propto \theta^{-5}\exp\left(-\theta^{-0.5}\sum_{j=1}^{10} x_j^{0.5}\right) \\
&= \theta^{-5}\exp(-488.97\theta^{-0.5}) \\
l(\theta) &= -5\ln\theta - 488.97\theta^{-0.5} \\
l'(\theta) &= -5\theta^{-1} + 244.485\theta^{-1.5} = 0 \\
0 &= -5\theta^{0.5} + 244.485
\end{aligned}
$$

and so $\hat{\theta} = (244.485/5)^2 = 2391$.

12.41 Each observation has a uniquely determined conditional probability. The contribution to the loglikelihood is given in Table 12.3. The total is $l(p) = 3\ln p - 11\ln(1 + p)$. Setting the derivative equal to zero gives $0 = l'(p) = 3p^{-1} - 11(1 + p)^{-1}$ and the solution is $\hat{p} = 3/8$.

12.42 $L = 2^n\theta^n(\Pi x_j)\exp(-\theta\Sigma x_j^2)$, $l = n\ln 2 + n\ln\theta + \Sigma\ln x_j - \theta\Sigma x_j^2$, $l' = n\theta^{-1} - \Sigma x_j^2 = 0$, $\hat{\theta} = n/\Sigma x_j^2$.

12.43 (a) $f(x) = px^{p-1}$, $L = p^n(\Pi x_j)^{p-1}$, $l = n\ln p + (p - 1)\Sigma\ln x_j$, $l' = np^{-1} + \Sigma\ln x_j = 0$, $\hat{p} = -n/\Sigma\ln x_j$.
(b) $E(X) = \int_0^1 px^p dx = p/(1 + p) = \bar{x}$. $\hat{p} = \bar{x}/(1 - \bar{x})$.

Table 12.3 Likelihood contributions for Exercise 12.41

Observation	Probability	Loglikelihood
1997-1	$\frac{\Pr(N=1)}{\Pr(N=1)+\Pr(N=2)} = \frac{(1-p)p}{(1-p)p+(1-p)p^2} = \frac{1}{1+p}$	$-3\ln(1+p)$
1997-2	$\frac{\Pr(N=2)}{\Pr(N=1)+\Pr(N=2)} = \frac{(1-p)p^2}{(1-p)p+(1-p)p^2} = \frac{p}{1+p}$	$\ln p - \ln(1+p)$
1998-0	$\frac{\Pr(N=0)}{\Pr(N=0)+\Pr(N=1)} = \frac{(1-p)}{(1-p)+(1-p)p} = \frac{1}{1+p}$	$-5\ln(1+p)$
1998-1	$\frac{\Pr(N=1)}{\Pr(N=0)+\Pr(N=1)} = \frac{(1-p)p}{(1-p)+(1-p)p} = \frac{p}{1+p}$	$2\ln p - 2\ln(1+p)$
1999-0	$\frac{\Pr(N=0)}{\Pr(N=0)} = 1$	0

12.44 (a) $L = (\Pi x_j)^{\alpha-1} \exp(-\Sigma x_j/\theta)[\Gamma(\alpha)]^{-n}\theta^{-n\alpha}$.

$$\begin{aligned}
l &= (\alpha-1)\Sigma \ln x_j - \theta^{-1}\Sigma x_j - n\ln\Gamma(\alpha) - n\alpha\ln\theta \\
&= 81.61837(\alpha-1) - 38,000\theta^{-1} - 10\ln\Gamma(\alpha) - 10\alpha\ln\theta. \\
\partial l/\partial\theta &= 38,000\theta^{-2} - 10\alpha\theta^{-1} = 0,
\end{aligned}$$

$\hat{\theta} = 38,000/(10 \cdot 12) = 316.67$.
(b) l is maximized at $\hat{\alpha} = 6.341$ and $\hat{\theta} = 599.3$ (with $l = -86.835$).

12.45 $\hat{\mu} = \frac{1}{5}\Sigma \ln x_i = 7.33429$. $\hat{\sigma}^2 = \frac{1}{5}\Sigma(\ln x_i)^2 - 7.33429^2 = 0.567405$,
$\hat{\sigma} = 0.753263$.

$$\begin{aligned}
\Pr(X > 4,500) &= 1 - \Phi[(\ln 4,500 - 7.33429)/0.753263] \\
&= 1 - \Phi(1.4305) = 0.076.
\end{aligned}$$

12.46 $L = \theta^{-n}\exp(-\Sigma x_j/\theta)$. $l = -n\ln\theta - \theta^{-1}\Sigma x_j$. $l' = -n\theta^{-1} + \theta^{-2}\Sigma x_j = 0$. $\hat{\theta} = \Sigma x_j/n$.

12.47 $L = \beta^{-10}(\Pi x_j)\exp[-\Sigma x_j^2/(2\beta^2)]$. $l = -10\ln\beta + \Sigma \ln x_j - \Sigma x_j^2/(2\beta^2)$. $l' = -10\beta^{-1} + \beta^{-3}\Sigma x_j^2 = 0$. $\hat{\beta} = \sqrt{\Sigma x_j^2/10} = 3.20031$.

12.48 $f(x) = \alpha x^{-\alpha-1}$. $L = \alpha^n(\Pi x_j)^{-\alpha-1}$. $l = n\ln\alpha - (\alpha+1)\Sigma \ln x_j$. $l' = n\alpha^{-1} - \Sigma \ln x_j = 0$. $\hat{\alpha} = n/\Sigma \ln x_j$.

12.49
$$\begin{aligned}
L &= \alpha^5\lambda^{5\alpha}[\Pi(\lambda + x_j)]^{-\alpha-1} \\
l &= 5\ln\alpha + 5\alpha\ln 1,000 - (\alpha+1)\Sigma\ln(1,000 + x_j) \\
l' &= 5\alpha^{-1} + 34.5388 - 35.8331 = 0. \ \hat{\alpha} = 3.8629.
\end{aligned}$$

12.50 (a) Three observations exceed 200. The empirical estimate is $3/20 = 0.15$.

(b) $E(X) = 100\alpha/(\alpha - 1) = \bar{x} = 154.5$. $\hat{\alpha} = 154.5/54.5 = 2.835$. $\Pr(X > 200) = (100/200)^{2.835} = 0.140$.

(c) $f(x) = \alpha 100^\alpha x^{-\alpha-1}$. $L = \alpha^{20} 100^{20\alpha} (\Pi x_j)^{-\alpha-1}$.

$$
\begin{aligned}
l &= 20 \ln \alpha + 20\alpha \ln 100 - (\alpha + 1)\Sigma \ln x_j \\
l' &= 20\alpha^{-1} + 20 \ln 100 - \Sigma \ln x_j = 0 \\
\hat{\alpha} &= 20/(\Sigma \ln x_j - 20 \ln 100) = 20/(99.125 - 92.103) = 2.848
\end{aligned}
$$

$\Pr(X > 200) = (100/200)^{2.848} = 0.139$.

12.51 The maximum likelihood estimate is $\hat{\theta} = 93.188$.

12.52 (a)
$$
\begin{aligned}
\sum \frac{(x_j - \mu)^2}{x_j} &= \sum \left(x_j - 2\mu + \frac{\mu^2}{x_j} \right) \\
&= \sum \left(\frac{\mu^2}{x_j} - \frac{\mu^2}{\bar{x}} \right) + \sum \left(\frac{\mu^2}{\bar{x}} - 2\mu + x_j \right) \\
&= \mu^2 \sum \left(\frac{1}{x_j} - \frac{1}{\bar{x}} \right) + \frac{n\mu^2}{\bar{x}} - 2n\mu + n\bar{x} \\
&= \mu^2 \sum \left(\frac{1}{x_j} - \frac{1}{\bar{x}} \right) + \frac{n}{\bar{x}}(\bar{x} - \mu)^2
\end{aligned}
$$

(b)
$$
\begin{aligned}
L &\propto \theta^{n/2} \exp \left[-\frac{\theta}{2\mu^2} \sum \frac{(x_j - \mu)^2}{x_j} \right] \\
l &= \ln L = \frac{n}{2} \ln \theta - \frac{\theta}{2\mu^2} \sum \frac{(x_j - \mu)^2}{x_j} \\
&= \frac{n}{2} \ln \theta - \frac{\theta}{2\mu^2} \left[\mu^2 \sum \left(\frac{1}{x_j} - \frac{1}{\bar{x}} \right) + \frac{n}{\bar{x}}(\bar{x} - \mu)^2 \right] \\
&= \frac{n}{2} \ln \theta - \frac{\theta}{2} \sum \left(\frac{1}{x_j} - \frac{1}{\bar{x}} \right) - \frac{n\theta}{2\mu^2 \bar{x}}(\bar{x} - \mu)^2 \\
\frac{\partial l}{\partial \mu} &= -\frac{n\theta}{2\bar{x}} \frac{-\mu^2 2(\bar{x} - \mu) - (\bar{x} - \mu)^2 2\mu}{\mu^4} = 0 \\
\hat{\mu} &= \bar{x}
\end{aligned}
$$

$$
\begin{aligned}
\frac{\partial l}{\partial \theta} &= \frac{n}{2\theta} - \frac{1}{2} \sum \left(\frac{1}{x_j} - \frac{1}{\bar{x}} \right) + \frac{n}{2\mu^2 \bar{x}}(\bar{x} - \mu)^2 = 0 \\
\hat{\theta} &= \frac{n}{\sum \left(\frac{1}{x_j} - \frac{1}{\bar{x}} \right)}
\end{aligned}
$$

12.53

$$L(\mu, \theta) = \prod_{j=1}^{n} f\left[x_j; \mu, (\theta m_j)^{-1}\right]$$

$$= \prod_{j=1}^{n} \left(\frac{2\pi}{\theta m_j}\right)^{-\frac{1}{2}} \exp\left[-\frac{(x_j - \mu)^2 m_j \theta}{2}\right]$$

$$\propto \theta^{n/2} \exp\left[-\frac{\theta}{2} \sum m_j (x_j - \mu)^2\right]$$

$$\ell(\mu, \theta) = \frac{n}{2} \ln \theta - \frac{\theta}{2} \sum m_j (x_j - \mu)^2 + \text{constant}$$

$$\frac{\partial \ell}{\partial \mu} = \theta \sum m_j (x_j - \mu) = 0 \Rightarrow \hat{\mu} = \frac{\sum m_j x_j}{\sum m_j} = \frac{\sum m_j x_j}{m}$$

$$\frac{\partial^2 \ell}{\partial \mu} = -\theta \sum m_j < 0, \text{ hence, maximum.}$$

$$\frac{\partial \ell}{\partial \theta} = \frac{n}{2}\frac{1}{\theta} - \frac{1}{2}\sum m_j(x_j - \mu)^2 = 0 \Rightarrow \hat{\theta}^{-1} = \frac{1}{n}\sum m_j(x_j - \hat{\mu})^2$$

$$\hat{\theta} = n\left[\sum m_j(x_j - \bar{x})^2\right]^{-1}$$

$$\frac{\partial^2 \ell}{\partial \theta^2} = -\frac{n}{2}\frac{1}{\theta^2} < 0, \text{ hence, maximum}$$

12.3 SECTION 12.3

12.54 In general, for the exponential distribution,

$$l'(\theta) = -n\theta^{-1} + n\bar{x}\theta^{-2}$$

$$l''(\theta) = n\theta^{-2} - 2n\bar{x}\theta^{-3}$$

$$E[l''(\theta)] = n\theta^{-2} - 2n\theta\theta^{-3} = -n\theta^{-2}$$

$$\text{Var}(\hat{\theta}) = \theta^2/n$$

where the third line follows from $E(\bar{X}) = E(X) = \theta$. The estimated variance for Data Set B is $\widehat{\text{Var}}(\hat{\theta}) = 1{,}424.4^2/20 = 101{,}445.77$ and the 95% confidence interval is $1{,}424.4 \pm 1.96(101{,}445.77)^{1/2}$ or $1{,}424.4 \pm 624.27$. Note that in this particular case, Theorem 12.13 gives the exact value of the variance. That is because

$$\text{Var}(\hat{\theta}) = \text{Var}(\bar{X}) = \text{Var}(X)/n = \theta^2/n.$$

For the gamma distribution,

$$l(\alpha, \theta) = (\alpha - 1) \sum_{j=1}^{n} \ln x_j - \sum_{j=1}^{n} x_j \theta^{-1} - n \ln \Gamma(\alpha) - n\alpha \ln \theta$$

$$\frac{\partial l(\alpha, \theta)}{\partial \alpha} = \sum_{j=1}^{n} \ln x_j - \frac{n\Gamma'(\alpha)}{\Gamma(\alpha)} - n \ln \theta$$

$$\frac{\partial l(\alpha, \theta)}{\partial \theta} = \sum_{j=1}^{n} x_j \theta^{-2} - n\alpha\theta^{-1}$$

$$\frac{\partial^2 l(\alpha, \theta)}{\partial \alpha^2} = -n \frac{\Gamma(\alpha)\Gamma''(\alpha) - \Gamma'(\alpha)^2}{\Gamma(\alpha)^2}$$

$$\frac{\partial^2 l(\alpha, \theta)}{\partial \alpha \partial \theta} = -n\theta^{-1}$$

$$\frac{\partial^2 l(\alpha, \theta)}{\partial \theta^2} = -2 \sum_{j=1}^{n} x_j \theta^{-3} + n\alpha\theta^{-2} = -2n\bar{x}\theta^{-3} + n\alpha\theta^{-2}.$$

The first two second partial derivatives do not contain x_j and so the expected value is equal to the indicated quantity. For the final second partial derivative, $E(\bar{X}) = E(X) = \alpha\theta$. Therefore,

$$I(\alpha, \theta) = \begin{bmatrix} n\frac{\Gamma(\alpha)\Gamma''(\alpha) - \Gamma'(\alpha)^2}{\Gamma(\alpha)^2} & n\theta^{-1} \\ n\theta^{-1} & n\alpha\theta^{-2} \end{bmatrix}.$$

The derivatives of the gamma function are available in some better computer packages, but are not available in Excel®. Using numerical derivatives of the gamma function yields

$$I(\hat{\alpha}, \hat{\theta}) = \begin{bmatrix} 82.467 & 0.0078091 \\ 0.0078091 & 0.0000016958 \end{bmatrix}$$

and the covariance matrix is

$$\begin{bmatrix} 0.021503 & -99.0188 \\ -99.0188 & 1{,}045{,}668 \end{bmatrix}.$$

Numerical second derivatives of the likelihood function (using $h_1 = 0.00005$ and $h_2 = 0.25$) yield

$$I(\hat{\alpha}, \hat{\theta}) = \begin{bmatrix} 82.467 & 0.0078091 \\ 0.0078091 & 0.0000016959 \end{bmatrix}$$

$$\text{and covariance matrix } \begin{bmatrix} 0.021502 & -99.0143 \\ -99.0143 & 1{,}045{,}620 \end{bmatrix}.$$

The confidence interval for α is $0.55616 \pm 1.96(0.021502)^{1/2}$ or 0.55616 ± 0.28741 and for θ is $2{,}561.1 \pm 1.96(1{,}045{,}620)^{1/2}$ or $2{,}561.1 \pm 2{,}004.2$.

12.55 The density function is $f(x|\theta) = \theta^{-1}$, $0 \leq x \leq \theta$. The likelihood function is

$$
\begin{aligned}
L(\theta) &= \theta^{-n}, \ 0 \leq x_1, \ldots, x_n \leq \theta \\
&= 0, \ \text{otherwise.}
\end{aligned}
$$

As a function of θ, the likelihood function is sometimes 0, and sometimes θ^{-n}. In particular, it is θ^{-n} only when θ is greater than or equal to all the xs. Equivalently, we have

$$
\begin{aligned}
L(\theta) &= 0, \ \theta < \max(x_1, \ldots, x_n) \\
&= \theta^{-n}, \ \theta \geq \max(x_1, \ldots, x_n).
\end{aligned}
$$

Therefore, the likelihood function is maximized at $\hat{\theta} = \max(x_1, \ldots, x_n)$. Note that the calculus technique of setting the derivative equal to zero does not work here because the likelihood function is not continuous (and therefore not differentiable) at the maximum. From Examples 9.7 and 9.10 we know that this estimator is asymptotically unbiased and consistent and we have its variance without recourse to Theorem 12.13. According to Theorem 12.13, we need

$$
\begin{aligned}
l(\theta) &= -n \ln \theta, \ \theta \geq \max(x_1, \ldots, x_n) \\
l'(\theta) &= -n\theta^{-1}, \ \theta \geq \max(x_1, \ldots, x_n) \\
l''(\theta) &= n\theta^{-2}, \ \theta \geq \max(x_1, \ldots, x_n).
\end{aligned}
$$

Then $E[l''(\theta)] = n\theta^{-2}$ because with regard to the random variables, $n\theta^{-2}$ is a constant and therefore its expected value is itself. The information is then the negative of this number and must be negative.

With regard to assumption (ii) of Theorem 12.13,

$$
\int_0^\theta \frac{\partial}{\partial \theta} \frac{1}{\theta} dx = \int_0^\theta -\theta^{-2} dx = -\frac{1}{\theta} \neq 0.
$$

12.56 From Exercise 12.54 we have $\hat{\alpha} = 0.55616$, $\hat{\theta} = 2,561.1$ and covariance matrix

$$
\begin{bmatrix} 0.021503 & -99.0188 \\ -99.0188 & 1,045,668 \end{bmatrix}.
$$

The function to be estimated is $g(\alpha, \theta) = \alpha\theta$ with partial derivatives of θ and α. The approximated variance is

$$
\begin{bmatrix} 2,561.1 & 0.55616 \end{bmatrix} \begin{bmatrix} 0.021503 & -99.0188 \\ -99.0188 & 1,045,668 \end{bmatrix} \begin{bmatrix} 2,561.1 \\ 0.55616 \end{bmatrix} = 182,402.
$$

The confidence interval is $1,424.4 \pm 1.96\sqrt{182,402}$ or $1,424.4 \pm 837.1$.

12.57 The partial derivatives of the mean are

$$\frac{\partial e^{\mu+\sigma^2/2}}{\partial \mu} = e^{\mu+\sigma^2/2} = 123.017$$

$$\frac{\partial e^{\mu+\sigma^2/2}}{\partial \sigma} = \sigma e^{\mu+\sigma^2/2} = 134.458.$$

The estimated variance is then

$$\begin{bmatrix} 123.017 & 134.458 \end{bmatrix} \begin{bmatrix} 0.1195 & 0 \\ 0 & 0.0597 \end{bmatrix} \begin{bmatrix} 123.017 \\ 134.458 \end{bmatrix} = 2,887.73.$$

12.58 The first partial derivatives are

$$\frac{\partial l(\alpha, \beta)}{\partial \alpha} = -5\alpha - 3\beta + 50$$

$$\frac{\partial l(\alpha, \beta)}{\partial \beta} = -3\alpha - 2\beta + 2.$$

The second partial derivatives are

$$\frac{\partial^2 l(\alpha, \beta)}{\partial \alpha^2} = -5$$

$$\frac{\partial^2 l(\alpha, \beta)}{\partial \beta^2} = -2$$

$$\frac{\partial^2 l(\alpha, \beta)}{\partial \alpha \partial \beta} = -3$$

and so the information matrix is

$$\begin{bmatrix} 5 & 3 \\ 3 & 2 \end{bmatrix}.$$

The covariance matrix is the inverse of the information, or

$$\begin{bmatrix} 2 & -3 \\ -3 & 5 \end{bmatrix}.$$

12.59 For the first case the observed loglikelihood and its derivatives are

$$l(\theta) = 62\ln[1 - e^{-1,000/\theta}] + 38\ln e^{-1,000/\theta}$$

$$l'(\theta) = \frac{-62e^{-1,000/\theta}(1,000/\theta^2)}{1 - e^{-1,000/\theta}} + 38,000/\theta^2$$

$$= \frac{-62,000e^{-1,000/\theta}\theta^{-2} + 38,000\theta^{-2} - 38,000e^{-1,000/\theta}\theta^{-2}}{1 - e^{-1,000/\theta}}$$

$$= \frac{38,000e^{1,000/\theta} - 100,000}{\theta^2(e^{1,000/\theta} - 1)}$$

$$l''(\theta) = \frac{-\theta^2(e^{1,000/\theta} - 1)38,000e^{1,000/\theta}1,000\theta^{-2}}{\theta^4(e^{1,000/\theta} - 1)^2}$$

Evaluating the second derivative at $\hat{\theta} = 1033.50$ and changing the sign gives $\hat{I}(\theta) = 0.00005372$. The reciprocal gives the variance estimate of 18,614.

Similarly, for the case with more information

$$l(\theta) = -62\ln\theta - 66,140\theta^{-1}$$
$$l'(\theta) = -62\theta^{-1} + 66,140\theta^{-2}$$
$$l''(\theta) = 62\theta^{-2} - 132,280\theta^{-3}$$
$$l''(1,066.77) = -0.000054482.$$

The variance estimate is the negative reciprocal, or 18,355.[1]

12.60 (a) $f(x) = px^{p-1}$. $\ln f(x) = \ln p + (p-1)\ln x$. $\partial^2 \ln f(x)/\partial p^2 = -p^{-2}$. $I(p) = nE(p^{-2}) = np^{-2}$. $\text{Var}(\hat{p}) \doteq p^2/n$.
(b) From Exercise 12.13, $\hat{p} = -n/\Sigma \ln x_j$. The CI is $\hat{p} \pm 1.96\hat{p}/\sqrt{n}$.
(c) $\mu = p/(1+p)$. $\hat{p}/(1+\hat{p})$. $\partial\mu/\partial p = (1+p)^{-2}$. $\text{Var}(\hat{\mu}) \doteq (1+p)^{-4}p^2/n$. The CI is $\hat{p}(1+\hat{p})^{-1} \pm 1.96\hat{p}(1+\hat{p})^{-2}/\sqrt{n}$.

12.61 (a) $\ln f(x) = -\ln\theta - x/\theta$. $\partial^2 \ln f(x)/\partial\theta^2 = \theta^{-2} - 2\theta^{-3}x$. $I(\theta) = nE(-\theta^{-2} + 2\theta^{-3}X) = n\theta^{-2}$. $\text{Var}(\hat{\theta}) \doteq \theta^2/n$.
(b) From Exercise 12.46, $\hat{\theta} = \bar{x}$. The CI is $\bar{x} \pm 1.96\bar{x}/\sqrt{n}$.
(c) $\text{Var}(X) = \theta^2$. $\partial\text{Var}(X)/\partial\theta = 2\theta$. $\widehat{\text{Var}(X)} = \bar{x}^2$. $\text{Var}[\widehat{\text{Var}(X)}] \doteq (2\theta)^2\theta^2/n = 4\theta^4/n$. The CI is $\bar{x}^2 \pm 1.96(2\bar{x}^2)/\sqrt{n}$.

12.62 $\ln f(x) = -(1/2)\ln(2\pi\theta) - x^2/(2\theta)$. $\partial^2 \ln f(x)/\partial\theta^2 = (2\theta^2)^{-1} - x^2(\theta^3)^{-1}$. $I(\theta) = nE[-(2\theta^2)^{-1} + X^2(\theta^3)^{-1}] = n(2\theta^2)^{-1}$ since $X \sim N(0,\theta)$. Then $\text{MSE}(\hat{\theta}) \doteq \text{Var}(\hat{\theta}) \doteq 2\theta^2/n \doteq 2\hat{\theta}^2/n = 8/40 = 0.2$.

---

[1] Comparing the variances at the same $\hat{\theta}$ value would be more useful.

12.63 (a) $L = F(2)[1 - F(2)]^3$. $F(2) = \int_0^2 2\lambda x e^{-\lambda x^2} dx = -e^{-\lambda x^2}\big|_0^2 = 1 - e^{-4\lambda}$. $l = \ln(1 - e^{-4\lambda}) - 12\lambda$. $\partial l/\partial\lambda = (1 - e^{-4\lambda})^{-1}4e^{-4\lambda} - 12 = 0$. $e^{-4\lambda} = 3/4$. $\hat{\lambda} = (1/4)\ln(4/3)$.
(b) $P_1(\lambda) = 1 - e^{-4\lambda}$, $P_2(\lambda) = e^{-4\lambda}$, $P_1'(\lambda) = 4e^{-4\lambda}$, $P_2'(\lambda) = -4e^{-4\lambda}$. $I(\lambda) = 4[16e^{-8\lambda}/(1 - e^{-4\lambda}) + 16e^{-8\lambda}/e^{-4\lambda}]$. $\widehat{\text{Var}(\hat{\lambda})} = \{4[16(9/16)/(1/4) + 16(9/16)/(3/4)]\}^{-1} = 1/192$.

12.64 From Exercise 12.14, $l = 81.61837(\alpha - 1) - 38{,}000\theta^{-1} - 10\ln\Gamma(\alpha) - 10\alpha\ln\theta$. Also, $\hat{\alpha} = 6.341$ and $\hat{\theta} = 599.3$. Using $v = 4$, we have

$$\frac{\partial^2 l(\alpha,\theta)}{\partial\alpha^2} \doteq \frac{l(6.3416341, 599.3) - 2l(6.341, 599.3) + l(6.3403659, 599.3)}{(.0006341)^2} = -1.70790$$

$$\frac{\partial^2 l(\alpha,\theta)}{\partial\alpha\partial\theta} \doteq \frac{l(6.34131705, 599.329965) - l(6.34131705, 599.270035)}{-l(6.34068295, 599.329965) + l(6.34068295, 599.270035)}{(.0006341)(.05993)}$$
$$= 0.0166861$$

$$\frac{\partial^2 l(\alpha,\theta)}{\partial\theta^2} \doteq \frac{l(6.341, 599.35993) - 2l(6.341, 599.3) + l(6.341, 599.25007)}{(.05993)^2} = -0.000176536$$

$$I(\hat{\alpha},\hat{\theta}) = \begin{bmatrix} 1.70790 & 0.0166861 \\ 0.0166861 & 0.000176536 \end{bmatrix}$$

and its inverse is

$$\widehat{\text{Var}} = \begin{bmatrix} 7.64976 & -723.055 \\ -723.055 & 74{,}007.7 \end{bmatrix}.$$

The mean is $\alpha\theta$ and so the derivative vector is $\begin{bmatrix} 599.3 & 6.341 \end{bmatrix}$. The variance of $\widehat{\alpha\theta}$ is estimated as 227,763 and a 95% CI is $3{,}800 \pm 1.97\sqrt{227{,}763} = 3{,}800 \pm 935$.

12.65 $\hat{\alpha} = 3.8629$. $\ln f(x) = \ln\alpha + \alpha\ln\lambda - (\alpha + 1)\ln(\lambda + x)$. $\partial^2\ln f(x)/\partial\alpha^2 = -\alpha^{-2}$. $I(\alpha) = n\alpha^{-2}$. $\text{Var}(\hat{\alpha}) \doteq \alpha^2/n$. Inserting the estimate gives 2.9844.

$$E(X \wedge 500) = \int_0^{500} x\alpha 1{,}000^\alpha (1{,}000 + x)^{-\alpha-1} dx$$
$$+ 500\int_{500}^\infty \alpha 1{,}000^\alpha (1{,}000 + x)^{-\alpha-1} dx$$
$$= \frac{1{,}000}{\alpha - 1} - (2/3)^\alpha \frac{1{,}500}{\alpha - 1}.$$

Evaluated at $\hat{\alpha}$ it is 239.88. The derivative with respect to α is

$$-\frac{1{,}000}{(\alpha - 1)^2} + (2/3)^\alpha \frac{1{,}500}{(\alpha - 1)^2} - (2/3)^\alpha \frac{1{,}500}{\alpha - 1}\ln(2/3)$$

which is -39.428 when evaluated at $\hat{\alpha}$. The variance of the LEV estimator is $(-39.4298)^2(2.9844) = 5{,}639.45$ and the CI is 239.88 ± 133.50.

12.66 (a) Let $\theta = \mu/\Gamma(1+\tau^{-1})$. From Appendix A, $E(X) = \theta\Gamma(1+\tau^{-1}) = \mu$.

(b) The density function is $f(x) = \exp\left\{-\left[\frac{\Gamma(1+\tau^{-1})x}{\mu}\right]^{\tau}\right\}\frac{\tau}{x}\left[\frac{\Gamma(1+\tau^{-1})x}{\mu}\right]^{\tau}$ and its logarithm is

$$\ln f(x) = -\left[\frac{\Gamma(1+\tau^{-1})x}{\mu}\right]^{\tau} + \ln\tau + \tau\ln[\Gamma(1+\tau^{-1})/\mu] - (\tau-1)\ln x.$$

The loglikelihood function is

$$l(\mu) = \sum_{j=1}^{n}\left\{-\left[\frac{\Gamma(1+\tau^{-1})x_j}{\mu}\right]^{\tau} + \ln\tau + \tau\ln[\Gamma(1+\tau^{-1})/\mu] - (\tau-1)\ln x_j\right\}$$

and its derivative is

$$l'(\mu) = \sum_{j=1}^{n}\left\{\tau\frac{[\Gamma(1+\tau^{-1})x_j]^{\tau}}{\mu^{\tau+1}} - \frac{\tau}{\mu}\right\}.$$

Setting the derivative equal to zero, moving the last term to the right hand side, multiplying by μ and dividing by τ produces the equation

$$\sum_{j=1}^{n}\left[\frac{\Gamma(1+\tau^{-1})x_j}{\mu}\right]^{\tau} = n$$

$$\left[\frac{\Gamma(1+\tau^{-1})}{\mu}\right]^{\tau}\sum_{j=1}^{n}x_j^{\tau} = n$$

$$\left[\frac{\Gamma(1+\tau^{-1})}{n^{1/\tau}}\right]^{\tau}\sum_{j=1}^{n}x_j^{\tau} = \mu^{\tau} \qquad (12.1)$$

and finally,

$$\hat{\mu} = \Gamma(1+\tau^{-1})\left(\sum_{j=1}^{n}\frac{x_j^{\tau}}{n}\right)^{1/\tau}.$$

(c) The second derivative of the loglikelihood function is

$$l''(\mu) = \sum_{j=1}^{n}\left\{-\tau(\tau+1)\frac{[\Gamma(1+\tau^{-1})x_j]^{\tau}}{\mu^{\tau+2}} + \frac{\tau}{\mu^2}\right\}$$

$$= \frac{n\tau}{\mu^2} - \tau(\tau+1)\Gamma(1+\tau^{-1})^{\tau}\mu^{-\tau-2}\sum_{j=1}^{n}x_j^{\tau}.$$

From (12.1), $\sum_{j=1}^{n} x_j^\tau = \left[\frac{n^{1/\tau}\hat{\mu}^\tau}{\Gamma(1+\tau^{-1})}\right]^\tau$ and therefore the observed information can be written as

$$
\begin{aligned}
l''(\hat{\mu}) &= \frac{n\tau}{\hat{\mu}^2} - \tau(\tau+1)\Gamma(1+\tau^{-1})^\tau \hat{\mu}^{-\tau-2}\left[\frac{n^{1/\tau}\hat{\mu}^\tau}{\Gamma(1+\tau^{-1})}\right]^\tau \\
&= \frac{n\tau}{\hat{\mu}^2} - \frac{\tau(\tau+1)n}{\hat{\mu}^2} = -\frac{\tau^2 n}{\hat{\mu}^2}
\end{aligned}
$$

and the negative reciprocal provides the variance estimate.

(d) The information requires the expected value of X^τ. From Appendix A it is $\theta^\tau \Gamma(1 + \frac{\tau}{\tau}) = \theta^\tau = [\mu/\Gamma(1+\tau^{-1})]^\tau$. Then

$$
\begin{aligned}
E[l''(\mu)] &= \frac{n\tau}{\mu^2} - \tau(\tau+1)\Gamma(1+\tau^{-1})^\tau \mu^{-\tau-2} n[\mu/\Gamma(1+\tau^{-1})]^\tau \\
&= \frac{n\tau}{\mu^2} - \frac{\tau(\tau+1)n}{\mu^2} = -\frac{\tau^2 n}{\mu^2}.
\end{aligned}
$$

Changing the sign, inverting, and substituting $\hat{\mu}$ for μ produces the same estimated variance as in part (c).

(e) To obtain the distribution of of $\hat{\mu}$, first obtain the distribution of $Y = X^\tau$. We have

$$
\begin{aligned}
S_Y(y) &= \Pr(Y > y) = \Pr(X^\tau > y) \\
&= \Pr(X > y^{1/\tau}) \\
&= \exp\left\{-\left[\frac{\Gamma(1+\tau^{-1})y^{1/\tau}}{\mu}\right]^\tau\right\} \\
&= \exp\left\{-\left[\frac{\Gamma(1+\tau^{-1})}{\mu}\right]^\tau y\right\}
\end{aligned}
$$

which is an exponential distribution with mean $[\mu/\Gamma(1+\tau^{-1})]^\tau$. Then $\sum_{j=1}^{n} X_j^\tau$ has a gamma distribution with parameters n and $[\mu/\Gamma(1+\tau^{-1})]^\tau$. Next look at

$$
\frac{\Gamma(1+\tau^{-1})^\tau}{\mu^\tau} \sum_{j=1}^{n} X_j^\tau.
$$

Multiplying by a constant changes the scale parameter, so the above variable has a gamma distribution with parameters n and 1. Now raise this expression to the $1/\tau$ power. Then

$$
\frac{\Gamma(1+\tau^{-1})}{\mu} \left(\sum_{j=1}^{n} X_j^\tau\right)^{1/\tau}
$$

has a transformed gamma distribution with parameters $\alpha = n$, $\theta = 1$, and $\tau = \tau$. To create $\hat{\mu}$, this function must be multiplied by $\mu/n^{1/\tau}$ which changes the scale parameter to $\theta = \mu/n^{1/\tau}$. From Appendix A,

$$E(\hat{\mu}) = \frac{\mu\Gamma(n + \tau^{-1})}{n^{1/\tau}\Gamma(n)}.$$

A similar argument provides the second moment and then a variance of

$$\text{Var}(\hat{\mu}) = \frac{\mu^2\Gamma(n + 2\tau^{-1})}{n^{2/\tau}\Gamma(n)} - \frac{\mu^2\Gamma(n + \tau^{-1})^2}{n^{2/\tau}\Gamma(n)^2}.$$

12.4   SECTION 12.4

12.67 $f(y) = \frac{12(4.801121)^{12}}{y(0.195951 + \ln y)^{13}}$. Let $W = \ln Y - 100 = \ln(Y/100)$. Then $y = 100e^w$ and $dy = 100e^w dw$. Thus,

$$f(w) = \frac{12(4.801121)^{12} 100e^w}{100e^w(0.195951 + w + \ln 100)^{13}} = \frac{12(4.801121)^{12}}{(4.801121 + w)^{13}}, \, y > 0$$

which is a Pareto density with $\alpha = 12$ and $\theta = 4.801121$.

12.68 $\pi(\alpha|\mathbf{x}) \propto \dfrac{\alpha^{10} 100^{10\alpha}}{\Pi x_j^{\alpha+1}} \dfrac{\alpha^{\gamma-1} e^{-\alpha/\theta}}{\theta^\gamma \Gamma(\gamma)}$

$$\propto \alpha^{10+\gamma-1} \exp[-\alpha(\theta^{-1} - 10\ln 100 + \Sigma \ln x_j)]$$

which is a gamma distribution with parameters $10 + \gamma$ and $(\theta^{-1} - 10\ln 100 + \Sigma \ln x_j)^{-1}$. The mean is $\hat{\alpha}_{Bayes} = (10 + \gamma)(\theta^{-1} - 10\ln 100 + \Sigma \ln x_j)^{-1}$. For the *mle*:

$$l = 10\ln\alpha + 10\alpha\ln 100 - (\alpha + 1)\Sigma \ln x_j,$$
$$l' = 10\alpha^{-1} + 10\ln 100 - \Sigma \ln x_j = 0$$

for $\hat{\alpha}_{mle} = 10(\Sigma \ln x_j - 10\ln 100)^{-1}$. The two estimators are equal when $\gamma = 0$ and $\theta = \infty$. This corresponds to $\pi(\alpha) = \alpha^{-1}$, an improper prior.

12.69 Generalizing from Exercise 12.68,

$$\hat{\alpha} = 100(\Sigma \ln x_j - 100\ln 100,000)^{-1}$$
$$= 100(1,208.4354 - 100\ln 100,000)^{-1} = 1.75.$$

12.70 (a) $\pi(\mu, \sigma|\mathbf{x}) \propto \sigma^{-n} \exp\left[-\Sigma \frac{1}{2}\left(\frac{\ln x_j - \mu}{\sigma}\right)^2\right]\sigma^{-1}$

(b) Let

$$l = \ln\pi(\mu, \sigma|\mathbf{x}) = -(n + 1)\ln\sigma - \frac{1}{2}\sigma^{-2}\sum(\ln x_j - \mu)^2.$$

Then

$$\partial l/\partial \mu = \frac{1}{2}\sigma^{-2} \sum 2(\ln x_j - \mu)(-1) = 0$$

and the solution is $\hat{\mu} = \frac{1}{n} \sum \ln x_j$. Also,

$$\partial l/\partial \sigma = -(n+1)\sigma^{-1} + \sigma^{-3} \sum (\ln x_j - \mu)^2 = 0$$

and so $\hat{\sigma} = \left[\frac{1}{n+1} \sum (\ln x_j - \hat{\mu})^2 \right]^{1/2}$.

(c)

$$\pi(\mu, \hat{\sigma}|\mathbf{x}) \propto \exp \left[-\sum \frac{1}{2} \left(\frac{\ln x_j - \mu}{\hat{\sigma}} \right)^2 \right]$$

$$= \exp \left(-\frac{1}{2} \frac{n\mu^2 - 2\mu\sum \ln x_j + \sum(\ln x_j)^2}{\hat{\sigma}^2} \right)$$

$$\propto \exp \left(-\frac{1}{2} \frac{\mu^2 - 2\mu\hat{\mu} + \hat{\mu}^2}{\hat{\sigma}^2/n} \right)$$

which is a normal *pdf* with mean $\hat{\mu}$ and variance $\hat{\sigma}^2/n$. The 95% HPD interval is $\hat{\mu} \pm 1.96\hat{\sigma}/\sqrt{n}$.

12.71 (a)

$$\pi(\theta|\mathbf{x}) \propto \frac{(\Pi x_j) \exp(-\theta^{-1}\Sigma x_j)}{\theta^{200}} \frac{\exp(-\lambda\theta^{-1})}{\theta^{\beta+1}}$$

$$\propto \frac{\exp[-\theta^{-1}(\lambda + \Sigma x_j)]}{\theta^{201+\beta}}$$

which is an inverse gamma pdf with parameters $200 + \beta$ and $30,000 + \lambda$.
(b) $E(2\theta|\mathbf{x}) = 2\frac{30,000+\lambda}{200+\beta-1}$. At $\beta = \lambda = 0$ it is $2\frac{30,000}{199} = 301.51$ while at $\beta = 2$ and $\lambda = 250$ it is $2\frac{30,250}{201} = 301.00$. For the first case, the inverse gamma parameters are 200 and 30,000. For the lower limit,

$$0.025 = \Pr(2\theta < a) = F(a/2) = 1 - \Gamma(200; 60,000/a)$$

for $a = 262.41$. Similarly the upper limit is 346.34. With parameters 202 and 30,250 the interval is $(262.14, 345.51)$.
(c) $\text{Var}(2\theta|\mathbf{x}) = 4\,\text{Var}(\theta|\mathbf{x}) = 4\left[\frac{(30,000+\lambda)^2}{(199+\beta)(198+\beta)} - \left(\frac{30,000+\lambda}{199+\beta} \right)^2 \right]$. The two variances are 459.13 and 452.99. The two CI's are 301.51 ± 42.00 and 301.00 ± 41.72
(d) $l = -\theta^{-1}30,000 - 200\ln\theta$. $l' = \theta^{-2}30,000 - 200\theta^{-1} = 0$. $\hat{\theta} = 150$. For the variance, $l' = \theta^{-2}\Sigma x_j - 200\theta^{-1}$, $l'' = -2\theta^{-3}\Sigma x_j + 200\theta^{-2}$, $E(-l'') = 2\theta^{-3}(200\theta) - 200\theta^{-2} = 200\theta^{-2}$ and so $\text{Var}(\hat{\theta}) \doteq \theta^2/200$ and $\text{Var}(2\theta) \doteq \theta^2/50$. An approximate CI is $300 \pm 1.96(150)/\sqrt{50} = 300 \pm 41.58$.

12.72 (a)

$$f(x) = \int_0^1 \binom{K}{x} \theta^x (1-\theta)^{K-x} \frac{\Gamma(a+b)}{\Gamma(a)\Gamma(b)} \theta^{a-1} (1-\theta)^{b-1} d\theta$$

$$= \binom{K}{x} \frac{\Gamma(a+b)}{\Gamma(a)\Gamma(b)} \frac{\Gamma(x+a)\Gamma(K-x+b)}{\Gamma(a+b+K)}$$

$$= \frac{K!}{x!(K-x)!} \frac{\Gamma(x+a)}{\Gamma(a)} \frac{\Gamma(K-x+b)}{\Gamma(b)} \frac{\Gamma(a+b)}{\Gamma(a+b+K)}$$

$$= \frac{a(a+1)\cdots(x+a-1)}{x!} \frac{b(b+1)\cdots(K-x+b-1)}{(K-x)!}$$

$$\times \frac{K!}{(a+b)\cdots(K+a+b-1)}$$

$$= \frac{(-1)^x \binom{-a}{x} (-1)^{K-x} \binom{-b}{K-x}}{(-1)^K \binom{-a-b}{K}} = \frac{\binom{-a}{x}\binom{-b}{K-x}}{\binom{-a-b}{K}}$$

$E(X|\theta) = K\theta$. $E(X) = E[E(X|\theta)] = E(K\theta) = K\frac{a}{a+b}$.

(b) $\pi(\theta|\mathbf{x}) \propto \theta^{\Sigma x_j}(1-\theta)^{\Sigma K_j - x_j}\theta^{a-1}(1-\theta)^{b-1}$ which is a beta density. Therefore the actual posterior distribution is

$$\pi(\theta|\mathbf{x}) = \frac{\Gamma(a+b+\Sigma K_j)}{\Gamma(a+\Sigma x_j)\Gamma(b+\Sigma K_j + \Sigma x_j)} \theta^{a+\Sigma x_j - 1}(1-\theta)^{b+\Sigma K_j - \Sigma x_j - 1}$$

with mean

$$E(\theta|\mathbf{x}) = \frac{a+\Sigma x_j}{a+b+\Sigma K_j}.$$

12.73 (a)

$$f(x) = \int_0^\infty \theta e^{-\theta x} \frac{\theta^{\alpha-1}e^{-\theta/\beta}}{\Gamma(\alpha)\beta^\alpha} d\theta$$

$$= \frac{1}{\Gamma(\alpha)\beta^\alpha} \int_0^\infty \theta^\alpha e^{-\theta(x+\beta^{-1})} d\theta$$

$$= \frac{1}{\Gamma(\alpha)\beta^\alpha}\Gamma(\alpha+1)(x+\beta^{-1})^{-\alpha-1}$$

$$= \alpha\beta^{-\alpha}(\beta^{-1}+x)^{-\alpha-1}$$

$E(X|\theta) = \theta^{-1}$.

$$E(X) = E[E(X|\theta)] = E(\theta^{-1})$$

$$= \int_0^\infty \theta^{-1}\frac{\theta^{\alpha-1}e^{-\theta/\beta}}{\Gamma(\alpha)\beta^\alpha} d\theta = \frac{\Gamma(\alpha-1)\beta^{\alpha-1}}{\Gamma(\alpha)\beta^\alpha} = \frac{1}{\beta(\alpha-1)}.$$

(b) $\pi(\theta|\mathbf{x}) \propto \theta^n e^{-\theta\Sigma x_j}\theta^{\alpha-1}e^{-\theta/\beta} = \theta^{n+\alpha-1}e^{-\theta(\Sigma x_j + \beta^{-1})}$ which is a gamma density. Therefore the actual posterior distribution is

$$\pi(\theta|\mathbf{x}) = \frac{\theta^{n+\alpha-1}e^{-\theta(\Sigma x_j + \beta^{-1})}}{\Gamma(n+\alpha)(\Sigma x_j + \beta^{-1})^{-n-\alpha}}$$

with mean

$$E(\theta|\mathbf{x}) = \frac{n + \alpha}{\Sigma x_j + \beta^{-1}}.$$

12.74 (a)

$$
\begin{aligned}
f(x) &= \int f(x|\theta)b(\theta)d\theta \\
&= \binom{r + x - 1}{x} \frac{\Gamma(a+b)}{\Gamma(a)\Gamma(b)} \int_0^1 \theta^{r+a-1}(1-\theta)^{b+x-1}d\theta \\
&= \binom{r + x - 1}{x} \frac{\Gamma(a+b)}{\Gamma(a)\Gamma(b)} \frac{\Gamma(r+a)\Gamma(b+x)}{\Gamma(r+a+b+x)} \\
&= \frac{\Gamma(r+x)}{\Gamma(r)x!} \frac{\Gamma(a+b)}{\Gamma(a)\Gamma(b)} \frac{\Gamma(a+r)\Gamma(b+x)}{\Gamma(a+r+b+x)}
\end{aligned}
$$

(b)

$$
\begin{aligned}
\pi(\theta|\mathbf{x}) &\propto \prod f(x_j|\theta)b(\theta) \\
&\propto \theta^{nr}(1-\theta)^{\Sigma x_j}\theta^{a-1}(1-\theta)^{b-1} \\
&= \theta^{a+nr-1}(1-\theta)^{b+\Sigma x_j-1}
\end{aligned}
$$

Hence, $\pi(\theta|\mathbf{x})$ is Beta with parameters

$$
\begin{aligned}
a^* &= \alpha + nr \\
b^* &= b + \sum x_j \\
E(\theta|\mathbf{x}) &= \frac{a^*}{a^* + b^*} = \frac{a + nr}{a + nr + b + \sum x_j}
\end{aligned}
$$

12.75 (a)

$$
\begin{aligned}
f(x) &= \int f(x|\theta)b(\theta)d\theta = \int_0^\infty \sqrt{\frac{\theta}{2\pi}} e^{-\frac{\theta}{2}(x-\mu)^2} \frac{\beta^\alpha}{\Gamma(\alpha)} \theta^{\alpha-1} e^{-\beta\theta} d\theta \\
&= \frac{\beta^\alpha}{(2\pi)^{1/2}\Gamma(\alpha)} \int_0^\infty \theta^{\frac{1}{2}+\alpha-1} e \exp\left\{-\theta\left[\frac{1}{2}(x-\mu)^2 + \beta\right]\right\} d\theta \\
&= \frac{\beta^\alpha}{(2\pi)^{1/2}\Gamma(\alpha)} \frac{\Gamma\left(\alpha + \frac{1}{2}\right)}{\left[\frac{1}{2}(x-\mu)^2 + \beta\right]^{\alpha+\frac{1}{2}}} \\
&= \frac{\Gamma\left(\alpha + \frac{1}{2}\right)}{\sqrt{2\pi\beta}\Gamma(\alpha)} \left[1 + \frac{1}{2\beta}(x-\mu)^2\right]^{-\alpha-\frac{1}{2}}
\end{aligned}
$$

(b)

$$
\begin{aligned}
\pi(\theta|\mathbf{x}) &\propto \left[\prod f(x_j|\theta)\right]\pi(\theta) \\
&\propto \theta^{n/2}\exp\left[-\frac{\theta}{2}\sum(x_j-\mu)^2\right]\theta^{\alpha-1}e^{-\beta\theta} \\
&= \theta^{\frac{n}{2}+\alpha-1}\exp\left\{-\theta\left[\frac{1}{2}\sum(x_j-\mu)^2 + \beta\right]\right\} = \theta^{\alpha^*-1}e^{-\theta\beta^*}
\end{aligned}
$$

where $\alpha^* = \alpha + \frac{n}{2}$, $\beta^* = \beta + \frac{1}{2}\sum(x_j - \mu)^2$. Therefore, $b(\theta|\mathbf{x})$ is gamma (α^*, β^*) and $\mathrm{E}(\theta|\mathbf{x}) = \frac{\alpha^*}{\beta^*} = \frac{\alpha + \frac{n}{2}}{\beta + \frac{1}{2}\sum(x_j - \mu)^2}$

12.76
$$f(x; p) = \binom{n}{x}p^x(1-p)^{n-x} = \binom{n}{x}(1-p)^n\left(\frac{p}{1-p}\right)^x$$
$$= \binom{n}{x}(1-p)^n\exp\{x\ln[p/(1-p)]\}$$

If we let $p(x) = \binom{n}{x}$, $q(\theta) = (1-p)^{-n}$, and $\theta = -\ln\frac{p}{1-p}$, then $p = \frac{1}{1+e^\theta}$ and $q(\theta) = (1-p)^{-n} = \left(\frac{e^\theta}{1+e^\theta}\right)^{-n}$.

12.77 $f(x) = \frac{\Gamma(\alpha+x)}{\Gamma(\alpha)x!}\frac{1}{\left(\frac{1+\beta}{\beta}\right)^\alpha}e^{\ln\left(\frac{1}{1+\beta}\right)}$. Then let $\theta = \ln(1+\beta)$. Then $\frac{1+\beta}{\beta} = \frac{1}{1-e^{-\theta}}$. The density function can be written $f(x) = \frac{\Gamma(\alpha+x)}{\Gamma(\alpha)x!}\frac{1}{\left(\frac{1}{1-e^{-\theta}}\right)^\alpha}e^{-x\theta}$. This is of the desired form with $p(x) = \frac{\Gamma(\alpha+x)}{\Gamma(\alpha)x!}$ and $q(\theta) = \left(\frac{1}{1-e^{-\theta}}\right)^\alpha$.

12.78
$$L(\theta) = \prod_{j=1}^{n} f(x_j; \theta) = \prod_{j=1}^{n}\frac{p(x_j)e^{-\theta x_j}}{q(\theta)}$$
$$\ell(\theta) = \sum_{j=1}^{n}\ln p(x_j) - \theta\sum_{j=1}^{n}x_j - n\ln q(\theta)$$
$$\ell'(\theta) = -\sum_{j=1}^{n}x_j - n\frac{q'(\theta)}{q(\theta)}$$

Therefore, $-\dfrac{q'(\hat{\theta})}{q(\hat{\theta})} = \overline{x}$

But, $-\dfrac{q'(\theta)}{q(\theta)} = E(x) = \mu(\theta)$

and so, $\mu(\hat{\theta}) = \overline{x}$

12.79 For the mean,

$$\ln f(x; \theta) = \ln p(m, x) - m\theta x - m\ln q(\theta)$$

$$\frac{\partial\ln f(x;\theta)}{\partial\theta} = \frac{\partial f(x;\theta)}{\partial\theta}\frac{1}{f(x;\theta)} = \left[-mx - \frac{mq'(\theta)}{q(\theta)}\right]$$

$$\frac{\partial f(x;\theta)}{\partial\theta} = \left[-mx - \frac{mq'(\theta)}{q(\theta)}\right]f(x;\theta)$$

$$0 = \int \frac{\partial f(x;\theta)}{\partial\theta}dx = -m\int xf(x;\theta)dx - \frac{mq'(\theta)}{q(\theta)}\int f(x;\theta)dx$$

$$= -m\mathrm{E}(X) - \frac{mq'(\theta)}{q(\theta)}$$

$$\mathrm{E}(X) = q'(\theta)/q(\theta) = \mu(\theta)$$

For the variance,

$$\frac{\partial f(x;\theta)}{\partial\theta} = -m[x - \mu(\theta)]f(x;\theta)$$

$$\frac{\partial^2 f(x;\theta)}{\partial\theta^2} = m\mu'(\theta)f(x;\theta) - m[x - \mu(\theta)]\frac{\partial f(x;\theta)}{\partial\theta}$$

$$= m\mu'(\theta)f(x;\theta) + m^2[x - \mu(\theta)]^2 f(x;\theta)$$

$$0 = \int \frac{\partial^2 f(x;\theta)}{\partial\theta^2}dx = m\mu'(\theta)\int f(x;\theta)dx + m^2\int [x - \mu(\theta)]^2 f(x;\theta)dx$$

$$= m\mu'(\theta) + m^2 \mathrm{Var}(X)$$

$$\mathrm{Var}(X) = -\mu'(\theta)/m$$

12.80 (a)

$$f(x|\theta) = \frac{p(x)e^{-\theta x}}{q(\theta)}$$

$$M_X(z|\theta) = \int \frac{p(x)e^{-\theta x}}{q(\theta)}e^{zx}dx$$

$$= \frac{1}{q(\theta)}\int p(x)e^{-(\theta-z)x}dx$$

$$= \frac{q(\theta - z)}{q(\theta)}.$$

Hence, $M_S(z) = [q(\theta - z)/q(\theta)]^n = q_*(\theta - z)/q_*(\theta)$ where $q_*(\theta) = [q(\theta)]^n$.

The distribution of S is of same form as X except that $p_*(x)$ may depend on n. Hence

$$f_{S|\Theta}(s|\theta) = p_n(s)\frac{e^{-\theta s}}{q(\theta)^n}$$

(b)

$$\pi(\theta|\mathbf{x}) \propto f(\mathbf{x},\theta) = f(\mathbf{x}|\theta)\,\pi(\theta)$$

$$= \prod f(x_j|\theta)\pi(\theta)$$

$$\propto \frac{e^{-\theta\Sigma x_j}}{[q(\theta)]^n}\pi(\theta)$$

$$= \frac{e^{-\theta s}}{[q(\theta)]^n}\pi(\theta)$$

But $\pi\left(\theta|S\right) \propto f\left(s|\theta\right)\pi(\theta) \propto \frac{e^{-\theta t}}{[q(\theta)]}\pi(\theta)$.

12.81 (a) Let N be Poisson(λ).

$$
\begin{aligned}
f(x) &= \sum_{n=x}^{\infty} \frac{n!}{x!(n-x)!}p^x(1-p)^{n-x}e^{-\lambda}\lambda^n/n! \\
&= \left(\frac{p}{1-p}\right)^x \frac{e^{-\lambda}}{x!} \sum_{n=x}^{\infty} \frac{[(1-p)\lambda]^n}{(n-x)!} \\
&= \left(\frac{p}{1-p}\right)^x \frac{e^{-\lambda}}{x!} \sum_{n=0}^{\infty} \frac{[(1-p)\lambda]^{n+x}}{n!} \\
&= \left(\frac{p}{1-p}\right)^x \frac{e^{-\lambda}}{x!} [(1-p)\lambda]^x e^{(1-p)\lambda} \\
&= e^{-p\lambda}(p\lambda)^x/x!, \text{ a Poisson distribution with parameter } p\lambda.
\end{aligned}
$$

(b) Let N be binomial(m,r).

$$
\begin{aligned}
f(x) &= \sum_{n=x}^{m} \frac{n!}{x!(n-x)!}p^x(1-p)^{n-x}\frac{m!}{n!(m-n)!}r^n(1-r)^{m-n} \\
&= \left(\frac{p}{1-p}\right)^x(1-r)^m\frac{m!}{x!}\sum_{n=x}^{m}\left(\frac{[1-p]r}{1-r}\right)^n\frac{1}{(n-x)!(m-n)!} \\
&= \left(\frac{p}{1-p}\right)^x(1-r)^m\frac{m!}{x!}\sum_{n=0}^{m-x}\left(\frac{[1-p]r}{1-r}\right)^{n+x}\frac{1}{n!(m-n-x)!} \\
&= \left(\frac{p}{1-p}\right)^x(1-r)^m\frac{m!}{x!}\left(\frac{[1-p]r}{1-r}\right)^x\frac{1}{(m-x)!} \\
&\quad \times\sum_{n=0}^{m-x}\left(\frac{[1-p]r}{1-rp}\right)^n\left(\frac{1-r}{1-rp}\right)^{-n}\frac{(m-x)!}{n!(m-n-x)!} \\
&= \left(\frac{pr}{1-r}\right)^x(1-r)^m\frac{m!}{x!(m-x)!}\left(\frac{1-r}{1-rp}\right)^{-m+x} \\
&\quad \times\sum_{n=0}^{m-x}\left(\frac{[1-p]r}{1-rp}\right)^n\left(\frac{1-r}{1-rp}\right)^{m-n-x}\frac{(m-x)!}{n!(m-n-x)!} \\
&= \frac{m!}{x!(m-x)!}(pr)^x(1-rp)^{m-x}, \text{ which is binomial } (m,pr).
\end{aligned}
$$

(c) Let N be negative binomial (r, β).

$$
\begin{aligned}
f(x) &= \sum_{n=x}^{\infty} \frac{n!}{x!(n-x)!} p^x (1-p)^{n-x} \\
&\quad \times \left(\frac{\beta}{1+\beta}\right)^n \left(\frac{1}{1+\beta}\right)^r \frac{r(r+1)\cdots(r+n-1)}{n!} \\
&= \left(\frac{p}{1-p}\right)^x \left(\frac{1}{1+\beta}\right)^r \frac{1}{x!} \sum_{n=x}^{\infty} \left[\frac{\beta(1-p)}{1+\beta}\right]^n \frac{r(r+1)\cdots(r+n-1)}{(n-x)!} \\
&= \left(\frac{p}{1-p}\right)^x \left(\frac{1}{1+\beta}\right)^r \frac{1}{x!} \sum_{n=0}^{\infty} \left[\frac{\beta(1-p)}{1+\beta}\right]^{n+x} \\
&\quad \times \frac{r(r+1)\cdots(r+n+x-1)}{n!} \\
&= \left(\frac{p\beta}{1+\beta}\right)^x \left(\frac{1}{1+\beta}\right)^r \frac{r(r+1)\cdots(r+x-1)}{x!} \\
&\quad \times \sum_{n=0}^{\infty} \left[\frac{\beta(1-p)}{1+\beta}\right]^n \frac{(r+x)\cdots(r+n+x-1)}{n!}
\end{aligned}
$$

and the summand is almost a negative binomial density with the term

$$
\left[1 - \frac{\beta(1-p)}{1+\beta}\right]^{r+x} = \left(\frac{1+p\beta}{1+\beta}\right)^{r+x}
$$

missing. Place it in the sum so the sum is one and then divide by it to produce

$$
\begin{aligned}
f(x) &= \left(\frac{1+p\beta}{1+\beta}\right)^{-r-x} \\
&= \left(\frac{p\beta}{1+p\beta}\right)^x \left(\frac{1}{1+p\beta}\right)^r \frac{r(r+1)\cdots(r+x-1)}{x!}
\end{aligned}
$$

which is negative binomial with parameters r and $p\beta$.

12.82 Let D be the die. Then

$$
\begin{aligned}
&\Pr(D = 2|2, 3, 4, 1, 4) \\
&= \frac{\Pr(2, 3, 4, 1, 4|D = 2)\Pr(D = 2)}{\Pr(2, 3, 4, 1, 4|D = 1)\Pr(D = 1) + \Pr(2, 3, 4, 1, 4|D = 2)\Pr(D = 2)} \\
&= \frac{\frac{1}{6}\frac{1}{6}\frac{3}{6}\frac{1}{6}\frac{3}{6}\frac{1}{2}}{\frac{3}{6}\frac{1}{6}\frac{1}{6}\frac{1}{6}\frac{1}{6}\frac{1}{2} + \frac{1}{6}\frac{1}{6}\frac{3}{6}\frac{1}{6}\frac{3}{6}\frac{1}{2}} = \frac{3}{4}.
\end{aligned}
$$

12.83 (a) $\Pr(Y = 0) = \int_0^1 e^{-\theta}(1)d\theta = 1 - e^{-1} = 0.63212 > 0.35$.

(b) $\Pr(Y = 0) = \int_0^1 \theta^2(1)d\theta = 1/3 < 0.35.$
(c) $\Pr(Y = 0) = \int_0^1 (1 - \theta)^2(1)d\theta = 1/3 < 0.35.$
  Only (a) is possible.

12.84 $\Pr(H = 1/4|d = 1)$

$$= \frac{\Pr(d = 1|H = 1/4)\Pr(H = 1/4)}{\Pr(d = 1|H = 1/4)\Pr(H = 1/4) + \Pr(d = 1|H = 1/2)\Pr(H = 1/2)}$$

$$= \frac{\frac{1}{4}\frac{4}{5}}{\frac{1}{4}\frac{4}{5} + \frac{1}{2}\frac{1}{5}} = \frac{2}{3}$$

12.85 The posterior pdf is proportional to

$$\frac{e^{-\theta}\theta^0}{0!}e^{-\theta} = e^{-2\theta}.$$

This is an exponential distribution. The pdf is $\pi(\theta|y = 0) = 2e^{-2\theta}$.

12.86 The posterior pdf is proportional to

$$\frac{e^{-\theta}\theta^1}{1!}\theta e^{-\theta} = \theta^2 e^{-2\theta}.$$

This is a gamma distribution with parameters 3 and 0.5. The pdf is $\pi(\theta|y = 1) = 4\theta^2 e^{-2\theta}$.

12.87 From Example 12.42 the posterior distribution is gamma with $\alpha = 50 + 177 = 227$ and $\theta = 0.002/[1,850(0.002) + 1] = 1/2,350$. The mean is $\alpha\theta = 0.096596$ and the variance is $\alpha\theta^2 = 0.000041105$. The coefficient of variation is $\sqrt{\alpha\theta^2}/(\alpha\theta) = 1/\sqrt{\alpha} = 0.066372$.

12.88 The posterior pdf is proportional to

$$\binom{3}{1}\theta^1(1 - \theta)^{3-1}6\theta(1 - \theta) \propto \theta^2(1 - \theta)^3.$$

This is a beta distribution with pdf $\pi(\theta|r = 1) = 60\theta^2(1 - \theta)^3$.

12.89 The equations are $\alpha\theta = 0.14$ and $\alpha\theta^2 = 0.0004$. The solution is $\alpha = 49$ and $\theta = 1/350$. From Example 12.42 the posterior distribution is gamma with $\alpha = 49 + 110 = 159$ and $\theta = (1/350)/[620(1/350) + 1] = 1/970$. The mean is $159/970 = 0.16392$ and the variance is $159/970^2 = 0.00016899$.

12.90 The prior exponential distribution is also a gamma distribution with $\alpha = 1$ and $\theta = 2$. From Example 12.42 the posterior distribution is gamma with $\alpha = 1 + 3 = 4$ and $\theta = 2/[1(2) + 1] = 2/3$. The pdf is $\pi(\lambda|y = 3) = 27\lambda^3 e^{-3\lambda/2}/32$.

12.91 (a) The posterior distribution is proportional to

$$\binom{3}{2}\theta^2(1 - \theta)280\theta^3(1 - \theta)^4 \propto \theta^5(1 - \theta)^5$$

which is a beta distribution. The pdf is $\pi(\theta|y = 2) = 2772\theta^5(1 - \theta)^5$.
(b) The mean is $6/(6 + 6) = 0.5$.

12.92 The posterior pdf is proportional to

$$te^{-t5}te^{-t} = t^2 e^{-t6}$$

which is a gamma distribution with $\alpha = 3$ and $\beta = 1/6$. The posterior pdf is $\pi(t|x = 5) = 108t^2 e^{-6t}$.

12.93 (a)
$$
\begin{aligned}
f(x|\theta_1, \theta_2) &= \sqrt{\frac{\theta_2}{2\pi}}\exp\left[-\frac{\theta_2}{2}(x - \theta_1)^2\right] \\
b(\theta_1|\theta_2) &= \sqrt{\frac{\theta_2}{2\pi\sigma^2}}\exp\left[-\frac{\theta_2}{2\sigma^2}(\theta_1 - \mu)^2\right] \\
b(\theta_2) &= \frac{\beta^\alpha}{\Gamma(\alpha)}\theta_2^{\alpha-1}e^{-\beta\theta_2}
\end{aligned}
$$

$$
\begin{aligned}
\pi(\theta_1, \theta_2|\mathbf{x}) &\propto \left[\prod_{j=1}^{r}f(x_j|\theta_1, \theta_2)\right]\pi(\theta_1|\theta_2)\pi(\theta_2) \\
&\propto \theta_2^{n/2}\exp\left[-\frac{\theta_2}{2}\sum(x_j - \theta_1)^2\right]\theta_2^{1/2} \\
&\quad \times \exp\left[-\frac{\theta_2}{2\sigma_2}(\theta_1 - \mu)^2\right]\theta_2^{\alpha-1}e^{-\beta\theta_2} \\
&= \theta_2^{\alpha + \frac{n+1}{2} - 1} \\
&\quad \times \exp\left\{-\theta_2\left[\beta + \frac{1}{2}\left(\frac{\theta_1 - \mu}{\sigma}\right)^2 + \frac{1}{2}\sum(x_j - \theta_1)^2\right]\right\}
\end{aligned}
$$

$$\pi\left(\theta_1|\theta_2,\mathbf{x}\right) \;\propto\; \pi\left(\theta_1,\theta_2|\mathbf{x}\right)$$

$$\propto\; \exp\left[-\frac{\theta_2}{2}\left(\frac{\theta_1^2}{\sigma^2} - \frac{2\mu\theta_1}{\sigma^2} + n\theta_1^2 - 2\theta_1\sum x_j\right)\right]$$

$$=\; \exp-\frac{1}{2}\left[\theta_1^2\left(\frac{\theta_2}{\sigma_2} + n\theta_2\right) - 2\theta_1\left(\frac{\mu\theta_2}{\sigma^2} + \theta_2\sum x_j\right)\right]$$

which is normal with variance $\sigma_*^2 = \left[\frac{\theta_2}{\sigma_2^2} + n\theta_2\right]^{-1} = \frac{\sigma^2}{\theta_2(1+n\sigma^2)}$ and mean μ_* which satisfies $\frac{\mu_*}{\sigma_*^2} = \frac{\mu\theta_2}{\sigma^2} + \theta_2 n\bar{x}$. Then, $\mu_* = \frac{\mu}{1+n\sigma^2} + \frac{n\sigma^2\bar{x}}{1+n\sigma^2}$.

For the posterior distribution of θ_2,

$$\pi\left(\theta_2|\mathbf{x}\right) \;\propto\; \int \pi\left(\theta_1,\theta_2|\mathbf{x}\right) d\theta_1$$

$$=\; \theta_2^{\alpha+\frac{n+1}{2}-1} e^{-\theta_2\beta}$$

$$\times \int \exp\left\{-\frac{\theta_2}{2}\left[\left(\frac{\theta_1-\mu}{\sigma}\right)^2 + \sum(x_j-\theta_1)^2\right]\right\} d\theta_1$$

Now $\sum(x_j-\theta_1)^2 = \sum(x_j-\bar{x})^2 + n\left(\bar{x}-\theta_1\right)^2$ and therefore

$$\pi\left(\theta_2|\mathbf{x}\right) \;\propto\; \theta_2^{\alpha+\frac{n+1}{2}-1} \exp\left\{-\theta_2\left[\beta + \frac{1}{2}\sum(x_j-\bar{x})^2\right]\right\}$$

$$\times \int \exp\left\{-\frac{\theta_2}{2}\left[\left(\frac{\theta_1-\mu}{\sigma}\right)^2 + n\left(\bar{x}-\theta_1\right)^2\right]\right\} d\theta_1$$

In order to evaluate the integral, complete the square as follows

$$-\frac{\theta_2}{2}\left[\left(\frac{\theta_1-\mu}{\sigma}\right)^2 + n\left(\bar{x}-\theta_1\right)^2\right]$$

$$=\; -\frac{\theta_2}{2}\left[\theta_1^2(1/\sigma^2 + n) - 2\theta_1(\mu/\sigma^2 + n\bar{x}) + \mu^2/\sigma^2 + n\bar{x}^2\right]$$

$$=\; -\frac{1}{2}\theta_2(1/\sigma^2 + n)\left(\theta_1 - \frac{\mu+n\sigma^2\bar{x}}{1+n\sigma^2}\right)^2 + \frac{\theta_2}{2}\left[\frac{(\mu+n\sigma^2\bar{x})^2}{\sigma^2(1+n\sigma^2)} - \frac{\mu^2}{\sigma^2} - n\bar{x}\right]$$

The first term is a normal density and integrates to $[\theta_2(1/\sigma^2 + n)]^{-1/2}$. The second term does not involve θ_1 and so factors out of the integral. The posterior density contains θ_2 raised to the $\alpha+\frac{n}{2}-1$ power and an exponential term involving θ_2 multiplied by

$$\beta + \frac{1}{2}\sum(x_j-\bar{x})^2 + \frac{1}{2}\left[\frac{(\mu+n\sigma^2\bar{x})^2}{\sigma^2(1+n\sigma^2)} - \frac{\mu^2}{\sigma^2} - n\bar{x}\right]$$

$$=\; \beta + \frac{1}{2}\sum(x_j-\bar{x})^2 + \frac{n(\bar{x}-\mu)^2}{2(1+n\sigma^2)}\;.$$

This constitutes a gamma density with the desired parameters.

(b) Because the mean of Θ_1 given Θ_2 and $\mathbf{x}$ does not depend on θ_2 it is also the mean of Θ_1 given just $\mathbf{x}$ which is μ_*. The mean of Θ_2 given $\mathbf{x}$ is the ratio of the parameters or

$$\frac{\alpha + n/2}{\beta + \frac{1}{2}\sum(x_j - \bar{x})^2 + \frac{n(\bar{x}-\mu)^2}{2(1+n\sigma^2)}}.$$

12.5   SECTION 12.5

12.94 (a) $\hat{q} = \bar{X}/m$, $E(\hat{q}) = E(X)/m = mq/m = q$.

(b)
$$\begin{aligned}
\mathrm{Var}(\hat{q}) &= \mathrm{Var}(\bar{X})/m^2 = \mathrm{Var}(X)/(nm^2) \\
&= mq(1-q)/(nm^2) = q(1-q)/(nm).
\end{aligned}$$

(c)
$$l = \sum_{j=1}^{n} \ln\binom{m}{x_j} + x_j \ln q + (m - x_j)\ln(1-q)$$

$$l' = \sum_{j=1}^{n} x_j q^{-1} - (m - x_j)(1-q)^{-1}$$

$$l'' = \sum_{j=1}^{n} -x_j q^{-2} - (m - x_j)(1-q)^{-2}$$

$$\begin{aligned}
I(q) &= E(-l'') = n[mqq^{-2} + (m - mq)(1-q)^{-2}] \\
&= nm[q^{-1} + (1-q)^{-1}].
\end{aligned}$$

The reciprocal is $(1-q)q/(nm)$.

(d) $\hat{q} \pm z_{\alpha/2}\sqrt{\hat{q}(1-\hat{q})/(nm)}$.

(e)
$$1 - \alpha = \Pr\left(-z_{\alpha/2} \le \frac{\hat{q} - q}{\sqrt{q(1-q)/(nm)}} \le z_{\alpha/2}\right)$$

and so

$$|\hat{q} - q| \le z_{\alpha/2}\sqrt{\frac{q(1-q)}{nm}}$$

which implies

$$nm(\hat{q} - q)^2 \le z_{\alpha/2}^2 q(1-q).$$

Then

$$(nm + z_{\alpha/2}^2)q^2 - (2nm\hat{q} + z_{\alpha/2}^2)q + nm\hat{q}^2 \le 0.$$

The boundaries of the CI are the roots of this quadratic:

$$\frac{2nm\hat{q} + z_{\alpha/2}^2 \pm z_{\alpha/2}\sqrt{1 + 4nm\hat{q}(1-\hat{q})}}{2(nm + z_{\alpha/2}^2)}.$$

12.95 Because $r = 1$, $\hat{\beta} = \bar{X}$.

$$
\begin{aligned}
\mathrm{Var}(\bar{X}) &= \mathrm{Var}(X)/n = \beta(1+\beta)/n. \\
l &= \sum_{j=1}^{n} \ln \mathrm{Pr}(N = x_j) = \sum_{j=1}^{n} \ln[\beta^{x_j}(1+\beta)^{-x_j-1}] \\
&= \sum_{j=1}^{n} x_j \ln(\beta) - (x_j + 1)\ln(1+\beta) \\
l'' &= \sum_{j=1}^{n} -x_j \beta^{-2} + (x_j + 1)(1+\beta)^{-2} \\
E(l'') &= -n\beta\beta^{-2} + n(\beta+1)(1+\beta)^{-2} = n/[\beta(1+\beta)]
\end{aligned}
$$

The reciprocal matches the true variance of the *mle*.

12.96 (a) The mle is the sample mean, $[905 + 2(45) + 3(2)]/10,000 = 0.1001$. and the CI is $0.1001 \pm 1.96\sqrt{0.1001/10,000} = 0.1001 \pm 0.0062$ or $(0.0939, 0.1063)$.
(b) The mle is the sample mean, 0.1001. The CI is $0.1001 \pm 1.96\sqrt{0.1001(1.1001}$ 0.1001 ± 0.0065 or $(0.0936, 0.1066)$.
(c) Numerical methods yield $\hat{r} = 56.1856$ and $\hat{\beta} = 0.00178159$.
(d) $\hat{q} = \bar{x}/4 = 0.025025$.
(e) $0.025025 \pm 1.96\sqrt{0.025025(0.974975)/40,000} = 0.025025 \pm 0.001531$ and $\frac{2(10,000)(4)(0.025025)+1.96^2 \pm 1.96\sqrt{1+4(10,000)(4)(0.025025(0.974975)}}{2[10,000(4)+1.96^2]}$ or 0.025071 ± 0.001
(f) The likelihood function increases as $m \to \infty$ and $q \to 0$.

12.97 (a) The sample means are – underinsured: $109/1,000 = 0.109$ and insured: $57/1,000 = 0.057$.
(b) The Poisson parameter is the sum of the individual parameters, $0.109 + 0.057 = 0.166$.

12.98 (a) $\hat{\lambda}$ is the sample mean, 0.166.
(b) Let n_{ij} be the number observations of j counts from population i where $j = 0, 1, \ldots$ and $i = 1, 2$. The individual estimators are $\hat{\lambda}_i = \sum_{j=0}^{\infty} j n_{ij}$. From the Theorem the estimator for the sum is the sum of the estimators which is $\hat{\lambda} = \sum_{j=0}^{\infty} j(n_{1j} + n_{2j})$ which is also the estimator from the combined sample.
(c) $\hat{\beta} = 0.166$.
(d) Numerical methods yield $\hat{r} = 0.656060$ and $\hat{\beta} = 0.253026$.
(e) $\hat{q} = 0.177/7 = 0.0237143$.
(f) The likelihood function increases as $m \to \infty$ and $q \to 0$.

12.99 (a) $\hat{\lambda} = 15.688$. When writing the likelihood function, a typical term is $(p_4 + p_5 + p_6)^{47}$ and the likelihood must be numerically maximized.
(b) $\hat{\beta} = 19.145$.
(c) $\hat{r} = 0.56418$ and $\hat{\beta} = 37.903$.

12.6 SECTION 12.6

12.100 Fitting Frank's copula produces scale parameter estimates of 5,886 and 218.2 and $\hat{\alpha} = 0.3035$.

12.7 SECTION 12.7

12.101 (a) With separate estimates, all but the female-nonsmoker group had 1 surrender out of a risk set of 8 lives (For example, the female-smoker group had seven observations with left truncation at zero. The remaining three observations were left truncated at 0.3, 2.1, and 3.4. At the time of the first year surrender, 0.8, the risk set had eight members.). For those three groups, we have $\hat{H}(1) = 1/8$, and $\hat{S}(1) = \exp(-1/8) = 0.88250$. For the female-nonsmoker group, there were no surrenders in the first year, so the estimate is $\hat{S}(1) = 1$.
(b) For the proportional hazards models, let $z_1 = 1$ for males (and 0 for females) and let $z_2 = 1$ for smokers (and 0 for nonsmokers). The maximum likelihood estimates for the exponential distribution are $\hat{\beta}_1 = 0.438274$, $\hat{\beta}_2 = 0.378974$, and $\hat{\theta} = 13.7843$. Letting the subscript indicate the z-values, we have

$$
\begin{aligned}
\hat{S}_{00}(1) &= \exp(-1/13.7843) = 0.930023 \\
\hat{S}_{01}(1) &= \exp(-e^{0.378974}/13.7843) = 0.899448 \\
\hat{S}_{10}(1) &= \exp(-e^{0.438274}/13.7843) = 0.893643 \\
\hat{S}_{11}(1) &= \exp(-e^{0.438274+0.378974}/13.7843) = 0.848518.
\end{aligned}
$$

(c) For the data-dependent approach, the two estimates are $\hat{\beta}_1 = 0.461168$ and $\hat{\beta}_2 = 0.374517$. The survival function estimates are

$$
\begin{aligned}
\hat{S}_{00}(1) &= \hat{S}_0(1) = 0.938855 \\
\hat{S}_{01}(1) &= 0.938855^{\exp(0.374517)} = 0.912327 \\
\hat{S}_{10}(1) &= 0.938855^{\exp(0.461168)} = 0.904781 \\
\hat{S}_{11}(1) &= 0.938855^{\exp(0.461168+0.374517)} = 0.864572.
\end{aligned}
$$

12.102 For this model, $S(t) = \exp(-e^{\beta z}t/\theta)$ where z is the index of industrial production. This is an exponential distribution with a mean of $\theta e^{-\beta z}$ and a median of $\theta e^{-\beta z} \ln 2$. The two facts imply that $0.2060 = \theta e^{-10\beta}$ and $0.0411 = \theta e^{-25\beta} \ln 2$. Dividing the first equation by the second equation (after dividing the second equation by $\ln 2$) produces $3.47417 = e^{15\beta}$ for $\beta = 0.083024$ and then $\theta = 0.47254$. Then, $S_5(1) = \exp[-e^{0.083024(5)}/0.47254] = 0.04055$.

12.103 The relative risk of a male child subject versus a female adult subject is $e^{\beta_1}/e^{\beta_2} = e^{\beta_1 - \beta_2}$. The variance of $\hat{\beta}_1 - \hat{\beta}_2$ can be estimated as

$$\begin{bmatrix} 1 & -1 \end{bmatrix} \begin{bmatrix} 0.36 & 0.10 \\ 0.10 & 0.20 \end{bmatrix} \begin{bmatrix} 1 \\ -1 \end{bmatrix} = 0.36$$

for a standard deviation of 0.6. Thus a 95% confidence interval is $0.25 + 0.45 \pm 1.96(0.6)$ or $(-0.476, 1.876)$. Exponentiating the endpoints provides the answer of $(0.621, 6.527)$.

12.104 The first death time had one death so the numerator is 1. The denominator is the sum of the c-values for all four subjects or $1 + 1 + e^b + e^b = 2 + 2e^b$. The second death time also had one death and the denominator is the sum of the c-values for the three members of the risk set, $1 + 2e^b$. Thus, $\hat{H}(3) = \frac{1}{2+2e^b} + \frac{1}{1+2e^b}$.

12.105 The contribution to the partial likelihood is the c-value for the one dying divided by the sum of the c-values for those in the risk set. Therefore

$$L = \frac{e^{\beta_1}}{e^{\beta_1} + e^{\beta_2} + e^{\beta_3}} \frac{e^{\beta_2}}{e^{\beta_2} + e^{\beta_3}} \frac{e^{\beta_3}}{e^{\beta_3}} = \frac{e^{\beta_1+\beta_2}}{(e^{\beta_1} + e^{\beta_2} + e^{\beta_3})(e^{\beta_2} + e^{\beta_3})}.$$

12.106 The parameter estimates are $\hat{b} = 0.5760$, $\hat{\beta}_0 = 0.2796$, and $\hat{\beta}_2 = 1.0688$. There is very little change from the results of Example 12.72.

12.107 The baseline Gompertz distribution has parameters $B = 0.003264$ and $c = 0.9501$. The covariate coefficients are $\beta_1 = -0.5465$ and $\beta_2 = 0.04247$. The signs are opposite those from the accelerated failure time models because of the way in which they are incorporated into the model.

12.108 The baseline gamma distribution has parameters $\alpha = 24.823$ and $\theta = 8.383$. The covariate coefficients are $\beta_1 = 0.0981$ and $\beta_2 = -0.00952$. These are not much different from the effects found with the Gompertz model.

13

Chapter 13 solutions

13.1 SECTION 13.3

13.1 For Data Set B truncated at 50 the maximum likelihood parameter estimates are $\hat{\tau} = 0.80990$ and $\hat{\theta} = 675.25$ leading to the graph in Figure 13.1

For Data Set B censored at 1,000, the estimates are $\hat{\tau} = 0.99984$ and $\hat{\theta} = 718.00$. The graph is in Figure 13.2.

For Data Set C the parameter estimates are $\hat{\tau} = 0.47936$ and $\hat{\theta} = 11,976$. The plot is given in Figure 13.3.

13.2 For Data Set B truncated at 50, the plot is given in Figure 13.4.

For Data Set B censored at 1,000, the plot is given in Figure 13.5.

13.3 The plot for Data Set B truncated at 50 is given in Figure 13.6.

For Data Set B censored at 1,000 the plot is given in Figure 13.7.

Loss Models: From Data to Decisions, Solutions Manual, Second Edition.
By Stuart A. Klugman, Harry H. Panjer, and Gordon E. Willmot
ISBN 0-471-22762-5   Copyright © 2004 John Wiley & Sons, Inc.

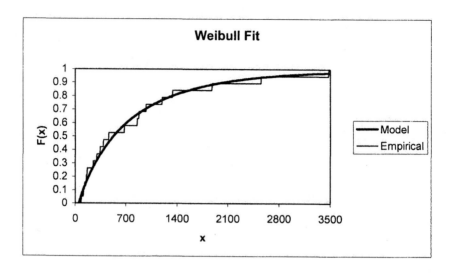

Fig. 13.1   Cdf plot for Data Set B truncated at 50.

13.2   SECTION 13.4

13.4 For Data Set B truncated at 50, the test statistic is 0.0887 while the critical value is unchanged from the example (0.3120). The null hypothesis is not rejected and it is plausible that the data came from a Weibull population. For Data Set B censored at 1,000, the test statistic is 0.0991 while the critical value is 0.3041. The null hypothesis is not rejected.

13.5 The first step is to obtain the distribution function. This can be recognized as an inverse exponential distribution, or the calculation done as

$$F(x) = \int_0^x 2y^{-2}e^{-2/y}dy = \int_{2/x}^\infty 2(2/z)^{-2}e^{-z}(2z^{-2})dz$$
$$= \int_{2/x}^\infty e^{-z}dz = e^{-2/x}.$$

In the first line the substitution $z = 2/y$ was used. The calculations are in Table 13.1. The test statistic is the maximum from the final column, or 0.168.

13.6 The distribution function is

$$F(x) = \int_0^x 2(1+y)^{-3}dy = -(1+y)^{-2}\big|_0^x = 1 - (1+x)^{-2}.$$

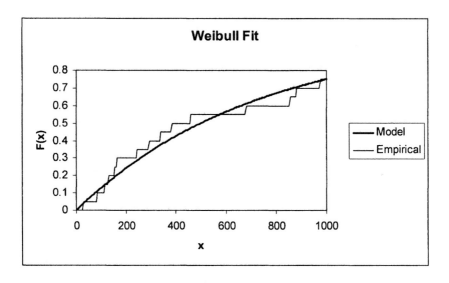

Fig. 13.2 Cdf plot for Data Set B censored at 1,000.

Table 13.1 Calculations for Exercise 13.5

x	$F(x)$	compare to	max difference
1	0.135	0, 0.2	0.135
2	0.368	0.2, 0.4	0.168
3	0.513	0.4, 0.6	0.113
5	0.670	0.6, 0.8	0.130
13	0.857	0.8, 1	0.143

The calculations are in Table 13.2. The test statistic is the maximum from the final column, 0.189.

13.7 For Data Set B truncated at 50, the test statistic is 0.1631 which is less than the critical value of 2.492 and the null hypothesis is not rejected. For Data Set B censored at 1,000, the test statistic is 0.1712 and the null hypothesis is again not rejected.

13.8 The calculations for Data Set B truncated at 50 are in Table 13.3. The sum is 0.3615. With three degrees of freedom, the critical value is 7.8147 and the Weibull model is not rejected. The p-value is 0.9481.

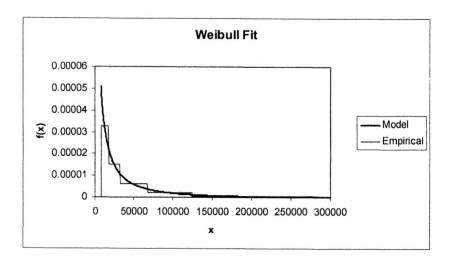

Fig. 13.3 Pdf and histogram for Data Set C.

Table 13.2   Calculations for Exercise 13.6

x	$F(x)$	compare to	max difference
0.1	0.174	0, 0.2	0.174
0.2	0.306	0.2, 0.4	0.106
0.5	0.556	0.4, 0.6	0.156
1.0	0.750	0.6, 0.8	0.150
1.3	0.811	0.8, 1	0.189

The calculations for Data Set B censored at 1,000 are in the Table 13.4. The sum is 0.5947. With two degrees of freedom, the critical value is 5.9915 and the Weibull model is not rejected. The p-value is 0.7428.

The calculations for Data Set C are in Table 13.5. The sum is 0.3698. With three degrees of freedom, the critical value is 7.8147 and the Weibull model is not rejected. The p-value is 0.9464.

13.9 The calculations are in Table 13.6. For the test there are three degrees of freedom (four groups less zero estimated parameters less one) and at a five percent significance level the critical value is 7.81. The null hypothesis is accepted and therefore the data may have come from a population with the given survival function.

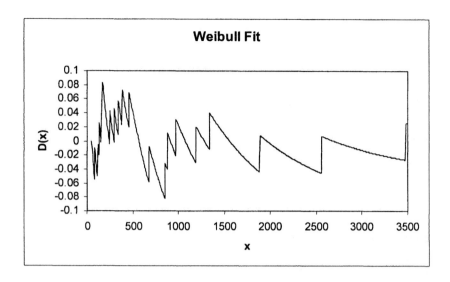

Fig. 13.4   Difference plot for Data Set B truncated at 50.

Table 13.3   Data Set B truncated at 50 for Exercise 13.8

Range	$\hat{p}$	Expected	Observed	χ^2
50–150	0.1599	3.038	3	0.0005
150–250	0.1181	2.244	3	0.2545
250–500	0.2064	3.922	4	0.0015
500–1,000	0.2299	4.368	4	0.0310
1,000–2,000	0.1842	3.500	3	0.0713
2,000–∞	0.1015	1.928	2	0.0027

13.10 Either recall that for a Poisson distribution the maximum likelihood estimator is the sample mean, or derive it from

$$L(\lambda) = \left(e^{-\lambda}\right)^{50} \left(\lambda e^{-\lambda}\right)^{122} \left(\frac{\lambda^2 e^{-\lambda}}{2}\right)^{101} \left(\frac{\lambda^3 e^{-\lambda}}{6}\right)^{92} \propto \lambda^{600} e^{-365\lambda}$$

$$\ln L(\lambda) = 600 \ln \lambda - 365\lambda$$

$$0 = 600\lambda^{-1} - 365$$

$$\hat{\lambda} = 600/365 = 1.6438.$$

For the goodness-of-fit test the calculations are in Table 13.7. The last two groups were combined. The total is 7.56. There are two degrees of freedom (4 groups less 1 estimated parameter less 1). At a 2.5% significance level the

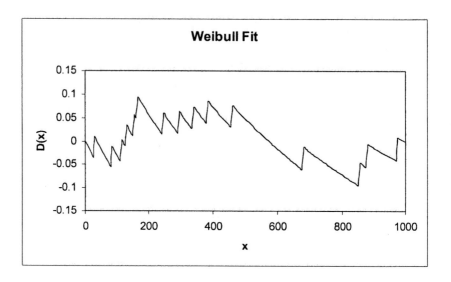

Fig. 13.5 Difference plot for Data Set B censored at 1,000.

Table 13.4 Data Set B censored at 1000 for Exercise 13.8

Range	$\hat{p}$	Expected	Observed	χ^2
0–150	0.1886	3.772	4	0.0138
150–250	0.1055	2.110	3	0.3754
250–500	0.2076	4.151	4	0.0055
500–1,000	0.2500	4.999	4	0.1997
1,000–∞	0.2484	4.968	5	0.0002

critical value is 7.38 and therefore the null hypothesis is rejected. The Poisson model is not appropriate.

13.11 With 365 observations, the expected count for k accidents is

$$365 \Pr(N = k) = \frac{365 e^{-0.6} 0.6^k}{k!}.$$

The test statistic is calculated in Table 13.8. The total of the last column is the test statistic of 2.85. With three degrees of freedom (four groups less one less zero estimated parameters) the critical value is 7.81 and the null hypothesis of a Poisson distribution cannot be rejected.

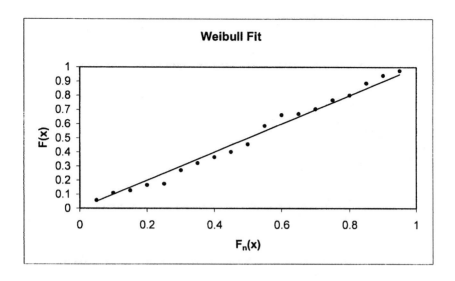

Fig. 13.6 $p - p$ plot for Data Set B truncated at 50.

Table 13.5 Data Set C truncated at 7500 for Exercise 13.8

Range	$\hat{p}$	Expected	Observed	χ^2
7,500–17,500	0.3299	42.230	42	0.0013
17,500–32,500	0.2273	29.096	29	0.0003
32,500–67,500	0.2178	27.878	28	0.0005
67,500–125,000	0.1226	15.690	17	0.1094
125,000–300,000	0.0818	10.472	9	0.2070
300,000–∞	0.0206	2.632	3	0.0513

13.12
$$L = \prod_{k=1}^{6} \frac{(n_k + e_k + 1)\cdots e_k}{n_k!} \left(\frac{1}{1+\beta}\right)^{e_k} \left(\frac{\beta}{1+\beta}\right)^{n_k}$$
$$\propto \beta^{\Sigma n_k}(1+\beta)^{-\Sigma(n_k+e_k)}.$$

The logarithm is

$$(\log\beta)\sum_{k=1}^{6} n_k - [\log(1+\beta)]\sum_{k=1}^{6}(n_k + e_k)$$

and setting the derivative equal to zero yields

$$\beta^{-1}\sum_{k=1}^{6} n_k - (1+\beta)^{-1}\sum_{k=1}^{6}(n_k + e_k) = 0$$

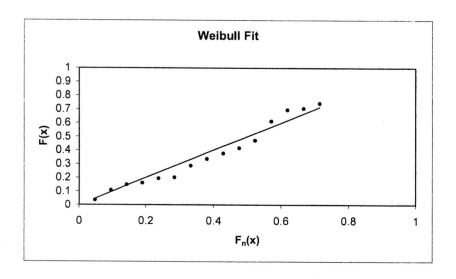

Fig. 13.7 $p - p$ plot for Data Set B censored at 1,000.

Table 13.6 Calculations for Exercise 13.9

Interval	Observed	Expected	Chi-square
0 to 1	21	$150F(1) = 150(2/20) = 15$	$\frac{6^2}{15} = 2.40$
1 to 2	27	$150[F(2) - F(1)] = 150(4/20) = 30$	$\frac{3^2}{30} = 0.30$
2 to 3	39	$150[F(3) - F(2)] = 150(6/20) = 45$	$\frac{6^2}{45} = 0.80$
3 to 4	63	$150[F(4) - F(3)] = 150(8/20) = 60$	$\frac{3^2}{60} = 0.15$
Total	150	150	3.65.

Table 13.7 Calculations for Exercise 13.10

No. of claims	No. of obs.	No. expected	Chi-square
0	50	$365e^{-1.6438} = 70.53$	$\frac{20.53^2}{70.53} = 5.98$
1	122	$365(1.6438)e^{-1.6438} = 115.94$	$\frac{6.06^2}{115.94} = 0.32$
2	101	$365(1.6438)^2 e^{-1.6438}/2 = 95.29$	$\frac{5.71^2}{95.29} = 0.34$
3 or more	92	$365 - 70.53 - 115.94 - 95.29 = 83.24$	$\frac{8.76^2}{83.24} = 0.92$

for $\hat{\beta} = \sum_{k=1}^{6} n_k / \sum_{k=1}^{6} e_k = 0.09772$. The expected number is $E_k = \hat{\beta}e_k$ which is exactly the same as for the Poisson model. Because the variance is $e_k \beta(1 + \beta)$, the goodness-of-fit test statistic equals the Poisson test statistic divided by $1 + \beta$ or $6.19/1.09772 = 5.64$. The geometric model is accepted.

Table 13.8 Calculations for Exercise 13.11

No. of accidents	Observed	Expected	Chi-square
0	209	200.32	0.38
1	111	120.19	0.70
2	33	36.06	0.26
3	7	7.21	1.51**
4	3	1.08	
5	2	0.14*	

*This is 365 less the sum of the other entries to reflect the expected for 5 or more accidents.
**The last three cells are grouped for an observed of 12 and an expected of 8.43.

13.13 The null hypothesis is that the data come from a gamma distribution with $\alpha = 1$, that is, from an exponential distribution. The alternative hypothesis is that α has some other value. From Example 12.8, for the exponential distribution, $\hat{\theta} = 1,424.4$ and the loglikelihood value is -165.230. For the gamma distribution, $\hat{\alpha} = 0.55616$ and $\hat{\theta} = 2,561.1$. The loglikelihood at the maximum is $L_0 = -162.293$. The test statistic is $2(-162.293 + 165.230) = 5.874$. The p-value based on one degree of freedom is 0.0154 indicating there is considerable evidence to support the gamma model over the exponential model.

13.14 For the exponential distribution, $\hat{\theta} = 29,721$ and the loglikelihood is -406.027. For the gamma distribution, $\hat{\alpha} = 0.37139$, $\hat{\theta} = 83,020$ and the loglikelihood is -360.496. For the transformed gamma distribution, $\hat{\alpha} = 3.02515$, $\hat{\theta} = 489.97$, $\hat{\tau} = 0.32781$ and the value of the loglikelihood function is -357.535. The models can only be compared in pairs. For exponential (null) vs. gamma (alternative), the test statistic is 91.061 and the p-value is essentially zero. The exponential model is convincingly rejected. For gamma (null) vs. transformed gamma (alternative), the test statistic is 5.923 with a p-value of 0.015 and there is strong evidence for the transformed gamma model. Exponential vs. transformed gamma could also be tested (using two degrees of freedom), but there is no point.

13.15 Poisson expected counts are:

$$0 \; : \; 10{,}000(e^{-0.1001}) = 9{,}047.47,$$
$$1 \; : \; 10{,}000(0.1001e^{-0.1001}) = 905.65,$$
$$2 \; : \; 10{,}000(0.1001^2 e^{-0.1001}/2) = 45.33,$$
$$3 \text{ or more} \; : \; 10{,}000 - 9{,}047.47 - 905.65 - 45.33 = 1.55.$$

The test statistic is

$$(9{,}048 - 9{,}047.47)^2/9{,}047.47 + (905 - 905.65)^2/906.65$$
$$+(45 - 45.33)^2/45.33 + (2 - 1.55)^2/1.44 = 0.14.$$

There are two degrees of freedom (four groups less one and less one estimated parameter) and so the 5% critical value is 5.99 and the null hypothesis (and therefore the Poisson model) is accepted.

Geometric expected counts are 9,090.08, 827.12, 75.26, and 7.54 and the test statistic is 23.77. With two degrees of freedom, the model is rejected.

Negative binomial expected counts are 9,048.28, 904.12, 45.97, and 1.63 and the test statistic is 0.11. With one degree of freedom the model is accepted.

Binomial ($m = 4$) expected counts are 9,035.95, 927.71, and 36.34 (extra grouping is needed to keep the counts above 1) and the test statistic is 3.70. With one degree of freedom the model is accepted (critical value is 3.84).

13.16 Poisson expected counts are 847.05, 140.61, and 12.34 (grouping needed to keep expected counts above 1) and the test statistic is 5.56. With one degree of freedom the model is rejected.

Geometric expected counts are 857.63, 122.10, 17.38, and 2.89 and the test statistic is 2.67. With two degrees of freedom the model is accepted.

Negative binomial expected counts are 862.45, 114.26, 19.10, and 4.19 and the test statistic is 2.50. With one degree of freedom, the model is accepted.

Binomial ($m = 7$) expected counts are 845.34, 143.74, and 10.92 and the test statistic is 8.48. With one degree of freedom the model is rejected.

13.17 (a) To achieve a reasonable expected count, the first three rows are combined as well as the last two. The test statistic is 16,308. With five degrees of freedom, the model is clearly rejected.
(b) All nine rows can now be used. The test statistic is 146.84. With seven degrees of freedom, the model is clearly rejected.
(c) The test statistic is 30.16. With six degrees of freedom, the model is clearly rejected.

13.18 $\bar{x} = 0.155140$ and $s^2 = 0.179314$. $E(N) = \lambda_1\lambda_2$ and $\text{Var}(N) = \lambda_1(\lambda_2 + \lambda_2^2)$. Solving the equations yields $\hat{\lambda}_1 = 0.995630$ and $\hat{\lambda}_2 = 0.155821$. For the secondary distribution, $f_j = e^{-0.155821}(0.155821)^j/j!$ and then $g_0 = exp[-0.99563(1 - e^{-0.155821})] = 0.866185$. Then,

$$g_k = \sum_{j=1}^{k} \frac{0.99563}{k} j f_j g_{k-j}.$$

For the goodness-of-fit test with 2 degrees of freedom, see Table 13.9, and the model is clearly rejected.

Table 13.9   Calculations for Exercise 13.18

Value	Obs.	Exp.	Chi-square
0	103,704	103,814.9	0.12
1	14,075	13,782.0	6.23
2	1,766	1,988.6	24.92
3	255	238.9	1.09
4+	53	28.6	20.82
Total			53.18

13.19 (a)

$$\chi^2 = \frac{(20{,}592-20{,}596.76)^2}{20{,}596.76} + \frac{(2{,}651-2{,}631.03)^2}{2{,}631.03} + \frac{(297-318.37)^2}{318.37}$$

$$+ \frac{(41-37.81)^2}{37.81} + \frac{(8-5.03)^2}{5.03}$$

$$= 0.0011 + 0.1516 + 1.4344 + 0.2691 + 1.7537 = 3.6099$$

$$df = 5 - 2 - 1 = 2, \text{ given } \alpha = 0.05, \Rightarrow$$

$$\chi^2_{2,0.05} = 5.99 > 3.6099 \Rightarrow \text{ fit is acceptable, or}$$

$$p = Pr(x^2_{(2)} > 3.6099) \approx 0.16 \Rightarrow \text{ fit is acceptable.}$$

(b)

$$a = \frac{\beta}{1+\beta}, \quad b = \frac{(r-1)\beta}{1+\beta}, \quad p_n = \left(a + \frac{b}{n}\right)p_{n-1}$$

$$\hat{p}_1 = (\hat{a}+\hat{b})\hat{p}_0 \Leftrightarrow \hat{a}+\hat{b} = \frac{\hat{r}\hat{\beta}}{1+\hat{\beta}} = \frac{\hat{p}_1}{\hat{p}_0} = \frac{2{,}631.03}{20{,}596.76} = 0.12774$$

$$\left(\hat{a}+\frac{\hat{b}}{2}\right) = \frac{(\hat{r}+1)}{2}\frac{\hat{\beta}}{1+\hat{\beta}} = \frac{\hat{p}_2}{\hat{p}_1} = \frac{318.37}{2{,}631.03} = 0.12101$$

$$\frac{2\hat{r}}{\hat{r}+1} = \frac{0.12774}{0.12101} = 1.05565 \Rightarrow \hat{r}(2-1.05565) = 1.05565 \Rightarrow$$

$$\hat{r} = 1.11786, \quad \hat{a} = \frac{\hat{\beta}}{1+\hat{\beta}} = \frac{0.12774}{\hat{r}} = 0.11427$$

$$\Rightarrow \hat{\beta} = \frac{0.11427}{1-0.11427} = 0.12901$$

13.3   SECTION 13.5

13.20 These are discrete data from a discrete population, so the normal and gamma models are not appropriate. There are two ways to distinguish among

Table 13.10   Tests for Exercise 13.21

Criterion	Exponential	Weibull	Trans gam
	B truncated at 50		
K-S	0.1340	0.0887	0.0775
A-D	0.4292	0.1631	0.1649
χ^2	1.4034	0.3615	0.5169
p-value	0.8436	0.9481	0.7723
loglikelihood	-146.063	-145.683	-145.661
SBC	-147.535	-148.628	-150.078
	B censored at 1,000		
K-S	0.0991	0.0991	N/A
A-D	0.1713	0.1712	N/A
χ^2	0.5951	0.5947	N/A
p-value	0.8976	0.7428	N/A
loglikelihood	-113.647	-113.647	N/A
SBC	-115.145	-116.643	N/A
	C		
K-S	N/A	N/A	N/A
A-D	N/A	N/A	N/A
χ^2	61.913	0.3698	0.3148
p-value	10^{-12}	0.9464	0.8544
loglikelihood	-214.924	-202.077	-202.077
SBC	-217.350	-206.929	-209.324

the three discrete options. One is to look at successive values of kn_k/n_{k-1}. They are 2.67, 2.33, 2.01, 1.67, 1.32, and 1.04. The sequence is linear and decreasing, indicating a binomial distribution is appropriate. An alternative is to compute the sample mean and variance. They are 2 and 1.494 respectively. The variance is considerably less than the mean, indicating a binomial model.

13.21 The various tests for the three data sets produce the following results. For Data Set B truncated at 50, the estimates are $\hat{\alpha} = 0.40982$, $\hat{\tau} = 1.24069$, and $\hat{\theta} = 1,642.31$. For Data Set B censored at 1,000 there is no maximum likelihood estimate. For Data Set C, the maximum likelihood estimate is $\hat{\alpha} = 4.50624$, $\hat{\tau} = 0.28154$, and $\hat{\theta} = 71.6242$. The results of the tests are in Table 13.10.

For Data Set B truncated at 50, there is no reason to use a three-parameter distribution. For Data Set C, the transformed gamma distribution does not provide sufficient improvement to drop the Weibull as the model of choice.

13.22 The loglikelihood values for the two models are -385.9 for the Poisson and -382.4 for the negative binomial. The test statistic is $2(-382.4+385.9) = 7.0$. There is one degree of freedom (two parameters minus one parameter) and so the critical value is 3.84. The null hypothesis is rejected and so the data favors the negative binomial distribution.

13.23 The penalty function subtracts $\ln(100)/2 = 2.3$ for each additional parameter. For the five models, the penalized loglikelihoods are — generalized Pareto: $-219.1 - 6.9 = -226.0$, Burr: $-219.2 - 6.9 = -226.1$, Pareto: $-221.2 - 4.6 = -225.8$, lognormal: $-221.4 - 4.6 = -226.0$, and inverse exponential: $-224.3 - 2.3 = -226.6$. The largest value is for the Pareto distribution.

13.24 The loglikelihood function for an exponential distribution is

$$l(\theta) = \ln \prod_{i=1}^{n} \theta^{-1} e^{-x_i/\theta} = \sum_{i=1}^{n} -\ln \theta - x_i/\theta = -n \ln \theta - n\bar{x}\theta^{-1}.$$

Under the null hypothesis that Sylvia's mean is double that of Phil's, the maximum likelihood estimates of the mean are 916.67 for Phil and 1833.33 for Sylvia. The loglikelihood value is

$$l_{null} = -20 \ln 916.67 - 20000/916.67 - 10 \ln 1833.33 - 15000/1833.33 = -241.55.$$

Under the alternative hypothesis of arbitrary parameters the loglikelihood value is

$$l_{alt} = -20 \ln 1000 - 20,000/1000 - 10 \ln 1500 - 15,000/1500 = -241.29.$$

The likelihood ratio test statistic is $2(-241.29 + 241.55) = 0.52$ which is not significant (the critical value is 3.84 with one degree of freedom). To add a parameter, the SBC requires an improvement of $\ln(30)/2 = 1.70$. Both procedures indicate that there is not sufficient evidence in the data to dispute Sylvia's claim.

13.25 Both the Poisson and negative binomial have acceptable p-values (0.93 and 0.74) with the Poisson favored. The Poisson has a higher loglikelihood value than the geometric. The negative binomial improves the loglikelihood by 0.01 over the Poisson. This is less than the 1.92 required by LRT or the 3.45 required by SBC. The Poisson is acceptable and preferred.

13.26 Both the geometric and negative binomial have acceptable p-vlaues (0.26 and 0.11) with the geometric favored. The geometric has a higher loglikelihood value than the Poisson. The negative binomial improves the loglikelihood by 0.71 over the geometric. This is less than the 1.92 required by

Table 13.11   Calculations for Exercise 13.28

Model	Parameters	NLL	Chi-square	df
Poisson	$\hat{\lambda} = 1.74128$	2,532.86	1,080.80	5
Geometric	$\hat{\beta} = 1.74128$	2,217.71	170.72	7
Negative binomial	$\hat{r} = .867043,\ \hat{\beta} = 2.00830$	2,216.07	165.57	6

LRT or the 2.30 required by SBC. The geometric model is acceptable and preferred.

13.27 The negative binomial distribution has the best p-value (0.000037) though it is clearly unacceptable. For the two one parameter distributions, the geometric distribution is a better loglikelihood and SBC than the Poisson. The negative binomial model improves the loglikelihood by $1132.25 - 1098.64 = 33.61$. This is more than the 1.92 required by the likelihood ratio test and is more than the $0.5 \ln 503 = 3.11$ required by the SBC. For the three models, the negative binomial is the best, but is not very good. It turns out that zero-modified models should be used.

13.28 (a) For $k = 1, 2, 3, 4, 5, 6, 7$ the values are 0.276, 2.315, 2.432, 2.891, 4.394, 2.828, and 4.268 which, if anything, are increasing. The negative binomial or geometric models may work well.
(b) The values appear in Table 13.11. Because the sample variance exceeds the sample mean, there is no *mle* for the binomial distribution.
(c) The geometric is better than the Poisson by both likelihood and chi-square measures. The negative binomial distribution is not an improvement over the geometric as the *NLL* decreases by only 1.64. When doubled, 3.28 does not exceed the critical value of 3.841. The best choice is geometric, but it does not pass the goodness-of-fit test.

13.29 For each data set and model, Table 13.12 first gives the negative loglikelihood and then the chi-square test statistic, degrees of freedom, and p-value. If there are not enough degrees of freedom to do the test, no p-value is given.

For Exercise 12.96, the Poisson is the clear choice. It is the only one parameter distribution acceptable by the goodness-of-fit test and no two parameter distribution improves the NLL by more than 0.03.

For Exercise 12.98, the geometric is the best one parameter distribution and is acceptable by the goodness-of-fit test. The best two parameter distribution is the negative binomial, but the improvement in the NLL is only .714 which is not significant. (The test statistic with one degree of freedom is 1.428). The three parameter ZM negative binomial improves the NLL by 3.577 over the

Table 13.12 Results for Exercise 13.29

	Ex. 12.96	Ex. 12.98	Ex. 12.99	Ex. 13.28
Poisson	3,339.66	488.241	3,578.58	2,532.86
	.00;1;.9773	5.56;1;.0184	16,308;4;0	1,081;5;0
Geometric	3,353.39	477.171	1,132.25	2,217.71
	23.76;2;0	.28;1;.5987	146.84;7;0	170.72;7;0
Neg. bin.	3,339.65	476.457	1,098.64	2,216.07
	.01;0	1.60;0	30.16;6;0	165.57;6;0
ZM Poisson	3,339.66	480.638	2,388.37	2,134.59
	.00;0	1.76;0	900.42;3;0	37.49;6;0
ZM geometric	3,339.67	476.855	1,083.56	2,200.56
	.00;0	1.12;0	1.52;6;.9581	135.43;6;0
ZM logarithmic	3,339.91	475.175	1,171.13	2,308.82
	.03;0	.66;0	186.05;6;0	361.18;6;0
ZM neg. bin.	3,339.63	473.594	1,083.47	2,132.42
	.00;-1	.05;0	1.32;5;.9331	28.43;5;0

geometric. This is significant (with two degrees of freedom). So an argument could be made for the ZM negative binomial, but the simpler geometric still looks to be a good choice.

For Exercise 12.99, the best one parameter distribution is the geometric, but it is not acceptable. The best two parameter distribution is the ZM geometric which does pass the goodness-of-fit test and has a much lower NLL. The ZM negative binomial lowers the NLL by 0.09 and is not a significant improvement.

For Exercise 13.28, none of the distributions fit well. According to the NLL, the ZM negative binomial is the best choice, but it does not look very promising.

13.30(a) The *mle* is $\hat{\rho} = 3.0416$ using numerical methods.
(b) The test statistic is 785.18 and with 3 degrees of freedom the model is clearly not acceptable.

13.31 Results appear in Table 13.13. The entries are the negative loglikelihood, the chi-square test statistic, degrees of freedom, and, the p-value (if the degrees of freedom are positive).

For Exercise 12.96, the Poisson cannot be topped. These four improve the loglikelihood by only 0.01 and all have more parameters.

Table 13.13   Results for Exercise 13.31

	Ex. 12.96	Ex. 12.98	Ex. 12.99	Ex. 13.28
Poisson-Poisson	3,339.65	478.306	1,198.28	2,151.88
	0.01;0	1.35;0	381.25;6;0	51.85;6;0
Polya-Aeppli	3,339.65	477.322	1,084.95	2,183.48
	0.01;0	1.58;0	4.32;6;0.6335	105.95;6;0
Poisson-I.G.	3,339.65	475.241	1,174.82	2,265.34
	0.01;0	1.30;0	206.08;6;0	262.74;6;0
Poisson-ETNB	3,339.65	473.624	1,083.56	did not
	0.01;−1	0.02;−1	1.52;5;0.9112	converge

For Exercise 12.98, both the Poisson-inverse Gaussian and Poisson-ETNB improve the loglikelihood over the geometric. The improvements are 1.93 and 3.547. When doubled, they are slightly (p-values of 0.04945 and 0.0288 respectively with 1 and 2 degrees of freedom) significant. The goodness-of-fit test cannot be done. The geometric model, which easily passed the goodness–of-fit test still looks good.

For Exercise 12.99, none of the models improved the loglikelihood over the ZM geometric (although the Poisson-ETNB, with one more parameter, tied). As well, the ZM geometric has the highest p-value and is clearly acceptable.

For Exercise 13.28, none of the models have a superior loglikelihood versus the ZM negative binomial. Although this model is not acceptable, it is the best one from among the available choices.

13.32 The coefficient discussed in the section is $\frac{(\mu_3 - 3\sigma^2 + 2\mu)\mu}{(\sigma^2 - \mu)^2}$. For the five data sets, use the empirical estimates. For the last two sets, the final category is for some number or more. For these cases, estimate by assuming the observations were all at that highest value. The five coefficient estimates are (a) −0.85689, (b) −1,817.27, (c) −5.47728, (d) 1.48726, (e) −0.42125. For all but data set (d) it appears that a compound Poisson model will not be appropriate. For data set (d) it appears that Polya-Aeppli model will do well. Table 13.14 summarizes a variety of fits. The entries are the negative loglikelihood, the chi-square test statistic, the degrees of freedom, and the p-value.
(a) All two-parameter distributions are superior to the two one-parameter distributions. The best two-parameter distributions are negative binomial (best loglikelihood) and Poisson-inverse Gaussian (best p-value). The three-parameter Poisson-ETNB is not a significant improvement by the likelihood ratio test. The simpler negative binomial is an excellent choice.

Table 13.14   Results for Exercise 13.32

	(a)	(b)	(c)	(d)	(e)
Poiss.	36,188.3 190.75;2;0	206.107 0.06;1;.8021	481.886 2.40;2;.3017	1,461.49 267.52;2;0	841.113 6.88;6;.3323
Geom.	36,123.6 41.99;3;0	213.052 14.02;2;0	494.524 24.03;3;0	1,309.64 80.13;4;0	937.975 189.47;9;0
NB	36,104.1 0.09;1;.7631	did not converge	481.054 0.31;1;.5779	1,278.59 1.57;4;.8139	837.455 3.46;6;.7963
P-bin. $m = 2$	36,106.9 2.38;1;.1228	did not converge	481.034 0.38;1;.5357	1,320.71 69.74;2;0	837.438 3.10;6;.7963
P-bin. $m = 3$	36,106.1 1.20;1;.2728	did not converge	481.034 0.35;1;.5515	1,303.00 63.10;3;0	837.442 3.19;6;.7853
Polya- Aeppli	36,104.6 0.15;1;.6966	did not converge	481.044 0.32;1;.5731	1,280.59 6.52;4;.1638	837.452 3.37;6;.7615
Ney.-A	36,105.3 0.49;1;.4820	did not converge	481.037 0.33;1;.5642	1,288.56 24.14;3;0	837.448 3.28;6;.7736
P-iG	36,103.6 0.57;1;.4487	did not converge	481.079 0.31;1;.5761	1,281.90 8.75;4;.0676	837.455 3.63;6;.7260
P-ETNB	36,103.5 5.43;1;.0198	did not converge	did not converge	1,278.58 1.54;3;.6740	did not converge

(b) Because the sample variance is less than the sample mean, mle's exist only for the Poisson and geometric distributions. The Poisson is clearly acceptable by the goodness-of-fit test.

(c) None of the two-parameter models are significant improvements over the Poisson according to the likelihood ratio test. Even though some have superior p-values, the Poisson is acceptable and should be our choice.

(d) The two-parameter models are better by the likelihood ratio test. The best is negative binomial on all measures. The Poisson-ETNB is not better and so use the negative binomial, which passes the goodness-of-fit test. The moment analysis supported the Polya-Aeppli, which was acceptable, but not as good as the negative binomial.

(e) The two-parameter models are better by the likelihood ratio test. The best is Poisson-binomial with $m = 2$, though the simpler and more popular negative binomial is a close alternative.

13.33 Excel® solver reports the following mle's to four decimals: $\hat{p} = 0.9312$, $\hat{\lambda}_1 = 0.1064$, and $\hat{\lambda}_2 = 0.6560$. The negative loglikelihood is 10,221.9. Rounding these numbers to two decimals produces a negative loglikelihood of 10,223.3

while Tröbliger's solution is superior at 10,222.1. A better two decimal solution is (0.94,0.11,0.69) which gives 10,222.0. The negative binomial distribution was found to have a negative loglikelihood of 10,223.4. The extra parameter for the two-point mixture cannot be justified (using the likelihood ratio test).

14

Chapter 14 solutions

14.1 SECTION 14.2

14.1 We have

$$
\begin{aligned}
60 - 0.6x &= \frac{\int_x^{100}(t-x)f(t)dt}{S(x)} \\
S(x)(60 - 0.6x) &= \int_x^{100}(t-x)f(t)dt \\
-f(x)(60 - 0.6x) - 0.6S(x) &= \int_x^{100} -f(t)dt = -S(x) \\
f(x)(60 - 0.6x) &= 0.4S(x) \\
\frac{f(x)}{S(x)} &= \frac{0.4}{60 - 0.6x}.
\end{aligned}
$$

Loss Models: From Data to Decisions, Solutions Manual, Second Edition.
By Stuart A. Klugman, Harry H. Panjer, and Gordon E. Willmot
ISBN 0-471-22762-5   Copyright © 2004 John Wiley & Sons, Inc.

The third line follows from differentiating both sides with respect to x. The last line yields the hazard rate. Then,

$$
\begin{aligned}
S(x) &= e^{-\int_0^x h(t)dt} \\
&= e^{-4\int_0^x (600-6t)^{-1}dt} \\
&= e^{(4/6)\ln(600-6t)|_0^x} \\
&= e^{(4/6)[\ln(600-6x)-\ln(600)]} \\
&= (1-0.01x)^{2/3}
\end{aligned}
$$

and

$$
f(x) = -S'(x) = \frac{2}{300}(1-0.01x)^{-1/3}.
$$

This can be recognized as a beta distribution with parameters $a = 1, b = 2/3$, and $\theta = 100$.

For the first problem, $S(65) = (0.35)^{2/3} = .4966$ and

$$
\begin{aligned}
E(Y) &= 1,000 \sum_{j=0}^{34} 1.06^{-j}(0.35 - 0.01j)^{2/3}/0.4966 \\
&= 11,540.56.
\end{aligned}
$$

For the second problem,

$$
\begin{aligned}
E(Z) &= 1,000 \int_0^{80} 1.06^{-x} f(20+x)dx/S(20) \\
&= 1,000 \int_0^{80} 1.06^{-x} \frac{2}{300}(0.8 - 0.01x)^{-1/3} dx/0.86177 \\
&= 157.14
\end{aligned}
$$

where numerical integration was used to get the answer.

14.2   SECTION 14.7

14.2 The value of 7 is treated as a left-truncation point. A typical term in the likelihood function is $\left(\frac{F(11)-F(10)}{1-F(7)}\right)^{37}$. Five parametric models were examined (others were also examined and rejected). Summary values are given in Table 14.1. All the two parameter models are clearly superior to the exponential distribution and the inverse transformed gamma model does not provide a significant improvement to warrant a third parameter. Based on the numbers, it is hard to choose from among the three two-parameter models. A graph (Figure 14.1) shows that the inverse Gaussian distribution provides a good fit (though not presented, graphs of the Weibull and gamma distributions do not match up as well).

Table 14.1   Fitted models for Exercise 14.2

Model	Parameters	NLL	χ^2	p-value
Exponential	$\theta = 4.272$	647.96	40.41	0
Gamma	$\alpha = 8.990$, $\theta = 1.158$	628.73	9.05	0.4331
Weibull	$\tau = 3.532$, $\theta = 10.57$	628.64	10.22	0.3330
inverse Gaussian	$\mu = 10.75$, $\theta = 112.7$	628.93	8.75	9.4611
Inv. trans. gamma	$\alpha = 1.942$, $\theta = 74.88$, $\tau = 1.950$	628.60	9.64	0.2911

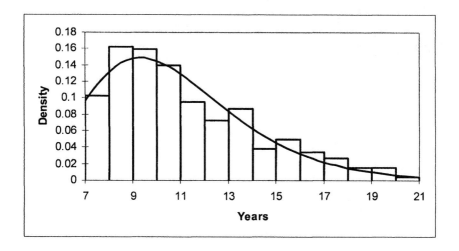

Fig. 14.1   Inverse Gaussian fit to data in Exercise 14.2.

14.3 The lognormal model fits well ($\mu = -0.36286$, $\sigma = 0.84691$) and passes the goodness-of-fit test with a p-value of 0.1863. The gamma distribution does better with an NLL of 364.32 (vs. 365.70 for the lognormal model) and a p-value of 0.4314. The best three and four parameter models do not show an improvement of 1.00 in the NLL, which is not sufficient. The inverse Burr distribution does show a higher p-value (0.5336). Figure 14.2 compares the lognormal and gamma models. It confirms that the gamma model provides a better fit.

14.4 Table 14.2 presents the NLL, SBC, and p-values for each of the four models to be considered. The mixture is superior to the lognormal, but by the SBC is not superior to the plain gamma distribution. On the other hand, the goodness-of-fit test favors the mixture distribution. A comparison of the expected counts shows that the mixture distribution provides a superior fit and is worth considering. For example, for the first four intervals, the observed

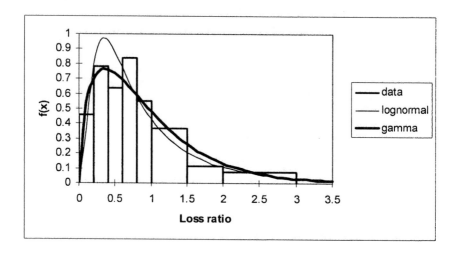

Fig. 14.2   Comparison of lognormal and gamma models for Exercise 14.3.

Table 14.2   Four models for Exercise 14.4

Model	NLL	SBC	p-value
lognormal	501.79	507.03	0.0198
gamma	491.78	497.03	0.7788
loggamma	512.21	517.45	0.0000
gamma/loggamma	487.52	500.62	0.9796

counts were 27, 4, 1, and 2. The expected counts were 23.3, 7.5, 5.4, and 4.4 for the gamma model and 27.0, 3.1, 2.7, and 2.7 for the mixture model.

14.5 An examination of numerous distributions, reveals that the inverse Burr distribution fits reasonably well for both data sets. It is significantly better than any two-parameter model and virtually identical to the transformed beta distribution. The NLL values are 48,394.61 for the 300,000 limit and 18,076.91 for the 500,000 limit. The total is 66,471.52. When a common inverse Burr distribution is fit to the combined data set, the NLL is 66,476.54. The difference of 5.02 is significant by the LRT (3 degrees of freedom), but not by the SBC ($1.5\ln(33643) = 15.635$ is required). The parameters for the three models are not that much different (see Table 14.3).Figures 14.3 and 14.4 show the quality of the inverse Burr fit to the combined data set.

Table 14.3 Inverse Burr fits for Exercise 14.5

Data set	τ	θ	γ
300,000 limit	0.21046	3401.75	1.4793
500,000 limit	0.18936	3754.42	1.5153
combined	0.20436	3497.41	1.4893

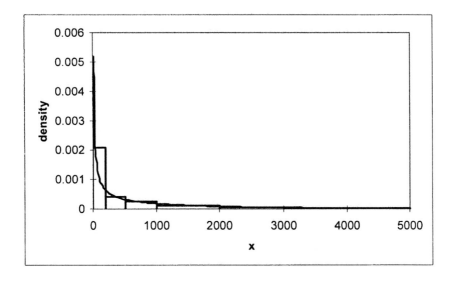

Fig. 14.3 Inverse Burr fit for Exercise 14.5.

14.6 The best one-parameter distribution is the Poisson with an NLL of 63.67 and a p-value of 0.69. The best two-parameter model is the negative binomial with an NLL of 61.05 and a p-value of 0.73. The improvement is 2.62 which is enough according to the LRT. The SBC requires an improvement of $0.5\ln(25) = 1.6094$ which also supports the negative binomial model. The zero-modified negative binomial model as an NLL of 60.95 and a p-value of 0.04. Thus the best model is not the Poisson, but is the negative binomial.

14.7 When individual negative binomial distributions are fit, the goodness-of-fit test statistics are all less than 0.013, so the model is clearly appropriate. The respective means are 0.09, 0.19, 0.27, 0.35, 0.43, and 0.55 and the expected increase is apparent. To see that a common negative binomial model is not appropriate, the NLL for the combined set is 44,779.6 while if the six separate NLLs are added, the sum is 41,976.9. The improvement is 2,802.7. The SBC

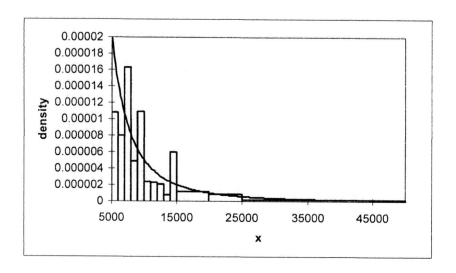

Fig. 14.4   Inverse Burr fit for Exercise 14.5.

requires an improvement of $5\ln(189878) = 60.8$ and separate models should be used.

14.8 The best one parameter model is the geometric with an NLL of 531.46 and a p-value of 0.0502. The two best two-parameter models are the negative binomial with an NLL of 528.77 and a p-value of 0.5405 and the Polya-Aeppli with an NLL of 528.47 and a p-value of 0.7239. The three parameter ZM negative binomial model is best with an NLL of 528.14 and a p-value of 0.6980. These numbers support the two-parameter models, not the ZM negative binomial.

15

Chapter 15 solutions

15.1 SECTION 15.2

15.1 Let the polynomial (a quadratic) be $f(x) = a(x-2)^2 + b(x-2) + c$.
Then $f(2) = c = 50$, $f(4) = 4a + 2b + c = 25$, and $f(5) = 9a + 3b + c = 20$.
Solving gives $a = 5/2, b = -35/2$ and $c = 50$. The quadratic is then $f(x) = 2.5(x-2)^2 - 17.5(x-2) + 50 = 2.5x^2 - 27.5x + 95$.

15.2 Let the line be $f(x) = ax + b$. We need to minimize $F = \sum_{j=1}^{3}[f(x_j) - y_j]^2$. Differentiating with respect to a and b, and setting the derivatives to zero yields the two equations

$$45a + 11b = 300$$
$$11a + 3b = 95.$$

The solution is $a = -145/14$ and $b = 975/14$, so that $f(x) = (975 - 145x)/14$.

Loss Models: From Data to Decisions, Solutions Manual, Second Edition.
By Stuart A. Klugman, Harry H. Panjer, and Gordon E. Willmot
ISBN 0-471-22762-5   Copyright © 2004 John Wiley & Sons, Inc.

15.2   SECTION 15.3

15.3 The clamped spline boundary conditions are replaced by the natural spline boundary conditions $f_0''(2) = 0$ and $f_1''(5) = 0$. The four equations resulting from the interpolating and smoothness conditions remain unchanged. The two equations resulting from the boundary conditions are replaced by

$$
\begin{aligned}
f_0''(2) &= 2c_0 = 0, \\
f_1''(5) &= 2c_1 + 6d_1 = 0.
\end{aligned}
$$

In matrix form, we have the six linear equations

$$
\begin{bmatrix}
2 & 4 & 8 & 0 & 0 & 0 \\
0 & 0 & 0 & 1 & 1 & 1 \\
1 & 4 & 12 & -1 & 0 & 0 \\
0 & 2 & 12 & 0 & -2 & 0 \\
0 & 2 & 0 & 0 & 0 & 0 \\
0 & 0 & 0 & 0 & 2 & 6
\end{bmatrix}
\begin{bmatrix}
b_0 \\ c_0 \\ d_0 \\ b_1 \\ c_1 \\ d_1
\end{bmatrix}
=
\begin{bmatrix}
-25 \\ -5 \\ 0 \\ 0 \\ 0 \\ 0
\end{bmatrix}.
$$

Solving this manually gives $c_0 = 0$ resulting in

$$
\begin{bmatrix}
2 & 8 & 0 & 0 & 0 \\
0 & 0 & 1 & 1 & 1 \\
1 & 12 & -1 & 0 & 0 \\
0 & 12 & 0 & -2 & 0 \\
0 & 0 & 0 & 2 & 6
\end{bmatrix}
\begin{bmatrix}
b_0 \\ d_0 \\ b_1 \\ c_1 \\ d_1
\end{bmatrix}
=
\begin{bmatrix}
-25 \\ -5 \\ 0 \\ 0 \\ 0
\end{bmatrix}.
$$

Take $b_0 = -12.5 - 4d_0$, then

$$
\begin{bmatrix}
0 & 1 & 1 & 1 \\
8 & -1 & 0 & 0 \\
12 & 0 & -2 & 0 \\
0 & 0 & 2 & 6
\end{bmatrix}
\begin{bmatrix}
d_0 \\ b_1 \\ c_1 \\ d_1
\end{bmatrix}
=
\begin{bmatrix}
-5 \\ 12.5 \\ 0 \\ 0
\end{bmatrix}.
$$

Take $c_1 = -3d_1$, then

$$
\begin{bmatrix}
0 & 1 & -2 \\
8 & -1 & 0 \\
12 & 0 & 6
\end{bmatrix}
\begin{bmatrix}
d_0 \\ b_1 \\ d_1
\end{bmatrix}
=
\begin{bmatrix}
-5 \\ 12.5 \\ 0
\end{bmatrix}.
$$

Take $d_1 = -2d_0$, then

$$
\begin{bmatrix}
4 & 1 \\
8 & -1
\end{bmatrix}
\begin{bmatrix}
d_0 \\ b_1
\end{bmatrix}
=
\begin{bmatrix}
-5 \\ 12.5
\end{bmatrix}
$$

from which $d_0 = \frac{5}{8}$ and $b_1 = -\frac{15}{2}$. Substitution yields $d_1 = -\frac{5}{4}, c_1 = \frac{15}{4}$ and $b_0 = -15$. Hence, the interpolating natural cubic spline is

$$
f(x) = \begin{cases}
50 - 15(x-2) + \frac{5}{8}(x-2)^3, & 2 \le x \le 4 \\
25 - \frac{15}{2}(x-4) + \frac{15}{4}(x-4)^2 - \frac{5}{4}(x-4)^3, & 4 \le x \le 5.
\end{cases}
$$

To check

$$
\begin{aligned}
f_0(2) &= 50 \\
f_0(4) &= 50 - 15(2) - \tfrac{5}{8}(8) = 25 \\
f_1(4) &= 25 \\
f_1(5) &= 25 - \tfrac{15}{2} + \tfrac{15}{4} - \tfrac{5}{4} = 20 \\
f_0'(4) &= -15 - 3(\tfrac{5}{8})4 = -\tfrac{15}{2} \\
f_1'(4) &= -\tfrac{15}{2} \\
f_0''(4) &= \tfrac{5}{8}(6)(2) = \tfrac{15}{2} \\
f_1''(4) &= \tfrac{15}{4}(2) = \tfrac{15}{2} \\
f_0''(2) &= 0 \\
f_1''(5) &= \tfrac{15}{4}(2) - \tfrac{5}{4}(3)(2) = 0.
\end{aligned}
$$

15.4 We have $n = 4$, $x_j = j - 2$, $h_j = 1$, $g_j = 4$, $u_1 = u_3 = -12$, and $u_2 = 12$. Then

$$
\mathbf{Hm} = \begin{bmatrix} 4 & 1 & 0 \\ 1 & 4 & 1 \\ 0 & 1 & 4 \end{bmatrix} \begin{bmatrix} m_1 \\ m_2 \\ m_3 \end{bmatrix} = 12 \begin{bmatrix} -1 \\ 1 \\ -1 \end{bmatrix} = \mathbf{v}
$$

from which, $m_1 = m_3 = -30/7$ and $m_2 = 36/7$. Thus

$$
\begin{aligned}
\mathbf{m} &= (0, -30/7, 36/7, -30/7, 0)' \\
\mathbf{c} &= (0, -15/7, 18/7, -15/7)' \\
\mathbf{d} &= (-5/7, 11/7, -11/7, 5/7)' \\
\mathbf{b} &= (12/7, -3/7, 0, 3/7)', \text{ and} \\
\mathbf{a} &= (0, 1, 0, 1)'.
\end{aligned}
$$

Thus the spline is

$$
f(x) = \begin{cases}
\tfrac{12}{7}(x+2) - \tfrac{5}{7}(x+2)^3, & -2 \le x \le -1 \\
1 - \tfrac{3}{7}(x+1) - \tfrac{15}{7}(x+1)^2 + \tfrac{11}{7}(x+1)^3, & -1 \le x \le 0 \\
\tfrac{18}{7}x^2 - \tfrac{11}{7}x^3, & 0 \le x \le 1 \\
1 + \tfrac{3}{7}(x-1) - \tfrac{15}{7}(x-1)^2 + \tfrac{5}{7}(x-1)^3, & 1 \le x \le 2.
\end{cases}
$$

15.5 (a)

$$
\begin{array}{ll}
f_0(0) = 0, & f_1(0) = 0 \\
f_1(1) = 2, & f_2(1) = 2 \\
f_0'(0) = 1, & f_1'(0) = 1 \\
f_1'(1) = 4, & f_2'(1) = 4 \\
f_0''(0) = 0, & f_1''(0) = 0 \\
f_1''(1) = 6, & f_2''(1) = 6
\end{array}
$$

YES

(b)

$$f_0(1) = 1, \quad f_1(1) = 1$$
$$f_1(2) = 7, \quad f_2(2) = 7$$
$$f_0'(1) = 3, \quad f_1'(1) = 3$$
$$f_1'(2) = 9, \quad f_2'(2) = 9$$
$$f_0''(1) = 6, \quad f_1''(1) = 6$$
$$f_1''(2) = 6, \quad f_2''(2) = 4$$

NO

(c)

$$f_0(0) = 0, \quad f_1(0) = 0$$
$$f_1(1) = 4, \quad f_2(1) = 4$$
$$f_0'(0) = 2, \quad f_1'(0) = 2$$
$$f_1'(1) = 6, \quad f_2'(1) = 6$$
$$f_0''(0) = 0, \quad f_1''(1) = 4$$
$$f_1''(1) = 4, \quad f_2''(1) = 4$$

NO

15.6

$$f_0(1) = 5, \quad f_1(1) = a \Rightarrow a = 5$$
$$f_0'(1) = 3, \quad f_1'(1) = b \Rightarrow b = 3$$
$$f_0''(1) = 6, \quad f_1''(1) = 2c \Rightarrow c = 3.$$

15.7 Let
$$f_0(x) = a_0 + b_0(x+1) + c_0(x+1)^2 + d_0(x+1)^3$$
$$f_1(x) = a_1 + b_1 x + c_1 x^2 + d_1 x^3.$$

$f_0(-1) = -1 \Rightarrow a_0 = -1$
$f_0(0) = f_1(0) \Rightarrow -1 + b_0 + c_0 + d_0 = a_1 = 0$
$f_1(1) = 1 \Rightarrow b_1 + c_1 + d_1 = 1$
$f_0'(-1) = 0 \Rightarrow b_0 = 0$
$f_1'(1) = 0 \Rightarrow b_1 + 2c_1 + 3d_1 = 0$
$f_0'(0) = f_1'(0) \Rightarrow b_0 + 2c_0 + 3d_0 = b_1$
$f_0''(0) = f_1''(0) \Rightarrow 2c_0 + 6d_0 = 2c_1.$
Solving $a_0 = -1, b_0 = 0, c_0 = 1.5, d_0 = -0.5, a_1 = 0, b_1 = 1.5, c_1 = 0, d_1 = -0.5$.
Therefore, $f_0(x) = -1 + 1.5(x+1)^2 - 0.5(x+1)^3 = 1.5x - 0.5x^3 = f_1(x)$.

Alternatively, $h_0 = h_1 = 1, g_1 = 2(1+1) = 4, u_1 = 6\left(\frac{1-0}{1} - \frac{0-(-1)}{1}\right) = 0$
and so (15.14) becomes $m_0 + 4m_1 + m_2 = 0$. The clamped spline condition
produces the two additional equations (from (15.22), $m_0 = \frac{3}{1}\left(\frac{0+1}{1} - 0\right) - \frac{m_1}{2}$
or $m_0 + 0.5m_1 = 3$ and $m_2 = \frac{3}{1}\left(0 - \frac{1-0}{1}\right) - \frac{m_1}{2}$ or $0.5m_1 + m_2 = -3$. The
solution is $m_0 = 3, m_1 = 0, m_2 = -3$. Then, $c_0 = \frac{3}{2} = 1.5, c_1 = \frac{0}{2} = 0, a_0 =$

-1, $a_1 = 0$, $d_0 = \frac{0-3}{6(1)} = -0.5$, $d_1 = \frac{-3-0}{6(1)} = -0.5$, $b_0 = \frac{0-(-1)}{1} - \frac{1(6+0)}{6} = 0$,
and $b_1 = \frac{1-0}{1} - \frac{1(0-3)}{6} = 1.5$.

15.8 (a) $f_0(-1) = f_1(-1) = 11$; $f_1(0) = f_2(0) = 26$; $f_2(3) = f_3(3) = 56$.
$f_0'(-1) = f_1'(-1) = 10$; $f_1'(0) = f_2'(0) = 19$; $f_2'(3) = f_3'(3) = -17$.
$f_0''(-1) = f_1''(-1) = 12$; $f_1''(0) = f_2''(0) = 6$; $f_2''(3) = f_3''(3) = -30$.
Case:

I. $m_0 = f''(-3) = 9(2) + 3(2)(-3) = 0$; $m_n = f''(4) = -60(2) + 5(3)(2)(4) = 0$. YES

II. $m_0 = m_n = 0$. YES

III. $m_1 = f''(-1) = 9(2) + 3(2)(-1) = 12 \neq m_0$. NO

IV. $f'''(x)$ changes at $x = -1$ and $x = 3$. NO

V. Because slopes at $x = -3$ and $x = 4$ could have been fixed. YES.

15.3 SECTION 15.4

15.9 The spline is

$$f(x) = \begin{cases} 50 - 15(x-2) + \frac{5}{8}(x-2)^3, & 2 \leq x \leq 4 \\ 25 - \frac{15}{2}(x-4) + \frac{15}{4}(x-4)^2 - \frac{5}{4}(x-4)^3, & 4 \leq x \leq 5 \end{cases}$$

and the second derivative is

$$f''(x) = \begin{cases} \frac{15}{4}(x-2), & 2 \leq x \leq 4 \\ \frac{15}{2} - \frac{15}{2}(x-4) = \frac{15}{2}(5-x), & 4 \leq x \leq 5. \end{cases}$$

The curvature is

$$\int_2^4 \frac{225}{16}(x-2)^2 dx + \int_4^5 \frac{225}{4}(5-x)^2 dx$$

$$= \left. \frac{225}{16}\frac{(x-2)^3}{3}\right|_2^4 + \left. \frac{225}{4}\frac{(5-x)^3}{-3}\right|_4^5$$

$$= \frac{75}{2} + \frac{75}{4} = 56.25.$$

15.4 SECTION 15.5

15.10 The spline in Exercise 15.3 is

$$f(x) = \begin{cases} 50 - 15(x-2) + \frac{5}{8}(x-2)^3, & 2 \leq x \leq 4 \\ 25 - \frac{15}{2}(x-4) + \frac{15}{4}(x-4)^2 - \frac{5}{4}(x-4)^3, & 4 \leq x \leq 5. \end{cases}$$

The slopes at $x_0 = 2$ and $x_2 = 5$ are

$$f'(2) = -15 \text{ and } f'(5) = -\frac{15}{2} + \frac{15}{4}(2) - \frac{5}{4}(3) = -\frac{15}{4}.$$

The extrapolation functions are

$$\begin{aligned}
f(x) &= 50 + 15(2 - x) = 80 - 15x, \ x < 2, \text{ and} \\
f(x) &= 20 - \frac{15}{4}(x - 5) = \frac{155 - 15x}{4}, \quad x > 5.
\end{aligned}$$

The extrapolated values are $80 - 15(0) = 80$ and $\frac{155 - 15(7)}{4} = 12.5$.

15.5   SECTION 15.6

15.11 (a) The following steps are followed:

$$\mathbf{H} = \begin{bmatrix} 4 & 1 \\ 1 & 4 \end{bmatrix}$$

$$\mathbf{R} = 6 \begin{bmatrix} 1 & -2 & 1 & 0 \\ 0 & 1 & -2 & 1 \end{bmatrix}.$$

Because $\sigma_j = 0.5, j = 0, 1, 2$, $\mathbf{\Sigma}$ is diagonal matrix with each diagonal element equal to 0.25. Then,

$$\mathbf{R\Sigma R}^T = 9 \begin{bmatrix} 6 & -4 \\ -4 & 6 \end{bmatrix}$$

$$\mathbf{H} + \frac{1-p}{6p}\mathbf{R\Sigma R}^T = \begin{bmatrix} 5 & 1/3 \\ 1/3 & 5 \end{bmatrix}$$

and the inverse of the second matrix is

$$\left(\mathbf{H} + \frac{1-p}{3p}\mathbf{R\Sigma R}^T\right)^{-1} = \begin{bmatrix} 0.2009 & -0.0134 \\ -0.0134 & 0.2009 \end{bmatrix}$$

which leads to

$$\mathbf{a} = \begin{bmatrix} 0.1071 \\ 1.6786 \\ 1.3214 \\ 2.8929 \end{bmatrix}.$$

(b) Using the nodes $(0, 0.1071)$, $(1, 1.6786)$, $(2, 1.3214)$ and $(3, 2.8929)$ in (15.15) results in

$$\mathbf{u} = \begin{bmatrix} -11.571 \\ 11.571 \end{bmatrix}$$

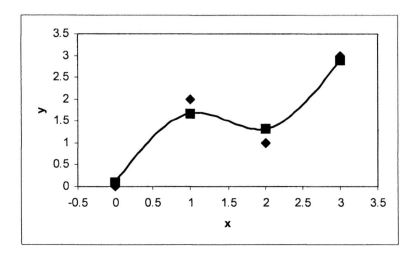

Fig. 15.1   Interpolating spline for Exercise 15.11.

and solving for **m** (in (15.17)) yields

$$\mathbf{m} = \left[\begin{array}{c} -3.857 \\ 3.857 \end{array} \right].$$

Substituting into (15.18) results in the following coefficients for the cubic spline segments.

j	x_j	a_j	b_j	c_j	d_j
0	0	0.1071	2.2143	0	-0.6429
1	1	1.6786	0.2857	-1.9286	1.2857
2	2	1.3214	0.2857	1.9286	-0.6429

(c) The resulting graph is shown in Figure 15.1

16

Chapter 16 solutions

16.1 SECTION 16.2

16.1

$$f(x|y) = \frac{f(x,y)}{f(y)} = \frac{\Pr(X = x,\ Z = y - x)}{\Pr(Y = y)}$$

$$= \frac{\binom{n_1}{x}p^x(1-p)^{n_1-x}\binom{n_2}{y-x}p^{y-x}(1-p)^{n_2-y+x}}{\binom{n_1+n_2}{y}p^y(1-p)^{n_1+n_2-y}}$$

$$= \frac{\binom{n_1}{x}\binom{n_2}{y-x}}{\binom{n_1+n_2}{y}}$$

This is the hypergeometric distribution.

16.2(a) $f_X(0) = 0.3,\ f_X(1) = 0.4,\ f_X(2) = 0.3.$
$f_Y(0) = 0.25,\ f_Y(1) = 0.3,\ f_Y(2) = 0.45.$
(b) The following array presents the values for $x = 0, 1, 2$

$$\begin{aligned}
f(x|Y=0) &= 0.2/0.25 = 0.8,\ 0/0.25 = 0,\ 0.05/0.25 = 0.2, \\
f(x|Y=1) &= 0/0.3 = 0,\ 0.15/0.3 = 0.5,\ 0.15/0.3 = 0.5, \\
f(x|Y=2) &= 0.1/0.45 = 0.22,\ 0.25/0.45 = 0.56,\ 0.1/0.45 = 0.22
\end{aligned}$$

Loss Models: From Data to Decisions, Solutions Manual, Second Edition.
By Stuart A. Klugman, Harry H. Panjer, and Gordon E. Willmot
ISBN 0-471-22762-5   Copyright © 2004 John Wiley & Sons, Inc.

(c)

$$
\begin{aligned}
\mathrm{E}(X|Y=0) &= 0(0.8) + 1(0) + 2(0.2) = 0.4 \\
\mathrm{E}(X|Y=1) &= 0(0) + 1(0.5) + 2(0.5) = 1.5 \\
\mathrm{E}(X|Y=2) &= 0(0.22) + 1(0.56) + 2(0.22) = 1 \\
\mathrm{E}(X^2|Y=0) &= 0(0.8) + 1(0) + 4(0.2) = 0.8 \\
\mathrm{E}(X^2|Y=1) &= 0(0) + 1(0.5) + 4(0.5) = 2.5 \\
\mathrm{E}(X^2|Y=2) &= 0(0.22) + 1(0.56) + 4(0.22) = 1.44 \\
\mathrm{Var}(X|Y=0) &= 0.8 - 0.4^2 = 0.64 \\
\mathrm{Var}(X|Y=1) &= 2.5 - 1.5^2 = 0.25 \\
\mathrm{Var}(X|Y=2) &= 1.44 - 1^2 = 0.44
\end{aligned}
$$

(d)

$$
\begin{aligned}
\mathrm{E}(X) &= 0.4(0.25) + 1.5(0.3) + 1(0.45) = 1 \\
\mathrm{E}[\mathrm{Var}(X|Y)] &= 0.64(0.25) + 0.25(0.3) + 0.44(0.45) = 0.433 \\
\mathrm{Var}[\mathrm{E}(X|Y)] &= 0.16(0.25) + 2.25(0.3) + 1(0.45) - 1^2 = 0.165 \\
\mathrm{Var}(X) &= 0.433 + 0.165 = 0.598
\end{aligned}
$$

16.3 (a)

$$
\begin{aligned}
f(x,y) &\propto \exp\left\{-\frac{1}{2(1-\rho^2)}\left[\left(\frac{x-\mu_1}{\sigma_1}\right)^2 - 2\rho\left(\frac{x-\mu_1}{\sigma_1}\right)\left(\frac{y-\mu_2}{\sigma_2}\right)\right]\right\} \\
&\propto \exp\left\{-\frac{1}{2(1-\rho^2)}\left[\frac{x^2}{\sigma_1^2} - 2x\left(\frac{\mu_1}{\sigma_1^2} + \rho\frac{y-u_2}{\sigma_1\sigma_2}\right)\right]\right\}.
\end{aligned}
$$

Now a normal density $N(\mu, \sigma^2)$ has pdf $f(x) \propto \exp\left[-\frac{1}{2\sigma^2}(x^2 - 2\mu x)\right]$. Then $f_{X|Y}(x|y) \propto f(x,y)$ is $N\left[\mu_1 + \rho\frac{\sigma_1}{\sigma_2}(y-\mu_2), (1-\rho^2)\sigma_1^2\right]$.

(b)

$$f_X(x) = \int f(x,y)\,dy$$

$$\propto \int \exp\left\{-\frac{1}{2(1-\rho^2)}\left[\left(\frac{x-\mu_1}{\sigma_1}\right)^2 - 2\rho\left(\frac{x-\mu_1}{\sigma_1}\right)\left(\frac{y-\mu_2}{\sigma_2}\right)\right.\right.$$
$$\left.\left. + \left(\frac{y-\mu_2}{\sigma_2}\right)^2\right]\right\}dy$$

$$= \exp\left[-\frac{1}{2}\left(\frac{x-\mu_1}{\sigma_1}\right)^2\right]$$

$$\times \int \exp\left[-\frac{1}{2}\left(\frac{y-\mu_2-\rho\frac{\sigma_2}{\sigma_1}(x-\mu_1)}{\sigma_2\sqrt{1-\rho^2}}\right)^2\right]dy$$

$$= \exp\left[-\frac{1}{2}\left(\frac{x-\mu_1}{\sigma_1}\right)^2\right]\sqrt{2\pi\sigma_2\sqrt{1-\rho^2}}$$

$$\propto \exp\left[-\frac{1}{2}\left(\frac{x-\mu_1}{\sigma_1}\right)^2\right]$$

Since the normal density is $\frac{1}{\sqrt{2\pi}\sigma}\exp\left[-\frac{1}{2}\left(\frac{x-\mu}{\sigma}\right)^2\right]$, in general, we have

$$f_X(x) = \frac{1}{\sqrt{2\pi}\sigma_1}\exp\left[-\frac{1}{2}\left(\frac{x-\mu_1}{\sigma_1}\right)^2\right] \sim N\left(\mu_1,\sigma_1^2\right)$$

(c) Suppose $f_X(x)f_Y(y) = f_{X,Y}(x,y)$. Then $f_X(x)f_Y(y) = f_{X,Y}(x,y) = f_{X|Y}(x|y)f_Y(y)$ Therefore, $f_X(x) = f_{X|Y}(x|y)$. From the results of (a) and (b), $\rho = 0$.
   Then

$$f_{X,Y}(x,y) \propto \exp\left\{-\frac{1}{2}\left[\left(\frac{x-\mu_1}{\sigma_1}\right)^2 + \left(\frac{y-\mu_2}{\sigma_2}\right)^2\right]\right\} \propto f_X(x)f_Y(x).$$

Therefore, $f_{X,Y}(x,y) = f_X(x)f_Y(y)$.

16.4 $\mathrm{E}\left[\sum b_j(Y_j - \bar{Y})^2\right] = \mathrm{E}\left[\sum b_j(Y_j - \gamma + \gamma - \bar{Y})^2\right]$

$$= \mathrm{E}\left[\sum b_j(Y_j - \gamma)^2 + \sum b_j(\gamma - \bar{Y})^2\right.$$
$$\left. + 2\sum b_j(Y_j - \gamma)(\gamma - \bar{Y})\right]$$

$$= \sum b_j(a_j + \sigma^2/b_j) + b\,\mathrm{Var}(\bar{Y})$$
$$+ 2\mathrm{E}\left[\gamma\sum b_j Y_j - b\gamma^2 + b\gamma\bar{Y} - \bar{Y}\sum b_j Y_j\right]$$

$$\mathrm{E}\left[\gamma \sum b_j Y_j - b\gamma^2 + b\gamma\bar{Y} - \bar{Y}\sum b_j Y_j\right] = \mathrm{E}[\gamma b\bar{Y} - b\gamma^2 + b\gamma\bar{Y} - b\bar{Y}^2]$$
$$= -\mathrm{E}[b(\bar{Y} - \gamma)^2]$$
$$= -b\,\mathrm{Var}(\bar{Y})$$

$$\mathrm{Var}(\bar{Y}) = \frac{1}{b^2}\sum b_j^2\,\mathrm{Var}(Y_j) = \frac{1}{b^2}\sum b_j^2(a_j + \sigma^2/b_j)$$
$$= \frac{1}{b^2}\sum b_j^2 a_j + \frac{1}{b}\sigma^2$$

$$\mathrm{E}\left[\sum b_j(Y_j - \bar{Y})^2\right] = \sum b_j(a_j + \sigma^2/b_j) - b\,\mathrm{Var}(\bar{Y})$$
$$= \sum b_j(a_j + \sigma^2/b_j) - \frac{1}{b}\sum b_j^2 a_j - \sigma^2$$
$$= \sum a_j(b_j - b_j^2/b) + (n-1)\sigma^2$$

16.5 (a)

$$\mathrm{E}(X) = \mathrm{E}[\mathrm{E}(X|\Theta_1,\Theta_2)] = \mathrm{E}(\Theta_1)$$
$$\mathrm{Var}(X) = \mathrm{E}[\mathrm{Var}(X|\Theta_1,\Theta_2)] + \mathrm{Var}[\mathrm{E}(X|\Theta_1,\Theta_2)]$$
$$= \mathrm{E}(\Theta_2) + \mathrm{Var}(\Theta_1)$$

(b) $f_{X|\Theta_1,\Theta_2}(x|\theta_1,\theta_2) = (2\pi\theta_2^2)^{-1/2}\exp\left[-\frac{1}{2\theta_2}(x-\theta_1)^2\right]$

$$f_X(x) = \int\int (2\pi\theta_2^2)^{-1/2}\exp\left[-\frac{1}{2\theta_2}(x-\theta_1)^2\right]\pi(\theta_1,\theta_2)\,d\theta_1 d\theta_2$$
$$= \int\int (2\pi\theta_2^2)^{-1/2}\exp\left[-\frac{1}{2\theta_2}(x-\theta_1)^2\right]\pi_1(\theta_1)\pi_2(\theta_2)\,d\theta_1 d\theta_2.$$

We are also given, $f_{Y|\Theta_2}(y|\theta_2) = (2\pi\theta_2^2)^{-1/2}\exp\left(-\frac{1}{2\theta_2}y^2\right)$. Let $Z = Y + \Theta_1$. Then

$$f_{Z,|\Theta_2}(z|\theta_2) = \int f_{Y|\theta_2}(z - \theta_1|\theta_2)\pi_1(\theta_1)d\theta_1$$

and

$$f_Z(z) = \int f_{Z,|\Theta_2}(z|\theta_2)\pi_2(\theta_2)d\theta_2$$
$$= \int\int f_{Y|\theta_2}(z - \theta_1|\theta_2)\pi_1(\theta_1)d\theta_1\pi_2(\theta_2)d\theta_2$$
$$= \int\int (2\pi\theta_2^2)^{-1/2}\exp\left[-\frac{1}{2\theta_2}(z-\theta_1)^2\right]\pi_1(\theta_1)d\theta_1\pi_2(\theta_2)d\theta_2$$
$$= f_X(x).$$

16.6
$$f_X(x) = \int \frac{e^{-\theta}\theta^x}{x!}\pi_1(\theta)d\theta = \int \frac{e^{-\theta}\theta^x}{x!}\pi(\theta-x)d\theta$$

$$f_Y(y) = \frac{e^{-\alpha}\alpha^y}{y!}$$

$$f_Z(z) = \int \frac{e^{-\theta}\theta^z}{z!}\pi(\theta)d\theta$$

Let $W = Y + Z$. Then

$$f_W(w) = \sum_{y=0}^{w} f_Y(y)f_Z(w-y)$$

$$= \sum_{y=0}^{w} \frac{e^{-\alpha}\alpha^y}{y!}\int \frac{e^{-\theta}\theta^{(w-y)}}{(w-y)!}\pi(\theta)d\theta$$

$$= \int \frac{e^{-(\alpha+\theta)}(\alpha+\theta)^w}{w!}\sum_{y=0}^{w}\binom{w}{y}\left(\frac{\alpha}{\alpha+\theta}\right)^y\left(\frac{\theta}{\alpha+\theta}\right)^{w-y}\pi(\theta)d\theta$$

$$= \int \frac{e^{-(\alpha+\theta)}(\alpha+\theta)^w}{w!}\pi(\theta)d\theta$$

with the last line following because the sum contains binomial probabilities. Let $r = \alpha + \theta$ and so

$$f_W(w) = \int \frac{e^{-r}r^w}{w!}\pi(r-\alpha)dr$$
$$= f_X(x).$$

16.2 SECTION 16.3

16.7
$$\lambda_0 = (1.96/0.05)^2 = 1,536.64$$

$$E(X) = \int_0^{100} \frac{100x - x^2}{5,000}dx = 33\frac{1}{3}$$

$$E(X^2) = \int_0^{100} \frac{100x^2 - x^3}{5,000}dx = 1,666\frac{2}{3}$$

$$\text{Var}(X) = 1,666\frac{2}{3} - (33\frac{1}{3})^2 = 555\frac{5}{9}$$

$$n\lambda = 1,536.64\left[1 + \left(\frac{\sqrt{555\frac{5}{9}}}{33\frac{1}{3}}\right)^2\right] = 2,304.96$$

2,305 claims are needed.

16.8 $0.81 = n\lambda/\lambda_0$. $0.64 = n\lambda\left[\lambda_0\left(1 + \frac{\alpha\beta^2}{\alpha^2\beta^2}\right)\right]^{-1} = 0.81(1 + \alpha^{-1})^{-1}$, $\alpha = 3.7647$. $\alpha\beta = 100$, $\beta = 26.5625$.

16.9 $\lambda_0 = 1{,}082.41$. $\mu = 600$, Estimate the variance as $\sigma^2 = \frac{0^2 + 75^2 + (-75)^2}{2} = 75^2$. The standard for full credibility is $1{,}082.41(75/600)^2 = 16.913$. $Z = \sqrt{3/16.913} = 0.4212$. The credibility pure premium is

$$0.4212(475) + 0.5788(600) = 547.35.$$

16.10 $\mu = s\beta\theta_Y$, $\sigma^2 = s\beta\sigma_Y^2 + s\beta(1+\beta)\theta_Y^2$ where s is used in place of the customary negative binomial parameter, r. Then

$$1.645 = \frac{r\mu\sqrt{n}}{\sigma} = \frac{0.05\sqrt{n}s\beta\theta_Y}{\sqrt{s\beta\sigma_Y^2 + s\beta(1+\beta)\theta_Y^2}}$$

and so

$$1{,}082.41 = \frac{ns^2\beta^2\theta_Y^2}{s\beta\sigma_Y^2 + s\beta(1+\beta)\theta_Y^2} = ns\beta\left(\frac{\theta_Y^2}{\sigma_Y^2 + \theta_Y^2(1+\beta)}\right).$$

The standard for full credibility is

$$ns\beta = 1{,}082.41\left(1 + \beta + \frac{\sigma_Y^2}{\theta_Y^2}\right).$$

Partial credibility is obtained by taking the square root of ratio of the number of claims to the standard for full credibility.

16.11 $\lambda_0 = (2.2414/.03)^2 = 5{,}582.08$. 5,583 claims are required.

16.12

$$\mathrm{E}(X) = \int_0^{200{,}000} \frac{x}{200{,}000}\,dx = 100{,}000$$

$$\mathrm{E}(X^2) = \int_0^{200{,}000} \frac{x^2}{200{,}000}\,dx = 13{,}333{,}333{,}333\frac{1}{3}$$

$$\mathrm{Var}(X) = 3{,}333{,}333{,}333\frac{1}{3}$$

The standard for full credibility is

$$1{,}082.41(1 + 3{,}333{,}333{,}333.33/10{,}000{,}000{,}000) = 1{,}443.21$$

$$Z = \sqrt{1{,}082/1{,}443.21} = 0.86586.$$

16.13 $(1.645/0.06)^2(1 + 7{,}500^2/1{,}500^2) = 19{,}543.51$ or 19,544 claims.

16.14 $Z = \sqrt{6{,}000/19{,}543.51} = 0.55408$. The credibility estimate is

$$0.55408(15{,}600{,}000) + 0.44592(16{,}500{,}000) = 16{,}001{,}328.$$

16.15 For the standard for estimating the number of claims, $800 = (y_p/0.05)^2$ and so $y_p = \sqrt{2}$.

$$E(X) = \int_0^{100} 0.0002x(100 - x)dx = 33\frac{1}{3},$$

$$E(X^2) = \int_0^{100} 0.0002x^2(100 - x)dx = 1,666\frac{2}{3},$$

$$Var(X) = 1,666\frac{2}{3} - (33\frac{1}{3})^2 = 555\frac{5}{9}.$$

The standard for full credibility is $(\sqrt{2}/0.1)^2[1 + 555\frac{5}{9}/(33\frac{1}{3})^2] = 300$

16.16 $1,000 = (1.96/0.1)^2(1 + c^2)$. The solution is the coefficient of variation, 1.2661.

16.17 $Z = \sqrt{10,000/17,500} = 0.75593$. The credibility estimate is

$$0.75593(25,000,000) + 0.24407(20,000,000) = 23,779,650.$$

16.18 The standard for estimating claim numbers is $(2.326/0.05)^2 = 2,164.11$. For estimating the amount of claims we have $E(X) = \int_1^\infty 2.5x^{-2.5}dx = 5/3$, $E(X^2) = \int_1^\infty 2.5x^{-1.5}dx = 5$, and $Var(X) = 5 - (5/3)^2 = 20/9$. Then $2164.11 = (1.96/K)^2[1 + (20/9)/(25/9)]$, $K = 0.056527$

16.19 $E(X) = 0.5(1) + 0.3(2) + 0.2(10) = 3.1$, $E(X^2) = 0.5(1) + 0.3(4) + 0.2(100) = 21.7$, $Var(X) = 21.7 - 3.1^2 = 12.09$. The standard for full credibility is $(1.645/.1)^2(1 + 12.09/3.1^2) = 611.04$ and so 612 claims are needed.

16.20 $3415 = (1.96/k)^2(1 + 4)$, $k = 0.075$ or 7.5%.

16.21 $Z = \sqrt{n/F}$, $R = ZO + (1 - Z)P$, $Z = (R - P)/(O - P) = \sqrt{n/F}$. $n/F = (R - P)^2/(O - P)^2$. $n = \frac{F(R-P)^2}{(O-P)^2}$.

16.3 SECTION 16.4

16.22 (a) $\pi(\theta_{ij}) = 1/6$ for die i and spinner j.
(b)(c) The calculations are in Table 16.1.
(d) $Pr(X_1 = 3) = (1 + 2 + 4 + 4 + 8 + 16)/(30 \cdot 6) = 35/180$.
(e) The calculations are in Table 16.2.
(f) The calculations are in Table 16.3.

Table 16.1   Calculations for Exercise 16.22(b) and (c)

i	j	$\Pr(X = 0|\theta_{ij})$	$\Pr(X = 3|\theta_{ij})$	$\Pr(X = 8|\theta_{ij})$	$\mu(\theta_{ij})$	$v(\theta_{ij})$
1	1	25/30	1/30	4/30	35/30	6,725/900
1	2	25/30	2/30	3/30	30/30	5,400/900
1	3	25/30	4/30	1/30	20/30	2,600/900
2	1	10/30	4/30	16/30	140/30	12,200/900
2	2	10/30	8/30	12/30	120/30	10,800/900
2	3	10/30	16/30	4/30	80/30	5,600/900

Table 16.2   Calculations for Exercise 16.22(e)

i	j	$\Pr(X_1 = 3|\theta_{ij})$	$\Pr(\Theta = \theta_{ij}|X_1 = 3) = \frac{\Pr(X_1=3|\theta_{ij})(1/6)}{35/180}$
1	1	1/30	1/35
1	2	2/30	2/35
1	3	4/30	4/35
2	1	4/30	4/35
2	2	8/30	8/35
2	3	16/30	16/35

Table 16.3   Calculations for Exercise 16.22(f)

x_2	$\Pr(X_2 = x_2|X_1 = 3) = \sum \Pr(X_2 = x_2|\Theta = \theta_{ij})\Pr(\Theta = \theta_{ij}|X_1 = 3)$
0	$\frac{1}{30}\frac{1}{35}[25(1) + 25(2) + 25(4) + 10(4) + 10(8) + 10(16)] = 455/1{,}050$
3	$\frac{1}{30}\frac{1}{35}[1(1) + 2(2) + 4(4) + 4(4) + 8(8) + 16(16)] = 357/1{,}050$
8	$\frac{1}{30}\frac{1}{35}[4(1) + 3(2) + 1(4) + 16(4) + 12(8) + 4(16)] = 238/1{,}050$

(g)

$$
\begin{aligned}
E(X_2|X_1 = 3) &= \frac{1}{30}\frac{1}{35}[35(1) + 30(2) + 20(4) + 140(4) + 120(8) + 80(16)] \\
&= \frac{2{,}975}{1{,}050}
\end{aligned}
$$

(h) $\Pr(X_2 = 0,\ X_1 = 3) = \left[\frac{1}{6}\frac{35(1)}{900} + \frac{25(2)}{900} + \frac{25(4)}{900}\right.$

$$
\left. + \frac{10(4)}{900} + \frac{10(8)}{900} + \frac{10(16)}{900}\right] = \frac{455}{5{,}400}.
$$

$\Pr(X_2 = 3|X_1 = 3) = \frac{357}{5,400}$. $\Pr(X_2 = 8|X_1 = 3) = \frac{238}{5,400}$.

(i) Divide answers to (h) by $\Pr(X_1 = 3) = 35/180$ to obtain the answers to (f).

(j) $E(X_2|X_1 = 3) = 0\frac{455}{1050} + 3\frac{357}{1050} + 8\frac{238}{1050} = \frac{2,975}{1,050}$

(k)

$$\mu = \frac{1}{6}\frac{1}{30}(35 + 30 + 20 + 140 + 120 + 80) = \frac{425}{180}$$

$$v = \frac{1}{6}\frac{1}{900}(5,725 + 5,400 + 2,600 + 12,200 + 10,800 + 5,600) = \frac{43,325}{5,400}$$

$$a = \frac{1}{6}\frac{1}{900}(35^2 + 30^2 + 20^2 + 140^2 + 120^2 + 80^2) - \left(\frac{425}{180}\right)^2 = \frac{76,925}{32,400}$$

(l)

$$Z = \left(1 + \frac{43,425/5,400}{76,925/32,400}\right)^{-1}$$
$$= 0.228349.$$
$$P_c = 0.228349(3) + 0.771651(425/180)$$
$$= 2.507.$$

16.23 (a) $\pi(\theta_i) = 1/3$, $i = 1, 2, 3$.

(b)(c) The calculations appear in Table 16.4.

Table 16.4 Calculations for Exercise 16.23(b) and (c)

i	1	2	3
$\Pr(X = 0|\theta_i)$	0.1600	0.0625	0.2500
$\Pr(X = 1|\theta_i)$	0.2800	0.0500	0.1500
$\Pr(X = 2|\theta_i)$	0.3225	0.3350	0.3725
$\Pr(X = 3|\theta_i)$	0.1750	0.1300	0.1050
$\Pr(X = 4|\theta_i)$	0.0625	0.4225	0.1225
$\mu(\theta_i)$	1.7	2.8	1.7
$v(\theta_i)$	1.255	1.480	1.655

(d) $\Pr(X_1 = 2) = \frac{1}{3}(0.3225 + 0.335 + 0.3725) = 0.34333$.

(e) The calculations appear in Table 16.5.

(f) The calculations appear in Table 16.6.

(g) $E(X_2|X_1 = 2) = 1.7(0.313107) + 2.8(0.325243) + 1.7(0.361650)$
$$= 2.057767.$$

(h) $\Pr(X_2 = 0, X_1 = 2) = [0.16(0.3225) + 0.0625(0.335) + 0.25(0.3725)]/3$
$$= 0.055221$$

$\Pr(X_2 = 1, X_1 = 2) = 0.054308$. $\Pr(X_2 = 2, X_1 = 2) = 0.118329$

$\Pr(X_2 = 3, X_1 = 2) = 0.046367$. $\Pr(X_2 = 4, X_1 = 2) = 0.069108$.

Table 16.5   Calculations for Exercise 16.23(e)

i	$\Pr(X_1 = 2|\theta_i)$	$\Pr(\Theta = \theta_i|X_1 = 2) = \frac{\Pr(X_1=2|\theta_i)(1/3)}{.34333}$
1	0.3225	0.313107
2	0.3350	0.325243
3	0.3725	0.361650

Table 16.6   Calculations for Exercise 16.23(f)

x_2	$\Pr(X_2 = x_2|X_1 = 2) = \sum \Pr(X_2 = x_2|\Theta = \theta_i)\Pr(\Theta = \theta_i|X_1 = 2)$
0	$0.16(0.313107) + 0.0625(0.325243) + 0.25(0.361650) = 0.160837$
1	$0.28(0.313107) + 0.05(0.325243) + 0.15(0.361650) = 0.158180$
2	$0.3225(0.313107) + 0.335(0.325243) + 0.3725(0.361650) = 0.344648$
3	$0.175(0.313107) + 0.13(0.325243) + 0.105(0.361650) = 0.135049$
4	$0.0625(0.313107) + 0.4225(0.325243) + 0.1225(0.361650) = 0.201286$

(i) Divide answers to (h) by $\Pr(X_1 = 2) = 0.343333$ to obtain the answers to (f).

(j)
$$\mathrm{E}(X_2|X_1 = 2) = 0(0.160837) + 1(0.158180) + 2(0.344648) + 3(0.135049)$$
$$+4(0.201286) = 2.057767.$$

(k)
$$\mu = \frac{1}{3}(1.7 + 2.8 + 1.7) = 2.06667$$
$$v = \frac{1}{3}(1.255 + 1.48 + 1.655) = 1.463333$$
$$a = \frac{1}{3}(1.7^2 + 2.8^2 + 1.7^2) - 2.06667^2 = 0.268889.$$

(l)
$$Z = \left(1 + \frac{1.463333}{.267779}\right)^{-1}$$
$$= 0.155228.$$
$$P_c = 0.155228(2) + 0.844772(2.06667)$$
$$= 2.056321$$

(m) Table 16.4 becomes Table 16.7 and the quantities become $\mu = 1.033333$, $v = 0.731667$, $\alpha = 0.067222$. $Z = \frac{2}{2+.731667/0.067222} = 0.155228$.

Table 16.7   Calculations for Exercise 16.23(m)

i	$\Pr(X = 0\|\theta_i)$	$\Pr(X = 1\|\theta_i)$	$\Pr(X = 2\|\theta_i)$	$\mu(\theta_i)$	$v(\theta_i)$
1	0.40	0.35	0.25	0.85	0.6275
2	0.25	0.10	0.65	1.40	0.7400
3	0.50	0.15	0.35	0.85	0.8275

16.24

$$\begin{aligned}
\mathrm{E}\,(S|\theta_A) &= \mathrm{E}\,(N|\theta_A)\,\mathrm{E}\,(X|\theta_A) = 0.2(200) = 40 \\
\mathrm{E}\,(S|\theta_B) &= 0.7(100) = 70 \\
\mathrm{Var}\,(S|\theta_A) &= \mathrm{E}\,(N|\theta_A)\,\mathrm{Var}\,(X|\theta_A) + \mathrm{Var}\,(N|\theta_A)\,[\mathrm{E}\,(X|\theta_A)]^2 \\
&= 0.2(400) + 0.2(40{,}000) = 8{,}800 \\
\mathrm{Var}\,(S|\theta_B) &= 0.7(1500) + 0.3(10{,}000) = 4{,}050 \\
\mu_S &= \frac{2}{3}40 + \frac{1}{3}70 = 50 \\
v_S &= \frac{2}{3}8{,}800 + \frac{1}{3}4{,}050 = 7{,}216.67 \\
a_S &= \mathrm{Var}[\mu(\theta)] = \frac{2}{3}40^2 + \frac{1}{3}70^2 - 50^2 = 200 \\
k &= \frac{v_S}{a_S} = 36.083 \\
Z &= \frac{4}{4 + 36.083} = 0.10 \\
P_c &= 0.10(125) + 0.90(50) = 57.50
\end{aligned}$$

16.25 Let S denote total claims. Then $\mu_S = \mu_N \mu_Y = 0.1(100) = 10$.

$$\begin{aligned}
v_S &= \mathrm{E}\{\mathrm{E}\,(N|\theta_1)\,\mathrm{Var}\,(Y|\theta_2) + \mathrm{Var}\,(N|\theta_1)\,\mathrm{E}[(Y|\theta_2)]^2\} \\
&= \mathrm{E}[\mathrm{E}\,(N|\theta_1)]\mathrm{E}[\mathrm{Var}\,(Y|\theta_2)] + \mathrm{E}[\mathrm{Var}\,(N|\theta_1)]\mathrm{E}\{[\mathrm{E}\,(Y|\theta_2)]^2\} \\
&= \mu_N v_Y + v_N \mathrm{E}\{[\mathrm{E}(Y|\theta_2)]^2\}
\end{aligned}$$

Since $a_Y = \mathrm{Var}[\mu_Y(\theta)] = \mathrm{E}\{[\mu_Y(\theta)]^2\} - \{\mathrm{E}[\mu_Y(\theta)]\}^2$, $v_S = \mu_N v_Y + v_N(a_Y + \mu_Y^2)$. Then $a_Y = \mathrm{Var}[\mathrm{E}(Y|\theta_2)] = \mathrm{Var}(\theta_2)$ since Y is exponentially distributed. But, again using the exponential distribution

$$\begin{aligned}
\mathrm{Var}(\theta_2) &= \mathrm{E}\,(\theta_2^2) - [\mathrm{E}(\theta_2)]^2 = \mathrm{E}[\mathrm{Var}(Y|\theta_2)] - \{\mathrm{E}[\mathrm{E}(Y|\theta_2)]\}^2 \\
&= v_Y - \mu_Y^2,
\end{aligned}$$

from which $a_Y + \mu_Y^2 = v_Y$. Then

$$\begin{aligned}
v_S &= \mu_N v_Y + v_N(v_Y - \mu_Y^2 + \mu_Y^2) = \mu_N v_Y + v_N v_Y \\
&= 0.1(25{,}000) + 0.1(25{,}000) = 5{,}000.
\end{aligned}$$

Also,

$$
\begin{aligned}
a_S &= \mathrm{Var}[\mu_S(\theta_1,\theta_2)] = \mathrm{E}\{[\mu_S(\theta_1,\theta_2)]^2\} - \{\mathrm{E}[\mu_S(\theta_1,\theta_2)]\}^2 \\
&= \mathrm{E}\{[\mu_N(\theta_1)]^2\}\mathrm{E}\{[(\mu_Y(\theta_2)]^2\} - \mu_N^2\mu_Y^2 \\
&= (a_N + \mu_N^2)(a_Y + \mu_Y^2) - \mu_N^2\mu_Y^2 \\
&= [0.05 + (0.01)^2](25{,}000) - (0.1)^2(100)^2 = 1{,}400.
\end{aligned}
$$

Therefore, $k = v_S/a_S = 5{,}000/1{,}400 = 3.5714$, $Z = \frac{3}{3+3.5714} = 0.4565$ and $P_c = 0.4565\left(\frac{200}{3}\right) + 0.5435(10) = 35.87.$

16.26 (a) $\mathrm{E}(X_j) = \mathrm{E}[\mathrm{E}(X_j|\Theta)] = \mathrm{E}[\beta_j\mu(\Theta)] = \beta_j\mathrm{E}[\mu(\Theta)] = \beta_j\mu.$

$$
\begin{aligned}
\mathrm{Var}(X_j) &= \mathrm{E}[\mathrm{Var}(X_j|\Theta)] + \mathrm{Var}[\mathrm{E}(X_j|\Theta)] \\
&= \mathrm{E}[\tau_j(\Theta) + \psi_j v(\Theta)] + \mathrm{Var}[\beta_j\mu(\Theta)] \\
&= \tau_j + \psi_j v + \beta_j^2 a.
\end{aligned}
$$

$$
\begin{aligned}
\mathrm{Cov}(X_i, X_j) &= \mathrm{E}(X_iX_j) - \mathrm{E}(X_i)\mathrm{E}(X_j) \\
&= \mathrm{E}[\mathrm{E}(X_iX_j|\Theta)] - \beta_i\beta_j\mu^2 \\
&= \mathrm{E}[\mathrm{E}\,(X_i|\Theta)\,\mathrm{E}(X_j|\Theta)] - \beta_i\beta_j\mu^2 \\
&= \mathrm{E}\{\beta_i\beta_j[\mu(\Theta)]^2\} - \beta_i\beta_j\mu^2 \\
&= \beta_i\beta_j(\mathrm{E}\{[\mu(\Theta)]^2\} - \{\mathrm{E}[\mu(\Theta)]\}^2) \\
&= \beta_i\beta_j a.
\end{aligned}
$$

(b) The normal equations are

$$
\mathrm{E}(X_{n+1}) = \tilde{\alpha}_0 + \sum_{j=1}^{n}\tilde{\alpha}_j\mathrm{E}(X_j)
$$

$$
\mathrm{Cov}\,(X_i, X_{n+1}) = \sum_{j=1}^{n}\tilde{\alpha}_j\,\mathrm{Cov}(X_i, X_j)
$$

where $\mathrm{E}(X_{n+1}) = \beta_{n+1}\mu$, $\mathrm{E}(X_j) = \beta_j\mu$ and $Cov\,(X_i, X_{n+1}) = \beta_i\beta_{n+1}a$, and $Cov\,(X_i, X_i) = \mathrm{Var}\,(X_i) = \tau_j + \psi_j v + \beta_j^2 a$. On substitution

$$
\beta_{n+1}\mu = \tilde{\alpha}_0 + \sum_{j=1}^{n}\tilde{\alpha}_j\beta_j\mu \tag{16.1}
$$

and

$$
\begin{aligned}
\beta_i\beta_{n+1}a &= \sum_{j=1}^{n}\tilde{\alpha}_j\beta_i\beta_j a + \tilde{\alpha}_1\left(\tau_i + \psi_i v\right) \\
&= \left(\beta_{n+1} - \frac{\tilde{\alpha}_0}{\mu}\right)\beta_i a + \tilde{\alpha}_i(\tau_i + \psi_i v) \text{ from (16.1).}
\end{aligned}
$$

Hence,

$$\frac{\tilde{\alpha}_0}{\mu}\beta_i a = \tilde{\alpha}_i \left(\tau_i + \psi_i v\right),$$

yielding

$$\tilde{\alpha}_i = \frac{\tilde{\alpha}_0}{\mu}\beta_i a \left(\tau_i + \psi_i v\right)^{-1}. \tag{16.2}$$

Then

$$\sum_{i=1}^{n} \tilde{\alpha}_i = \frac{\tilde{\alpha}_0}{\mu}a \sum_{i=1}^{n} \left(\tau_i + \psi_i v\right)^{-1}.$$

From (16.1) and (16.2),

$$\tilde{\alpha}_0 = \beta_{n+1}\mu - \sum_{j=1}^{n} \tilde{\alpha}_j \beta_j \mu = \beta_{n+1}\mu - \tilde{\alpha}_0 a \sum_{j=1}^{n} \frac{\beta_j^2}{\tau_j + \psi_j v}$$

which gives

$$\tilde{\alpha}_0 = \frac{\beta_{n+1}\mu}{1 + a \sum_{j=1}^{n} \frac{\beta_j^2}{\tau_j + \psi_j v}} = \frac{\beta_{n+1}\mu}{1 + a \sum_{j=1}^{n} m_j} = \frac{\beta_{n+1}\mu}{1 + am}$$

and

$$\tilde{\alpha}_i = \frac{\beta_i \beta_{n+1}}{1 + am}\frac{a}{\tau_i + \psi_i v}.$$

The credibility premium is

$$
\begin{aligned}
\tilde{\alpha}_0 + \sum_{j=1}^{n} \tilde{\alpha}_j X_j &= \frac{\beta_{n+1}\mu}{1 + am} + \frac{\beta_{n+1}a}{1 + am} \sum_{j=1}^{n} \frac{\beta_j}{\tau_j + \psi_j v} X_j \\
&= \frac{E(X_{n+1})}{1 + am} + \frac{\beta_{n+1}a}{1 + am} \sum_{j=1}^{n} \frac{m_j}{\beta_j} X_j \\
&= \frac{E(X_{n+1})}{1 + am} + \frac{\beta_{n+1}am}{1 + am}\overline{X} \\
&= (1 - Z)E\left(X_{n+1}\right) + Z\beta_{n+1}\overline{X}.
\end{aligned}
$$

16.27 The posterior distribution is

$$
\begin{aligned}
\pi\left(\theta|\mathbf{x}\right) &\propto \left[\prod_{j=1}^{n} f(x_j|\theta)\right] \pi(\theta) \propto \prod_{j=1}^{n} \left[\theta^{x_j}(1 - \theta)^{K_j - x_j}\right] \theta^{a-1}(1 - \theta)^{b-1} \\
&= \theta^{\Sigma x_j + a - 1}(1 - \theta)^{\Sigma(K_j - x_j) + b - 1} \\
&= \theta^{a_*}(1 - \theta)^{b_*}
\end{aligned}
$$

which is the kernel of the beta distribution with parameters $a_* = \sum x_j + a$ and $b_* = \sum(K_j - x_j) + b$. So

$$
\begin{aligned}
\mathrm{E}(X_{n+1}|\mathbf{x}) &= \int_0^1 \mu_{n+1}(\theta)\pi(\theta|x)d\theta \\
&= \int_0^1 K_{n+1}\theta\frac{\Gamma(a_*+b_*)}{\Gamma(a_*)\Gamma(b_*)}\theta^{a_*-1}(1-\theta)^{b_*-1}d\theta \\
&= K_{n+1}\frac{\Gamma(a_*+b_*)}{\Gamma(a_*)\Gamma(b_*)}\int_0^1 \theta^{a_*+1-1}(1-\theta)^{b_*-1}d\theta \\
&= K_{n+1}\frac{\Gamma(a_*+b_*)}{\Gamma(a_*)\Gamma(b_*)}\frac{\Gamma(a_*+1)\Gamma(b_*)}{\Gamma(a_*+1+b_*)} \\
&= K_{n+1}\frac{a_*}{a_*+b_*} \\
&= K_{n+1}\frac{\sum x_j + a}{\sum x_j + a + \sum(K_j - x_j) + b} \\
&= K_{n+1}\left(\frac{\sum x_j}{\sum K_j + a + b}\frac{\sum K_j}{\sum K_j} + \frac{a}{\sum K_j + a + b}\frac{a+b}{a+b}\right) \\
&= K_{n+1}\left(\frac{\sum x_j}{\sum K_j}\frac{\sum K_j}{\sum K_j + a + b} + \frac{a}{a+b}\frac{a+b}{\sum K_j + a + b}\right)
\end{aligned}
$$

Let

$$
Z = \frac{\Sigma K_j}{\Sigma K_j + a + b}, \quad \overline{X} = \frac{\Sigma X_j}{\Sigma K_j}, \quad \mu = \frac{a}{a+b}.
$$

Then $\mathrm{E}(X_{n+1}|\mathbf{x}) = K_{n+1}[Z\overline{X} + (1-Z)\mu]$. Normalizing, $\mathrm{E}\left(\frac{X_{n+1}}{K_{n+1}}\bigg|\mathbf{x}\right) = Z\overline{X} + (1-Z)\mu$, the credibility premium.

16.28 The posterior distribution is

$$
\pi(\theta|\mathbf{x}) \propto \left[\prod_{j=1}^n f(x_j|\theta)\right]\pi(\theta) \propto \theta^n e^{-\theta\Sigma x_j}\theta^{\alpha-1}e^{-\theta/\beta} = \theta^{n+\alpha-1}e^{-\theta(\Sigma x_j + \beta^{-1})}
$$

which is the kernel of the gamma distribution. So, noting that $\mu(\theta) = \theta^{-1}$,

$$
\begin{aligned}
E(X_{n+1}|\mathbf{x}) &= \int_0^\infty \mu_{n+1}(\theta)\pi(\theta|\mathbf{x})d\theta \\
&= \frac{\left(\sum x_j + \beta^{-1}\right)^{n+\alpha}}{\Gamma(n+\alpha)} \int_0^\infty \frac{1}{\theta}\theta^{n+\alpha-1}e^{-\theta\left(\Sigma x_j + \beta^{-1}\right)}d\theta \\
&= \frac{\left(\sum x_j + \beta^{-1}\right)^{n+\alpha}}{\Gamma(n+\alpha)} \int_0^\infty \theta^{n+\alpha-2}e^{-\theta\left(\Sigma x_j + \beta^{-1}\right)}d\theta \\
&= \frac{\left(\sum x_j + \beta^{-1}\right)^{n+\alpha}}{\Gamma(n+\alpha)} \frac{\Gamma(n+\alpha-1)}{\left(\sum x_j + \beta^{-1}\right)^{n+\alpha-1}} \\
&= \frac{\sum x_j + \beta^{-1}}{n+\alpha-1} \\
&= \frac{n\beta}{(n+\alpha-1)\beta}\bar{x} + \left(1 - \frac{n\beta}{(n+\alpha-1)\beta}\right)\frac{1}{\beta(\alpha-1)} \\
&= Z\bar{x} + (1-Z)\mu
\end{aligned}
$$

where

$$
\mu = \int_0^\infty \frac{1}{\theta}\frac{\theta^{\alpha-1}e^{-\theta/\beta}}{\Gamma(\alpha)\beta^\alpha}d\theta = \frac{1}{\beta(\alpha-1)}.
$$

16.29 The posterior distribution is

$$
\begin{aligned}
\pi(\theta|\mathbf{x}) &\propto \left[\prod_{j=1}^n f(x_j|\theta)\right]\pi(\theta) \\
&\propto \prod_{j=1}^n \left[\theta^r(1-\theta)^{x_j}\right]\theta^{a-1}(1-\theta)^{b-1} \\
&= \theta^{nr+a-1}(1-\theta)^{\Sigma x_j + b-1}
\end{aligned}
$$

which is the kernel of the beta distribution.

$$
\begin{aligned}
E(X_{n+1}|\mathbf{x}) &= \int_0^1 \mu(\theta)\pi(\theta|\mathbf{x})d\theta \\
&= \int_0^1 r\frac{1-\theta}{\theta}\frac{\Gamma\left(nr+a+\sum x_j + b\right)}{\Gamma(nr+a)\Gamma\left(\sum x_j + b\right)}\theta^{nr+a-1}(1-\theta)^{\Sigma x_j + b-1}d\theta \\
&= r\frac{\Gamma\left(nr+a+\sum x_j + b\right)}{\Gamma(nr+a)\Gamma\left(\sum x_j + b\right)}\frac{\Gamma(nr+a-1)\Gamma\left(\sum x_j + b+1\right)}{\Gamma\left(nr+a+\sum x_j + b\right)} \\
&= r\frac{\sum x_j + b}{nr+a-1} = \frac{nr}{nr+a-1}\bar{x} + \left(1 - \frac{nr}{nr+a-1}\right)\frac{rb}{a-1}.
\end{aligned}
$$

But,

$$\mu = \mathrm{E}[\mathrm{E}\left(X|\theta\right)] = \int_0^1 r\frac{1-\theta}{\theta}\frac{\Gamma(a+b)}{\Gamma(a)\Gamma(b)}\theta^{a-1}(1-\theta)^{b-1}d\theta = \frac{rb}{a-1}$$

and so $\mathrm{E}(X_{n+1}|\mathbf{x}) = Z\overline{X} + (1-Z)\mu$ where $Z = \frac{nr}{nr+a-1}$.

16.30 (a) The posterior distribution is

$$\pi(\theta|\mathbf{x}) \quad \propto \quad \left[\prod_{j=1}^n \frac{\exp(-m\theta x_j)}{[q(\theta)]^m}\right][q(\theta)]^{-k}\exp(-\theta\mu k)$$

$$= \quad [q(\theta)]^{-k-mn}\exp\left[-\theta\left(m\sum x_j + \mu k\right)\right].$$

This is of the same form as the prior distribution, with

$$k_* = k + mn \text{ and } \mu_* = \frac{m\sum x_j + \mu k}{mn + k}$$

The Bayesian premium is

$$\begin{aligned} \mathrm{E}(X_{n+1}|\mathbf{x}) &= -\int_{\theta_0}^{\theta_1}\frac{q'(\theta)}{q(\theta)}[q(\theta)]^{-k_*}\exp(-\theta\mu_* k_*)c(\mu_*, k_*)^{-1}d\theta \\ &= -\int_{\theta_0}^{\theta_1}q'(\theta)[q(\theta)]^{-k_*-1}\exp(-\theta\mu_* k_*)c(\mu_*, k_*)^{-1}d\theta \\ &= -\left.[q(\theta)]^{-k_*}\exp(-\theta\mu_* k_*)c(\mu_*, k_*)^{-1}\right|_{\theta_0}^{\theta_1} \\ &\quad + \int_{\theta_0}^{\theta_1}q(\theta)\{-(k_*+1)[q(\theta)]^{-k_*-2}q'(\theta)\exp(-\theta\mu_* k_*) \\ &\quad -[q(\theta)]^{-k_*-1}\exp(-\theta\mu_* k_*)\mu_* k_*\}c(\mu_*, k_*)^{-1}d\theta \\ &= 0 + (k_*+1)\mathrm{E}(X_{n+1}|\mathbf{x}) + \mu_* k_*. \end{aligned}$$

and so

$$\mathrm{E}(X_{n+1}|\mathbf{x}) = \mu_* = \frac{m\sum x_j + \mu k}{mn + k} = \frac{mn}{mn+k}\bar{x} + \frac{k}{mn+k}\mu.$$

(b) The Bühlmann premium must be the same because the Bayesian premium is linear in the observations.

(c) The inverse Gaussian distribution can be written

$$f(x) = \left(\frac{\theta}{2\pi x^3}\right)^{1/2}\exp\left(-\frac{\theta x}{2\mu^2} + \frac{\theta}{\mu} - \frac{\theta}{2x}\right).$$

Replace θ with m and μ with $(2\theta)^{-1/2}$ to obtain

$$f(x) = \left(\frac{m}{2\pi x^3}\right)^{1/2}\exp\left[-m\theta x + m(2\theta)^{1/2} - \frac{m}{2x}\right].$$

Now let $p(m, x) = \left(\frac{m}{2\pi x^3}\right)^{1/2} \exp\left(\frac{m}{2x}\right)$ and $q(\theta) = \exp[-(2\theta)^{1/2}]$ to see that $f(x)$ has the desired form.

16.31 (a) It is true when $X_1, X_2, \ldots$ represent values in successive years and τ is an inflation factor for each year.

(b) This is a special case of Exercise 16.26 with $\beta_j = \tau^j$, $\tau_j(\theta) = 0$, $\psi_j = \tau^{2j}/m_j$ for $j = 1, \ldots, n$.

(c) From Exercise 16.26(b)

$$\tilde{\alpha}_0 + \sum_{j=1}^{n} \tilde{\alpha}_j X_j = (1 - Z)\mathrm{E}(X_{n+1}) + Z\tau^{n+1}\overline{X}$$

where

$$\overline{X} = \sum_{j=1}^{n} \frac{\tau^{2j}}{\frac{\tau^{2j}}{m_j}} \frac{X_j}{\tau_j} \bigg/ \left[\sum_{j=1}^{m} \frac{\tau^{2j}}{\frac{\tau^{2j}}{m_j}}\right] = \sum_{j=1}^{n} \frac{m_j X_j}{\tau^j} \bigg/ \sum m_j = \sum_{j=1}^{n} \frac{m_j}{m} \frac{X_j}{\tau_j}$$

and

$$Z = \frac{a \sum_{j=1}^{n} \frac{m_j}{v}}{1 + a \sum_{j=1}^{n} \frac{m_j}{v}} = \frac{m}{k + m}.$$

Then

$$\tilde{\alpha}_0 + \sum_{j=1}^{n} \tilde{\alpha}_j X_j = \frac{k}{k + m}\mathrm{E}(X_{n+1}) + \frac{m}{k + m}\tau^{n+1}\overline{X}$$

$$= \frac{k}{k + m}\tau^{n+1}\mu + \frac{m}{k + m} \sum_{j=1}^{n} \frac{m_j}{m}\tau^{n-1-j}X_j.$$

(d) As in Exercise 16.26, the credibility premium equals the Bayesian premium.

(e)
$$\frac{\frac{\partial}{\partial\theta} f(x_j|\theta)}{f(x_j|\theta)} = -m_j\tau^{-j}x_j - m_j\frac{q'(\theta)}{q(\theta)}$$

Therefore,

$$\int \frac{\partial}{\partial\theta} f(x_j|\theta)dx_j = -m_j\tau^{-j}\int x_j f(x_j|\theta)dx_j + m_j\mu(\theta)\int f(x_j|\theta)dx_j$$

which leads to

$$0 = -m_j\tau^{-j}\mathrm{E}(X_j|\theta) + m_j\mu(\theta)$$

so that $\mathrm{E}(X_j|\theta) = \tau^j\mu(\theta)$. Also,

$$\frac{\partial^2}{\partial\theta^2} f(x_j|\theta) = m_j\mu'(\theta)f(x_j|\theta) + [m_j\tau^{-j}x_j - m_j\mu(\theta)]^2 f(x_j|\theta)$$

$$= m_j\mu'(\theta)f(x_j|\theta) + (m_j\tau^{-j})^2[x_j - \tau^j\mu(\theta)]^2 f(x_j|\theta).$$

Integrating leads to

$$0 = m_j \mu'(\theta) + (m_j \tau^{-j})^2 \operatorname{Var}(X_j | \theta)$$

from which

$$\operatorname{Var}(X_j | \theta) = \frac{\tau^{2j}}{m_j} v(\theta).$$

(f) As in Exercise 16.26, $E[\mu(\theta)] = \mu$. Then

$$\pi(\theta | \mathbf{x}) \quad \propto \quad \left[\prod_{j=1}^{n} f(x_j | \theta) \right] \pi(\theta) \propto \prod_{j=1}^{n} \left\{ \frac{e^{-m_j \tau^{-j} x_j \theta}}{[q(\theta)]^{m_j}} \right\} [q(\theta)]^{-k} e^{-\theta u k}$$

$$= \quad [q(\theta)]^{-k-m} \exp\left[-\theta \left(\sum_{j=1}^{n} \tau^{-j} m_j x_j + \mu k \right) \right] = [q(x)]^{-k_*} e^{-\theta \mu_* k_*}$$

which is of the same form as the prior with

$$k_* = k + m \text{ and } k_* \mu_* = k\mu + \sum_{j=1}^{n} m_j \tau^{-j} X_j$$

so that

$$\mu_* = \frac{k}{k+m} \mu + \frac{m}{k+m} \sum_{j=1}^{n} \frac{m_j}{m} \tau^{-j} X_j.$$

Therefore $E[X_{n+1} | \mathbf{x}]$ is linear in the X_j's. Hence, credibility is exact.

16.32 (a) The Poisson pgf of each X_j is $P_{X_j}(z | \theta) = e^{-\theta(z-1)}$ and so the pgf of S is $P_S(z | \theta) = e^{-n\theta(z-1)}$ which is Poisson with mean $n\theta$. Hence,

$$f_{S|\theta}(s | \theta) = \frac{(n\theta)^s e^{-n\theta}}{s!}$$

and so

$$f_S(s) = \int \frac{(n\theta)^s e^{-n\theta}}{s!} \pi(\theta) d\theta.$$

(b) $\mu(\theta) = E(X | \theta) = \theta$ and $\pi(\theta | \mathbf{x}) = \left[\prod_{j=1}^{n} f(x_j | \theta) \right] \pi(\theta) / f(x)$. We have,

$$f(x) \quad = \quad \int \left[\prod_{j=1}^{n} f(x_j | \theta) \right] \pi(\theta) d\theta$$

$$= \quad \frac{\int \theta^{\Sigma x_j} e^{-n\theta} \pi(\theta) d\theta}{\prod_{j=1}^{n} x_j!}$$

Therefore,

$$\pi(\theta|\mathbf{x}) = \frac{\theta^{\Sigma x_j} e^{-n\theta} \pi(\theta)}{\int\limits_0^\infty \theta^{\Sigma x_j} e^{-n\theta} \pi(\theta) d\theta}$$

The Bayesian premium is

$$
\begin{aligned}
\mathrm{E}(X_{n+1}|\mathbf{x}) &= \int_0^\infty \mu(\theta)\pi(\theta|x) d\theta = \frac{\int\limits_0^\infty \theta^{\Sigma x_j + 1} e^{-n\theta} \pi(\theta) d\theta}{\int\limits_0^\infty \theta^{\Sigma x_j} e^{-n\theta} \pi(\theta) d\theta} \\
&= \frac{\frac{(s+1)!}{n^{s+1}} \int\limits_0^\infty \frac{n^{s+1}}{(s+1)!} \theta^{s+1} e^{-n\theta} \pi(\theta) d\theta}{\frac{s!}{n^s} \int\limits_0^\infty \frac{n^s}{s!} \theta^s e^{-n\theta} \pi(\theta) d\theta} = \frac{s+1}{n} \frac{f_S(s+1)}{f_S(s)}.
\end{aligned}
$$

(c)

$$
\begin{aligned}
f_S(s) &= \int\limits_0^\infty \frac{(n\theta)^s e^{-n\theta}}{s!} \frac{\beta^{-\alpha}}{\Gamma(\alpha)} \theta^{\alpha-1} e^{-\theta/\beta} d\theta \\
&= \frac{n^s}{s!} \frac{\beta^{-\alpha}}{\Gamma(\alpha)} \int\limits_0^\infty \theta^{s+\alpha-1} e^{-(n+\beta^{-1})\theta} d\theta \\
&= \frac{n^s}{s!} \frac{\beta^{-\alpha}}{\Gamma(\alpha)} \frac{\Gamma(s+\alpha)}{(n+\beta^{-1})^{s+\alpha}} \\
&= \frac{\Gamma(s+\alpha)}{\Gamma(s+1)\Gamma(\alpha)} \left(\frac{1}{1+n\beta}\right)^\alpha \left(\frac{n\beta}{1+n\beta}\right)^s \\
&= \binom{r+s-1}{s} \left(\frac{1}{1+\beta_*}\right)^r \left(\frac{\beta_*}{1+\beta_*}\right)^s
\end{aligned}
$$

where $\beta_* = n\beta$ and $r = \alpha$. This is a negative binomial distribution.

16.33 The posterior distribution is

$$
\begin{aligned}
\pi(\theta|\mathbf{x}) &\propto \left\{\prod_{j=1}^n \exp\left[-\frac{1}{2v}(x_j - \theta)^2\right]\right\} \exp\left[-\frac{1}{2a}(\theta - \mu)^2\right] \\
&= \exp\left[(2v)^{-1}(-\Sigma x_j^2 + 2\theta n\bar{x} - n\theta^2) - (2a)^{-1}(\theta^2 - 2\theta\mu + \mu^2)\right] \\
&\propto \exp\left[-\theta^2\left(\frac{n}{2v} + \frac{1}{2a}\right) + 2\theta\left(\frac{n\bar{x}}{2v} + \frac{\mu}{2a}\right)\right].
\end{aligned}
$$

Let $p = \frac{n}{2v} + \frac{1}{2a}$ and $q = \frac{n\bar{x}}{2v} + \frac{\mu}{2a}$ and then note that $-p\theta^2 + 2q\theta = -(p^{1/2}\theta - qp^{-1/2})^2 - q^2 p^{-1}$. Then

$$
\begin{aligned}
\pi(\theta|\mathbf{x}) &\propto \exp\left[-(p^{1/2}\theta - qp^{-1/2})^2\right] \\
&= \exp\left[-\frac{1}{2}\left(\frac{\theta - qp^{-1}}{(2p)^{-1/2}}\right)^2\right]
\end{aligned}
$$

and the posterior distribution is normal with mean

$$
\mu_* = qp^{-1} = \frac{\dfrac{n\bar{x}}{v} + \dfrac{\mu}{a}}{\dfrac{n}{v} + \dfrac{1}{a}}
$$

and variance

$$
a_* = \frac{1}{2p} = \left(\frac{n}{v} + \frac{1}{a}\right)^{-1}.
$$

Then (16.25) implies that $X_{n+1}|\mathbf{x}$ is a mixture with $X_{n+1}|\Theta$ having a normal distribution with mean Θ, and $\Theta|\mathbf{x}$ is normal with mean μ_* and variance a_*. From Example 4.30, this means that $X_{n+1}|\mathbf{x}$ is normally distributed with mean μ_* and variance $a_* + v$, that is

$$
f_{X_{n+1}|\mathbf{x}}(x_{n+1}|\mathbf{x}) = [2\pi(a_* + v)]^{-1/2} \exp\left[-\frac{(x_{n+1} - \mu_*)^2}{2(a_* + v)}\right], \quad -\infty < x_{n+1} < \infty.
$$

The Bayesian estimate is the mean of the predictive distribution, μ_* which can be written as $Z\bar{x} + (1 - Z)\mu$, where

$$
Z = \frac{n/v}{n/v + 1/a} = \frac{na}{na + v} = \frac{n}{n + v/a}.
$$

Because the Bayesian estimate is a linear function of the data, it must be the Bühlmann estimate as well. To see this directly,

$$
\begin{aligned}
\mu(\Theta) &= \Theta,\ \mu = E(\Theta) = \mu \\
v(\Theta) &= v\ (\text{not random}),\ v = E(v) = v \\
a &= \text{Var}(\Theta) = a
\end{aligned}
$$

thus indicating that the quantities in the question were chosen to align with the text. Then, $k = v/a$ and $Z = n/(n + k)$.

16.34 (a) Let Θ represent the selected urn. Then, $f_X(x|\Theta = 1) = \frac{1}{4}$, $x = 1, 2, 3, 4$ and $f_X(x|\Theta = 2) = \frac{1}{6}$, $x = 1, 2, \ldots, 6$. Then, $\mu(1) = E(X|\Theta = 1) = 2.5$ and $\mu(2) = E(X|\theta = 2) = 3.5$.

For the Bayesian solution, the marginal probability of drawing a 4 is, $f_X(4) = \frac{1}{2} \times \frac{1}{4} + \frac{1}{2} \times \frac{1}{6} = \frac{5}{24}$ and the posterior probability for urn 1 is

$$\pi(\theta = 1|X = 4) = \frac{f_{X|\Theta}(4|1)\pi(1)}{f_X(4)} = \frac{\frac{1}{4}\frac{1}{2}}{\frac{5}{24}} = \frac{3}{5}$$

and for urn 2 is

$$\pi(\theta = 2|X = 4) = 1 - \frac{3}{5} = \frac{2}{5}.$$

The expected value of the next observation is

$$\mathrm{E}(X_2|X_1 = 4) = 2.5\left(\frac{3}{5}\right) + 3.5\left(\frac{2}{5}\right) = 2.9.$$

(b) Using Bühlmann credibility,

$$\mu = \frac{1}{2}(2.5 + 3.5) = 3$$

$$v(1) = \frac{1}{4}(1^2 + 2^2 + 3^2 + 4^2) - (2.5)^2 = 1.25$$

$$v(2) = \frac{1}{6}(1^2 + \cdots + 6^2) - (3.5)^2 = 2.917$$

$$v = \frac{1}{2}v(1) + \frac{1}{2}v(2) = 2.0835$$

$$a = \mathrm{Var}[\mu(\theta)] = \mathrm{E}\{[\mu(\theta)]^2\} - \{\mathrm{E}[\mu(\theta)]\}^2 = \frac{1}{2}[2.5^2 + 3.5^2] - 3^2$$

$$= 0.25$$

$$k = \frac{v}{a} = \frac{2.0835}{0.25} = 8.334$$

$$Z = \frac{1}{1 + 8.334} = 0.1071352.$$

The credibility premium is $P_c = Z\bar{x} + (1-Z)\mu = 0.1071352(4) + 0.8927648(3) = 3.10709$.

16.35 (a)

$$\mu(\theta) = \theta, v(\theta) = \theta$$

$$\mu = \mathrm{E}(\theta) = \int_1^\infty 3\theta^{-3}d\theta = 1.5$$

$$v = \mathrm{E}(\theta) = 1.5$$

$$a = \mathrm{Var}(\theta) = \int_1^\infty 3\theta^{-2}d\theta - 2.25 = 0.75$$

$$k = 1.5/0.75 = 2$$

$$Z = \frac{2}{2+2} = 0.5$$

$$P_c = 0.5(10) + 0.5(1.5) = 5.75.$$

(b) Because the support of the prior distribution is $\theta > 1$, that is also the support of the posterior distribution. Therefore, the posterior distribution is not gamma. $\pi(\theta|N_1 + N_2 = 20) \propto e^{-2\theta}\theta^{20}\theta^{-4} = e^{-2\theta}\theta^{16}$. The required constant is

$$\int_1^\infty e^{-2\theta}\theta^{16}d\theta = e^{-2}\left[\frac{1}{2} + \frac{17}{4} + \frac{17(16)}{8} + \cdots + \frac{16!}{2^{17}}\right] = 1{,}179{,}501{,}863e^{-2}$$

and the posterior distribution is $\pi(\theta|N_1+N_2 = 20) = e^{-2\theta}\theta^{16}/1{,}179{,}501{,}863e^{-2}$. The posterior mean is

$$\frac{\int_1^\infty \theta e^{-2\theta}\theta^{16}d\theta}{1{,}179{,}501{,}863e^{-2}} = 8.5.$$

The mean is actually slightly less than 8.5 (which would be the exact answer if integrals from zero to infinity were used to create a gamma posterior.

16.36 $Z = \frac{0.5}{0.5+k} = 0.5$, $k = 0.5$, $Z = \frac{3}{3+0.5} = 6/7$.

16.37 (a)
$$\begin{aligned}
\Pr(X_1 = 1|A) &= 3(0.1^2)(0.9) = 0.027 \\
\Pr(X_1 = 1|B) &= 3(0.6^2)(0.4) = 0.432 \\
\Pr(X_1 = 1|C) &= 3(0.8^2)(0.2) = 0.384 \\
\Pr(A|X_1 = 1) &= 0.027/(0.027 + 0.432 + 0.384) = 27/843 = 9/281 \\
\Pr(B|X_1 = 1) &= 144/281 \\
\Pr(C|X_1 = 1) &= 128/281 \\
\mu(A) &= 3(0.9) = 2.7 \\
\mu(B) &= 3(0.4) = 1.2 \\
\mu(C) &= 3(0.2) = 0.6 \\
E(X_2|X_1 = 1) &= [9(2.7) + 144(1.2) + 128(0.6)]/281 = 0.97473.
\end{aligned}$$

(b)
$$\begin{aligned}
\mu &= (2.7 + 1.2 + 0.6)/3 = 1.5 \\
a &= (2.7^2 + 1.2^2 + 0.6^2)/3 - 2.25 = 0.78 \\
v(A) &= 3(0.9)(0.1) = 0.27,\ v(B) = 0.72,\ v(C) = 0.48 \\
v &= (0.27 + 0.72 + 0.48)/3 = 0.49 \\
k &= 49/78,\ Z = (1 + 49/78)^{-1} = 78/127 \\
P_c &= \frac{78}{127}(1) + \frac{49}{127}(1.5) = 1.19291.
\end{aligned}$$

16.38 (a)

$$\mu(\lambda) = \lambda, \ v(\lambda) = \lambda$$

$$\mu = E(\lambda) = \int_1^\infty 4\lambda^{-4} d\lambda = 4/3$$

$$v = E(\lambda) = 4/3$$

$$a = \text{Var}(\lambda) = \int_1^\infty 4\lambda^{-3} d\lambda - 16/9 = 2/9$$

$$k = (4/3)/(2/9) = 6, \ Z = \frac{3}{3+6} = 1/3$$

$$P_c = (1/3)(1) + (2/3)(4/3) = 11/9$$

(b)

$$\mu = \int_0^1 \lambda d\lambda = 1/2$$

$$v = \mu = 1/2$$

$$a = \int_0^1 \lambda^2 d\lambda - 1/4 = 1/12$$

$$k = (1/2)/(1/12) = 6, \ Z = \frac{3}{3+6} = 1/3$$

$$P_c = (1/3)(1) + (2/3)(1/2) = 2/3.$$

16.39 $\mu(h) = h$, $\mu = E(h) = 2$, $v(h) = h$, $v = E(h) = 2$, $a = \text{Var}(h) = 2$, $k = 2/2 = 1$, $Z = \frac{1}{1+1} = 1/2$.

16.40 (a) $r \sim bin(3, \theta)$, $\pi(\theta) = 6\theta(1 - \theta)$.

$$\pi(\theta | X = 1) \propto 3\theta(1 - \theta)^2 6\theta(1 - \theta) \propto \theta^2 (1 - \theta)^3$$

and so the posterior distribution is beta with parameters 3 and 4. Then the expected next observation is $E(3\theta | X = 1) = 3(3/7) = 9/7$.

(b)

$$\mu(\theta) = 3\theta, \ v(\theta) = 3\theta(1 - \theta)$$

$$\mu = E(3\theta) = 3 \int_0^1 \theta 6\theta(1 - \theta) d\theta = 1.5$$

$$v = E[3\theta(1 - \theta)] = 3 \int_0^1 \theta(1 - \theta) 6\theta(1 - \theta) d\theta = 0.6$$

$$a = \text{Var}(3\theta) = 9 \int_0^1 \theta^2 6\theta(1 - \theta) d\theta - 2.25 = 0.45$$

$$k = 0.6/0.45 = 4/3, \ Z = (1 + 4/3)^{-1} = 3/7$$

$$P_c = (3/7)(1) + (4/7)(1.5) = 9/7.$$

16.41 (a)
$$
\begin{aligned}
\mu(A) &= 20,\ \mu(B) = 12,\ \mu(C) = 10 \\
v(A) &= 416,\ v(B) = 288,\ v(C) = 308 \\
\mu &= (20 + 12 + 10)/3 = 14 \\
v &= (416 + 288 + 308)/3 = 337\tfrac{1}{3} \\
a &= (20^2 + 12^2 + 10^2)/3 - 14^2 = 18\tfrac{2}{3} \\
k &= 337\tfrac{1}{3}/18\tfrac{2}{3} = 18\tfrac{1}{14} \\
Z &= (1 + 18\tfrac{1}{14})^{-1} = 14/267 \\
P_c &= (14/267)(0) + (253/267)(14) = 13.2659.
\end{aligned}
$$

(b)
$$
\begin{aligned}
\pi(A|X = 0) &= 2/(2 + 3 + 4) = 2/9 \\
\pi(B|X = 0) &= 3/9,\ \pi(C|X = 0) = 4/9 \\
\mathrm{E}(X_2|X_1 = 0) &= (2/9)20 + (3/9)12 + (4/9)10 = 12\tfrac{8}{9}.
\end{aligned}
$$

16.42 (a) $\Pr(N = 0) = \int_1^3 e^{-\lambda}(0.5)d\lambda = (e^{-1} - e^{-3})/2 = 0.159046.$

(b)
$$
\mu = v = \mathrm{E}(\lambda) = \int_1^3 \lambda(0.5)d\lambda = 2
$$
$$
a = \mathrm{Var}(\lambda) = \int_1^3 \lambda^2(0.5)d\lambda - 4 = 1/3
$$
$$
k = 2/(1/3) = 6,\ Z = \frac{1}{1 + 6} = 1/7
$$
$$
P_c = (1/7)(1) + (6/7)(2) = 13/7.
$$

(c) $\pi(\lambda|X_1 = 1) = e^{-\lambda}\lambda(.5)/\int_1^3 e^{-\lambda}\lambda(.5)d\lambda = e^{-\lambda}\lambda/(2e^{-1} - 4e^{-3}),$

$$
\begin{aligned}
\mathrm{E}(\lambda|X_1 = 1) &= \int_1^3 e^{-\lambda}\lambda^2 d\lambda/(2e^{-1} - 4e^{-3}) \\
&= (5e^{-1} - 17e^{-3})/(2e^{-1} - 4e^{-3}) = 1.8505.
\end{aligned}
$$

16.43 (a)
$$
\begin{aligned}
\mu(A) &= (1/6)(4) = 2/3,\ \mu(B) = (5/6)(2) = 5/3 \\
v(A) &= (1/6)(20) + (5/36)(16) = 50/9 \\
v(B) &= (5/6)(5) + (5/36)(4) = 85/18 \\
\mu &= [(2/3) + (5/3)]/2 = 7/6 \\
v &= [(50/9) + (85/18)]/2 = 185/36 \\
a &= [(2/3)^2 + (4/3)^2]/2 - 49/36 = 1/4 \\
k &= (185/36)/(1/4) = 185/9 \\
Z &= \frac{4}{4 + 185/9} = 36/221.
\end{aligned}
$$

(b) $(36/221)(0.25) + (185/221)(7/6) = 1{,}349/1{,}326 = 1.01735.$

16.44
$$
\begin{aligned}
E(X_2) &= (1 + 8 + 12)/3 = 7 \\
&= E[E(X_2|X_1)] \\
&= [2.6 + 7.8 + E(X_2|X_1 = 12)]/3. \\
E(X_2|X_1 = 12) &= 10.6.
\end{aligned}
$$

16.45 (a) $X \sim$ Poisson(λ), $\pi(\lambda) = e^{-\lambda/2}/2$. The posterior distribution with three claims is proportional to $e^{-\lambda}\lambda^3 e^{-\lambda/2} = \lambda^3 e^{-1.5\lambda}$ which is gamma with parameters 4 and $1/1.5$. The mean is $4/1.5 = 2\frac{2}{3}$.

(b)
$$
\begin{aligned}
\mu(\lambda) &= v(\lambda) = \lambda \\
\mu &= v = E(\lambda) = 2 \\
a &= \text{Var}(\lambda) = 4 \\
k &= 2/4 = 0.5, \quad Z = \frac{1}{1 + 0.5} = \frac{2}{3} \\
P_c &= \frac{2}{3}(3) + \frac{1}{3}(2) = \frac{8}{3} = 2\frac{2}{3}.
\end{aligned}
$$

16.46 (a) $r \sim bin(3, \theta)$, $\pi(\theta) = 280\theta^3(1 - \theta)^4$ which is beta(4,5).

$$
\pi(\theta|X = 2) \propto 3\theta^2(1 - \theta)280\theta^3(1 - \theta)^4 \propto \theta^5(1 - \theta)^5
$$

and so the posterior distribution is beta with parameters 6 and 6. Then the expected next observation is $E(3\theta|X = 2) = 3(6/12) = 1.5.$

(b)
$$
\begin{aligned}
\mu(\theta) &= 3\theta, \ v(\theta) = 3\theta(1 - \theta) \\
\mu &= E(3\theta) = 3(4/9) = 4/3 \\
v &= E[3\theta(1 - \theta)] = 3\int_0^1 \theta(1 - \theta)280\theta^3(1 - \theta)^4 d\theta \\
&= 840\frac{\Gamma(5)\Gamma(6)}{\Gamma(11)} = 2/3 \\
a &= \text{Var}(3\theta) = 9\int_0^1 \theta^2 280\theta^3(1 - \theta)^4 d\theta - 16/9 \\
&= 2{,}520\frac{\Gamma(6)\Gamma(5)}{\Gamma(11)} - 16/9 = 2/9 \\
k &= (2/3)/(2/9) = 3 \\
Z &= (1 + 3)^{-1} = 1/4 \\
P_c &= (1/4)(2) + (3/4)(4/3) = 1.5.
\end{aligned}
$$

16.47 (a)

$$\mu(A_1) = 0.15, \; \mu(A_2) = 0.05$$
$$v(A_1) = 0.1275, \; v(A_2) = 0.0475$$
$$\mu = (0.15 + 0.05)/2 = 0.1$$
$$v = (0.1275 + 0.0475)/2 = 0.0875$$
$$a = (0.15^2 + 0.05^2)/2 - 0.1^2 = 0.0025$$
$$k = 0.0875/0.0025 = 35$$
$$Z = \frac{3}{3 + 35} = 3/38,$$

estimated frequency is $(3/38)(1/3) + (35/38)(0.1) = 9/76$.

$$\mu(B_1) = 24, \; \mu(B_2) = 34$$
$$v(B_1) = 64, \; v(B_2) = 84$$
$$\mu = (24 + 34)/2 = 29$$
$$v = (64 + 84)/2 = 74$$
$$a = (24^2 + 34^2)/2 - 29^2 = 25$$
$$k = 74/25$$
$$Z = \frac{1}{1 + 74/25} = 25/99,$$

estimated severity is $(25/99)(20) + (74/99)(29) = 294/11$.

The estimated total is $(9/76)(294/11) = 1323/418 = 3.1651$.

(b) Information about the various spinner combinations is given in Table 16.8

Table 16.8 Calculations for Exercise 16.47

Spinners	μ	v
A_1, B_1	3.6	83.04
A_1, B_2	5.1	159.99
A_2, B_1	1.2	30.56
A_2, B_2	1.7	59.11

$$\mu = (3.6 + 5.1 + 1.2 + 1.7)/4 = 2.9$$
$$v = (83.04 + 159.99 + 30.56 + 59.11)/4 = 83.175$$
$$a = (3.6^2 + 5.1^2 + 1.2^2 + 1.7^2)/4 - 2.9^2 = 2.415$$
$$k = 83.175/2.415 = 34.441, \; Z = \frac{3}{3 + 34.441} = 0.080126,$$

estimated total is $(0.080126)(20/3) + 0.919874(2.9) = 3.2018$.

(c) For part (a),

$$\begin{aligned}
\Pr(1|A_1) &= 3(0.15)(0.85)^2 = 0.325125 \\
\Pr(1|A_2) &= 3(0.05)(0.95)^2 = 0.135375 \\
\Pr(A_1|1) &= \frac{0.325125}{0.325125 + 0.135375} = 0.706026 \\
\Pr(A_2|1) &= 1 - 0.706026 = 0.293974.
\end{aligned}$$

Estimated frequency is $0.706026(0.15) + 0.293974(0.05) = 0.120603$.

$$\begin{aligned}
\Pr(20|B_1) &= 0.8 \\
\Pr(20|B_2) &= 0.3 \\
\Pr(B_1|20) &= \frac{0.8}{0.8 + 0.3} = 8/11 \\
\Pr(B_2|20) &= 3/11.
\end{aligned}$$

Estimated severity is $(8/11)(24) + (3/11)(34) = 26.727272$.
  Estimated total is $0.120603(26.727272) = 3.2234$.
  For part (b),

$$\begin{aligned}
\Pr(0, 20, 0|A_1, B_1) &= (0.85)^2(0.12) = 0.0867 \\
\Pr(0, 20, 0|A_1, B_2) &= (0.85)^2(0.045) = 0.0325125 \\
\Pr(0, 20, 0|A_2, B_1) &= (0.95)^2(0.04) = 0.0361 \\
\Pr(0, 20, 0|A_2, B_2) &= (0.95)^2(0.015) = 0.0135375.
\end{aligned}$$

The posterior probabilities are 0.51347, 0.19255, 0.21380, 0.08017 and the estimated total is

$$0.51347(3.6) + 0.19255(5.1) + 0.21380(1.2) + 0.08017(1.7) = 3.2234.$$

(d)
$$\begin{aligned}
\Pr(X_1 = 0, \ldots, X_{n-1} = 0|A_1, B_1) &= (0.85)^{n-1} \\
\Pr(X_1 = 0, \ldots, X_{n-1} = 0|A_1, B_2) &= (0.85)^{n-1} \\
\Pr(X_1 = 0, \ldots, X_{n-1} = 0|A_2, B_1) &= (0.95)^{n-1} \\
\Pr(X_1 = 0, \ldots, X_{n-1} = 0|A_2, B_2) &= (0.95)^{n-1}
\end{aligned}$$

$$\begin{aligned}
&E(X_n|X_1 = 0, \ldots, X_{n-1} = 0) \\
&= \frac{(0.85)^{n-1}(3.6) + (0.85)^{n-1}(5.1) + (0.95)^{n-1}(1.2) + (0.95)^{n-1}(1.7)}{(0.85)^{n-1} + (0.85)^{n-1} + (0.95)^{n-1} + (0.95)^{n-1}} \\
&= \frac{2.9 + 8.7(0.85/0.95)^{n-1}}{2 + 2(0.85/0.95)^{n-1}}
\end{aligned}$$

and the limit as $n \to \infty$ is $2.9/2 = 1.45$.

16.48 $\Pr(X = 0.12|A) = \dfrac{1}{\sqrt{2\pi}(0.03)} \exp\left[-\dfrac{(0.12 - 0.1)^2}{2(0.0009)}\right] = 10.6483,$

$\Pr(X = 0.12|B) = (X = 0.12|C) = 0$ (actually, just very close to zero), so $\Pr(A|X = 0.12) = 1$. The Bayesian estimate is $\mu(A) = 0.1$.

16.49 $\mathrm{E}(X|X_1 = 4) = 2 = Z(4) + (1 - Z)(1)$, $Z = 1/3 = \frac{1}{1+k}$, $k = 2 = v/a = 3/a$, $a = 1.5$.

16.50 $v = \mathrm{E}(v) = 8$, $a = \mathrm{Var}(\mu) = 4$, $k = 8/4 = 2$, $Z = \frac{3}{3+2} = 0.6$.

16.51 (a)

$$f(y) = \int_0^\infty \lambda^{-1} e^{-y/\lambda} 400\lambda^{-3} e^{-20/\lambda} d\lambda = 400 \int_0^\infty \lambda^{-4} e^{-(20+y)/\lambda} d\lambda.$$

Let $\theta = (20 + y)/\lambda$, $\lambda = (20 + y)/\theta$, $d\lambda = -(20 + y)/\theta^2 d\theta$, and so

$$f(y) = 400 \int_0^\infty (20 + y)^{-3}\theta^2 e^{-\theta} d\theta = 800(20 + y)^{-3}$$

which is Pareto with parameters 2 and 20 and so the mean is $20/(2 - 1) = 20$.
(b) $\mu(\lambda) = \lambda$, $v(\lambda) = \lambda^2$. The distribution of λ is inverse gamma with $\alpha = 2$ and $\theta = 20$. Then $\mu = \mathrm{E}(\lambda) = 20/(2 - 1) = 20$ and $v = \mathrm{E}(\lambda^2)$ which does not exist. The Bühlmann estimate does not exist.
(c) $\pi(\lambda|15, 25) \propto \lambda^{-1} e^{-15/\lambda}\lambda^{-1}e^{-25/\lambda}400\lambda^{-3}e^{-20/\lambda} \propto \lambda^{-5}e^{-60/\lambda}$ which is inverse gamma with $\alpha = 4$ and $\theta = 60$. The posterior mean is $60/(4 - 1) = 20$.

16.52

$$
\begin{aligned}
\mu(\theta) &= \theta,\ v(\theta) = \theta(1 - \theta) \\
a &= \mathrm{Var}(\theta) = 0.07 \\
v &= \mathrm{E}(\theta - \theta^2) = \mathrm{E}(\theta) - \mathrm{Var}(\theta) - [\mathrm{E}(\theta)]^2 \\
&= 0.25 - 0.07 - (0.25)^2 = 0.1175 \\
k &= 0.1175/0.07 = 1.67857, \\
Z &= \frac{1}{1 + 1.67857} = 0.37333.
\end{aligned}
$$

16.53 (a) means are 0, 2, 4, and 6 while the variances are all 9. Thus

$$
\begin{aligned}
\mu &= (0 + 2 + 4 + 6)/4 = \\
v &= 9,\ a = (0 + 4 + 16 + 36)/4 - 9 = 5 \\
Z &= \frac{1}{1 + 9/5} = 5/14 = 0.35714.
\end{aligned}
$$

(b)(i) $v = 9$, $a = 20$, $Z = \frac{1}{1+9/20} = 20/29 = 0.68966$.

(b)(ii) $v = 3.24$, $a = 5$, $Z = \frac{1}{1+3.24/5} = 5/8.24 = 0.60680$.

(b)(iii) $v = 9$, $a = (4+4+100+100)/4-36 = 16$, $Z = \frac{1}{1+9/16} = 16/25 = 0.64$.

(b)(iv) $Z = \frac{3}{3+9/5} = 15/24 = 0.625$.

(b)(v) $a = 5$, $v = (9+9+2.25+2.25)/4 = 5.625$, $Z = \frac{2}{2+5.625/5} = 10/15.625 = 0.64$.

The answer is (i).

16.54 (a) Preliminary calculations are given in Table 16.9.

Table 16.9 Calculations for Exercise 16.54

Risk	100	1,000	20,000	μ	v
1	0.5	0.3	0.2	4,350	61,382,500
2	0.7	0.2	0.1	2,270	35,054,100

$$\text{Pr}(100|1) = 0.5, \ \text{Pr}(100|2) = 0.7$$
$$\text{Pr}(1|100) = \frac{0.5(2/3)}{0.5(2/3) + 0.7(1/3)} = 10/17, \ \text{Pr}(2|100) = 7/17.$$

Expected value is $(10/17)(4350) + (7/17)(2,270) = 3,493.53$.

(b)
$$\mu = (2/3)(4,350) + (1/3)(2,270) = 3,656.33$$
$$v = (2/3)(61,382,500) + (1/3)(35,054,100) = 52,606,366.67$$
$$a = (2/3)(4,350)^2 + (1/3)(2,270)^2 - 3,656.33^2 = 963,859.91$$
$$k = 54.579, \ Z = 1/55.579 = 0.017992.$$

Estimate is $0.017992(100) + 0.982008(3,656.33) = 3,592.34$.

16.55 (a)
$$v(\mu, \lambda) = \mu(2\lambda^2) = 2\mu\lambda^2$$
$$v = 2E(\mu\lambda^2) = 2E(\mu)[\text{Var}(\lambda) + E(\lambda)^2]$$
$$= 2(0.1)(640,000 + 1,000^2)$$
$$= 328,000.$$

(b)
$$\mu(\mu, \lambda) = \mu\lambda$$
$$a = \text{Var}(\mu\lambda) = E(\mu^2\lambda^2) - E(\mu)^2E(\lambda)^2$$
$$= [\text{Var}(\mu) + E(\mu)^2][\text{Var}(\lambda) + E(\lambda)^2] - E(\mu)^2E(\lambda)^2$$
$$= (0.0025 + 0.1^2)(640,000 + 1,000^2) - 0.1^2 1,000^2$$
$$= 10,500.$$

16.56 If $\rho = 0$ then the claims from successive years are uncorrelated and hence the past data $\mathbf{x} = (X_1, \ldots, X_n)$ are of no value in helping to predict X_{n+1} so more reliance should be placed on μ. (Unlike most models in this chapter, here we get to know μ as opposed to only knowing a probability distribution concerning μ.) Conversely, if $\rho = 1$, then X_{n+1} is a perfect linear function of $\mathbf{x}$. Thus no reliance need be placed on μ.

16.57 (a)
$$\frac{\Gamma'(\alpha)}{\Gamma(\alpha)} = \frac{\frac{d}{d\alpha} \int_0^\infty x^{\alpha-1} e^{-x} dx}{\Gamma(\alpha)} = \frac{\int_0^\infty (\ln x) x^{\alpha-1} e^{-x} dx}{\Gamma(\alpha)}$$

(b)
$$\Psi'(\alpha) = \frac{d}{d\alpha} \frac{\Gamma'(\alpha)}{\Gamma(\alpha)} = \frac{\Gamma(\alpha)\Gamma''(\alpha) - [\Gamma'(\alpha)]^2}{[\Gamma(\alpha)]^2}$$

$$= \frac{\Gamma''(\alpha)}{\Gamma(\alpha)} - [\Psi(\alpha)]^2$$

$$= \frac{\int_0^\infty (\ln x)^2 x^{\alpha-1} e^{-x} dx}{\Gamma(\alpha)} - [\Psi(\alpha)]^2$$

$$\int_0^\infty (\ln x)^2 x^{\alpha-1} e^{-x} dx = \Gamma(\alpha)\{\Psi'(\alpha) + [\Psi(\alpha)]^2\}$$

16.58 The Bayes estimator is found from the posterior distribution,

$$\pi_{\Theta|\mathbf{X}}(\theta|\mathbf{x}) \propto \exp\left[-\frac{1}{2}\sum_{j=1}^{25}\left(\frac{\ln x_j - \theta}{2}\right)^2 - \frac{1}{2}(\theta-5)^2\right]$$

$$\propto \exp\left\{-\frac{1}{2}\left[\frac{\theta - \frac{2}{29}(10 + \frac{1}{2}\sum \ln x_j)}{\sqrt{4/29}}\right]^2\right\}$$

which implies that the posterior distribution of Θ is normal with mean $\frac{2}{29}(10 + \frac{1}{2}\sum \ln x_j)$ and variance $4/29$. We are trying to estimate the mean of X and with a lognormal distribution, it is $\exp(\theta + 2)$. The Bayes estimator is the posterior expected value of this quantity which is e^2 times the moment generating function of a normal random variable evaluated at 1 (recall that the normal mgf is $M(t) = \exp(\mu t + \sigma^2 t^2/2)$ and so

$$\hat{\mu}_{Bayes} = \exp\left[2 + \frac{2}{29}(10 + \frac{1}{2}\sum \ln x_j) + \frac{2}{29}\right]$$

$$= \exp\left(\frac{80}{29} + \frac{25}{29}\bar{W}\right)$$

where $\bar{W} = \frac{1}{25}\sum \ln x_j$.

The credibility estimator is found from

$$
\begin{aligned}
\mu(\Theta) &= e^{\Theta+2} \\
\mu &= E(e^{\Theta+2}) = e^{2+5+0.5} = e^{7.5} \\
v(\Theta) &= e^{2\Theta+8} - e^{2\Theta+4} \\
v &= E(e^{2\Theta+8} - e^{2\Theta+4}) = e^{10+2+8} - e^{10+2+4} = e^{16}(e^4 - 1) \\
a &= E(e^{2\Theta+4}) - e^{15} = e^{16} - e^{15} = e^{16}(e - 1) \\
Z &= \frac{25}{25 + \frac{e^4-1}{e-1}} = .44490 \\
\hat{\mu}_{cred} &= .44490\bar{X} + .55510e^{7.5}.
\end{aligned}
$$

The log-credibility estimator is found from

$$
\begin{aligned}
\mu(\Theta) &= E(\ln X|\Theta) = \Theta \\
\mu &= E(\Theta) = 5 \\
v(\Theta) &= \text{Var}(\ln X|\Theta) = 4 \\
v &= E(4) = 4 \\
a &= \text{Var}(\Theta) = 1 \\
Z &= \frac{25}{25 + \frac{4}{1}} = \frac{25}{29} \\
\hat{\mu}_{\ln-cred} &= c\exp\left(\frac{25}{29}\bar{W} + \frac{4}{29}5\right).
\end{aligned}
$$

We know that the Bayes estimator is unbiased and because the log-credibility and Bayes estimators both involve $\exp(25\bar{W}/29)$ and both are unbiased, they must be identical. Therefore

$$
\hat{\mu}_{\ln-cred} = \exp\left(\frac{25}{29}\bar{W} + \frac{80}{29}\right).
$$

With regard to bias and mean squared error, for the Bayes and log-credibility estimators,

$$\begin{aligned}
\mathrm{E}(\hat{\mu}|\theta) &= e^{80/29}\mathrm{E}(e^{25\bar{W}/29}|\theta)\\
&= e^{80/29}[\mathrm{E}(X^{1/29}|\theta)]^{25}\\
&= e^{80/29}\left\{\exp\left[\frac{1}{29}\theta + \frac{1}{2}\left(\frac{1}{29}\right)^2 4\right]\right\}^{25}\\
&= \exp\left(\frac{25}{29}\theta + \frac{2370}{841}\right)\\
bias &= \exp\left(\frac{25}{29}\theta + \frac{2370}{841}\right) - \exp(\theta + 2)\\
\mathrm{E}(\hat{\mu}^2|\theta) &= e^{160/29}\mathrm{E}(e^{50\bar{W}/29}|\theta)\\
&= e^{160/29}[\mathrm{E}(X^{2/29}|\theta)]^{25}\\
&= e^{160/29}\left\{\exp\left[\frac{2}{29}\theta + \frac{1}{2}\left(\frac{2}{29}\right)^2 4\right]\right\}^{25}\\
&= \exp\left(\frac{50}{29}\theta + \frac{4840}{841}\right)\\
variance &= \exp\left(\frac{50}{29}\theta + \frac{4840}{841}\right) - \exp\left(\frac{50}{29}\theta + \frac{4740}{841}\right)\\
mse &= varaiance + bias^2
\end{aligned}$$

For the credibility estimator

$$\begin{aligned}
\mathrm{E}(\hat{\mu}|\theta) &= \mathrm{E}(0.4449\bar{X} + 0.5551e^{7.5})\\
&= 0.4449e^{\theta+2} + 0.5551e^{7.5}\\
bias &= 0.5551(e^{7.5} - e^{\theta+2})\\
\mathrm{Var}(\hat{\mu}|\theta) &= 0.4449^2\,\mathrm{Var}(\bar{X})\\
&= 0.4449^2(e^{2\theta+8} - e^{2\theta+4})/25
\end{aligned}$$

Values of the bias and mean squared error are given for various percentiles in Table 16.10.

16.59 (a)

$$\begin{aligned}
\mathrm{E}\{[X_{n+1} - g(\mathbf{X})]^2\} &= \mathrm{E}\{[X_{n+1} - \mathrm{E}(X_{n+1}|\mathbf{X}) + \mathrm{E}(X_{n+1}|\mathbf{X}) - g(\mathbf{X})]^2\}\\
&= \mathrm{E}\{[X_{n+1} - \mathrm{E}(X_{n+1}|\mathbf{X})]^2\}\\
&\quad + \mathrm{E}\{[\mathrm{E}(X_{n+1}|\mathbf{X}) - g(\mathbf{X})]^2\}\\
&\quad + 2\mathrm{E}\{[X_{n+1} - \mathrm{E}(X_{n+1}|\mathbf{X})][\mathrm{E}(X_{n+1}|\mathbf{X}) - g(\mathbf{X})]\}
\end{aligned}$$

Table 16.10   Results for Exercise 16.58

Percentile	θ	mean	Bayes/log-cred bias	mse	credibility bias	mse
1	2.674	107	61	6,943	944	893,379
5	3.355	212	90	18,691	886	804,248
10	3.718	304	109	31,512	835	735,976
25	4.326	559	138	75,310	694	613,435
50	5.000	1,097	150	202,165	395	666,286
75	5.674	2,153	78	580,544	−191	2,003,192
90	6.282	3,950	−186	1,671,092	−1,189	8,036,278
95	6.645	5,681	−533	3,345,035	−2,150	18,316,467
99	7.326	11,230	−1,966	13,777,997	−5,230	80,871,171

The third term is

$$2\mathrm{E}\{[X_{n+1} - \mathrm{E}(X_{n+1}|\mathbf{X})][\mathrm{E}(X_{n+1}|\mathbf{X}) - g(\mathbf{X})]\}$$
$$= 2\mathrm{E}(\mathrm{E}\{[X_{n+1} - \mathrm{E}(X_{n+1}|\mathbf{X})][\mathrm{E}(X_{n+1}|\mathbf{X}) - g(\mathbf{X})]|\mathbf{X}\})$$
$$= 2\mathrm{E}\{[\mathrm{E}(X_{n+1}|\mathbf{X}) - \mathrm{E}(X_{n+1}|\mathbf{X})][\mathrm{E}(X_{n+1}|\mathbf{X}) - g(\mathbf{X})]\}$$
$$= 0$$

completing the proof.
(b) The objective function is minimized when $\mathrm{E}\{[\mathrm{E}(X_{n+1}|\mathbf{X}) - g(\mathbf{X})]^2\}$ is minimized. If $g(\mathbf{X})$ is set equal to $\mathrm{E}(X_{n+1}|\mathbf{X})$ the expectation is of a random variable which is identically zero and so is zero. Because an expected square cannot be negative, this is the minimum. But this is the Bayesian premium.
(c) Inserting a linear function, the mean squared error to minimize is

$$\mathrm{E}\{[\mathrm{E}(X_{n+1}|\mathbf{X}) - \alpha_0 - \sum_{j=1}^{n} \alpha_j X_j]^2\}.$$

But this is (16.34) which is minimized by the linear credibility premium.

16.4   SECTION 16.5

16.60 $\bar{X}_1 = 733\frac{1}{3}$, $\bar{X}_2 = 633\frac{1}{3}$, $\bar{X}_3 = 900$, $\bar{X} = 755\frac{5}{9}$

$$\hat{v}_1 = (16\frac{2}{3}^2 + 66\frac{2}{3}^2 + 83\frac{1}{3}^2)/2 = 5,833\frac{1}{3}$$

$$\hat{v}_2 = (8\frac{1}{3}^2 + 33\frac{1}{3}^2 + 41\frac{2}{3}^2)/2 = 1,458\frac{1}{3}$$

$$\hat{v}_3 = (0^2 + 50^2 + 50^2)/2 = 2,500$$

$$\hat{v} = 3,263\frac{8}{9}$$

$$\hat{a} = \frac{1}{2}(22\frac{2}{9}^2 + 122\frac{2}{9}^2 + 144\frac{4}{9}^2) - 3,263\frac{8}{9}/3 = 17,060\frac{5}{27}$$

$$\hat{k} = 3,263\frac{8}{9}/17,060\frac{5}{27} = 0.191316$$

$$Z = 3/(3 + 0.191316) = 0.94005$$

The three estimates are

$$0.94005(733\frac{1}{3}) + 0.05995(755\frac{5}{9}) = 734.67$$

$$0.94005(633\frac{1}{3}) + 0.05995(755\frac{5}{9}) = 640.66$$

$$0.94005(900) + 0.05995(755\frac{5}{9}) = 891.34.$$

16.61
$$\bar{X}_1 = 45,000/220 = 204.55$$
$$\bar{X}_2 = 54,000/235 = 229.79$$
$$\bar{X}_3 = 91,000/505 = 180.20$$
$$\hat{\mu} = \bar{X} = 190,000/960 = 197.91.$$

$$\hat{v} = [100(4.55)^2 + 120(3.78)^2 + 90(18.68)^2 + 75(10.21)^2 + 70(13.07)^2$$
$$+150(6.87)^2 + 175(8.77)^2 + 180(14.24)^2/(1+2+2)$$
$$= 22,401,$$

$$\hat{a} = \frac{220(204.55 - 197.91)^2 + 235(229.79 - 197.91)^2 + 505(180.20 - 197.91)^2 - 22,401(2)}{960 - (220^2 + 235^2 + 505^2)/960} = 617.54.$$

$\hat{k} = 36.27$, $Z_1 = 0.8585$, $Z_2 = 0.8663$, $Z_3 = 0.9330$. The estimates are

$$0.8585(204.55) + 0.1415(197.91) = 203.61$$
$$0.8663(229.79) + 0.1337(197.91) = 225.53$$
$$0.9330(180.20) + 0.0670(197.91) = 181.39.$$

Using the alternative method,

$$\hat{\mu} = \frac{0.8585(204.55) + 0.8663(229.79) + 0.9330(180.20)}{0.8585 + 0.8663 + 0.9330} = 204.32$$

and the estimates are

$$0.8585(204.55) + 0.1415(204.32) = 204.50$$
$$0.8663(229.79) + 0.1337(204.32) = 226.37$$
$$0.9330(180.20) + 0.0670(204.32) = 181.81.$$

16.62 $\bar{X} = 475$, $\hat{v} = (0^2 + 75^2 + 75^2)/2 = 5{,}625$. With μ known to be 600, $\tilde{a} = (475 - 600)^2 - 5{,}625/3 = 13{,}750$, $\hat{k} = 5{,}625/13{,}750 = 0.4091$, $Z = 3/3.4091 = 0.8800$. The premium is $0.88(475) + 0.12(600) = 490$.

16.63 (a)
$$\begin{aligned} \mathrm{Var}(X_{ij}) &= \mathrm{E}[\mathrm{Var}(X_{ij}|\Theta_i)] + \mathrm{Var}[\mathrm{E}(X_{ij}|\Theta_i)] \\ &= \mathrm{E}[v(\Theta_i] + \mathrm{Var}[\mu(\Theta_i)] = v + a. \end{aligned}$$

(b) This follows from (16.9).
(c)

$$\begin{aligned} \sum_{i=1}^{r}\sum_{j=1}^{n}(X_{ij} - \bar{X})^2 &= \sum_{i=1}^{r}\sum_{j=1}^{n}(X_{ij} - \bar{X}_i + \bar{X}_i - \bar{X})^2 \\ &= \sum_{i=1}^{r}\sum_{j=1}^{n}(X_{ij} - \bar{X}_i)^2 + 2\sum_{i=1}^{r}\sum_{j=1}^{n}(X_{ij} - \bar{X}_i)(\bar{X}_i - \bar{X}) \\ &\quad + \sum_{i=1}^{r}\sum_{j=1}^{n}(\bar{X}_i - \bar{X})^2 \\ &= \sum_{i=1}^{r}\sum_{j=1}^{n}(X_{ij} - \bar{X}_i)^2 + 2\sum_{i=1}^{r}(\bar{X}_i - \bar{X})\sum_{j=1}^{n}(X_{ij} - \bar{X}_i) \\ &\quad + n\sum_{i=1}^{r}(\bar{X}_i - \bar{X})^2 \\ &= \sum_{i=1}^{r}\sum_{j=1}^{n}(X_{ij} - \bar{X}_i)^2 + n\sum_{i=1}^{r}(\bar{X}_i - \bar{X})^2 \end{aligned}$$

The middle term is zero because $\sum_{j=1}^{n}(X_{ij} - \bar{X}_i) = \sum_{j=1}^{n}X_{ij} - n\bar{X}_i = 0$.
(d)
$$\mathrm{E}\left[\frac{1}{nr-1}\sum_{i=1}^{r}\sum_{j=1}^{n}(X_{ij} - \bar{X})^2\right]$$

$$= \mathrm{E}\left[\frac{1}{nr-1}\sum_{i=1}^{r}\sum_{j=1}^{n}(X_{ij} - \bar{X}_i)^2 + \frac{n}{nr-1}\sum_{i=1}^{r}(\bar{X}_i - \bar{X})^2\right]$$

We know that $\frac{1}{n-1}\sum_{j=1}^{n}(X_{ij}-\bar{X}_i)^2$ is an unbiased estimator of $v(\theta_i)$ and so the expected value of the first term is

$$
E\left[\frac{1}{nr-1}\sum_{i=1}^{r}\sum_{j=1}^{n}(X_{ij}-\bar{X}_i)^2\right]
$$

$$
= E\left\{E\left[\frac{1}{nr-1}\sum_{i=1}^{r}\sum_{j=1}^{n}(X_{ij}-\bar{X}_i)^2|\Theta_i\right]\right\}
$$

$$
= E\left[\frac{n-1}{nr-1}\sum_{i=1}^{r}v(\Theta_i)\right] = \frac{r(n-1)}{nr-1}v.
$$

For the second term note that $\mathrm{Var}(\bar{X}_i) = E[v(\Theta_i)/n] + \mathrm{Var}[\mu(\Theta_i)] = v/n + a$ and $\frac{1}{r-1}\sum_{i=1}^{r}(\bar{X}_i - \bar{X})^2$ is an unbiased estimator of $v/n + a$. Then, for the second term,

$$
E\left[\frac{n}{nr-1}\sum_{i=1}^{r}(\bar{X}_i - \bar{X})^2\right] = \frac{n(r-1)}{nr-1}\left(\frac{v}{n} + a\right).
$$

Then the total is

$$
\frac{r(n-1)}{nr-1}v + \frac{n(r-1)}{nr-1}\left(\frac{v}{n} + a\right) = v + a - \frac{n-1}{nr-1}a.
$$

(e) Unconditionally, all of the X_{ij} are assumed to have the same mean, when in fact they do not. They also have a conditional variance which is smaller and so the variance from $\bar{X}$ is not as great as it appears from (b).

16.64 $\bar{X} = 333/2{,}787 = 0.11948 = \hat{v}$. The sample variance is $447/2{,}787 -$ $0.11948^2 = 0.14611$ and so $\hat{a} = 0.14611 - 0.11948 = 0.02663$. Then, $\hat{k} = 0.11948/0.02663 = 4.4867$ and $Z = 1/5.4867 = 0.18226$. The premiums are given in Table 16.11.

Table 16.11   Calculations for Exercise 16.64

No. of claims	Premium
0	$0.18226(0) + 0.81774(0.11948) = 0.09770$
1	$0.18226(1) + 0.81774(0.11948) = 0.27996$
2	$0.18226(2) + 0.81774(0.11948) = 0.46222$
3	$0.18226(3) + 0.81774(0.11948) = 0.64448$
4	$0.18226(4) + 0.81774(0.11948) = 0.82674$

16.65 (a) See Appendix B.

(b)
$$a = \text{Var}[\mu(\Theta)] = \text{Var}(\Theta)$$
$$v = \text{E}[v(\Theta)] = \text{E}[\Theta(1+\Theta)]$$
$$\mu = \text{E}[\mu(\Theta)] = \text{E}(\Theta)$$
$$v - \mu - \mu^2 = \text{E}(\Theta) - \text{E}(\Theta^2) - \text{E}(\Theta) - \text{E}(\Theta)^2 = \text{Var}(\Theta) = a.$$

(c)
$$\hat{\mu} = \bar{X} = 0.11948$$
$$\hat{a} + \hat{v} = 0.14611$$
$$\hat{a} = \hat{v} - 0.11948 - 0.11948^2$$
$$\hat{a} - \hat{v} = -0.133755$$

The solution is $\hat{a} = 0.0061775$ and $\hat{v} = 0.1399325$. Then

$$\hat{k} = 0.1399325/0.0061775 = 22.652$$

and $Z = 1/23.652 = 0.04228$. The premiums are given in Table 16.12

Table 16.12 Calculations for Exercise 16.65

No. of claims	Premium
0	$0.04228(0) + 0.95772(0.11948) = 0.11443$
1	$0.04228(1) + 0.95772(0.11948) = 0.15671$
2	$0.04228(2) + 0.95772(0.11948) = 0.19899$
3	$0.04228(3) + 0.95772(0.11948) = 0.24127$
4	$0.04228(4) + 0.95772(0.11948) = 0.28355$

16.66

$$f_{\mathbf{X}_i}(\mathbf{x}_i) = \int_0^\infty \prod_{j=1}^{n_i} \left[\frac{(m_{ij}\theta_i)^{t_{ij}} e^{-m_{ij}\theta_i}}{t_{ij}!} \right] \frac{1}{\mu} e^{-\theta_i/\mu} d\theta_i$$

$$= \frac{1}{\mu} \left(\prod_{j=1}^{n_i} \frac{m_{ij}^{t_{ij}}}{t_{ij}!} \right) \int_0^\infty e^{-\theta_i(\mu^{-1}+m_i)} \theta_i^{t_i} d\theta_i$$

$$= \frac{1}{\mu} \left(\prod_{j=1}^{n_i} \frac{m_{ij}^{t_{ij}}}{t_{ij}!} \right) \frac{t_i!}{(\mu^{-1}+m_i)^{t_i+1}} \propto \mu^{-1}(\mu^{-1}+m_i)^{-t_i-1}$$

where $t_i = \sum_{j=1}^{n_i} t_{ij}$. Then the likelihood function is

$$L(\mu) \propto \mu^{-r} \prod_{i=1}^{r} (\mu^{-1}+m_i)^{-t_i-1}$$

and the logarithm is

$$l(\mu) = -r\ln(\mu) - \sum_{i=1}^{r}(t_i + 1)\ln(\mu^{-1} + m_i)$$

and

$$l'(\mu) = -r\mu^{-1} - \sum_{i=1}^{r}(t_i + 1)(\mu^{-1} + m_i)^{-1}(-\mu^{-2}) = 0.$$

The equation to be solved is

$$r\mu = \sum_{i=1}^{r} \frac{t_i + 1}{\mu^{-1} + m_i}.$$

16.67 (a)

$$
\begin{aligned}
\sum_{i=1}^{r}\sum_{j=1}^{n_i} m_{ij}(X_{ij} - \bar{X})^2 &= \sum_{i=1}^{r}\sum_{j=1}^{n_i} m_{ij}(X_{ij} - \bar{X}_i + \bar{X}_i - \bar{X})^2 \\
&= \sum_{i=1}^{r}\sum_{j=1}^{n_i} m_{ij}(X_{ij} - \bar{X}_i)^2 \\
&\quad + 2\sum_{i=1}^{r}\sum_{j=1}^{n_i} m_{ij}(X_{ij} - \bar{X}_i)(\bar{X}_i - \bar{X}) \\
&\quad + \sum_{i=1}^{r}\sum_{j=1}^{n_i} m_{ij}(\bar{X}_i - \bar{X})^2 \\
&= \sum_{i=1}^{r}\sum_{j=1}^{n_i} m_{ij}(X_{ij} - \bar{X}_i)^2 + \sum_{i=1}^{r} m_i(\bar{X}_i - \bar{X})^2.
\end{aligned}
$$

The middle term vanishes because $\sum_{j=1}^{n_i} m_{ij}(X_{ij} - \bar{X}_i) = 0$ from the definition of $\bar{X}_i$.

(b)

$$
\begin{aligned}
\hat{a} &= (m - m^{-1}\sum_{i=1}^{r} m_i^2)^{-1}\left[\sum_{i=1}^{r}\sum_{j=1}^{n_i} m_{ij}(X_{ij} - \bar{X})^2 \right. \\
&\quad \left. - \sum_{i=1}^{r}\sum_{j=1}^{n_i} m_{ij}(X_{ij} - \bar{X}_i)^2 - (r-1)\hat{v} \right] \\
&= (m - m^{-1}\sum_{i=1}^{r} m_i^2)\left[^{-1}\sum_{i=1}^{r}\sum_{j=1}^{n_i} m_{ij}(X_{ij} - \bar{X})^2 \right. \\
&\quad \left. - \hat{v}\sum_{i=1}^{r}(n_i - 1) - (r-1)\hat{v} \right].
\end{aligned}
$$

Also

$$m_* = \frac{\sum_{i=1}^{r} m_i \left(1 - \frac{m_i}{m}\right)}{\sum_{i=1}^{r} n_i - 1} = \frac{m - m^{-1} \sum_{i=1}^{r} m_i^2}{\sum_{i=1}^{r} n_i - 1}.$$

Then

$$
\begin{aligned}
\hat{a} &= \frac{m_*^{-1}}{\sum_{i=1}^{r} n_i - 1} \left[\sum_{i=1}^{r} \sum_{j=1}^{n_i} m_{ij} (X_{ij} - \bar{X})^2 - \hat{v} \left(\sum_{i=1}^{r} n_i - 1 \right) \right] \\
&= m_*^{-1} \left[\frac{\sum_{i=1}^{r} \sum_{j=1}^{n_i} m_{ij} (X_{ij} - \bar{X})^2}{\sum_{i=1}^{r} n_i - 1} - \hat{v} \right].
\end{aligned}
$$

16.68 The sample mean is 21/34 and the sample variance is $370/340 - (21/34)^2 = 817/1{,}156$. Then $\hat{v} = 21/34$ and $\hat{a} = 817/1{,}156 - 21/34 = 103/1{,}156$. $\hat{k} = (21/34)/(103/1{,}156) = 714/103$ and $Z = 1/(1 + 714/103) = 103/817$. The estimate is $(103/817)(2) + (714/817)(21/34) = 0.79192$.

17

Chapter 17 solutions

17.1 SECTION 17.1

17.1 The first 7 values of the cumulative distribution function for a Poisson(3) variable are 0.0498, 0.1991, 0.4232, 0.6472, 0.8153, 0.9161, and 0.9665. With $0.0498 \leq 0.1247 < 0.1991$ the first simulated value is $x = 1$. With $0.9161 \leq 0.9321 < 0.9665$ the second simulated value is $x = 6$. With $0.6472 \leq 0.6873 < 0.8153$ the third simulated value is $x = 4$.

17.2 The cumulative distribution function is

$$F_X(x) = \begin{cases} 0.25x, & 0 \leq x < 2 \\ 0.5, & 2 \leq x < 4 \\ 0.1x + 0.1, & 4 \leq x < 9. \end{cases}$$

For $u = 0.2$, solve $0.2 = 0.25x$ for $x = 0.8$. The function is constant at 0.5 from 2 to 4, so the second simulated value is $x = 4$. For the third value solve $0.7 = 0.1x + 0.1$ for $x = 6$.

17.3 The requested probability is the same as the probability that at least a of the observations are at or below $\pi_{0.9}$ and at most b are at or below $\pi_{0.9}$.

Loss Models: From Data to Decisions, Solutions Manual, Second Edition.
By Stuart A. Klugman, Harry H. Panjer, and Gordon E. Willmot
ISBN 0-471-22762-5   Copyright © 2004 John Wiley & Sons, Inc.

The number of such observations has a binomial distribution with a sample size of n and a success probability of $\Pr(X \leq \pi_{0.9}) = 0.9$. Let N be this binomial variable. We want $0.95 = \Pr(a \leq N \leq b)$. From the central limit theorem,

$$0.95 = \Pr\left[\frac{a - 0.9n}{\sqrt{0.09n}} \leq Z \leq \frac{b - 0.9n}{\sqrt{0.09n}}\right]$$

and a symmetric interval implies

$$-1.96 = \frac{a - 0.9n}{\sqrt{0.09n}}$$

giving $a = 0.9n - 1.96\sqrt{0.9(0.1)n}$. Because a must be an integer, the result should be rounded down. A similar calculation can be done for b.

17.4 The mean and standard deviation are both 100. The analog of (17.1) is

$$\frac{0.02\mu}{\sigma/\sqrt{n}} = 1.645.$$

Substituting the mean and standard deviation produces $n = (1.645/0.02)^2 = 6{,}766$ where the answer has been rounded up for safety. For the probability at 200, the true value is $F(200) = 1 - \exp(-2) = 0.8647$. The equation to solve is

$$\frac{0.02(0.8647)}{\sqrt{\frac{0.8647(0.1353)}{n}}} = 1.645$$

for $n = 1{,}059$. When doing these simulations, the goal should be achieved 90% of the time.

17.5 The answer depends on the particular simulation.

17.6 The sample variance for the five observations is

$$\frac{(1 - 3)^2 + (2 - 3)^2 + (3 - 3)^2 + (4 - 3)^2 + (5 - 3)^2}{4} = 2.5.$$

The estimate is the sample mean and its standard deviation is $\sigma/\sqrt{n}$ which is approximated by $\sqrt{2.5/n}$. Setting this equal to the goal of 0.05 gives the answer, $n = 1000$.

17.2   SECTION 17.2

17.7 The inversion method requires a solution to $u = \Phi\left(\frac{x - 15{,}000}{2{,}000}\right)$ where $\Phi(x)$ is the standard normal cdf. For $u = 0.5398$, the equation to solve is

$\frac{x-15,000}{2,000} = 0.1$ for $x = 15,200$. After the deductible is applied, the insurer's cost for the first month is 5,200. The next equation is $-1.2 = \frac{x-15,000}{2,000}$ for $x = 12,600$ and a cost of 2,600. The third month's equation is $-3.0 = \frac{x-15,000}{2,000}$ for $x = 9,000$ and a cost of 0. The final month uses $0.8 = \frac{x-15,000}{2,000}$ for $x = 16,600$ and a cost of 6,600. The total cost is 14,400.

17.8 The equation to solve for the inversion method is $u = \Phi\left(\frac{\ln x - 0.01}{0.02}\right)$. When $u = 0.1587$, the equation is $-1 = \frac{\ln x - 0.01}{0.02}$ for $x = 0.99005$ and the first year's price is 99.005. For the second year, solve $1.5 = \frac{\ln x - 0.01}{0.02}$ for $x = 1.04081$ and the price is 103.045.

17.9 For this binomial distribution, the probability of no claims is 0.03424 and so if $0 \le u < 0.03424$, the simulated value is 0. The probability of one claim is 0.11751 and so for $0.03424 \le u < 0.15175$, the simulated value is 1. The probability of 2 claims is 0.19962 and so for $0.15175 \le u < 0.35137$. Because the value of 0.18 is in this interval, the simulated value is 2.

17.10 For claim times, the equation to solve is $u = 1 - \exp(-x/2)$ for $x = -0.5\ln(1-u)$. The simulated times are 0.886, 0.388 and two more we don't need. The first claim is at time 0.886 and the second claim is after time 1, so there is only one claim in the simulated year. For the amount of that claim, the equation to solve is $0.89 = 1 - \left(\frac{1000}{1000+x}\right)^2$ for $x = 2015$. At the time of the first claim, the surplus is $2000 + 2200(0.886) - 2015 = 1934.2$. Because ruin has not occurred, premiums continue to be collected for an ending surplus of $1934.2 + 2200(0.114) = 2185$.

17.11 The empirical distribution places probability $1/2$ on each of the two points. The mean of this distribution is 2 and the variance of this distribution is 1. There are four possible bootstrap samples: (1,1), (3,1), (1,3), (3,3). The value of the estimator for each is 0, 1, 1, and 0. The mean squared error is $(1/4)[(0-1)^2 + (1-1)^2 + (1-1)^2 + (0-1)^2] = 0.5$.

17.12 (a) The distribution function is $F(x) = x/10$ and so is 0.2, 0.4, and 0.7 at the three sample value. These are to be compared with the empirical values of 0, 1/3, 2/3, and 1. The maximum difference is 0.7 versus 1 for a test statistic of 0.3.

(b) Simulations by the author produced an estimated p-value of 0.8882.

17.13 (a) The estimate is $4(7)/3 = 9.33$. The estimated mean squared error is $(28/3)^2/15 = 5.807$.

(b) There are twenty seven equally weighted bootstrap samples. For example, the sample 2, 2, 4 produces an estimate of $4(4)/3 = 5.33$ and a contribution to the mean squared error of $(5.33 - 8.0494)^2 = 7.3769$. Averaging the 27 values produces an estimated mean squared error of 4.146.